BRITISH PARLIAMENTARY
ELECTION RESULTS 1983-1997

British Parliamentary Election Results 1983-1997

Compiled and Edited by
COLIN RALLINGS AND MICHAEL THRASHER

Ashgate

Aldershot • Brookfield USA • Singapore • Sydney

Published by
Ashgate Publishing Limited
Gower House
Croft Road
Aldershot
Hants GU11 3HR
England

Ashgate Publishing Company
Old Post Road
Brookfield
Vermont 05036
USA

British Library Cataloguing in Publication Data
Rallings, Colin
    British parliamentary election results, 1983-1997
    1.Great Britain. Parliament - Elections - Statistics
    I.Title II.Thrasher, Michael
    324.9'41'0858

Library of Congress Cataloging-in-Publication Data
Rallings, Colin
    British parliamentary election results, 1983-1997 / Colin Rallings.
Michael Thrasher.
        p.   cm.
    ISBN 1-84014-058-5 (hb)
        1. Great Britain. Parliament–Elections–Statistics.
    2. Elections–Great Britain–Statistics. I. Thrasher, Michael.
    II. Title.
    JN956.R35   1998
    324.941'0858'021–dc21   98-47263
                                                         CIP

ISBN 1 84014 058 5

Printed in Great Britain by The Book Company, Suffolk

CONTENTS

PREFACE

This is the sixth volume in a series of definitive reference books recording constituency results in British parliamentary elections since 1832. It includes all elections between the 1983 general election and the dissolution of parliament in March 1997. Interim cumulative supplements have been published since 1983 under the general title of 'Britain Votes'. The latest volume, *Britain Votes 6,* covers the 1997 general election, which was fought on new boundaries. It was published by Ashgate in 1998.

Previous volumes in this series were compiled and edited by the late Fred Craig. This volume has retained the overall layout developed by Craig but some modifications have been introduced. Parliamentary constituencies have been ordered according to the identification number used by the Press Association. This has been done simply because most of those now using this reference work are more familiar with this particular method of organising general election results. For those readers with a preference for Craig's method of grouping constituencies, viz. Greater London, England (excluding Greater London), Wales, Scotland and Northern Ireland, there is an appendix which contains a listing of constituencies which follows this order. Another development from previous volumes has been to calculate the percentage change for each party between elections. We have also dispensed with the descriptions Mrs. or Miss to denote the marital status of women candidates, preferring instead to use the more common Ms.

A number of people have helped in the compilation of these results. We would like to thank the Returning Officers and their staffs who responded to our requests for information. At Plymouth all those who have worked with us on this project, especially Brian Cheal, Pamela Hookway and Lawrence Ware, deserve our thanks.

Despite our efforts to avoid mistakes, some will remain. We take full responsibility for those and we are happy for attentive readers to bring such errors to our attention so that future editions may be corrected.

Colin Rallings and Michael Thrasher
University of Plymouth
August 1998

INTRODUCTORY NOTES

All constituencies in the United Kingdom are listed in alphabetical order following the practice of the Press Association. This number is in square brackets immediately following each constituency name.

Between the 1987 and 1992 general elections, however, major boundary changes took place in Milton Keynes and an additional constituency was created. This meant that for the 1983 and 1987 elections there were a total of 650 constituencies but for the 1992 election the total rose to 651. The former constituencies of Milton Keynes and Buckingham were sub-divided between the new constituencies of Buckingham, Milton Keynes North East and Milton Keynes South West. In *Britain Votes 5*, which recorded the results of the 1992 general election, the constituency numbering system was altered to accommodate this change. For this volume, however, we decided to retain the constituency order which had been in place for both the 1983 and 1987 elections. The results for the two Milton Keynes constituencies in 1992, therefore, will be found listed under the old Milton Keynes constituency. Following constituencies retain the 1983/1987 numbering system and not that used in 1992.

Under the name of each constituency are eight columns:

1. **The year of election.** In constituencies where a by-election took place, printed directly above the year is the cause of the by-election, for example the death or resignation of the sitting Member, and printed directly below the year we have recorded the day and month on which the by-election occured.

2. **Electors.** In the case of the 1983 and 1987 results, this figure is an estimate of the electorate at the time of the election based on the Electoral Register as first published. An explanation and description of the formula used can be found in F.W.S. Craig (ed.) *British Electoral Facts, 1832-1987* (Aldershot, Dartmouth, 1989, 5th edition), p. xiii and p.80. For the 1992 election we took advantage of the fact that an increasing number of election officers could supply more exact counts of their electorates on the day of the election. Wherever possible we have used these, not least because in a number of constituencies the 'on the day' electorate differs quite sharply from that 'as first published' owing to a high incidence of late claims. Where the Craig formula has been applied to 1992 electorates a † symbol appears.

3. **Turnout.** The number of valid votes expressed as a percentage of the total electorate.

4. **Candidate.** The surname and initials of the candidate. For the 1992 election we reported only candidates' initials as listed on the actual ballot paper. Where this has proved incompatible with Craig's practice of reporting each candidate's full set of initials we have altered our own data to comply with his. All women are listed as Ms. except where Craig identified them as Dr. In such cases a ‡ symbol appears. Candidates who were elected at the previous general election or, in the case of the 1979-1983 parliament, were members at dissolution, have an * following their name.

5. **Party.** The party affiliation of the candidate. Those Labour party candidates that were also sponsored by the Co-operative Party are listed in a separate appendix. Between the 1987 and 1992 general elections the Ecology Party changed its name to the Green Party. To facilitate comparisons across elections we have used the more recent description 'Green' to identify Ecology Party candidates at the 1983 and 1987 elections.

6. **Vote.** The number of votes polled by the candidate as recorded by election Returning Officers. At the foot of each set of voting figures we have listed the majority of the winning candidate over the second-placed candidate.

7. **Share.** The number of votes polled by the candidate expressed as a percentage of the total valid votes cast. Percentages do not always sum exactly to 100 because of rounding. Where a candidate lost his/her deposit an * follows the percentage share. Until the coming into effect of Section 13 of the Representation of the People Act (1985) on October 1, 1985, a candidate forfeited his/her deposit of £150 if not elected and did not poll more than one-eighth of the total votes cast, exclusive of spoilt ballot papers. Following that date the deposit was raised to £500 but the minimum number of votes required to retain the deposit fell to one-twentieth. Below each set of share figures we have listed the percentage majority of the winning candidate over the second-placed candidate. The rounding of percentages originally calculated to two or more decimal places sometimes results in the percentage majority figure differing by +/- 0.1% from that obtained by subtracting the share of the first-placed party from that of the second-placed party.

8. **Change.** The percentage change in share of the vote for the party since the previous election. Because of boundary changes no calculations were made for the 1983 election. At both the 1983 and 1987 general elections there was an alliance between the Liberal Party and the newly-formed Social Democratic Party (SDP). Following the 1987 general election this alliance broke up and there emerged a new party, the Liberal Democratic Party. Some Liberals refused to recognise the new party and in 1992 candidates representing the Liberal Party challenged in seats also contested by the Liberal Democrats. When calculating percentage change we have assumed that the Liberal Democrat Party is the successor party to both the Liberals and SDP. Where the

continuing Liberal Party fielded candidates in 1992 the figure for change will correspond to the party's vote share. In 1992 a number of candidates stood as joint Plaid Cymru/Green and in such cases the percentage change is based on the vote for Plaid Cymru at the previous election.

Where by-elections took place we have recorded the percentage change for a party only if it contested the previous election. Where relevant the percentage change recorded at a subsequent general election is based not on the by-election result but rather the previous general election.

Constituency Boundaries

Details of the area included within constituency boundaries will be found in Statutory Instruments, 1982, No. 1838 (Northern Ireland); 1983 Nos. 417 (England); 418 (Wales); 422 (Scotland). Maps showing constituency boundaries were included with the Boundary Commissions' reports published in November 1982 (Northern Ireland) and February 1983 (England, Wales and Scotland).

Between 1985 and 1987 the Boundary Commissions carried out interim reviews of 183 constituencies but only 107 of the changes had been approved by Parliament before it was dissolved. Of these 107 changes only two involved 5% or more of the electorate (Crawley and Reading East). Details of the area within each constituency after these changes will be found in Statutory Instruments, 1985, No. 1776; 1986, Nos. 597 and 2231; 1987, Nos. 462, 469 and 937.

There were minor changes to the boundaries of 98 constituencies between the general elections of 1987 and 1992. These were usually designed to ensure consistency with changes in local government boundaries. Details can be found in Statutory Instruments, 1987, Nos. 2050, 2208 and 2209; 1988, No. 1992. A more significant change involved the creation of an additional seat in Buckinghamshire. The boundaries of the two existing seats of Buckingham and Milton Keynes were re-drawn to create three new constituencies - Buckingham, Milton Keynes North East, and Milton Keynes South West. Details of the changes can be found in House of Commons Paper, 1990, No. 298. The figures for the change in share of the vote in these constituencies are based on estimates of the likely 1987 'result' in the new seats provided by the authors for the BBC and ITN.

General Election Polling Dates

The 1983 general election took place on June 9, that in 1987 on June 11 and that in 1992 on April 9.

PARTY LABELS AND ABBREVIATIONS

AFE	Anti-Federal Europe
AFL	Anti-Federalist League
AP	Alliance Party of Northern Ireland
BNP	British National Party
CDP	Christian Democratic Party
CL	Communist League
CNP	Cornish Nationalist Party
Comm	Communist
Con	Conservative
CPGB	Communist Party of Great Britain
FAIA	For the Anglo-Irish Agreement
FP	Fellowship Party
FTACMP	Free Trade Anti-Common Market Party
GP/PC	Green Party/Plaid Cymru
Green	Green Party (formerly Ecology Party)
Green/WFLOE	Green/Women for Life on Earth
HP	Humanist Party
ICP	International Communist Party
Ind	Independent (when placed before a party label indicates an unofficial candidate)
Islam	Islamic Party
Lab	Labour
LD	Liberal Democrat
Lib	Liberal
LTU	Labour and Trade Union Party
MK	Mebyon Kernow
MRLP	Monster Raving Loony Party
N Lab P	National Labour Party
NA	New Agenda
Nat	Nationalist
NBP	New Britain Party
ND	National Democrat

NF	National Front
NIEP	Northern Ireland Ecology Party
NLP	Natural Law Party
OSM	Orkney and Shetland Movement
PAL	Party of Associates with Licensees
PC	Plaid Cymru
PC/GP	Plaid Cymru/Green Party
PS	Progressive Socialist
RCP	Revolutionary Communist Party
Ref	Referendum Party
RF	Red Front (candidates of the Revolutionary Communist Party)
RLGG	Raving Loony Green Giant Party
Scot Soc	Scottish Socialist
SD	Social Democrat
SDLP	Social Democratic and Labour Party
SDP	Social Democratic Party
SF	Sinn Fein
SML	Scottish Militant Labour
SNP	Scottish National Party
Soc	Socialist
SPGB	Socalist Party of Great Britain
UDP	Ulster Democratic Party
UDUP	Ulster Democratic Unionist Party
UKI	UK Independence Party
UKU	United Kingdom Unionist Party
UPUP	Ulster Popular Unionist Party
UU	Ulster Unionist Party
WFLOE	Women for Life on Earth
WKP	Workers Party
WP	Workers Party of Northern Ireland
WR	Wessex Regionalist
WRP	Workers Revolutionary Party

PARLIAMENTARY CONSTITUENCY RESULTS

ABERAVON [1]

Election	Electors	T'out	Candidate	Party	Votes	% Sh	% Ch
1983	53,443	75.6	Morris J.*	Lab	23,745	58.8	
			Cutts S.M. Ms.	Lib	8,206	20.3	
			Bailey G.N.A.	Con	6,605	16.3	
			Phillips A.G.	PC	1,859	4.6*	
					15,539	38.4	
1987	52,280	77.7	Morris J.*	Lab	27,126	66.8	+8.0
			Harris M. Ms.	Lib	6,517	16.0	-4.3
			Warwick P.T.P.	Con	5,861	14.4	-1.9
			Howells A.L. Ms.	PC	1,124	2.8*	-1.8
					20,609	50.7	
1992	51,655	77.6	Morris J.*	Lab	26,877	67.1	+0.3
			Williams W.H.	Con	5,567	13.9	-0.5
			Harris M. Ms.	LD	4,999	12.5	-3.6
			Saunders D.W.J.	PC	1,919	4.8*	+2.0
			Beany C.	Ind	707	1.8*	
					21,310	53.2	

ABERDEEN NORTH [2]

Election	Electors	T'out	Candidate	Party	Votes	% Sh	% Ch
1983	63,049	65.0	Hughes R.*	Lab	19,262	47.0	
			Deans C.S.	SDP	10,118	24.7	
			Scanlan G.E.C. Ms.	Con	7,426	18.1	
			McGugan J.A.	SNP	3,790	9.3*	
			Harty M.E. Ms.	Green	367	0.9*	
					9,144	22.3	
1987	63,214	69.9	Hughes R.*	Lab	24,145	54.7	+7.6
			Smith R.	SDP	7,867	17.8	-6.9
			Scanlan G.E.C. Ms.	Con	6,330	14.3	-3.8
			Greenhorn P.B.	SNP	5,827	13.2	+3.9
					16,278	36.9	
1992	59,911	66.9	Hughes R.*	Lab	18,845	47.0	-7.6
			McGugan J.A.	SNP	9,608	24.0	+10.8
			Cook P.S.	Con	6,836	17.1	+2.7
			Ford M.A.	LD	4,772	11.9	-5.9
					9,237	23.1	

ABERDEEN SOUTH [3]

Election	Electors	T'out	Candidate	Party	Votes	% Sh	% Ch
1983	57,540	68.7	Malone P.G.	Con	15,393	38.9	
			Middleton R.	Lab	11,812	29.9	
			Philip I.G.	SDP	10,372	26.2	
			Coull S.	SNP	1,974	5.0*	
					3,581	9.1	
1987	62,943	67.1	Doran F.	Lab	15,917	37.7	+7.8
			Malone P.G.*	Con	14,719	34.8	-4.1
			Philip I.G.	SDP	8,844	20.9	-5.3
			Weir M.F.	SNP	2,776	6.6	+1.6
					1,198	2.8	
1992	58,494	70.2	Robertson R.S.	Con	15,808	38.5	+3.6
			Doran F.*	Lab	14,291	34.8	-2.9
			Davidson J.C.	SNP	6,223	15.1	+8.6
			Keith I. Ms.	LD	4,767	11.6	-9.3
					1,517	3.7	

ALDERSHOT [4]

Election	Electors	T'out	Candidate	Party	Votes	% Sh	% Ch
1983	77,593	72.7	Critchley J.M.G.*	Con	31,288	55.4	
			Westbrook N.S.E.	Lib	19,070	33.8	
			Crawford A.H.	Lab	6,070	10.8*	
					12,218	21.7	
1987	80,803	74.0	Critchley J.M.G.*	Con	35,272	59.0	+3.6
			Hargreaves R.A.	Lib	17,488	29.2	-4.6
			Pearson I.H.	Lab	7,061	11.8	+1.0
					10,427	17.4	
1992	81,755†	78.7	Critchley J.M.G.*	Con	36,974	57.5	-1.5
			Collett A.P.	LD	17,786	27.6	-1.6
			Smith J.A.	Lab	8,552	13.3	+1.5
			Robinson D.H.	Lib	1,038	1.6*	+1.6
					19,188	29.8	

ALDRIDGE-BROWNHILLS [5]

Election	Electors	T'out	Candidate	Party	Votes	% Sh	% Ch
1983	60,803	78.3	Shepherd R.C.S.*	Con	24,148	50.7	
			Burford R.T.	Lab	11,864	24.9	
			Gunn P.G.	SDP	11,599	24.4	
					12,284	25.8	
1987	62,129	79.8	Shepherd R.C.S.*	Con	26,434	53.3	+2.6
			Duncan C.P.	Lab	14,038	28.3	+3.4
			Betteridge G.J.	SDP	9,084	18.3	-6.0
					12,396	25.0	
1992	63,404†	82.6	Shepherd R.C.S.*	Con	28,431	54.3	+1.0
			Fawcett N.E.	Lab	17,407	33.3	+4.9
			Reynolds S.	LD	6,503	12.4	-5.9
					11,024	21.1	

ALTRINCHAM AND SALE [6]

Election	Electors	T'out	Candidate	Party	Votes	% Sh	% Ch
1983	65,984	73.0	Montgomery W.F.*	Con	25,321	52.5	
			Clancy B.P.	Lib	14,410	29.9	
			Erwin A.	Lab	7,684	15.9	
			Marsh C.M.H. Ms.	Green	629	1.3*	
			Wolstenholme L.J.	Ind	152	0.3*	
					10,911	22.6	
1987	67,611	76.7	Montgomery W.F. Sir.*	Con	27,746	53.5	+0.9
			Mulholland J.H.	Lib	13,518	26.1	-3.8
			Hinder D.	Lab	10,617	20.5	+4.5
					14,228	27.4	
1992	66,248†	80.2	Montgomery W.F. Sir.*	Con	29,066	54.7	+1.2
			Atherton M.E. Ms.	Lab	12,275	23.1	+2.6
			Mulholland J.H.	LD	11,601	21.8	-4.2
			Renwick J.C.	NLP	212	0.4*	+0.4
					16,791	31.6	

ALYN AND DEESIDE [7]

Election	Electors	T'out	Candidate	Party	Votes	% Sh	% Ch
1983	56,618	78.1	Jones S.B.*	Lab	17,806	40.3	
			Burns S.H.M.	Con	16,438	37.2	
			Owen E.C.H.	SDP	9,535	21.6	
			Shore K.A.	PC	413	0.9*	
					1,368	3.1	
1987	58,373	80.9	Jones S.B.*	Lab	22,916	48.6	+8.3
			Twilley N.J.	Con	16,533	35.0	-2.2
			Owen E.C.H.	SDP	7,273	15.4	-6.2
			Rogers J.D.	PC	478	1.0*	+0.1
					6,383	13.5	
1992	60,478†	80.1	Jones S.B.*	Lab	25,206	52.0	+3.5
			Riley J.J.	Con	17,355	35.8	+0.8
			Britton R.A.	LD	4,687	9.7	-5.7
			Rogers J.D.	PC	551	1.1*	+0.1
			Button V.J.	Green	433	0.9*	+0.9
			Cooksey J.M.	Ind	200	0.4*	
					7,851	16.2	

AMBER VALLEY [8]

Election	Electors	T'out	Candidate	Party	Votes	% Sh	% Ch
1983	66,720	77.2	Oppenheim P.A.C.L.	Con	21,502	41.7	
			Bookbinder D.M.	Lab	18,184	35.3	
			Johnson B.M.	Lib	10,989	21.3	
			Griffiths P.F.	Ind	856	1.7*	
					3,318	6.4	
1987	68,487	81.2	Oppenheim P.A.C.L.*	Con	28,603	51.4	+9.7
			Bookbinder D.M.	Lab	19,103	34.4	-0.9
			Reynolds S.	Lib	7,904	14.2	-7.1
					9,500	17.1	
1992	70,156†	84.7	Oppenheim P.A.C.L.*	Con	27,418	46.1	-5.3
			Cooper J.G.	Lab	26,706	44.9	+10.6
			Brocklebank G.	LD	5,294	8.9	-5.3
					712	1.2	

ANGUS EAST [9]

Election	Electors	T'out	Candidate	Party	Votes	% Sh	% Ch
1983	59,359	73.5	Fraser P.L.*	Con	19,218	44.1	
			Welsh A.P.	SNP	15,691	36.0	
			Hammond P.M. Ms.	SDP	4,978	11.4*	
			McConnell C.S.	Lab	3,497	8.0*	
			Ross P.M. Ms.	Green	239	0.5*	
					3,527	8.1	
1987	61,060	75.5	Welsh A.P.	SNP	19,536	42.4	+6.4
			Fraser P.L.*	Con	17,992	39.0	-5.0
			Mennie R.A.	Lab	4,971	10.8	+2.8
			Mortimer I.N.	SDP	3,592	7.8	-3.6
					1,544	3.3	
1992	63,170†	75.0	Welsh A.P.*	SNP	19,006	40.1	-2.3
			Harris R.O.	Con	18,052	38.1	-0.9
			Taylor D.G.	Lab	5,994	12.6	+1.9
			McLeod C.A.	LD	3,897	8.2	+0.4
			McCabe D.M.	Green	449	0.9*	+0.4
					954	2.0	

ANTRIM EAST [10]

Election	Electors	T'out	Candidate	Party	Votes	% Sh	% Ch
1983	58,671	65.1	Beggs J.R.	UU	14,293	37.4	
			Allister J.H.	UDUP	13,926	36.4	
			Neeson S.	APNI	7,620	19.9	
			O'Cleary M.	SDLP	1,047	2.7*	
			Cunning W.A.	Ind	741	1.9*	
			Kelly A.K.	WP	581	1.5*	
					367	1.0	

[Seeks Re-election]

Election	Electors	T'out	Candidate	Party	Votes	% Sh	% Ch
1986 (23/1)	60,780	58.9	Beggs J.R.*	UU	30,386	84.9	+47.5
			Neeson S.	APNI	5,405	15.1	-4.9
					24,981	69.8	
1987	60,587	55.2	Beggs J.R.*	UU	23,942	71.6	+34.1
			Neeson S.	APNI	8,582	25.6	+5.7
			Kelly A.K.	WP	936	2.8*	+1.3
					15,360	45.9	
1992	62,864	62.4	Beggs J.R.*	UU	16,966	43.2	-28.3
			Dodds N.A.	UDUP	9,544	24.3	-12.1
			Neeson S.	APNI	9,132	23.3	-2.4
			Boal M.M. Ms.	Con	3,359	8.6	+8.6
			Palmer A. Ms.	NLP	250	0.6*	+0.6
					7,422	18.9	

ANTRIM NORTH [11]

Election	Electors	T'out	Candidate	Party	Votes	% Sh	% Ch
1983	63,228	69.9	Paisley I.R.K. Rev.*	UDUP	23,922	54.2	
			Coulter R.J. Rev.	UU	10,749	24.3	
			Farren S.N.	SDLP	6,193	14.0	
			McMahon P.	SF	2,860	6.5*	
			Samuel M.H.	NIEP	451	1.0*	
					13,173	29.8	

[Seeks Re-election]

1986	65,157	53.5	Paisley I.R.K. Rev.*	UDUP	33,937	97.4	+43.2
(23/1)			Barry P.	FAIA	913	2.6*	
					33,024	94.8	

1987	65,733	62.8	Paisley I.R.K. Rev.*	UDUP	28,383	68.7	+14.6
			Farren S.N.	SDLP	5,149	12.5	-1.6
			Williams J.G.	APNI	5,140	12.4	+12.4
			Regan S.	SF	2,633	6.4	-0.1
					23,234	56.2	

1992	69,114	65.8	Paisley I.R.K. Rev.*	UDUP	23,152	50.9	-17.8
			Gaston J.A.	UU	8,216	18.1	+18.1
			Farren S.N.	SDLP	6,512	14.3	+1.8
			Williams J.G.	APNI	3,442	7.6	-4.9
			Sowler T.R.H.	Con	2,263	5.0*	+5.0
			McCarry J.K.	SF	1,916	4.2*	-2.2
					14,936	32.8	

7

ANTRIM SOUTH [12]

Election	Electors	T'out	Candidate	Party	Votes	% Sh	% Ch
1983	59,233	65.6	Forsythe C.	UU	17,727	45.7	
			Thompson R.	UDUP	10,935	28.2	
			Mawhinney G.H.	APNI	4,612	11.9*	
			Maginness A.	SDLP	3,377	8.7*	
			Laverty S.H.	SF	1,629	4.2*	
			Smyth K.	WP	549	1.4*	
					6,792	17.5	

[Seeks Re-election]

Election	Electors	T'out	Candidate	Party	Votes	% Sh	% Ch
1986	61,238	52.2	Forsythe C.*	UU	30,087	94.1	+48.4
(23/1)			Barry P.	FAIA	1,870	5.9	
					28,217	88.3	

Election	Electors	T'out	Candidate	Party	Votes	% Sh	% Ch
1987	61,649	59.1	Forsythe C.*	UU	25,395	69.8	+24.1
			Mawhinney G.H.	APNI	5,808	16.0	+4.1
			McClelland S.D.	SDLP	3,611	9.9	+1.2
			Cushinan H.J.	SF	1,592	4.4*	+0.2
					19,587	53.8	

Election	Electors	T'out	Candidate	Party	Votes	% Sh	% Ch
1992	67,192	62.9	Forsythe C.*	UU	29,956	70.9	+1.2
			McClelland S.D.	SDLP	5,397	12.8	+2.9
			Blair J.K.	APNI	5,224	12.4	-3.6
			Cushinan H.J.	SF	1,220	2.9*	-1.5
			Dino-Martin D.J.	Ind	442	1.0*	
					24,559	58.1	

ARGYLL AND BUTE [13]

Election	Electors	T'out	Candidate	Party	Votes	% Sh	% Ch
1983	47,497	72.9	Mackay J.J.*	Con	13,380	38.6	
			Michie J.R. Ms.	Lib	9,536	27.5	
			Smith I.	SNP	8,514	24.6	
			McCafferty C.	Lab	3,204	9.3*	
					3,844	11.1	
1987	48,700	75.5	Michie J.R. Ms.	Lib	13,726	37.3	+9.8
			Mackay J.J.*	Con	12,332	33.5	-5.1
			Shaw R.R.	SNP	6,297	17.1	-7.5
			Tierney D.	Lab	4,437	12.1	+2.8
					1,394	3.8	
1992	47,921	76.1	Michie J.R. Ms.*	LD	12,739	34.9	-2.4
			Corrie J.A.	Con	10,117	27.7	-5.8
			MacCormick D.N.	SNP	8,689	23.8	+6.7
			Browne D.	Lab	4,946	13.6	+1.5
					2,622	7.2	

ARUNDEL [14]

Election	Electors	T'out	Candidate	Party	Votes	% Sh	% Ch
1983	74,849	69.7	Marshall R.M.*	Con	31,096	59.6	
			Walsh J.M.M. Dr.	Lib	15,391	29.5	
			Rees G.C.	Lab	4,302	8.2*	
			Wadman J.H.	Ind Con	1,399	2.7*	
					15,705	30.1	
1987	77,406	72.4	Marshall R.M.*	Con	34,356	61.3	+1.8
			Walsh J.M.M. Dr.	Lib	15,476	27.6	-1.9
			Slowe P.M.	Lab	6,177	11.0	+2.8
					18,880	33.7	
1992	79,299	77.0	Marshall R.M.*	Con	35,405	58.0	-3.4
			Walsh J.M.M.Dr.	LD	15,542	25.5	-2.2
			Nash R.A.	Lab	8,321	13.6	+2.6
			Renson D.A. Ms.	Lib	1,103	1.8*	+1.8
			Corbin R.D.	Green	693	1.1*	+1.1
					19,863	32.5	

ASHFIELD [15]

Election	Electors	T'out	Candidate	Party	Votes	% Sh	% Ch
1983	69,791	73.7	Haynes D.F.*	Lab	21,859	42.5	
			Seligman R.J.R.	Con	15,772	30.7	
			Stein F.B. Ms.	Lib	13,812	26.8	
					6,087	11.8	
1987	70,937	77.2	Haynes D.F.*	Lab	22,812	41.7	-0.8
			Coleman B.G.	Con	18,412	33.6	+3.0
			Stein F.B. Ms.	Lib	13,542	24.7	-2.1
					4,400	8.0	
1992	72,528	80.4	Hoon G.W.	Lab	32,018	54.9	+13.2
			Robertson L.A.	Con	19,031	32.6	-1.0
			Turton J.S.	LD	7,291	12.5	-12.2
					12,987	22.3	

ASHFORD [16]

Election	Electors	T'out	Candidate	Party	Votes	% Sh	% Ch
1983	65,442	73.2	Speed H.K.*	Con	27,230	56.8	
			Hawkes J.C. Ms.	SDP	13,319	27.8	
			Lewis P.A.	Lab	6,167	12.9	
			Porter C.A. Dr.	Green	569	1.2*	
			King J.W.	Ind Lab	456	1.0*	
			Lockwood R.E.	BNP	195	0.4*	
					13,911	29.0	
1987	70,052	75.7	Speed H.K.*	Con	29,978	56.5	-0.3
			Macmillan N.N.	SDP	14,490	27.3	-0.5
			Wiggins M.J.	Lab	7,775	14.7	+1.8
			Porter C.A. Dr.	Green	778	1.5*	+0.3
					15,488	29.2	
1992	71,768†	79.2	Speed H.K.*	Con	31,031	54.6	-1.9
			Headley C.L.B. Ms.	LD	13,672	24.1	-3.3
			Cameron D.A. Ms.	Lab	11,365	20.0	+5.3
			Porter C.A. Dr.	Green	773	1.4*	-0.1
					17,359	30.5	

ASHTON-UNDER-LYNE [17]

Election	Electors	T'out	Candidate	Party	Votes	% Sh	% Ch
1983	58,963	71.6	Sheldon R.E.*	Lab	20,987	49.7	
			Spring R.J.G.	Con	13,290	31.5	
			Adler J.	SDP	7,521	17.8	
			Hallsworth D.P.	RCP	407	1.0*	
					7,697	18.2	
1987	58,440	74.0	Sheldon R.E.*	Lab	22,389	51.8	+2.0
			Cadman H.L.	Con	13,103	30.3	-1.2
			Hunter M.J.	Lib	7,760	17.9	+0.1
					9,286	21.5	
1992	58,702†	73.9	Sheldon R.E.*	Lab	24,550	56.6	+4.8
			Pinniger J.R.	Con	13,615	31.4	+1.1
			Turner C.W.	LD	4,005	9.2	-8.7
			Hall C.L.	Lib	907	2.1*	+2.1
			Brannigan J.	NLP	289	0.7*	+0.7
					10,935	25.2	

AYLESBURY [18]

Election	Electors	T'out	Candidate	Party	Votes	% Sh	% Ch
1983	72,792	71.5	Raison T.H.F.*	Con	30,230	58.1	
			Soole M.A.	SDP	15,308	29.4	
			Moran M.P.	Lab	6,354	12.2*	
			Chapman T.J.	Ind	166	0.3*	
					14,922	28.7	
1987	76,919	74.5	Raison T.H.F.*	Con	32,970	57.5	-0.5
			Soole M.A.	SDP	16,412	28.6	-0.8
			Larner J. Ms.	Lab	7,936	13.8	+1.6
					16,558	28.9	
1992	79,090†	80.4	Lidington D.R.	Con	36,500	57.4	-0.1
			Bowles S.M. Ms.	LD	17,640	27.7	-0.9
			Priest R.	Lab	8,517	13.4	-0.5
			Foster N.A.	Green	702	1.1*	+1.1
			D'Arcy B.H.M.	NLP	239	0.4*	+0.4
					18,860	29.7	

AYR [19]

Election	Electors	T'out	Candidate	Party	Votes	% Sh	% Ch
1983	65,010	76.7	Younger G.K.H. Hon.*	Con	21,325	42.8	
			MacDonald K.	Lab	13,338	26.8	
			Brodie C.G.	Lib	12,740	25.6	
			Goldie I.R.	SNP	2,431	4.9*	
					7,987	16.0	
1987	66,450	79.9	Younger G.K.H. Hon.*	Con	20,942	39.4	-3.4
			MacDonald K.	Lab	20,760	39.1	+12.3
			Moody K.W.	Lib	7,859	14.8	-10.8
			Weir C.T.	SNP	3,548	6.7	+1.8
					182	0.3	
1992	65,534	83.0	Gallie P.R.	Con	22,172	40.8	+1.3
			Osborne A.G.	Lab	22,087	40.6	+1.5
			Mullin B.A. Ms.	SNP	5,949	10.9	+4.3
			Boss J.A.	LD	4,067	7.5	-7.3
			Scott R.B.	NLP	132	0.2*	+0.2
					85	0.2	

BANBURY [20]

Election	Electors	T'out	Candidate	Party	Votes	% Sh	% Ch
1983	65,324	75.2	Baldry A.B.	Con	26,225	53.4	
			Fitchett K.E.	SDP	13,200	26.9	
			Hodgson J.B.	Lab	9,343	19.0	
			Brough D.N.	MRLP	383	0.8*	
					13,025	26.5	
1987	69,381	76.2	Baldry A.B.*	Con	29,716	56.2	+2.8
			Rowland D.C.	SDP	12,386	23.4	-3.4
			Honeybone J.A.	Lab	10,789	20.4	+1.4
					17,330	32.8	
1992	71,847	81.5	Baldry A.B.*	Con	32,215	55.0	-1.2
			Billingham A.T. Ms.	Lab	15,495	26.5	+6.1
			Fisher G.J.	LD	10,602	18.1	-5.3
			Ticciati R.	NLP	250	0.4*	+0.4
					16,720	28.6	

BANFF AND BUCHAN [21]

Election	Electors	T'out	Candidate	Party	Votes	% Sh	% Ch
1983	60,403	67.0	McQuarrie A.*	Con	16,072	39.7	
			Henderson D.	SNP	15,135	37.4	
			Needham E.A.	SDP	6,084	15.0	
			Lloyd I.F.R.	Lab	3,150	7.8*	
					937	2.3	
1987	62,149	70.8	Salmond A.E.A.	SNP	19,462	44.3	+6.8
			McQuarrie A.*	Con	17,021	38.7	-1.0
			Burness G.M.	SDP	4,211	9.6	-5.5
			Livie J.M.	Lab	3,281	7.5	-0.3
					2,441	5.6	
1992	64,472	71.6	Salmond A.E.A.*	SNP	21,954	47.5	+3.3
			Manson S.P.	Con	17,846	38.6	-0.1
			Balcombe B.R.	Lab	3,803	8.2	+0.8
			Kemp R.C. Ms.	LD	2,588	5.6	-4.0
					4,108	8.9	

BARKING [22]

Election	Electors	T'out	Candidate	Party	Votes	% Sh	% Ch
1983	52,362	65.4	Richardson J. Ms.	Lab	14,415	42.1	
			Summerson H.H.F.	Con	10,389	30.4	
			Gibb J.K.	Lib	8,770	25.6	
			Newport I.R.	NF	646	1.9*	
					4,026	11.8	
1987	51,639	66.9	Richardson J. Ms.*	Lab	15,307	44.3	+2.2
			Sharp W.K.	Con	11,898	34.4	+4.1
			Gibb J.K.	Lib	7,336	21.2	-4.4
					3,409	9.9	
1992	50,480	70.0	Richardson J. Ms.*	Lab	18,224	51.6	+7.3
			Kennedy J.	Con	11,956	33.9	-0.6
			Churchman S.W.	LD	5,133	14.5	-6.7
					6,268	17.7	
[Death]							
1994 (9/6)	49,635	38.3	Hodge M. Ms.	Lab	13,704	72.1	20.5
			White G.	LD	2,290	12.0	-2.5
			May T.M. Ms.	Con	1,976	10.4	-23.5
			Needs G.	NF	551	2.9*	
			Batten G.	UKI	406	2.1*	
			Butensky H. Ms.	NLP	90	0.5*	
					11,414	60.0	

13

BARNSLEY CENTRAL [23]

Election	Electors	T'out	Candidate	Party	Votes	% Sh	% Ch
1983	55,115	66.3	Mason R.*	Lab	21,847	59.8	
			Oldfield H.S.	Con	7,674	21.0	
			Reid G.C. Rev.	Lib	7,011	19.2	
					14,173	38.8	
1987	55,902	70.0	Illsley E.E.	Lab	26,139	66.8	+7.0
			Prais V. Ms.	Con	7,088	18.1	-2.9
			Holland S.A.M. Ms.	Lib	5,928	15.1	-4.1
					19,051	48.7	
1992	55,374†	70.5	Illsley E.E.*	Lab	27,048	69.3	+2.5
			Senior D.N.	Con	7,687	19.7	+1.6
			Cowton S.R.	LD	4,321	11.1	-4.1
					19,361	49.6	

BARNSLEY EAST [24]

Election	Electors	T'out	Candidate	Party	Votes	% Sh	% Ch
1983	53,611	66.5	Patchett T.	Lab	23,505	65.9	
			Tomlinson P.W.	Lib	6,413	18.0	
			England G.	Con	5,749	16.1	
					17,092	47.9	
1987	53,505	72.6	Patchett T.*	Lab	28,948	74.5	+8.6
			Clappison W.J.	Con	5,437	14.0	-2.1
			Griffiths G.J.	Lib	4,482	11.5	-6.4
					23,511	60.5	
1992	53,956†	72.9	Patchett T.*	Lab	30,346	77.2	+2.7
			Procter J.M.	Con	5,569	14.2	+0.2
			Anginotti S. Ms.	LD	3,399	8.6	-2.9
					24,777	63.0	
[Death]							
1996	53, 215	33.6	Ennis J.	Lab	13,683	76.4	-0.7
(12/12)			Willis D.	LD	1,502	8.4	-0.3
			Ellison J. Ms.	Con	1,299	7.3	-6.9
			Capstick W.	SLP	949	5.3	
			Tolstoy N.	UKI	378	2.1*	
			Hyland J. Ms.	Ind	89	0.5*	
					12,181	68.1	

BARNSLEY WEST AND PENISTONE [25]

Election	Electors	T'out	Candidate	Party	Votes	% Sh	% Ch
1983	60,648	73.2	McKay A.*	Lab	22,560	50.8	
			Hartley T.G.	Con	12,218	27.5	
			Evans J.W.	SDP	9,624	21.7	
					10,342	23.3	
1987	61,091	75.6	McKay A.*	Lab	26,498	57.3	+6.5
			Duncan A.J.C.	Con	12,307	26.6	-0.9
			Hall R.	SDP	7,409	16.0	-5.6
					14,191	30.7	
1992	63,391†	75.7	Clapham M.	Lab	27,965	58.3	+0.9
			Sawyer G.	Con	13,461	28.0	+1.4
			Nicolson I.H.	LD	5,610	11.7	-4.3
			Jones D.	Green	970	2.0*	+2.0
					14,504	30.2	

BARROW AND FURNESS [26]

Election	Electors	T'out	Candidate	Party	Votes	% Sh	% Ch
1983	67,896	75.2	Franks C.S.	Con	22,284	43.6	
			Booth A.E.*	Lab	17,707	34.7	
			Cottier D.K.	SDP	11,079	21.7	
					4,577	9.0	
1987	69,288	79.0	Franks C.S.*	Con	25,432	46.5	+2.8
			Phizacklea P.	Lab	21,504	39.3	+4.6
			Phelps R.W.	SDP	7,799	14.2	-7.4
					3,928	7.2	
1992	67,835	82.0	Hutton J.M.P.	Lab	26,568	47.7	+8.5
			Franks C.S.*	Con	22,990	41.3	-5.1
			Crane C.J.	LD	6,089	10.9	-3.3
					3,578	6.4	

15

BASILDON [27]

Election	Electors	T'out	Candidate	Party	Votes	% Sh	% Ch
1983	65,604	69.0	Amess D.A.A.	Con	17,516	38.7	
			Fulbrook J.G.H.	Lab	16,137	35.6	
			Slipman S. Ms.	SDP	11,634	25.7	
					1,379	3.0	
1987	67,985	73.8	Amess D.A.A.*	Con	21,858	43.5	+4.9
			Fulbrook J.G.H.	Lab	19,209	38.3	+2.6
			Auvray R.M.	Lib	9,139	18.2	-7.5
					2,649	5.3	
1992	67,442	79.8	Amess D.A.A.*	Con	24,159	44.9	+1.4
			Potter J.R.	Lab	22,679	42.2	+3.9
			Williams G.	LD	6,963	12.9	-5.3
					1,480	2.8	

BASINGSTOKE [28]

Election	Electors	T'out	Candidate	Party	Votes	% Sh	% Ch
1983	71,975	76.8	Hunter A.R.F.	Con	28,381	51.3	
			Hudson Davies G.E.*	SDP	15,931	28.8	
			McAllister J.S.	Lab	10,646	19.3	
			Wilson I.S.	BNP	344	0.6*	
					12,450	22.5	
1987	78,003	77.0	Hunter A.R.F.*	Con	33,657	56.0	+4.7
			Bennett D.A.	SDP	15,764	26.3	-2.6
			Daden P.F.	Lab	10,632	17.7	-1.5
					17,893	29.8	
1992	82,962	82.8	Hunter A.R.F.*	Con	37,521	54.6	-1.4
			Bull D.J.C.	Lab	16,323	23.8	+6.1
			Curtis C.I.	LD	14,119	20.6	-5.7
			Oldaker V.J. Ms.	Green	714	1.0*	+1.0
					21,198	30.8	

BASSETLAW [29]

Election	Electors	T'out	Candidate	Party	Votes	% Sh	% Ch
1983	65,721	74.2	Ashton J.W.*	Lab	22,231	45.6	
			Cleasby M.A.	Con	18,400	37.7	
			Withnall B.	SDP	8,124	16.7	
					3,831	7.9	
1987	68,043	77.6	Ashton J.W.*	Lab	25,385	48.1	+2.5
			Selves D.R.J.	Con	19,772	37.5	-0.3
			Smith W.G.	SDP	7,616	14.4	-2.2
					5,613	10.6	
1992	68,583†	79.4	Ashton J.W.*	Lab	29,061	53.4	+5.3
			Spelman C.A. Ms.	Con	19,064	35.0	-2.5
			Reynolds M.J.	LD	6,340	11.6	-2.8
					9,997	18.4	

BATH [30]

Election	Electors	T'out	Candidate	Party	Votes	% Sh	% Ch
1983	64,325	74.4	Patten C.F.*	Con	22,544	47.1	
			Dean J.M.	SDP	17,240	36.0	
			Pott A.J.	Lab	7,259	15.2	
			Grimes D.P.	Green	441	0.9*	
			Wardle R.S.	Ind Lib	319	0.7*	
			Young G.S.	Ind	67	0.1*	
					5,304	11.1	
1987	65,246	79.4	Patten C.F.*	Con	23,515	45.4	-1.7
			Dean J.M.	SDP	22,103	42.7	+6.6
			Smith J. Ms.	Lab	5,507	10.6	-4.5
			Wall D.N.	Green	687	1.3*	+0.4
					1,412	2.7	
1992	63,838	82.4	Foster D.M.E.	LD	25,718	48.9	+6.3
			Patten C.F.*	Con	21,950	41.8	-3.6
			Richards P.R. Ms.	Lab	4,102	7.8	-2.8
			McCanlis D.	Green	433	0.8*	-0.5
			Barker M.J. Ms.	Lib	172	0.3*	+0.3
			Sked A. Dr.	AFL	117	0.2*	
			Rumming J.A.S.	Ind	79	0.2*	
					3,768	7.2	

17

BATLEY AND SPEN [31]

Election	Electors	T'out	Candidate	Party	Votes	% Sh	% Ch
1983	73,798	73.4	Peacock E.J. Ms.	Con	21,433	39.6	
			Woolmer K.J.*	Lab	20,563	38.0	
			Woolley E.S.	SDP	11,678	21.6	
			Lord C.R.	Green	493	0.9*	
					870	1.6	
1987	74,347	79.0	Peacock E.J. Ms.*	Con	25,512	43.4	+3.9
			Woolmer K.J.	Lab	24,150	41.1	+3.2
			Burke K.	SDP	8,372	14.3	-7.3
			Harrison A.	Ind Lab	689	1.2*	
					1,362	2.3	
1992	76,387	79.7	Peacock E.J. Ms.*	Con	27,629	45.4	+2.0
			Durkin E.A. Ms.	Lab	26,221	43.1	+2.0
			Beever G.J.	LD	6,380	10.5	-3.8
			Lord C.R.	Green	628	1.0*	+0.1
					1,408	2.3	

BATTERSEA [32]

Election	Electors	T'out	Candidate	Party	Votes	% Sh	% Ch
1983	65,938	66.6	Dubs A.*	Lab	19,248	43.8	
			Allason R.W.S.	Con	15,972	36.4	
			Harris M.F.	SDP	7,675	17.5	
			Salt M.J.	NF	539	1.2*	
			Willington S.G. Ms.	Green	377	0.9*	
			Jackson T.A.	Ind	86	0.2*	
			Purie-Harwell K. Ms.	Ind	22	0.1*	
					3,276	7.5	
1987	66,979	70.7	Bowis J.C.	Con	20,945	44.2	+7.9
			Dubs A.*	Lab	20,088	42.4	-1.4
			Harries D.I.	SDP	5,634	11.9	-5.6
			Willington S.G. Ms.	Green	559	1.2*	+0.3
			Bell A.B.	WRP	116	0.2*	
					857	1.8	
1992	68,207†	76.7	Bowis J.C.*	Con	26,390	50.5	+6.2
			Dubs A.	Lab	21,550	41.2	-1.2
			O'Brien R.	LD	3,659	7.0	-4.9
			Wingrove I.B.	Green	584	1.1*	-0.1
			Stevens W.A.	NLP	98	0.2*	+0.2
					4,840	9.3	

18

BEACONSFIELD [33]

Election	Electors	T'out	Candidate	Party	Votes	% Sh	% Ch
1983	66,186	72.4	Smith T.J.*	Con	30,552	63.8	
			Ive D.H.	Lib	12,252	25.6	
			Smith J.S.	Lab	5,107	10.7*	
					18,300	38.2	
1987	67,713	74.6	Smith T.J.*	Con	33,324	66.0	+2.2
			Ive D.H.	Lib	11,985	23.7	-1.8
			Harper K.J.	Lab	5,203	10.3	-0.4
					21,339	42.2	
1992	66,899†	79.0	Smith T.J.*	Con	33,817	64.0	-2.0
			Purse P.A. Ms.	LD	10,220	19.3	-4.4
			Smith D.G.	Lab	7,163	13.5	+3.2
			Foulds W.F.	Ind Con	1,317	2.5*	
			Foss A.P.O.	NLP	196	0.4*	+0.4
			Martin J. Ms.	Ind	166	0.3*	
					23,597	44.6	

BECKENHAM [34]

Election	Electors	T'out	Candidate	Party	Votes	% Sh	% Ch
1983	58,719	70.0	Goodhart P.C. Sir.*	Con	23,606	57.4	
			Forrest C.M. Ms.	Lib	10,936	26.6	
			Dowd J.P.	Lab	6,386	15.5	
			Younger G.W.	BNP	203	0.5*	
					12,670	30.8	
1987	60,110	73.6	Goodhart P.C. Sir.*	Con	24,903	56.3	-1.1
			Darracott C.G.	Lib	11,439	25.9	-0.7
			Ritchie K.G.H.	Lab	7,888	17.8	+2.3
					13,464	30.4	
1992	59,469	77.8	Merchant P.R.G.	Con	26,323	56.9	+0.6
			Ritchie K.G.H.	Lab	11,038	23.8	+6.0
			Williams M.C. Ms.	LD	8,038	17.4	-8.5
			Williams G.	Lib	643	1.4*	+1.4
			Shaw P.J.	NLP	243	0.5*	+0.5
					15,285	33.0	

BEDFORDSHIRE MID [35]

Election	Electors	T'out	Candidate	Party	Votes	% Sh	% Ch
1983	75,558	76.9	Lyell N.W.*	Con	33,042	56.8	
			Howes M. Ms.	Lib	15,661	26.9	
			Tizard J.N.	Lab	9,420	16.2	
					17,381	29.9	
1987	80,675	78.6	Lyell N.W.*	Con	37,411	59.0	+2.1
			Hills N.C.	SDP	14,560	23.0	-4.0
			Heywood J.	Lab	11,463	18.1	+1.9
					22,851	36.0	
1992	81,950†	84.4	Lyell N.W. Sir.*	Con	40,230	58.2	-0.8
			Clayton R.A.	Lab	15,092	21.8	+3.8
			Hills N.C.	LD	11,957	17.3	-5.7
			Cottier D.P.	Lib	1,582	2.3*	+2.3
			Lorys M.J.	NLP	279	0.4*	+0.4
					25,138	36.4	

BEDFORDSHIRE NORTH [36]

Election	Electors	T'out	Candidate	Party	Votes	% Sh	% Ch
1983	71,491	75.2	Skeet T.H.H.*	Con	27,969	52.0	
			Gibbons B.K.W.	Lib	14,120	26.3	
			Healy P. Ms.	Lab	11,323	21.1	
			Hughes N.J.	Ind	344	0.6*	
					13,849	25.8	
1987	73,536	77.2	Skeet T.H.H. Sir.*	Con	29,845	52.6	+0.6
			Lennon J.V. Ms.	Lib	13,340	23.5	-2.8
			Henderson C.B.	Lab	13,140	23.2	+2.1
			Slee C.D.	Ind	435	0.8*	
					16,505	29.1	
1992	73,789†	80.1	Skeet T.H.H. Sir.*	Con	29,970	50.7	-1.9
			Hall P.	Lab	18,302	31.0	+7.8
			Smithson M.	LD	10,014	16.9	-6.6
			Smith L. Ms.	Green	643	1.1*	+1.1
			Bence B.H.	NLP	178	0.3*	+0.3
					11,668	19.7	

Election	Electors	T'out	Candidate	Party	Votes	% Sh	% Ch
1983	76,298	75.6	Madel W.D.*	Con	31,767	55.1	
			Byfield R.	SDP	16,036	27.8	
			Cochrane W.	Lab	9,899	17.2	
					15,731	27.3	
1987	79,336	78.3	Madel W.D.*	Con	36,140	58.2	+3.1
			Burrow J.R.	SDP	13,835	22.3	-5.5
			Dimoldenberg P.H.	Lab	11,352	18.3	+1.1
			Rollings P.J.	Green	822	1.3*	+1.3
					22,305	35.9	
1992	80,120	81.9	Madel W.D.*	Con	37,498	57.1	-1.0
			Elliott B.E.	Lab	16,225	24.7	+6.5
			Freeman J.M.	LD	10,988	16.7	-5.5
			Rollings P.J.	Green	689	1.0*	-0.3
			Gilmour J.D.	NLP	239	0.4*	+0.4
					21,273	32.4	

BELFAST EAST [38]

Election	Electors	T'out	Candidate	Party	Votes	% Sh	% Ch
1983	55,539	70.1	Robinson P.D.*	UDUP	17,631	45.3	
			Burchill D.J.M.	UU	9,642	24.8	
			Napier O.J.	APNI	9,373	24.1	
			Donaldson D.	SF	682	1.8*	
			Tang M. Ms.	Ind Lab	584	1.5*	
			Prendiville P.M.	SDLP	519	1.3*	
			Cullen F.J.	WP	421	1.1*	
			Boyd H.	Ind	59	0.2*	
					7,989	20.5	

[Seeks Re-election]

Election	Electors	T'out	Candidate	Party	Votes	% Sh	% Ch
1986	55,256	61.7	Robinson P.D.*	UDUP	27,607	81.0	+35.7
(23/1)			Oliver J.N.	APNI	5,917	17.4	-6.7
			Cullen F.J.	WP	578	1.7*	+0.6
					21,690	63.6	

Election	Electors	T'out	Candidate	Party	Votes	% Sh	% Ch
1987	54,628	60.2	Robinson P.D.*	UDUP	20,372	61.9	+16.6
			Alderdice J.T. Dr.	APNI	10,574	32.1	+8.0
			Cullen F.J.	WP	1,314	4.0*	+2.9
			O'Donnell J.	SF	649	2.0*	+0.2
					9,798	29.8	

Election	Electors	T'out	Candidate	Party	Votes	% Sh	% Ch
1992	52,869	67.7	Robinson P.D.*	UDUP	18,437	51.5	+6.2
			Alderdice J.T. Dr.	APNI	10,650	29.8	-2.4
			Greene D.	Con	3,314	9.3	+9.3
			Dunlop D. Ms.	Ind U	2,256	6.3	
			O'Donnell J.	SF	679	1.9*	-0.1
			Bell J.	WP	327	0.9*	-3.1
			Redden G.F.	NLP	128	0.4*	+0.4
					7,787	21.8	

BELFAST NORTH [39]

Election	Electors	T'out	Candidate	Party	Votes	% Sh	% Ch
1983	61,087	69.4	Walker A.C.	UU	15,339	36.2	
			Seawright G.	UDUP	8,260	19.5	
			Feeney B.	SDLP	5,944	14.0	
			Austin J.	SF	5,451	12.9	
			Maguire P.	APNI	3,879	9.1*	
			Lynch S.	WP	2,412	5.7*	
			Gault W.H.S.	Ind UDUP	1,134	2.7*	
					7,079	16.7	

[Seeks Re-election]

Election	Electors	T'out	Candidate	Party	Votes	% Sh	% Ch
1986	59,791	50.6	Walker A.C.*	UU	21,649	71.5	+35.3
(23/1)			Maguire P.	APNI	5,072	16.7	+7.6
			Lynch S.	WP	3,563	11.8	+6.1
					16,577	54.7	
1987	59,124	62.3	Walker A.C.*	UU	14,355	39.0	+2.8
			Maginness A.	SDLP	5,795	15.7	+1.7
			Seawright G.	Ind UDUP	5,671	15.4	
			McManus P.	SF	5,062	13.7	+0.9
			Lynch S.	WP	3,062	8.3	+2.6
			Campbell T.	APNI	2,871	7.8	-1.3
					8,560	23.3	
1992	55,068	65.2	Walker A.C.*	UU	17,240	48.0	+9.0
			Maginness A.	SDLP	7,615	21.2	+5.5
			McManus T.P.	SF	4,693	13.1	-0.7
			Campbell T.	APNI	2,246	6.3	-1.5
			Redpath M.R. Ms.	Con	2,107	5.9	+5.9
			Lynch S.	NA	1,386	3.9*	+3.9
			Smith M. Ms.	WP	419	1.2*	-7.1
			O'Leary D.	NLP	208	0.6*	+0.6
					9,625	26.8	

Election	Electors	T'out	Candidate	Party	Votes	% Sh	% Ch
1983	53,674	69.6	Smyth W.M. Rev.*	UU	18,669	50.0	
			Cook D.S.	APNI	8,945	23.9	
			McCrea R.S.	UDUP	4,565	12.2*	
			McDonnell A. Dr.	SDLP	3,216	8.6*	
			McKnight S.	SF	1,107	3.0*	
			Carr G.	WP	856	2.3*	
					9,724	26.0	

[Seeks Re-election]

Election	Electors	T'out	Candidate	Party	Votes	% Sh	% Ch
1986	53,944	56.6	Smyth W.M. Rev.*	UU	21,771	71.3	+21.4
(23/1)			Cook D.S.	APNI	7,635	25.0	+1.1
			Carr G.	WP	1,109	3.6*	+1.3
					14,136	46.3	

Election	Electors	T'out	Candidate	Party	Votes	% Sh	% Ch
1987	54,208	60.3	Smyth W.M. Rev.*	UU	18,917	57.8	+7.9
			Cook D.S.	APNI	6,963	21.3	-2.7
			McDonnell A. Dr.	SDLP	4,268	13.0	+4.4
			Carr G.	WP	1,528	4.7*	+2.4
			McKnight S.	SF	1,030	3.1*	+0.2
					11,954	36.5	

Election	Electors	T'out	Candidate	Party	Votes	% Sh	% Ch
1992	52,050	64.5	Smyth W.M. Rev.*	UU	16,336	48.6	-9.2
			McDonnell A. Dr.	SDLP	6,266	18.7	+5.6
			Montgomery J.A.	APNI	5,054	15.0	-6.2
			Fee A.L.	Con	3,356	10.0	+10.0
			Hayes S.	SF	1,123	3.3*	+0.2
			Hadden P.	LTU	875	2.6*	+2.6
			Lynn P.J.T.	WP	362	1.1*	+1.1
			Mullan T.M.M. Ms.	NLP	212	0.6*	+0.6
					10,070	30.0	

BELFAST WEST [41]

Election	Electors	T'out	Candidate	Party	Votes	% Sh	% Ch
1983	59,675	74.3	Adams G.	SF	16,379	36.9	
			Hendron J.G. Dr.	SDLP	10,934	24.6	
			Fitt G.*	Soc	10,326	23.3	
			Passmore T.	UU	2,435	5.5*	
			Haffey G.A.	UDUP	2,399	5.4*	
			McMahon M. Ms.	WP	1,893	4.3*	
					5,445	12.3	
1987	59,324	69.1	Adams G.*	SF	16,862	41.2	+4.2
			Hendron J.G. Dr.	SDLP	14,641	35.7	+11.1
			Millar F.	UU	7,646	18.7	+13.2
			McMahon M. Ms.	WP	1,819	4.4*	+0.2
					2,221	5.4	
1992	54,644	73.1	Hendron J.G. Dr.	SDLP	17,415	43.6	+7.8
			Adams G.*	SF	16,826	42.1	+0.9
			Cobain F.	UU	4,766	11.9	-6.7
			Lowry J.T.	WP	750	1.9*	+1.9
			Kennedy M.F.	NLP	213	0.5*	+0.5
					589	1.5	

BERKSHIRE EAST [42]

Election	Electors	T'out	Candidate	Party	Votes	% Sh	% Ch
1983	82,216	72.7	MacKay A.J.	Con	33,967	56.8	
			O'Sullivan K.P.	SDP	17,868	29.9	
			Rogers E.G. Ms.	Lab	7,953	13.3	
					16,099	26.9	
1987	87,820	73.8	MacKay A.J.*	Con	39,094	60.3	+3.5
			Murray L.A. Ms.	SDP	16,468	25.4	-4.5
			Evans R.J.E.	Lab	9,287	14.3	+1.0
					22,626	34.9	
1992	90,414	81.4	MacKay A.J.*	Con	43,898	59.7	-0.6
			Murray L.A. Ms.	LD	15,218	20.7	-4.7
			Dibble K.	Lab	14,458	19.7	+5.3
					28,680	39.0	

BERWICK-UPON-TWEED [43]

Election	Electors	T'out	Candidate	Party	Votes	% Sh	% Ch
1983	53,585	77.8	Beith A.J.*	Lib	21,958	52.7	
			Brazier J.W.H.	Con	13,743	33.0	
			Baird V. Ms.	Lab	5,975	14.3	
					8,215	19.7	
1987	54,378	77.3	Beith A.J.*	Lib	21,903	52.1	-0.6
			Middleton J.T.	Con	12,400	29.5	-3.5
			Lambert S.	Lab	7,360	17.5	+3.2
			Pamphilion N.D.	Green	379	0.9*	+0.9
					9,503	22.6	
1992	54,937†	79.1	Beith A.J.*	LD	19,283	44.4	-7.7
			Henfrey A.W.	Con	14,240	32.8	+3.3
			Adam G.J.	Lab	9,933	22.9	+5.4
					5,043	11.6	

BETHNAL GREEN AND STEPNEY [44]

Election	Electors	T'out	Candidate	Party	Votes	% Sh	% Ch
1983	55,333	55.6	Shore P.D.*	Lab	15,740	51.2	
			Charters S.J.	Lib	9,382	30.5	
			Argyropulo D.C.	Con	4,323	14.1	
			Clark V.J.	NF	800	2.6*	
			Rees J.	Comm	243	0.8*	
			Chaudhuri B.N.	Ind	214	0.7*	
			Mahoney P.J.	Ind	36	0.1*	
					6,358	20.7	
1987	55,769	57.6	Shore P.D.*	Lab	15,490	48.2	-3.0
			Shaw J.A.	Lib	10,206	31.8	+1.3
			Maitland O.H. Ms.	Con	6,176	19.2	+5.2
			Gasquoine S.L. Ms.	Comm	232	0.7*	-0.1
					5,284	16.5	
1992	55,675†	65.5	Shore P.D.*	Lab	20,350	55.8	+7.6
			Shaw J.A.	LD	8,120	22.3	-9.5
			Emmerson J.E. Ms.	Con	6,507	17.9	-1.4
			Edmonds R.C.	BNP	1,310	3.6*	+3.6
			Kelsey S.E.	Comm	156	0.4*	-0.3
					12,230	33.6	

BEVERLEY [45]

Election	Electors	T'out	Candidate	Party	Votes	% Sh	% Ch
1983	75,813	73.2	Wall P.H.B. Sir.*	Con	31,233	56.3	
			Pitts M.F.	Lib	17,364	31.3	
			Morley E.A.	Lab	6,921	12.5*	
					13,869	25.0	
1987	78,923	76.3	Cran J.D.	Con	31,459	52.2	-4.0
			Bryant J.W.	Lib	18,864	31.3	+0.0
			Shaw M.	Lab	9,901	16.4	+4.0
					12,595	20.9	
1992	81,033	79.9	Cran J.D.*	Con	34,503	53.3	+1.1
			Collinge A.	LD	17,986	27.8	-3.5
			Challen C.R.	Lab	12,026	18.6	+2.1
			Hetherington D.	NLP	199	0.3*	+0.3
					16,517	25.5	

BEXHILL AND BATTLE [46]

Election	Electors	T'out	Candidate	Party	Votes	% Sh	% Ch
1983	61,785	72.9	Wardle C.F.	Con	30,329	67.3	
			Smith P.R.	Lib	10,583	23.5	
			Pearson I.P.	Lab	3,587	8.0*	
			Rix A.P.M. Ms.	Green	538	1.2*	
					19,746	43.8	
1987	65,288	77.4	Wardle C.F.*	Con	33,570	66.4	-0.9
			Kiernan R.	SDP	13,051	25.8	+2.3
			Watts D.K.	Lab	3,903	7.7	-0.2
					20,519	40.6	
1992	65,829†	79.1	Wardle C.F.*	Con	31,380	60.3	-6.2
			Prochak S.M. Ms.	LD	15,023	28.9	+3.0
			Taylor F.	Lab	4,883	9.4	+1.7
			Prus J.L.	Green	594	1.1*	+1.1
			Smith M.F. Ms.	Ind	190	0.4*	
					16,357	31.4	

BEXLEYHEATH [47]

Election	Electors	T'out	Candidate	Party	Votes	% Sh	% Ch
1983	59,263	74.5	Townsend C.D.*	Con	23,411	53.1	
			Standen B.C.	Lib	13,153	29.8	
			Erlam A.B.	Lab	7,560	17.1	
					10,258	23.2	
1987	59,448	77.8	Townsend C.D.*	Con	24,866	53.7	+0.7
			Standen B.C.	Lib	13,179	28.5	-1.3
			Little J.F.	Lab	8,218	17.8	+0.6
					11,687	25.3	
1992	57,684†	82.2	Townsend C.D.*	Con	25,606	54.0	+0.3
			Browning R.J.	Lab	11,520	24.3	+6.5
			Chaplin A.W. Ms.	LD	10,107	21.3	-7.2
			Cundy R.W.C.	Ind	170	0.4*	
					14,086	29.7	

BILLERICAY [48]

Election	Electors	T'out	Candidate	Party	Votes	% Sh	% Ch
1983	74,779	73.8	Proctor K.H.*	Con	29,635	53.7	
			Bonner P.M.A.E.	Lib	15,020	27.2	
			Sewell C.W.	Lab	10,528	19.1	
					14,615	26.5	
1987	79,535	77.2	Gorman T.E. Ms.	Con	33,741	54.9	+1.2
			Birch M.	SDP	15,725	25.6	-1.6
			Howitt R.S.	Lab	11,942	19.4	+0.4
					18,016	29.3	
1992	80,287	82.5	Gorman T.E. Ms.*	Con	37,406	56.5	+1.6
			Bellard F.	LD	14,912	22.5	-3.1
			Miller A.F. Ms.	Lab	13,880	21.0	+1.5
					22,494	34.0	

BIRKENHEAD [49]

Election	Electors	T'out	Candidate	Party	Votes	% Sh	% Ch
1983	67,293	69.7	Field F.E.*	Lab	23,249	49.6	
			Peet T.	Con	13,535	28.9	
			Lindsay G.C.	Lib	9,782	20.9	
			Clarke H.I. Ms.	Green	337	0.7*	
					9,714	20.7	
1987	65,662	72.3	Field F.E.*	Lab	27,883	58.7	+9.1
			Costa K.J.	Con	12,511	26.3	-2.5
			Kemp R.	Lib	7,095	14.9	-5.9
					15,372	32.4	
1992	62,673	73.0	Field F.E.*	Lab	29,098	63.6	+4.9
			Hughes R.G.M.	Con	11,485	25.1	-1.2
			Williams P.M. Ms.	LD	4,417	9.7	-5.3
			Fox T.R. Ms.	Green	543	1.2*	+1.2
			Griffiths B. Ms.	NLP	190	0.4*	+0.4
					17,613	38.5	

BIRMINGHAM EDGBASTON [50]

Election	Electors	T'out	Candidate	Party	Votes	% Sh	% Ch
1983	55,063	66.2	Knight J.C.J. Ms.*	Con	19,585	53.7	
			Binns J.C.	SDP	8,167	22.4	
			Bilson P.A.	Lab	7,647	21.0	
			Hurdley J. Dr.	Green	516	1.4*	
			Hardwick S.T.	Ind Con	293	0.8*	
			Davis P.A. Ms.	Comm	169	0.5*	
			Howlett D.C. Ms.	Ind	97	0.3*	
					11,418	31.3	
1987	54,416	68.6	Knight J.C.J. Dame*	Con	18,595	49.8	-3.9
			Wilton J.F.	Lab	10,014	26.8	+5.9
			Binns J.C.	SDP	7,843	21.0	-1.4
			Simpson P.M.	Green	559	1.5*	+0.1
			Hardwick S.T.	Ind Con	307	0.8*	
					8,581	23.0	
1992	53,058	71.3	Knight J.C.J. Dame*	Con	18,529	49.0	-0.8
			Wilton J.F.	Lab	14,222	37.6	+10.8
			Robertson-Steel I.R.S.	LD	4,419	11.7	-9.3
			Simpson P.M.	Green	643	1.7*	+0.2
					4,307	11.4	

BIRMINGHAM, ERDINGTON [51]

Election	Electors	T'out	Candidate	Party	Votes	% Sh	% Ch
1983	56,019	67.0	Corbett R.	Lab	14,930	39.8	
			Moylan D.M.G.	Con	14,699	39.2	
			Barber C.B.	SDP	7,915	21.1	
					231	0.6	
1987	54,179	68.5	Corbett R.*	Lab	17,037	45.9	+6.1
			Johnston P.J.	Con	14,570	39.2	+0.1
			Biddlestone N.A.	SDP	5,530	14.9	-6.2
					2,467	6.6	
1992	52,414	70.1	Corbett R.*	Lab	18,549	50.5	+4.6
			Hope S.N.	Con	13,814	37.6	-1.7
			Campbell J.R.B.	LD	4,398	12.0	-2.9
					4,735	12.9	

BIRMINGHAM, HALL GREEN [52]

Election	Electors	T'out	Candidate	Party	Votes	% Sh	% Ch
1983	61,023	70.6	Eyre R.E.*	Con	21,142	49.1	
			Willis M.H.	Lab	11,769	27.3	
			Hemming J.A.M.	Lib	10,175	23.6	
					9,373	21.8	
1987	61,148	74.7	Hargreaves A.R.	Con	20,478	44.9	-4.2
			Brook F.E. Ms.	Lab	12,857	28.2	+0.8
			Wilkes F.M.	SDP	12,323	27.0	+3.4
					7,621	16.7	
1992	60,103	78.2	Hargreaves A.R.*	Con	21,649	46.1	+1.2
			Slowey J.E. Ms.	Lab	17,984	38.3	+10.1
			McGrath D.A.	LD	7,342	15.6	-11.4
					3,665	7.8	

BIRMINGHAM, HODGE HILL [53]

Election	Electors	T'out	Candidate	Party	Votes	% Sh	% Ch
1983	61,234	67.6	Davis T.A.G.*	Lab	19,692	47.6	
			Roe P.M.	Con	14,600	35.3	
			Gopsill G.A.	Lib	6,557	15.8	
			Tomkinson N.D.W.	NF	529	1.3*	
					5,092	12.3	
1987	59,296	68.8	Davis T.A.G.*	Lab	19,872	48.7	+1.1
			Eyre S.J.A.	Con	15,083	36.9	+1.7
			Hardeman K.G.	Lib	5,868	14.4	-1.5
					4,789	11.7	
1992	57,581	70.9	Davis T.A.G.*	Lab	21,895	53.6	+4.9
			Gibson E.M. Ms.	Con	14,827	36.3	-0.6
			Hagan S.C.G.	LD	3,740	9.2	-5.2
			Whicker E.J.	NF	370	0.9*	+0.9
					7,068	17.3	

BIRMINGHAM, LADYWOOD [54]

Election	Electors	T'out	Candidate	Party	Votes	% Sh	% Ch
1983	60,441	62.6	Short C. Ms.	Lab	19,278	51.0	
			Le Hunte P. Ms.	Con	10,248	27.1	
			Hardeman K.G.	Lib	7,758	20.5	
			Bakhtaura B.	Ind	335	0.9*	
			Atkinson R.W.	WRP	198	0.5*	
					9,030	23.9	
1987	58,761	64.8	Short C. Ms.*	Lab	21,971	57.7	+6.7
			Lee S.T.	Con	11,943	31.3	+4.3
			Sangha G.S.	SDP	3,532	9.3	-11.2
			Millington J.H.M. Ms.	Green	650	1.7*	+1.7
					10,028	26.3	
1992	56,995	65.9	Short C. Ms.*	Lab	24,887	66.3	+8.6
			Ashford B.S. Ms.	Con	9,604	25.6	-5.8
			Worth B.L.	LD	3,068	8.2	-1.1
					15,283	40.7	

31

BIRMINGHAM, NORTHFIELD [55]

Election	Electors	T'out	Candidate	Party	Votes	% Sh	% Ch
1983	74,326	71.2	King R.D.	Con	22,596	42.7	
			Spellar J.F.*	Lab	19,836	37.5	
			Webb D.	Lib	10,045	19.0	
			Sheppard P.R.	Comm	420	0.8*	
					2,760	5.2	
1987	73,319	72.6	King R.D.*	Con	24,024	45.1	+2.4
			Spellar J.F.	Lab	20,889	39.2	+1.7
			Gordon J.C.	SDP	8,319	15.6	-3.4
					3,135	5.9	
1992	70,563	76.1	Burden R.H.	Lab	24,433	45.5	+6.3
			King R.D.*	Con	23,803	44.4	-0.8
			Cropp D.L.	LD	5,431	10.1	-5.5
					630	1.2	

BIRMINGHAM, PERRY BARR [56]

Election	Electors	T'out	Candidate	Party	Votes	% Sh	% Ch
1983	74,371	69.2	Rooker J.W.*	Lab	27,061	52.6	
			Portillo M.D.X.	Con	19,659	38.2	
			Williams C.E.	Lib	4,773	9.3*	
					7,402	14.4	
1987	73,767	69.6	Rooker J.W.*	Lab	25,894	50.4	-2.1
			Taylor J.D.B.	Con	18,961	36.9	-1.3
			Webb D.	Lib	6,514	12.7	+3.4
					6,933	13.5	
1992	72,186	71.6	Rooker J.W.*	Lab	27,507	53.2	+2.8
			Green G.G.	Con	18,917	36.6	-0.3
			Philpott T.P.J.G.	LD	5,261	10.2	-2.5
					8,590	16.6	

BIRMINGHAM, SELLY OAK [57]

Election	Electors	T'out	Candidate	Party	Votes	% Sh	% Ch
1983	71,671	71.5	Beaumont-Dark A.M.*	Con	23,008	44.9	
			Turner J.R.H.	Lab	17,612	34.4	
			Wheldall K.W.	SDP	10,613	20.7	
					5,396	10.5	
1987	72,213	73.1	Beaumont-Dark A.M.*	Con	23,305	44.2	-0.7
			Bore A.	Lab	20,721	39.3	+4.9
			Cane C.K.B. Ms.	Lib	8,128	15.4	-5.3
			Hackett W.M. Ms.	Green	611	1.2*	+1.2
					2,584	4.9	
1992	72,195	76.6	Jones L.M. Ms.	Lab	25,430	46.0	+6.7
			Beaumont-Dark A.M.*	Con	23,370	42.3	-1.9
			Osborne D.	LD	5,679	10.3	-5.1
			Slatter P.G.	Green	535	1.0*	-0.2
			Barwood C.W.	NLP	178	0.3*	+0.3
			Malik K.	RCP	84	0.2*	+0.2
					2,060	3.7	

BIRMINGHAM, SMALL HEATH [58]

Election	Electors	T'out	Candidate	Party	Votes	% Sh	% Ch
1983	59,376	60.4	Howell D.H.*	Lab	22,874	63.8	
			Nischal P.	Con	7,262	20.3	
			Bostock A.M.	SDP	5,722	16.0	
					15,612	43.5	
1987	56,722	60.6	Howell D.H.*	Lab	22,787	66.3	+2.5
			Nischal P.	Con	7,266	21.1	+0.9
			Hemming J.A.M.	Lib	3,600	10.5	-5.5
			Clawley A.	Green	559	1.6*	+1.6
			Sheppard P.R.	Comm	154	0.4*	+0.4
					15,521	45.2	
1992	55,233	62.8	Godsiff R.D.	Lab	22,675	65.3	-1.0
			Chaudhary A.Q.	Con	8,686	25.0	+3.9
			Thomas H.A.	LD	2,515	7.2	-3.2
			Clawley H.M. Ms.	Green	824	2.4*	+0.7
					13,989	40.3	

BIRMINGHAM, SPARKBROOK [59]

Election	Electors	T'out	Candidate	Party	Votes	% Sh	% Ch
1983	53,612	61.5	Hattersley R.S.G.*	Lab	19,757	59.9	
			Douglas-Osborn P.E.	Con	9,209	27.9	
			Parmar O.S.	SDP	3,416	10.4*	
			Eden F. Ms.	RCP	305	0.9*	
			Chinn C.S.A.	Ind	281	0.9*	
					10,548	32.0	
1987	53,093	63.5	Hattersley R.S.G.*	Lab	20,513	60.8	+0.9
			Khan N.A.	Con	8,654	25.7	-2.3
			Dimmick R.J.C.	SDP	3,803	11.3	+0.9
			Ambler R.A.	Green	526	1.6*	+1.6
			Khan P.	RF	229	0.7*	
					11,859	35.2	
1992	51,682	66.8	Hattersley R.S.G.*	Lab	22,116	64.1	+3.2
			Khamisa M.J.	Con	8,544	24.8	-0.9
			Parry D.J.	LD	3,028	8.8	-2.5
			Alldrick C.J.	Green	833	2.4*	+0.9
					13,572	39.3	

BIRMINGHAM, YARDLEY [60]

Election	Electors	T'out	Candidate	Party	Votes	% Sh	% Ch
1983	57,707	72.2	Bevan A.D.G.*	Con	17,986	43.2	
			Godsiff R.D.	Lab	15,141	36.4	
			Bennett D.A.	SDP	8,109	19.5	
			Jones R.P.	NF	415	1.0*	
					2,845	6.8	
1987	56,957	73.9	Bevan A.D.G.*	Con	17,931	42.6	-0.6
			Edge G.	Lab	15,409	36.6	+0.3
			Smith L.W.	Lib	8,734	20.8	+1.3
					2,522	6.0	
1992	54,755	78.0	Morris E. Ms.	Lab	14,884	34.9	-1.8
			Bevan A.D.G.*	Con	14,722	34.5	-8.1
			Hemming J.A.M.	LD	12,899	30.2	+9.5
			Read P. Ms.	NF	192	0.4*	+0.4
					162	0.4	

BISHOP AUCKLAND [61]

Election	Electors	T'out	Candidate	Party	Votes	% Sh	% Ch
1983	71,142	72.2	Foster D.*	Lab	22,850	44.5	
			Legg B.C.	Con	18,444	35.9	
			Collinge A.	Lib	10,070	19.6	
					4,406	8.6	
1987	72,106	74.1	Foster D.*	Lab	25,648	48.0	+3.5
			Wight R.	Con	18,613	34.8	-1.1
			Irwin G.	Lib	9,195	17.2	-2.4
					7,035	13.2	
1992	72,573†	76.5	Foster D.*	Lab	27,763	50.0	+2.0
			Williamson D.R.	Con	17,676	31.8	-3.0
			Wade W.P.	LD	10,099	18.2	+1.0
					10,087	18.2	

BLABY [62]

Election	Electors	T'out	Candidate	Party	Votes	% Sh	% Ch
1983	71,930	77.4	Lawson N.*	Con	32,689	58.7	
			Lustig R.E.	Lib	15,573	28.0	
			Wrigley C.J.	Lab	6,838	12.3*	
			Gegan P.E.	NF	568	1.0*	
					17,116	30.7	
1987	77,094	80.9	Lawson N.*	Con	37,732	60.5	+1.8
			Lustig R.E.	Lib	15,556	25.0	-3.0
			Roberts J.M.	Lab	9,046	14.5	+2.2
					22,176	35.6	
1992	81,791†	83.4	Robathan A.R.G.	Con	39,498	57.9	-2.6
			Ranson E.M. Ms.	Lab	14,151	20.7	+6.2
			Lewin M. Ms.	LD	13,780	20.2	-4.8
			Peacock J.A.	BNP	521	0.8*	+0.8
			Lincoln S.I. Ms.	NLP	260	0.4*	+0.4
					25,347	37.2	

BLACKBURN [63]

Election	Electors	T'out	Candidate	Party	Votes	% Sh	% Ch
1983	76,073	74.6	Straw J.W.*	Lab	25,400	44.7	
			Mather G.C.S.	Con	22,345	39.4	
			Fairbrother E.B.	SDP	8,174	14.4	
			Riley D.A.	NF	864	1.5*	
					3,055	5.4	
1987	74,801	74.9	Straw J.W.*	Lab	27,965	49.9	+5.2
			Cheetham A.C. Ms.	Con	22,468	40.1	+0.7
			Ali M.A.	SDP	5,602	10.0	-4.4
					5,497	9.8	
1992	73,337	75.0	Straw J.W.*	Lab	26,633	48.4	-1.5
			Coates R.M.	Con	20,606	37.5	-2.6
			Mann D.E.	LD	6,332	11.5	+1.5
			Field R.R.C.	Green	878	1.6*	+1.6
			Carmichael-Grimshaw M. Ms.	Ind	334	0.6*	
			Ayliffe W.J.	NLP	195	0.4*	+0.4
					6,027	11.0	

BLACKPOOL NORTH [64]

Election	Electors	T'out	Candidate	Party	Votes	% Sh	% Ch
1983	57,576	70.0	Miscampbell N.A.*	Con	20,592	51.1	
			Heyworth C.J.	Lib	10,440	25.9	
			Hindley M.J.	Lab	8,730	21.7	
			Hanson A.S.	NF	514	1.3*	
					10,152	25.2	
1987	58,893	73.1	Miscampbell N.A.*	Con	20,680	48.0	-3.1
			Kirton E.T.	Lab	13,359	31.0	+9.3
			Heyworth C.J.	Lib	9,032	21.0	-5.0
					7,321	17.0	
1992	58,142	77.5	Elletson H.D.H.	Con	21,501	47.7	-0.3
			Kirton E.T.	Lab	18,461	41.0	+10.0
			Lahiff A.P.	LD	4,786	10.6	-10.3
			Francis Sir G.	MRLP	178	0.4*	+0.4
			Walker H.B.	NLP	125	0.3*	+0.3
					3,040	6.7	

BLACKPOOL SOUTH [65]

Election	Electors	T'out	Candidate	Party	Votes	% Sh	% Ch
1983	56,201	69.8	Blaker P.A.R.*	Con	19,852	50.6	
			Jackson F.J.	Lab	9,714	24.8	
			Cox A.G.	SDP	9,417	24.0	
			Smith W.	NF	263	0.7*	
					10,138	25.8	
1987	57,567	73.5	Blaker P.A.R. Sir.*	Con	20,312	48.0	-2.5
			Baugh S.M. Ms.	Lab	13,568	32.1	+7.3
			Allit J.B.	SDP	8,405	19.9	-4.1
					6,744	15.9	
1992	56,829	77.3	Hawkins N.J.	Con	19,880	45.2	-2.8
			Marsden G.	Lab	18,213	41.4	+9.4
			Wynne R.E.	LD	5,675	12.9	-7.0
			Henning D.	NLP	173	0.4*	+0.4
					1,667	3.8	

BLAENAU GWENT [66]

Election	Electors	T'out	Candidate	Party	Votes	% Sh	% Ch
1983	55,948	76.9	Foot M.M.*	Lab	30,113	70.0	
			Atkinson G.M.	Lib	6,488	15.1	
			Morgan T.P.	Con	4,816	11.2*	
			Morgan S.	PC	1,624	3.8*	
					23,625	54.9	
1987	56,011	77.2	Foot M.M.*	Lab	32,820	75.9	+5.9
			Taylor A.R.	Con	4,959	11.5	+0.3
			McBride D.I.	Lib	3,847	8.9	-6.2
			Morgan S.	PC	1,621	3.7*	-0.0
					27,861	64.4	
1992	55,643†	78.1	Smith L.T.	Lab	34,333	79.0	+3.1
			Melding D.R.M.	Con	4,266	9.8	-1.7
			Burns A.	LD	2,774	6.4	-2.5
			Davies T.A.R.	PC/GP	2,099	4.8*	+1.1
					30,067	69.2	

37

BLAYDON [67]

Election	Electors	T'out	Candidate	Party	Votes	% Sh	% Ch
1983	65,481	73.2	McWilliam J.D.*	Lab	21,285	44.4	
			Williams A.C.	Con	14,063	29.3	
			Carr M.C.	SDP	12,607	26.3	
					7,222	15.1	
1987	66,301	75.7	McWilliam J.D.*	Lab	25,277	50.3	+6.0
			Nunn V.P.	SDP	12,789	25.5	-0.8
			Pescod P.R.	Con	12,147	24.2	-5.1
					12,488	24.9	
1992	66,044†	77.7	McWilliam J.D.*	Lab	27,028	52.7	+2.3
			Pescod P.R.	Con	13,685	26.7	+2.5
			Nunn V.P.	LD	10,602	20.7	-4.8
					13,343	26.0	

BLYTH VALLEY [68]

Election	Electors	T'out	Candidate	Party	Votes	% Sh	% Ch
1983	57,639	72.8	Ryman J.*	Lab	16,583	39.5	
			Brownlow R.M. Ms.	SDP	13,340	31.8	
			Hargreaves A.R.	Con	11,657	27.8	
			Robinson S.	Ind	406	1.0*	
					3,243	7.7	
1987	59,104	78.1	Campbell R.	Lab	19,604	42.5	+3.0
			Brownlow R.M. Ms.	SDP	18,751	40.6	+8.8
			Kinghorn R.R.F.	Con	7,823	16.9	-10.8
					853	1.8	
1992	60,975	80.7	Campbell R.*	Lab	24,542	49.9	+7.4
			Tracey P.M.	LD	16,498	33.5	-7.1
			Revell M.J.	Con	7,691	15.6	-1.3
			Tyley S.P.	Green	470	1.0*	+1.0
					8,044	16.3	

BOLSOVER [69]

Election	Electors	T'out	Candidate	Party	Votes	% Sh	% Ch
1983	64,769	72.7	Skinner D.E.*	Lab	26,514	56.3	
			Roberts S.	Con	12,666	26.9	
			Reddish S.C.	SDP	7,886	16.8	
					13,848	29.4	
1987	65,659	77.1	Skinner D.E.*	Lab	28,453	56.2	-0.1
			Lingens M.R.	Con	14,333	28.3	+1.4
			Fowler M.H.	SDP	7,836	15.5	-1.3
					14,120	27.9	
1992	66,551	79.1	Skinner D.E.*	Lab	33,978	64.5	+8.3
			James T.D.R.	Con	13,323	25.3	-3.0
			Barber S.P. Ms.	LD	5,368	10.2	-5.3
					20,655	39.2	

BOLTON NORTH EAST [70]

Election	Electors	T'out	Candidate	Party	Votes	% Sh	% Ch
1983	58,918	77.1	Thurnham P.G.	Con	19,632	43.2	
			Taylor W.A. Ms.*	Lab	17,189	37.8	
			Alcock J.H.	SDP	8,311	18.3	
			Ball D.P.	BNP	186	0.4*	
			Keen T.L.	Ind	104	0.2*	
					2,443	5.4	
1987	59,382	78.7	Thurnham P.G.*	Con	20,742	44.4	+1.2
			White F.R.	Lab	19,929	42.6	+4.8
			Alcock J.H.	SDP	6,060	13.0	-5.3
					813	1.7	
1992	58,660†	82.3	Thurnham P.G.*	Con	21,644	44.9	+0.5
			Crausby D.A.	Lab	21,459	44.5	+1.8
			Dunning B.F.	LD	4,971	10.3	-2.7
			Tong P.	NLP	181	0.4*	+0.4
					185	0.4	

BOLTON SOUTH-EAST [71]

Election	Electors	T'out	Candidate	Party	Votes	% Sh	% Ch
1983	67,527	73.6	Young D.W.*	Lab	23,984	48.3	
			Walsh J.	Con	15,231	30.7	
			Rothwell M.P. Ms.	Lib	10,157	20.4	
			Keen T.L.	Ind	296	0.6*	
					8,753	17.6	
1987	65,932	74.9	Young D.W.*	Lab	26,791	54.3	+6.0
			Windle S.	Con	15,410	31.2	+0.6
			Harasiwka F.	Lib	7,161	14.5	-5.9
					11,381	23.1	
1992	65,600†	75.5	Young D.W.*	Lab	26,906	54.3	+0.0
			Wood-Dow N.J.S.	Con	14,215	28.7	-2.5
			Lee D.S.	LD	5,244	10.6	-3.9
			Hardman W.	Ind Lab	2,894	5.8	
			Walch L.J.	NLP	290	0.6*	+0.6
					12,691	25.6	

BOLTON WEST [72]

Election	Electors	T'out	Candidate	Party	Votes	% Sh	% Ch
1983	67,353	78.1	Sackville T.G. Hon.	Con	23,731	45.1	
			Green G.D.	Lab	16,579	31.5	
			Baker R.H.	SDP	12,321	23.4	
					7,152	13.6	
1987	69,843	80.0	Sackville T.G. Hon.*	Con	24,779	44.3	-0.8
			Harkin G.J.	Lab	20,186	36.1	+4.6
			Eccles D.T.	SDP	10,936	19.6	-3.8
					4,593	8.2	
1992	71,345†	83.5	Sackville T.G. Hon.*	Con	26,452	44.4	+0.1
			Morris C.	Lab	25,373	42.6	+6.5
			Ronson B.O. Ms.	LD	7,529	12.6	-6.9
			Phillips J.R. Ms.	NLP	240	0.4*	+0.4
					1,079	1.8	

BOOTHFERRY [73]

Election	Electors	T'out	Candidate	Party	Votes	% Sh	% Ch
1983	72,370	73.1	Bryan P.E.O. Sir.*	Con	30,536	57.7	
			Ellis A.S.	Lib	13,116	24.8	
			Geraghty T.	Lab	9,271	17.5	
					17,420	32.9	
1987	75,176	75.8	Davis D.M.	Con	31,716	55.7	-2.0
			Davies J.D. Ms.	Lib	12,746	22.4	-2.4
			Donson R.	Lab	12,498	21.9	+4.4
					18,970	33.3	
1992	80,561	79.9	Davis D.M.*	Con	35,266	54.8	-0.9
			Coubrough L. M. Ms.	Lab	17,731	27.5	+5.6
			Goss J.M.	LD	11,388	17.7	-4.7
					17,535	27.2	

41

Election	Electors	T'out	Candidate	Party	Votes	% Sh	% Ch
1983	75,354	68.3	Roberts A.*	Lab	27,282	53.0	
			Watson R.M.	Con	12,143	23.6	
			Wall J.F.	SDP	12,068	23.4	
					15,139	29.4	
1987	71,765	72.9	Roberts A.*	Lab	34,975	66.9	+13.9
			Papworth P.R.	Con	10,498	20.1	-3.5
			Denham P.V.	SDP	6,820	13.0	-10.4
					24,477	46.8	

[Death]

Election	Electors	T'out	Candidate	Party	Votes	% Sh	% Ch
1990	70,718	50.6	Carr M.	Lab	26,737	75.4	+8.5
(24/5)			Clappison W.J.	Con	3,220	9.1	-11.0
			Cunningham J.J.	LD	3,179	9.0	-4.0
			Brady F.P.S.	Green	1,267	3.6*	
			White K.J.	Lib	474	1.3*	
			Sutch D.E.	MRLP	418	1.2*	
			Holmes J.	SDP	155	0.4*	
			Schofield T.J.	Ind	27	0.1*	
					23,517	66.3	

[Death]

Election	Electors	T'out	Candidate	Party	Votes	% Sh	% Ch
1990	70,881	39.7	Benton J.E.	Lab	22,052	78.4	+11.5
(8/11)			Clappison W.J.	Con	2,587	9.2	-10.9
			Cunningham J.J.	LD	2,216	7.9	-5.1
			Brady F.P.S.	Green	557	2.0*	
			Sutch D.E.	MRLP	310	1.1*	
			White K.J.	Lib	291	1.0*	
			Black D.	Ind	132	0.5*	
					19,465	69.2	
1992	69,308†	72.5	Benton J.E.	Lab	37,464	74.6	+7.7
			Varley C.J.	Con	8,022	16.0	-4.1
			Cunningham J.J.	LD	3,301	6.6	-6.5
			Hall M.G. Ms.	Lib	1,174	2.3*	+2.3
			Haynes T.P.	NLP	264	0.5*	+0.5
					29,442	58.6	

BOSWORTH [75]

Election	Electors	T'out	Candidate	Party	Votes	% Sh	% Ch
1983	73,097	78.2	Butler A.C. Hon.*	Con	31,663	55.4	
			Fox M.F.	SDP	14,369	25.1	
			Janner D.J.M.	Lab	11,120	19.5	
					17,294	30.3	
1987	77,206	81.2	Tredinnick D.A.S.	Con	34,145	54.4	-1.0
			Bill D.C.	Lib	17,129	27.3	+2.2
			Hall R.S.	Lab	10,787	17.2	-2.3
			Freer D.G. Ms.	Green	660	1.1*	+1.1
					17,016	27.1	
1992	80,260†	84.1	Tredinnick D.A.S.*	Con	36,618	54.2	-0.2
			Everitt D.B.	Lab	17,524	26.0	+8.8
			Drozdz G.M.	LD	12,643	18.7	-8.6
			Fewster B.	Green	716	1.1*	+0.0
					19,094	28.3	

BOURNEMOUTH EAST [76]

Election	Electors	T'out	Candidate	Party	Votes	% Sh	% Ch
1983	70,771	66.6	Atkinson D.A.*	Con	25,176	53.4	
			Millward J. Dr.	Lib	13,760	29.2	
			Shutler M.J.	Lab	4,026	8.5*	
			Hogarth P.M. Ms.	Ind Con	3,644	7.7*	
			Dykes T.D.	Green	273	0.6*	
			Stooks J.	Ind	225	0.5*	
					11,416	24.2	
1987	75,232	70.5	Atkinson D.A.*	Con	30,925	58.3	+4.8
			Millward J. Dr.	Lib	16,242	30.6	+1.4
			Taylor I.A.	Lab	5,885	11.1	+2.5
					14,683	27.7	
1992	75,131	72.8	Atkinson D.A.*	Con	30,820	56.4	-1.9
			Russell N.R.	LD	15,998	29.3	-1.4
			Brushett P.	Lab	7,541	13.8	+2.7
			Holmes S.T. Ms.	NLP	329	0.6*	+0.6
					14,822	27.1	

BOURNEMOUTH WEST [77]

Election	Electors	T'out	Candidate	Party	Votes	% Sh	% Ch
1983	72,297	69.2	Butterfill J.V.	Con	28,466	56.9	
			James R.M.	Lib	15,135	30.3	
			Horrocks K.	Lab	6,243	12.5*	
			Morse J.H.	BNP	180	0.4*	
					13,331	26.6	
1987	74,444	73.3	Butterfill J.V.*	Con	30,117	55.2	-1.7
			Craven P.G.M.	SDP	17,466	32.0	+1.7
			Jones R.W.	Lab	7,018	12.9	+0.4
					12,651	23.2	
1992	74,729	75.7	Butterfill J.V.*	Con	29,820	52.7	-2.5
			Dover J. Ms.	LD	17,117	30.2	-1.7
			Grower B.B.	Lab	9,423	16.7	+3.8
			Springham A.R.	NLP	232	0.4*	+0.4
					12,703	22.4	

BOW AND POPLAR [78]

Election	Electors	T'out	Candidate	Party	Votes	% Sh	% Ch
1983	57,768	55.4	Mikardo I.*	Lab	15,878	49.6	
			Flounders E.	Lib	10,017	31.3	
			Eyres S.R.	Con	5,129	16.0	
			Bartlett S. Ms.	NF	596	1.9*	
			Snooks A.J.	Ind Lab	266	0.8*	
			Scotcher K.R.	WRP	117	0.4*	
					5,861	18.3	
1987	59,178	57.4	Gordon M. Ms.	Lab	15,746	46.4	-3.2
			Flounders E.	Lib	11,115	32.7	+1.4
			Hughes D.C.	Con	6,810	20.1	+4.0
			Chappel P.S.	WRP	276	0.8*	+0.4
					4,631	13.6	
1992	56,685†	65.8	Gordon M. Ms.*	Lab	18,487	49.5	+3.1
			Hughes P.J.	LD	10,083	27.0	-5.7
			Pearce S.N.C.	Con	6,876	18.4	-1.6
			Tyndall J.H.	BNP	1,107	3.0*	+3.0
			Petter S.	Green	612	1.6*	+1.6
			Hite W.R.	NLP	158	0.4*	+0.4
					8,404	22.5	

Election	Electors	T'out	Candidate	Party	Votes	% Sh	% Ch
1983	66,349	70.8	Lawler G.J.	Con	16,094	34.3	
			Wall C.P.	Lab	14,492	30.9	
			Birkby P.D.	SDP	11,962	25.5	
			Ford B.T.*	Ind Lab	4,018	8.6*	
			Howarth A.M.	MRLP	194	0.4*	
			Easter M.D.S.	BNP	193	0.4*	
					1,602	3.4	
1987	67,430	72.7	Wall C.P.	Lab	21,009	42.8	+12.0
			Lawler G.J.*	Con	19,376	39.5	+5.2
			Berkeley A.M.	SDP	8,656	17.7	-7.8
					1,633	3.3	

[Death]

Election	Electors	T'out	Candidate	Party	Votes	% Sh	% Ch
1990	67,444	53.4	Rooney T.H.	Lab	18,619	51.7	+8.9
(8/11)			Ward D.	LD	9,105	25.3	+7.6
			Atkin M.E.J. Ms.	Con	6,048	16.8	-22.7
			Pidcock D.M.	Islam	800	2.2*	
			Knott M.L.	Green	447	1.2*	
			Tenney R.I.	NF	305	0.8*	
			Floyd J.	Ind	219	0.6*	
			Beckett W.	MRLP	210	0.6*	
			Nowosielski N.A.B.	Lib	187	0.5*	
			Wigglesworth M.	Ind Con	89	0.2*	
					9,514	26.4	
1992	66,711	73.4	Rooney T.H.	Lab	23,420	47.8	+5.0
			Riaz M.	Con	15,756	32.2	-7.3
			Ward D.	LD	9,133	18.7	+1.0
			Beckett W.	MRLP	350	0.7*	+0.7
			Nasr M.H.	Islam	304	0.6*	+0.6
					7,664	15.7	

BRADFORD SOUTH [80]

Election	Electors	T'out	Candidate	Party	Votes	% Sh	% Ch
1983	69,588	71.0	Torney T.W.*	Lab	18,542	37.5	
			Hall G.T.	Con	18,432	37.3	
			Pearl D.A.	SDP	12,143	24.6	
			Adsett R.	Green	308	0.6*	
					110	0.2	
1987	69,588	73.7	Cryer G.R.	Lab	21,230	41.4	+3.9
			Hall G.T.	Con	20,921	40.8	+3.5
			Lindley T.	SDP	9,109	17.8	-6.8
					309	0.6	
1992	69,930	75.6	Cryer G.R.*	Lab	25,185	47.6	+6.2
			Popat S.	Con	20,283	38.4	-2.4
			Boulton B.J.	LD	7,243	13.7	-4.1
			Naseem M.	Islam	156	0.3*	+0.3
					4,902	9.3	
[Death]							
1994	69,521	44.2	Sutcliffe G.	Lab	17,014	55.3	+7.7
(9/6)			Wright H. Ms.	LD	7,350	23.9	+10.2
			Farley R.	Con	5,475	17.8	-20.6
			Sutch D.E.	MRLP	727	2.4*	
			Laycock K.	NLP	187	0.6*	
					9,664	31.4	

BRADFORD WEST [81]

Election	Electors	T'out	Candidate	Party	Votes	% Sh	% Ch
1983	71,296	68.9	Madden M.F.	Lab	19,499	39.7	
			Day S.R.	Con	16,162	32.9	
			Lyons E.*	SDP	13,301	27.1	
			Slaughter B.E. Ms.	WRP	139	0.3*	
					3,337	6.8	
1987	70,763	70.2	Madden M.F.*	Lab	25,775	51.9	+12.2
			Duncan Smith G.I.	Con	18,224	36.7	+3.8
			Moghal M.E.	SDP	5,657	11.4	-15.7
					7,551	15.2	
1992	70,017	69.9	Madden M.F.*	Lab	26,046	53.2	+1.3
			Ashworth A.J.	Con	16,544	33.8	-2.9
			Griffiths A.O.	LD	5,150	10.5	-0.9
			Braham P.	Green	735	1.5*	+1.5
			Pidcock D.M.	Islam	471	1.0*	+1.0
					9,502	19.4	

BRAINTREE [82]

Election	Electors	T'out	Candidate	Party	Votes	% Sh	% Ch
1983	73,548	76.2	Newton A.H.*	Con	29,462	52.6	
			Bing I.G.	SDP	16,021	28.6	
			Dyson J.M. Ms.	Lab	10,551	18.8	
					13,441	24.0	
1987	76,994	79.0	Newton A.H.*	Con	32,978	54.2	+1.6
			Bing I.G.	SDP	16,121	26.5	-2.1
			Stapleton B.L.	Lab	11,764	19.3	+0.5
					16,857	27.7	
1992	78,880†	83.4	Newton A.H.*	Con	34,415	52.3	-1.9
			Willmore I.	Lab	16,921	25.7	+6.4
			Wallis D.P. Ms.	LD	13,603	20.7	-5.8
			Abbott J.E.	Green	855	1.3*	+1.3
					17,494	26.6	

BRECON AND RADNOR [83]

Election	Electors	T'out	Candidate	Party	Votes	% Sh	% Ch
1983	47,277	80.1	Hooson T.E.*	Con	18,255	48.2	
			Morris D.R. Rev.	Lab	9,471	25.0	
			Livsey R.A.L.	Lib	9,226	24.4	
			Meredudd S.R. Ms.	PC	640	1.7*	
			Booth R.G.W.P.	Ind	278	0.7*	
					8,784	23.2	

[Death]

Election	Electors	T'out	Candidate	Party	Votes	% Sh	% Ch
1985	48,371	79.4	Livsey R.A.L.	Lib	13,753	35.8	+11.4
(4/7)			Willey F.R.	Lab	13,194	34.4	+9.4
			Butler C.J.	Con	10,631	27.7	-20.5
			Davies J.M. Ms.	PC	435	1.1*	-0.6
			Sutch D.E.	MRLP	202	0.5*	
			Everest R.J.	Ind Con	154	0.4*	
			Genillard A.C.L.	Ind	43	0.1*	
					559	1.4	
1987	49,410	84.3	Livsey R.A.L.	Lib	14,509	34.8	+10.5
			Evans J.P.	Con	14,453	34.7	-13.5
			Willey F.R.	Lab	12,180	29.2	+4.2
			Davies J.H.	PC	535	1.3*	-0.4
					56	0.1	
1992	51,564	85.9	Evans J.P.	Con	15,977	36.1	+1.4
			Livsey R.A.L.*	LD	15,847	35.8	+1.0
			Mann C.J.	Lab	11,634	26.3	-2.9
			Meredudd S.R. Ms.	PC	418	0.9*	-0.3
			Richards H.W.	Green	393	0.9*	+0.9
					130	0.3	

BRENT EAST [84]

Election	Electors	T'out	Candidate	Party	Votes	% Sh	% Ch
1983	61,489	63.6	Freeson R.*	Lab	18,363	47.0	
			Lacey R.M.	Con	13,529	34.6	
			Rosen M.H. Dr.	SDP	6,598	16.9	
			O'Leary J.	Ind	289	0.7*	
			Downing G.J.	WRP	222	0.6*	
			Radclyffe K.	Ind	88	0.2*	
					4,834	12.4	
1987	61,020	64.5	Livingstone K.R.	Lab	16,772	42.6	-4.4
			Crawley H.S. Ms.	Con	15,119	38.4	+3.8
			Finkelstein D.W.	SDP	5,710	14.5	-2.4
			Dooley R.Q.	Ind Lab	1,035	2.6*	
			Litvinoff M.	Green	716	1.8*	+1.8
					1,653	4.2	
1992	53,436	68.7	Livingstone K.R.*	Lab	19,387	52.8	+10.2
			Green D.H.	Con	13,416	36.6	-1.9
			Cummins M.	LD	3,249	8.9	-5.7
			Dean T.M. Ms.	Green	548	1.5*	-0.3
			Murphy A.G. Ms.	CPGB	96	0.3*	+0.3
					5,971	16.3	

BRENT NORTH [85]

Election	Electors	T'out	Candidate	Party	Votes	% Sh	% Ch
1983	62,679	70.4	Boyson R.*	Con	24,842	56.3	
			Jackson S.M. Ms.	Lab	10,191	23.1	
			Mann T.J. Dr.	SDP	9,082	20.6	
					14,651	33.2	
1987	63,081	71.0	Boyson R.*	Con	26,823	59.9	+3.6
			Patel P.	Lab	11,103	24.8	+1.7
			Mularczyk C.	SDP	6,868	15.3	-5.3
					15,720	35.1	
1992	58,923	70.6	Boyson R.*	Con	23,445	56.4	-3.5
			Moher J.	Lab	13,314	32.0	+7.2
			Lorber P.	LD	4,149	10.0	-5.4
			Thakore V.D.	Ind	356	0.9*	
			Davids T.F.	NLP	318	0.8*	+0.8
					10,131	24.4	

BRENT SOUTH [86]

Election	Electors	T'out	Candidate	Party	Votes	% Sh	% Ch
1983	62,783	63.6	Pavitt L.A.*	Lab	21,259	53.3	
			Smedley C.W.O.	Con	10,740	26.9	
			Billins R.G.	Lib	7,557	18.9	
			Sawh R.	Ind	356	0.9*	
					10,519	26.4	
1987	62,772	64.9	Boateng P.Y.	Lab	21,140	51.9	-1.4
			Paterson A.J.	Con	13,209	32.4	+5.5
			Harskin M.T.	Lib	6,375	15.7	-3.3
					7,931	19.5	
1992	56,054	64.1	Boateng P.Y.*	Lab	20,662	57.5	+5.6
			Blackman R.J.	Con	10,957	30.5	-1.9
			Harskin M.T.	LD	3,658	10.2	-5.5
			Johnson D.P.	Green	479	1.3*	+1.3
			Jani C.I.	NLP	166	0.5*	+0.5
					9,705	27.0	

BRENTFORD AND ISLEWORTH [87]

Election	Electors	T'out	Candidate	Party	Votes	% Sh	% Ch
1983	69,170	74.7	Hayhoe B.J.*	Con	24,515	47.4	
			Rowlands P.L.	Lab	15,128	29.3	
			Wilks D.M.W. Dr.	SDP	11,438	22.1	
			Andrews P.	NF	427	0.8*	
			Simmerson R.E.G.	Ind Con	179	0.3*	
					9,387	18.2	
1987	71,715	76.7	Hayhoe B.J. Sir.*	Con	26,230	47.7	+0.3
			Keen A.L. Ms.	Lab	18,277	33.2	+4.0
			Wilks D.M.W. Dr.	SDP	9,626	17.5	-4.6
			Cooper T.H.	Green	849	1.5*	+1.5
					7,953	14.5	
1992	72,193	74.8	Deva N.J.A.	Con	24,752	45.8	-1.9
			Keen A.L. Ms.	Lab	22,666	42.0	+8.7
			Salmon J.C.N. Ms.	LD	5,683	10.5	-7.0
			Bradley J.W.	Green	927	1.7*	+0.2
					2,086	3.9	

BRENTWOOD AND ONGAR [88]

Election	Electors	T'out	Candidate	Party	Votes	% Sh	% Ch
1983	65,975	76.6	McCrindle R.A.*	Con	29,484	58.4	
			Amor N.R	Lib	15,282	30.3	
			Orpe J.W.	Lab	5,739	11.4*	
					14,202	28.1	
1987	67,521	79.0	McCrindle R.A.*	Con	32,258	60.5	+2.1
			Amor N.R.	Lib	13,337	25.0	-5.2
			Orpe J.W.	Lab	7,042	13.2	+1.8
			Willis M.E. Ms.	Green	686	1.3*	+1.3
					18,921	35.5	
1992	65,884	84.7	Pickles E.J.	Con	32,145	57.6	-2.9
			Bottomley E.T. Ms.	LD	17,000	30.5	+5.5
			Keohane J.F.	Lab	6,080	10.9	-2.3
			Bartley C. Ms.	Green	555	1.0*	-0.3
					15,145	27.2	

BRIDGEND [89]

Election	Electors	T'out	Candidate	Party	Votes	% Sh	% Ch
1983	53,918	77.0	Hubbard-Miles P.C.	Con	15,950	38.4	
			Fellows J.A.	Lab	14,623	35.2	
			Smart R.	SDP	9,630	23.2	
			Bush K.	PC	1,312	3.2*	
					1,327	3.2	
1987	57,163	80.6	Griffiths W.J.	Lab	21,893	47.5	+12.3
			Hubbard-Miles P.C.*	Con	17,513	38.0	-0.4
			Smart R.	SDP	5,590	12.1	-11.1
			McAllister L.J. Ms.	PC	1,065	2.3*	-0.8
					4,380	9.5	
1992	58,518†	80.5	Griffiths W.J.*	Lab	24,143	51.3	+3.7
			Unwin D.A.	Con	16,817	35.7	-2.3
			Mills D.	LD	4,827	10.3	-1.9
			Jones A.L.	PC	1,301	2.8*	+0.5
					7,326	15.6	

BRIDGWATER [90]

Election	Electors	T'out	Candidate	Party	Votes	% Sh	% Ch
1983	64,225	74.8	King T.J.*	Con	25,107	52.3	
			Farley R.H. Ms.	SDP	14,410	30.0	
			May A.J.	Lab	8,524	17.7	
					10,697	22.3	
1987	67,400	78.3	King T.J.*	Con	27,177	51.5	-0.7
			Clarke C.J.	SDP	15,982	30.3	+0.3
			Turner J.	Lab	9,594	18.2	+0.4
					11,195	21.2	
1992	71,575	79.5	King T.J.*	Con	26,610	46.8	-4.8
			Revans W.J.	LD	16,894	29.7	-0.6
			James P.E.	Lab	12,365	21.7	+3.5
			Dummett G.M.J.	Green	746	1.3*	+1.3
			Body A.C.	Ind	183	0.3*	
			Sanson G.F. Ms.	NLP	112	0.2*	+0.2
					9,716	17.1	

BRIDLINGTON [91]

Election	Electors	T'out	Candidate	Party	Votes	% Sh	% Ch
1983	76,718	70.6	Townend J.E.*	Con	31,284	57.8	
			Martin E. Ms.	SDP	14,675	27.1	
			Craven M.A.	Lab	7,370	13.6	
			Tooke S.J.O.	Green	803	1.5*	
					16,609	30.7	
1987	80,126	73.7	Townend J.E.*	Con	32,351	54.8	-3.0
			Marshall E.I.	SDP	15,030	25.5	-1.6
			Bird L.M.	Lab	10,653	18.1	+4.4
			Myerscough R.D.	Green	983	1.7*	+0.2
					17,321	29.3	
1992	84,950	77.8	Townend J.E.*	Con	33,604	50.8	-4.0
			Leeman J.A.	LD	17,246	26.1	+0.6
			Hatfield S.M.	Lab	15,263	23.1	+5.0
					16,358	24.7	

BRIGG AND CLEETHORPES [92]

Election	Electors	T'out	Candidate	Party	Votes	% Sh	% Ch
1983	77,471	73.6	Brown M.R.*	Con	28,893	50.7	
			Wigginton G.S.S.	Lib	16,704	29.3	
			Hough J.D.	Lab	11,404	20.0	
					12,189	21.4	
1987	80,096	76.3	Brown M.R.*	Con	29,725	48.7	-2.0
			Powney I.G.	Lib	17,475	28.6	-0.7
			Geraghty T.	Lab	13,876	22.7	+2.7
					12,250	20.1	
1992	83,510	77.0	Brown M.R.*	Con	31,673	49.2	+0.6
			Cawsey I.A.	Lab	22,494	35.0	+12.2
			Cockbill M.R. Ms.	LD	9,374	14.6	-14.0
			Jacques D.N.	Green	790	1.2*	+1.2
					9,179	14.3	

BRIGHTON, KEMPTOWN [93]

Election	Electors	T'out	Candidate	Party	Votes	% Sh	% Ch
1983	60,877	71.5	Bowden A.*	Con	22,265	51.1	
			Fitch R.	Lab	12,887	29.6	
			Burke D.T.	SDP	8,098	18.6	
			Budden E.	NF	290	0.7*	
					9,378	21.5	
1987	60,271	74.5	Bowden A.*	Con	24,031	53.5	+2.4
			Bassam J.S.	Lab	14,771	32.9	+3.3
			Berry C.J.	Lib	6,080	13.5	-5.1
					9,260	20.6	
1992	57,649†	76.1	Bowden A.*	Con	21,129	48.1	-5.4
			Haynes G.O. Ms.	Lab	18,073	41.2	+8.3
			Scott P.D.	LD	4,461	10.2	-3.4
			Overall E.J. Ms.	NLP	230	0.5*	+0.5
					3,056	7.0	

BRIGHTON, PAVILION [94]

Election	Electors	T'out	Candidate	Party	Votes	% Sh	% Ch
1983	59,769	69.3	Amery H.J.*	Con	21,323	51.5	
			Neves M.W.J.	SDP	10,191	24.6	
			Spillman H.	Lab	9,879	23.9	
					11,132	26.9	
1987	58,910	73.7	Amery H.J.*	Con	22,056	50.8	-0.7
			Hill D.S.	Lab	12,914	29.7	+5.9
			Carey K.F.	SDP	8,459	19.5	-5.1
					9,142	21.1	
1992	57,618†	76.8	Spencer D.H.	Con	20,630	46.6	-4.2
			Lepper D.	Lab	16,955	38.3	+8.6
			Pearce T.H.	LD	5,606	12.7	-6.8
			Brodie I.M.	Green	963	2.2*	+2.2
			Turner E.J. Ms.	NLP	103	0.2*	+0.2
					3,675	8.3	

BRISTOL EAST [95]

Election	Electors	T'out	Candidate	Party	Votes	% Sh	% Ch
1983	66,296	73.8	Sayeed J.	Con	19,844	40.5	
			Benn A.N.W.*	Lab	18,055	36.9	
			Tyrer P.E.	Lib	10,404	21.3	
			Andrews E.H.	NF	343	0.7*	
			Dorey G.A. Ms.	Green	311	0.6*	
					1,789	3.7	
1987	63,840	78.7	Sayeed J.*	Con	21,906	43.6	+3.1
			Thomas R.R.	Lab	17,783	35.4	-1.5
			Foster D.M.E.	Lib	10,247	20.4	-0.8
			Kingston P.M.	Ind NF	286	0.6*	
					4,123	8.2	
1992	62,659	80.3	Corston J.A. Ms.	Lab	22,418	44.6	+9.1
			Sayeed J.*	Con	19,726	39.2	-4.4
			Kiely J.F.	LD	7,903	15.7	-4.7
			Anderson I.H.M.	NF	270	0.5*	+0.5
					2,692	5.4	

BRISTOL NORTH WEST [96]

Election	Electors	T'out	Candidate	Party	Votes	% Sh	% Ch
1983	72,996	76.9	Stern M.C.	Con	24,617	43.9	
			Palmer S.R. Ms.	Lab	18,290	32.6	
			Long H.S. Ms.	SDP	13,228	23.6	
					6,327	11.3	
1987	72,876	79.4	Stern M.C.*	Con	26,953	46.6	+2.7
			Walker T.W.	Lab	20,001	34.6	+2.0
			Kirkcaldy J.M.G.	SDP	10,885	18.8	-4.7
					6,952	12.0	
1992	72,760	82.3	Stern M.C.*	Con	25,354	42.3	-4.3
			Naysmith J.D.	Lab	25,309	42.3	+7.7
			Taylor J.D.	LD	8,498	14.2	-4.6
			Long H.S. Ms.	SD	729	1.2*	
					45	0.1	

BRISTOL SOUTH [97]

Election	Electors	T'out	Candidate	Party	Votes	% Sh	% Ch
1983	72,067	68.8	Cocks M.F.L.*	Lab	21,824	44.0	
			Gammell A.B.	Con	17,405	35.1	
			Stanbury D.M.	SDP	9,674	19.5	
			Collard G.	Green	352	0.7*	
			Chester A.	Comm	224	0.5*	
			Byrne L.J. Ms.	WRP	113	0.2*	
					4,419	8.9	
1987	68,733	74.0	Primarolo D. Ms.	Lab	20,798	40.9	-3.1
			Cutcher P.S.	Con	19,394	38.1	+3.0
			Long H.S. Ms.	SDP	9,952	19.6	+0.0
			Vowles G.R.	Green	600	1.2*	+0.5
			Meghji C.M. Ms.	RF	149	0.3*	+0.3
					1,404	2.8	
1992	64,403	77.8	Primarolo D. Ms.*	Lab	25,164	50.2	+9.3
			Bercow J.S.	Con	16,245	32.4	-5.7
			Crossley P.N.	LD	7,822	15.6	-3.9
			Boxall J.H.	Green	756	1.5*	+0.3
			Phillips N.D.	NLP	136	0.3*	+0.3
					8,919	17.8	

BRISTOL WEST [98]

Election	Electors	T'out	Candidate	Party	Votes	% Sh	% Ch
1983	73,190	70.7	Waldegrave W.A. Hon.*	Con	25,400	49.1	
			Ferguson G.R.P.	Lib	15,222	29.4	
			Tatlow P.R. Ms.	Lab	10,094	19.5	
			Scott J.F.K.	Green	872	1.7*	
			Boyle S.	Ind	142	0.3*	
					10,178	19.7	
1987	72,357	75.0	Waldegrave W.A. Hon.*	Con	24,695	45.5	-3.6
			Ferguson G.R.P.	Lib	16,992	31.3	+1.9
			Georghiou M.C. Ms.	Lab	11,337	20.9	+1.4
			Dorey G.A. Ms.	Green	1,096	2.0*	+0.3
			Ralph V. Ms.	Comm	134	0.2*	+0.2
					7,703	14.2	
1992	70,945	74.0	Waldegrave W.A. Hon.*	Con	22,169	42.2	-3.3
			Boney C.R.	LD	16,098	30.7	-0.7
			Bashforth H.	Lab	12,992	24.8	+3.9
			Sawday G.A.	Green	906	1.7*	-0.3
			Cross D.J.	NLP	104	0.2*	+0.2
			Brent B.	RCP	92	0.2*	+0.2
			Hammond P.J.	Ind	87	0.2*	
			Hedges T.P.E.	AFL	42	0.1*	+0.1
					6,071	11.6	

BROMSGROVE [99]

Election	Electors	T'out	Candidate	Party	Votes	% Sh	% Ch
1983	66,146	75.1	Miller H.D.*	Con	27,911	56.2	
			Millington A.J.	SDP	10,736	21.6	
			Titley G.	Lab	10,280	20.7	
			Churchman J.C.	Green	716	1.4*	
					17,175	34.6	
1987	69,494	76.4	Miller H.D.*	Con	29,051	54.7	-1.5
			Ward J.D.	Lab	12,366	23.3	+2.6
			Cropp D.L.	SDP	11,663	22.0	+0.3
					16,685	31.4	
1992	71,085†	82.5	Thomason K.R.	Con	31,709	54.1	-0.7
			Mole C.M.V. Ms.	Lab	18,007	30.7	+7.4
			Cassin A.J. Ms.	LD	8,090	13.8	-8.2
			Churchman J.C.	Green	856	1.5*	+1.5
					13,702	23.4	

56

BROXBOURNE [100]

Election	Electors	T'out	Candidate	Party	Votes	% Sh	% Ch
1983	67,387	74.0	Roe M.A. Ms.	Con	29,328	58.8	
			Pollock B.R.	Lib	11,862	23.8	
			Stears M.J.	Lab	8,159	16.4	
			Smith J.R.	BNP	502	1.0*	
					17,466	35.0	
1987	70,631	75.2	Roe M.A. Ms.*	Con	33,567	63.2	+4.4
			Yates E. Ms.	Lib	10,572	19.9	-3.9
			Parry P.W.	Lab	8,984	16.9	+0.5
					22,995	43.3	
1992	72,127	79.9	Roe M.A. Ms.*	Con	36,094	62.6	-0.6
			Hudson M.	Lab	12,124	21.0	+4.1
			Davies J.M. Ms.	LD	9,244	16.0	-3.9
			Woolhouse G.	NLP	198	0.3*	+0.3
					23,970	41.6	

BROXTOWE [101]

Election	Electors	T'out	Candidate	Party	Votes	% Sh	% Ch
1983	69,760	76.5	Lester J.T.*	Con	28,522	53.5	
			Melton K.M.	Lib	13,444	25.2	
			Warner M.	Lab	11,368	21.3	
					15,078	28.3	
1987	71,780	79.2	Lester J.T.*	Con	30,462	53.6	+0.1
			Fleet K.J.	Lab	13,811	24.3	+3.0
			Melton K.M.	Lib	12,562	22.1	-3.1
					16,651	29.3	
1992	73,124†	83.4	Lester J.T.*	Con	31,096	51.0	-2.6
			Walker J.R.W.	Lab	21,205	34.8	+10.5
			Ross J.D.	LD	8,395	13.8	-8.3
			Lukehurst D.	NLP	293	0.5*	+0.5
					9,891	16.2	

BUCKINGHAM [102]

Election	Electors	T'out	Candidate	Party	Votes	% Sh	% Ch
1983	62,758	77.1	Walden G.G.H.	Con	27,552	56.9	
			Ryder R.H.J.D.	Lib	13,584	28.1	
			Groucutt M.	Lab	7,272	15.0	
					13,968	28.9	
1987	70,036	78.3	Walden G.G.H.*	Con	32,162	58.6	+1.7
			Burke C.M.	Lib	13,636	24.9	-3.2
			Groucutt M.	Lab	9,053	16.5	+1.5
					18,526	33.8	

During the 1987-1992 Parliament the boundaries of the two existing seats of Buckingham and Milton Keynes were re-drawn to create three new constituencies - Buckingham, Milton Keynes North East and Milton Keynes South West. The figures for change in share of the vote in 1992 are based on the estimates of the likely 1987 'result' in the new seat.

Election	Electors	T'out	Candidate	Party	Votes	% Sh	% Ch
1992	56,064†	84.2	Walden G.G.H.*	Con	29,496	62.5	+1.1
			Jones H.T.	LD	9,705	20.6	-6.2
			White K.M.	Lab	7,662	16.2	+4.3
			Sheaff L.R.	NLP	353	0.7*	+0.7
					19,791	41.9	

BURNLEY [103]

Election	Electors	T'out	Candidate	Party	Votes	% Sh	% Ch
1983	66,542	76.3	Pike P.L.	Lab	20,178	39.8	
			Bruce I.C.	Con	19,391	38.2	
			Steed M.	Lib	11,191	22.0	
					787	1.6	
1987	65,956	78.8	Pike P.L.*	Lab	25,140	48.4	+8.6
			Elletson H.D.H.	Con	17,583	33.8	-4.4
			Baker R.H.	SDP	9,241	17.8	-4.3
					7,557	14.5	
1992	69,128†	74.2	Pike P.L.*	Lab	27,184	53.0	+4.6
			Binge B. Ms.	Con	15,693	30.6	-3.2
			Birtwistle G.	LD	8,414	16.4	-1.4
					11,491	22.4	

BURTON [104]

Election	Electors	T'out	Candidate	Party	Votes	% Sh	% Ch
1983	71,849	75.9	Lawrence I.J.*	Con	27,874	51.1	
			Slater R.E.G.	Lab	16,227	29.8	
			Garner W.J. Ms.	Lib	10,420	19.1	
					11,647	21.4	
1987	73,252	78.5	Lawrence I.J.*	Con	29,160	50.7	-0.4
			Heptonstall D.	Lab	19,330	33.6	+3.8
			Hemsley K.A.	Lib	9,046	15.7	-3.4
					9,830	17.1	
1992	75,293†	82.4	Lawrence I.J.*	Con	30,845	49.7	-1.0
			Muddyman P.K. Ms.	Lab	24,849	40.0	+6.4
			Renold R.C.	LD	6,375	10.3	-5.5
					5,996	9.7	

BURY NORTH [105]

Election	Electors	T'out	Candidate	Party	Votes	% Sh	% Ch
1983	66,065	79.6	Burt A.J.H.	Con	23,923	45.5	
			White F.R.*	Lab	21,131	40.2	
			Wilson E.M. Ms.	Lib	7,550	14.4	
					2,792	5.3	
1987	67,961	82.5	Burt A.J.H.*	Con	28,097	50.1	+4.6
			Crausby D.A.	Lab	21,168	37.8	-2.4
			Vasmer D.	Lib	6,804	12.1	-2.2
					6,929	12.4	
1992	69,531†	84.8	Burt A.J.H.*	Con	29,266	49.7	-0.5
			Dobbin J.	Lab	24,502	41.6	+3.8
			McGrath C.F.L.	LD	5,010	8.5	-3.6
			Sullivan M.S.	NLP	163	0.3*	+0.3
					4,764	8.1	

59

BURY SOUTH [106]

Election	Electors	T'out	Candidate	Party	Votes	% Sh	% Ch
1983	64,827	76.1	Sumberg D.A.G.	Con	21,718	44.0	
			Boden D.	Lab	17,998	36.5	
			Evans K.J.	SDP	9,628	19.5	
					3,720	7.5	
1987	65,043	79.7	Sumberg D.A.G.*	Con	23,878	46.1	+2.0
			Boden D.	Lab	21,199	40.9	+4.4
			Eyre D.A.	SDP	6,772	13.1	-6.5
					2,679	5.2	
1992	65,793†	82.1	Sumberg D.A.G.*	Con	24,873	46.0	-0.0
			Blears H-A. Ms.	Lab	24,085	44.6	+3.7
			Cruden A.H.	LD	4,832	8.9	-4.1
			Sullivan N.A. Ms.	NLP	228	0.4*	+0.4
					788	1.5	

BURY ST. EDMUNDS [107]

Election	Electors	T'out	Candidate	Party	Votes	% Sh	% Ch
1983	72,875	72.3	Griffiths E.W.*	Con	31,081	59.0	
			Harland R.E.W. Sir.	SDP	14,959	28.4	
			Moszczynski W.	Lab	6,666	12.6	
					16,122	30.6	
1987	76,619	74.1	Griffiths E.W. Sir.*	Con	33,672	59.3	+0.3
			Harland R.E.W. Sir.	SDP	12,214	21.5	-6.9
			Greene C.L.	Lab	9,841	17.3	+4.7
			Wakelam I.M.J. Ms.	Green	1,057	1.9*	+1.9
					21,458	37.8	
1992	79,462†	78.9	Spring R.J.G.	Con	33,554	53.5	-5.8
			Sheppard T.	Lab	14,767	23.6	+6.2
			Williams J.B.	LD	13,814	22.0	+0.5
			Lillis J.B. Ms.	NLP	550	0.9*	+0.9
					18,787	30.0	

CAERNARFON [108]

Election	Electors	T'out	Candidate	Party	Votes	% Sh	% Ch
1983	44,147	78.6	Wigley D.W.*	PC	18,308	52.7	
			Jones D.T.	Con	7,319	21.1	
			Williams B.H. Ms.	Lab	6,736	19.4	
			Griffiths O.G.	Lib	2,356	6.8*	
					10,989	31.7	
1987	45,661	78.0	Wigley D.W.*	PC	20,338	57.1	+4.4
			Aubel F.F.E.	Con	7,526	21.1	+0.0
			Williams D.R.	Lab	5,652	15.9	-3.5
			Parsons J.H.	Lib	2,103	5.9	-0.9
					12,812	36.0	
1992	45,348	80.1	Wigley D.W.*	PC	21,439	59.0	+1.9
			Fowler P.E.H.	Con	6,963	19.2	-2.0
			Mainwaring S. Ms.	Lab	5,641	15.5	-0.3
			Williams R.A.W.	LD	2,101	5.8	-0.1
			Evans G.	NLP	173	0.5*	+0.5
					14,476	39.9	

CAERPHILLY [109]

Election	Electors	T'out	Candidate	Party	Votes	% Sh	% Ch
1983	63,479	74.5	Davies R.	Lab	21,570	45.6	
			Lambert A.	Lib	10,017	21.2	
			Welby C.W.H.	Con	9,295	19.7	
			Whittle L.G.	PC	6,414	13.6	
					11,553	24.4	
1987	64,154	76.5	Davies R.*	Lab	28,698	58.4	+12.8
			Powell M.E.	Con	9,531	19.4	-0.2
			Butlin M.G.	Lib	6,923	14.1	-7.1
			Whittle L.G.	PC	3,955	8.1	-5.5
					19,167	39.0	
1992	64,555†	77.2	Davies R.*	Lab	31,713	63.7	+5.2
			Philpott H.L.	Con	9,041	18.1	-1.3
			Whittle L.G.	PC	4,821	9.7	+1.6
			Wilson S.W.	LD	4,247	8.5	-5.6
					22,672	45.5	

CAITHNESS AND SUTHERLAND [110]

Election	Electors	T'out	Candidate	Party	Votes	% Sh	% Ch
1983	30,871	75.4	Maclennan R.A.R.*	SDP	12,119	52.0	
			Scouller A.M.	Con	5,276	22.7	
			Carrigan D.	Lab	3,325	14.3	
			Ingram J.	SNP	2,568	11.0*	
					6,843	29.4	
1987	31,279	73.6	Maclennan R.A.R.*	SDP	12,338	53.6	+1.6
			Hamilton R.L.	Con	3,844	16.7	-5.9
			Byron A.	Lab	3,437	14.9	+0.7
			MacGregor A.W.K.	SNP	2,371	10.3	-0.7
			Mowat W.A.	Ind Lib	686	3.0*	
			Planterose B.R.	Green	333	1.4*	+1.4
					8,494	36.9	
1992	30,677	72.5	Maclennan R.A.R.*	LD	10,032	45.1	-8.5
			Bruce G.	Con	4,667	21.0	+4.3
			MacGregor A.W.K.	SNP	4,049	18.2	+7.9
			Coyne M.F.	Lab	3,483	15.7	+0.7
					5,365	24.1	

CALDER VALLEY [111]

Election	Electors	T'out	Candidate	Party	Votes	% Sh	% Ch
1983	71,309	78.5	Thompson D.*	Con	24,439	43.7	
			Shutt D.T.	Lib	16,440	29.4	
			Holmes P.A. Ms.	Lab	15,108	27.0	
					7,999	14.3	
1987	73,398	81.1	Thompson D.*	Con	25,892	43.5	-0.1
			Chaytor D.M.	Lab	19,847	33.4	+6.4
			Shutt D.T.	Lib	13,761	23.1	-6.2
					6,045	10.2	
1992	74,418†	82.1	Thompson D.*	Con	27,753	45.4	+1.9
			Chaytor D.M.	Lab	22,875	37.4	+4.1
			Pearson S.J.	LD	9,842	16.1	-7.0
			Smith V.P. Ms.	Green	622	1.0*	+1.0
					4,878	8.0	

CAMBRIDGE [112]

Election	Electors	T'out	Candidate	Party	Votes	% Sh	% Ch
1983	67,018	75.2	Rhodes James R.V.*	Con	20,931	41.5	
			Oakeshott M.A.	SDP	14,963	29.7	
			Jones J.D. Ms.	Lab	14,240	28.2	
			Dougrez-Lewis J.D.I.	MRLP	286	0.6*	
					5,968	11.8	
1987	69,336	78.0	Rhodes James R.V.*	Con	21,624	40.0	-1.5
			Williams S.V.T.B. Ms.	SDP	16,564	30.6	+0.9
			Howard C.J.	Lab	15,319	28.3	+0.1
			Wright M.E. Ms.	Green	597	1.1*	+1.1
					5,060	9.4	
1992	69,011	73.2	Campbell A. Ms.	Lab	20,039	39.7	+11.4
			Bishop M.A.	Con	19,459	38.5	-1.4
			Howarth D.R.	LD	10,037	19.9	-10.7
			Cooper T.H.	Green	720	1.4*	+0.3
			Brettell-Winnington N.J.	MRLP	175	0.3*	+0.3
			Chalmers R.A.	NLP	83	0.2*	+0.2
					580	1.1	

CAMBRIDGESHIRE NORTH EAST [113]

Election	Electors	T'out	Candidate	Party	Votes	% Sh	% Ch
1983	69,894	76.3	Freud C.R.*	Lib	26,936	50.5	
			Duval N.C.	Con	21,741	40.8	
			Harris R.J.	Lab	4,629	8.7*	
					5,195	9.7	
1987	74,231	77.4	Moss M.D.	Con	26,983	47.0	+6.2
			Freud C.R.*	Lib	25,555	44.5	-6.0
			Harris R.J.	Lab	4,891	8.5	-0.2
					1,428	2.5	
1992	79,991	79.3	Moss M.D.*	Con	34,288	54.0	+7.1
			Leeke M.L.	LD	19,195	30.3	-14.2
			Harris R.J.	Lab	8,746	13.8	+5.3
			Ash C.D.	Lib	998	1.6*	+1.6
			Chalmers M.J. Ms.	NLP	227	0.4*	+0.4
					15,093	23.8	

63

CAMBRIDGESHIRE SOUTH EAST [114]

Election	Electors	T'out	Candidate	Party	Votes	% Sh	% Ch
1983	66,885	74.2	Pym F.L.*	Con	28,555	57.6	
			Slee C.J.	SDP	14,791	29.8	
			Jackson M.E. Ms.	Lab	6,261	12.6	
					13,764	27.7	
1987	73,210	76.5	Paice J.E.T.	Con	32,901	58.8	+1.2
			Lee P.C.	SDP	15,399	27.5	-2.3
			Ling T.S.	Lab	7,694	13.7	+1.1
					17,502	31.3	
1992	78,601†	80.6	Paice J.E.T.*	Con	36,693	57.9	-0.8
			Wotherspoon R.E.	LD	12,883	20.3	-7.2
			Jones A.M.	Lab	12,688	20.0	+6.3
			Marsh J.W.	Green	836	1.3*	+1.3
			Langridge B.D. Ms.	NLP	231	0.4*	+0.4
					23,810	37.6	

CAMBRIDGESHIRE SOUTH WEST [115]

Election	Electors	T'out	Candidate	Party	Votes	% Sh	% Ch
1983	76,228	75.9	Grant J.A. Sir.*	Con	32,521	56.2	
			Nicholls D.C.	Lib	18,654	32.2	
			Gluza J.L.	Lab	6,703	11.6*	
					13,867	24.0	
1987	81,658	77.7	Grant J.A. Sir.*	Con	36,622	57.7	+1.5
			Nicholls D.C.	Lib	18,371	29.0	-3.3
			Billing J. Ms.	Lab	8,434	13.3	+1.7
					18,251	28.8	
1992	84,419†	81.1	Grant J.A. Sir.*	Con	38,902	56.8	-0.9
			Sutton S.M. Ms.	LD	19,263	28.1	-0.8
			Price K.A.	Lab	9,378	13.7	+0.4
			Whitebread L. Ms.	Green	699	1.0*	+1.0
			Chalmers F.C.	NLP	225	0.3*	+0.3
					19,639	28.7	

CANNOCK AND BURNTWOOD [116]

Election	Electors	T'out	Candidate	Party	Votes	% Sh	% Ch
1983	66,188	77.4	Howarth J.G.D.	Con	20,976	40.9	
			Roberts G.E.*	Lab	18,931	36.9	
			Withnall J.W.	SDP	11,336	22.1	
					2,045	4.0	
1987	68,137	79.8	Howarth J.G.D.*	Con	24,186	44.5	+3.5
			Roberts G.E.	Lab	21,497	39.5	+2.6
			Stanley N.K.	Lib	8,698	16.0	-6.1
					2,689	4.9	
1992	72,522	84.3	Wright A.W.	Lab	28,139	46.0	+6.5
			Howarth J.G.D.*	Con	26,633	43.6	-0.9
			Treasaden P.W.	LD	5,899	9.6	-6.3
			Hartshorne M.	MRLP	469	0.8*	+0.8
					1,506	2.5	

CANTERBURY [117]

Election	Electors	T'out	Candidate	Party	Votes	% Sh	% Ch
1983	73,464	70.0	Crouch D.L.*	Con	29,029	56.5	
			Purchese J.	Lib	13,287	25.8	
			Gould J.R Ms.	Lab	7,906	15.4	
			Conder D.R.	Green	962	1.9*	
			White J.M. Ms.	Ind	226	0.4*	
					15,742	30.6	
1987	75,973	74.0	Brazier J.W.H.	Con	30,273	53.8	-2.6
			Purchese J.	Lib	15,382	27.3	+1.5
			Keen L.A. Ms.	Lab	9,494	16.9	+1.5
			Dawe S.M.	Green	947	1.7*	-0.2
			White J.M. Ms.	Ind	157	0.3*	
					14,891	26.5	
1992	75,180	78.1	Brazier J.W.H.*	Con	29,827	50.8	-3.0
			Vye M.J.	LD	19,022	32.4	+5.0
			Whitemore M.F.	Lab	8,936	15.2	-1.7
			Arnall W.J. Ms.	Green	747	1.3*	-0.4
			Curphey S.E. Ms.	NLP	203	0.3*	+0.3
					10,805	18.4	

CARDIFF CENTRAL [118]

Election	Electors	T'out	Candidate	Party	Votes	% Sh	% Ch
1983	53,815	72.1	Grist I.*	Con	16,090	41.4	
			German M.J.	Lib	12,638	32.6	
			Davies R.T.	Lab	9,387	24.2	
			Morgan A.P.	PC	704	1.8*	
					3,452	8.9	
1987	52,980	77.6	Grist I.*	Con	15,241	37.1	-4.4
			Jones J.O.	Lab	13,255	32.3	+8.1
			German M.J.	Lib	12,062	29.4	-3.2
			Caiach S.M. Dr.‡	PC	535	1.3*	-0.5
					1,986	4.8	
1992	57,780†	74.3	Jones J.O.	Lab	18,014	42.0	+9.7
			Grist I.*	Con	14,549	33.9	-3.2
			Randerson J.E. Ms.	LD	9,170	21.4	-8.0
			Marshall H.	PC	748	1.7*	+0.4
			Von Ruhland C.J.	Green	330	0.8*	+0.8
			Francis B.M.	NLP	105	0.2*	+0.2
					3,465	8.1	

CARDIFF NORTH [119]

Election	Electors	T'out	Candidate	Party	Votes	% Sh	% Ch
1983	53,377	77.3	Jones G.H.	Con	19,433	47.1	
			Jeremy A.W.	SDP	12,585	30.5	
			Hutt J.E. Ms.	Lab	8,256	20.0	
			Hughes D.J.L. Dr.	PC	974	2.4*	
					6,848	16.6	
1987	54,704	81.0	Jones G.H.*	Con	20,061	45.3	-1.8
			Tarbet S.H.	Lab	11,827	26.7	+6.7
			Jeremy A.W.	SDP	11,725	26.5	-4.0
			Bush E.M. Ms.	PC	692	1.6*	-0.8
					8,234	18.6	
1992	56,757†	84.1	Jones G.H.*	Con	21,547	45.1	-0.1
			Morgan J. Ms.	Lab	18,578	38.9	+12.2
			Warlow E. Ms.	LD	6,487	13.6	-12.9
			Bush E.M. Ms.	PC	916	1.9*	+0.4
			Morse J.H.	BNP	121	0.3*	+0.3
			Palmer D.L.	NLP	86	0.2*	+0.2
					2,969	6.2	

CARDIFF SOUTH AND PENARTH [120]

Election	Electors	T'out	Candidate	Party	Votes	% Sh	% Ch
1983	59,520	71.0	Callaghan L.J.*	Lab	17,448	41.3	
			Tredinnick D.A.S.	Con	15,172	35.9	
			Roddick G.W.	Lib	8,816	20.9	
			Edwards S.A. Ms.	PC	673	1.6*	
			Lewis B.T.	Ind	165	0.4*	
					2,276	5.4	
1987	58,714	76.4	Michael A.E.	Lab	20,956	46.7	+5.5
			Neale G.J.J.	Con	16,382	36.5	+0.6
			Randerson J.E. Ms.	Lib	6,900	15.4	-5.5
			Edwards S.A. Ms.	PC	599	1.3*	-0.3
					4,574	10.2	
1992	61,490†	77.2	Michael A.E.*	Lab	26,383	55.5	+8.8
			Jarvie T.H.	Con	15,958	33.6	-2.9
			Verma P.K.	LD	3,707	7.8	-7.6
			Anglezarke B.A. Ms.	PC	776	1.6*	+0.3
			Davey L.	Green	676	1.4*	+1.4
					10,425	21.9	

CARDIFF WEST [121]

Election	Electors	T'out	Candidate	Party	Votes	% Sh	% Ch
1983	58,538	69.6	Terlezki S.	Con	15,472	38.0	
			Seligman D.J.	Lab	13,698	33.6	
			Thomas J.*	SDP	10,388	25.5	
			Parri M.	PC	848	2.1*	
			Jones G.P.	Green	352	0.9*	
					1,774	4.4	
1987	57,363	77.8	Morgan H.R.	Lab	20,329	45.5	+11.9
			Terlezki S.*	Con	16,284	36.5	-1.5
			Drake R.G.	SDP	7,300	16.3	-9.1
			Keelan P.J.	PC	736	1.6*	-0.4
					4,045	9.1	
1992	58,936†	77.5	Morgan H.R.*	Lab	24,306	53.2	+7.7
			Prior M.J.	Con	15,015	32.9	-3.6
			Gasson J-A. Ms.	LD	5,002	10.9	-5.4
			Bestic P.M. Ms.	PC	1,177	2.6*	+0.9
			Harding A.E.	NLP	184	0.4*	+0.4
					9,291	20.3	

CARLISLE [122]

Election	Electors	T'out	Candidate	Party	Votes	% Sh	% Ch
1983	54,515	76.4	Lewis R.H.*	Lab	15,618	37.5	
			Sowler T.R.H.	Con	15,547	37.3	
			Hunt R.S.	SDP	10,471	25.1	
					71	0.2	
1987	55,053	78.8	Martlew E.A.	Lab	18,311	42.2	+4.7
			Hodgson W.G.	Con	17,395	40.1	+2.8
			Hunt R.S.	SDP	7,655	17.7	-7.5
					916	2.1	
1992	55,140†	79.4	Martlew E.A.*	Lab	20,479	46.8	+4.5
			Condie C.W.	Con	17,371	39.7	-0.4
			Aldersey R.E.	LD	5,740	13.1	-4.5
			Robinson N.E. Ms.	NLP	190	0.4*	+0.4
					3,108	7.1	

CARMARTHEN [123]

Election	Electors	T'out	Candidate	Party	Votes	% Sh	% Ch
1983	63,468	82.1	Thomas R.G. Dr.*	Lab	16,459	31.6	
			Thomas N.M.	Con	15,305	29.4	
			Evans G.R.	PC	14,099	27.0	
			Colin J.R. Ms.	SDP	5,737	11.0*	
			Kingzett B.	Green	374	0.7*	
			Grice C.D.	BNP	154	0.3*	
					1,154	2.2	
1987	65,315	82.8	Williams A.W.	Lab	19,128	35.4	+3.8
			Richards R.	Con	14,811	27.4	-2.0
			Edwards H.T.	PC	12,457	23.0	-4.0
			Jones G.G.	SDP	7,203	13.3	+2.3
			Oubridge G.E.	Green	481	0.9*	+0.2
					4,317	8.0	
1992	68,920	82.7	Williams A.W.*	Lab	20,879	36.6	+1.3
			Thomas H.R.G.	PC	17,957	31.5	+8.5
			Cavenagh S.J.	Con	12,782	22.4	-5.0
			Hughes J.M-J. Ms.	LD	5,353	9.4	-3.9
					2,922	5.1	

CARRICK, CUMNOCK AND DOON VALLEY [124]

Election	Electors	T'out	Candidate	Party	Votes	% Sh	% Ch
1983	55,925	74.3	Foulkes G.*	Lab	21,394	51.5	
			McInnes J.	Con	10,024	24.1	
			Logan R.	SDP	7,421	17.9	
			Wyllie R.	SNP	2,694	6.5*	
					11,370	27.4	
1987	56,360	75.8	Foulkes G.*	Lab	25,669	60.1	+8.6
			Stevenson S.J.S.	Con	8,867	20.7	-3.4
			Ali M. Ms.	SDP	4,106	9.6	-8.3
			Calman C.D.	SNP	4,094	9.6	+3.1
					16,802	39.3	
1992	55,332	77.0	Foulkes G.*	Lab	25,182	59.1	-1.0
			Boswell J.A.D.	Con	8,516	20.0	-0.8
			Douglas C.E.	SNP	6,910	16.2	+6.6
			Paris M.C. Ms.	LD	2,005	4.7*	-4.9
					16,666	39.1	

CARSHALTON AND WALLINGTON [125]

Election	Electors	T'out	Candidate	Party	Votes	% Sh	% Ch
1983	68,682	72.0	Forman F.N.*	Con	25,396	51.3	
			Ensor B.J.M.	SDP	14,641	29.6	
			Baker J.G. Ms.	Lab	8,655	17.5	
			Steel R.W.	Green	784	1.6*	
					10,755	21.7	
1987	69,120	75.0	Forman F.N.*	Con	27,984	54.0	+2.6
			Grant J.D.	SDP	13,575	26.2	-3.4
			Baker J.G. Ms.	Lab	9,440	18.2	+0.7
			Steel R.W.	Green	843	1.6*	+0.0
					14,409	27.8	
1992	65,209	80.9	Forman F.N.*	Con	26,243	49.7	-4.2
			Brake T.A.	LD	16,300	30.9	+4.7
			Moran M. Ms.	Lab	9,333	17.7	-0.5
			Steel R.W.	Green	614	1.2*	-0.5
			Bamford D.J.B.	RLGG	266	0.5*	+0.5
					9,943	18.8	

CASTLE POINT [126]

Election	Electors	T'out	Candidate	Party	Votes	% Sh	% Ch
1983	64,023	71.3	Braine B.R. Sir.*	Con	26,730	58.5	
			Bastow A.P. Ms.	SDP	11,313	24.8	
			Cunningham L. Ms.	Lab	7,621	16.7	
					15,417	33.8	
1987	66,514	74.5	Braine B.R. Sir.*	Con	29,681	59.9	+1.4
			Bastow A.P. Ms.	SDP	10,433	21.1	-3.7
			Deal W.A.	Lab	9,422	19.0	+2.3
					19,248	38.9	
1992	66,229†	80.4	Spink R.M.	Con	29,629	55.6	-4.3
			Flack D.F.L.	Lab	12,799	24.0	+5.0
			Petchey A.R.K.	LD	10,208	19.2	-1.9
			Willis I.L. Ms.	Green	643	1.2*	+1.2
					16,830	31.6	

CEREDIGION AND PEMBROKE NORTH [127]

Election	Electors	T'out	Candidate	Party	Votes	% Sh	% Ch
1983	60,523	77.8	Howells G.W.*	Lib	19,677	41.8	
			Raw-Rees W.T.K.	Con	14,038	29.8	
			Hughes G.E.	Lab	6,840	14.5	
			Davies C.G.	PC	6,072	12.9	
			Smith M.A. Ms.	Green	431	0.9*	
					5,639	12.0	
1987	63,141	76.5	Howells G.W.*	Lib	17,683	36.6	-5.2
			Williams O.J.	Con	12,983	26.9	-3.0
			Davies J.R.	Lab	8,965	18.6	+4.0
			Davies C.G.	PC	7,848	16.2	+3.3
			Wakefield M.A. Ms.	Green	821	1.7*	+0.8
					4,700	9.7	
1992	66,166†	77.4	Dafis C.G.	PC/Green	16,020	31.3*	+15.1
			Howells G.W.*	LD	12,827	25.1	-11.6
			Williams O.J.	Con	12,718	24.8	-2.0
			Davies J.R.	Lab	9,637	18.8	+0.3
					3,193	6.2	

*C.G. Davies, a candidate in 1983 and 1987, is the same as C.G. Dafis, the winner in 1992.

CHEADLE [128]

Election	Electors	T'out	Candidate	Party	Votes	% Sh	% Ch
1983	66,474	76.8	Normanton T.*	Con	28,452	55.7	
			Clark P.R.	Lib	19,072	37.3	
			Parker K.	Lab	3,553	7.0*	
					9,380	18.4	
1987	68,332	81.0	Day S.R.	Con	30,484	55.1	-0.7
			Leah A.B.	Lib	19,853	35.9	-1.5
			Coffey A. Ms.	Lab	5,037	9.1	+2.1
					10,631	19.2	
1992	66,131†	84.4	Day S.R.*	Con	32,504	58.2	+3.2
			Calton P. Ms.	LD	16,726	30.0	-5.9
			Broadhurst S.R. Ms.	Lab	6,442	11.5	+2.4
			Whittle P.M. Ms.	NLP	168	0.3*	+0.3
					15,778	28.3	

CHELMSFORD [129]

Election	Electors	T'out	Candidate	Party	Votes	% Sh	% Ch
1983	78,849	79.4	St. John-Stevas N.A.F.*	Con	29,824	47.6	
			Mole S.G.	Lib	29,446	47.0	
			Playford C.E.	Lab	3,208	5.1*	
			Waite P.D.P.	Ind	127	0.2*	
					378	0.6	
1987	82,564	82.2	Burns S.H.M.	Con	35,231	51.9	+4.3
			Mole S.G.	Lib	27,470	40.5	-6.5
			Playford C.E.	Lab	4,642	6.8	+1.7
			Slade A.C.	Green	486	0.7*	+0.7
					7,761	11.4	
1992	83,440	84.6	Burns S.H.M.*	Con	39,043	55.3	+3.4
			Nicholson H.P.	LD	20,783	29.4	-11.1
			Chad R.K.	Lab	10,010	14.2	+7.3
			Burgess E.J. Ms.	Green	769	1.1*	+0.4
					18,260	25.9	

CHELSEA [130]

Election	Electors	T'out	Candidate	Party	Votes	% Sh	% Ch
1983	53,864	56.1	Scott N.P.*	Con	19,122	63.2	
			Fryer J.H.	Lib	7,101	23.5	
			Palmer N.D.	Lab	3,876	12.8	
			Feilding A.C.M. Ms.	Ind	139	0.5*	
					12,021	39.8	
1987	49,534	57.7	Scott N.P.*	Con	18,443	64.6	+1.3
			Ware J.M. Ms.	Lib	5,124	17.9	-5.5
			Ward D.J.	Lab	4,406	15.4	+2.6
			Kortvelyessy N. Ms.	Green	587	2.1*	+2.1
					13,319	46.6	
1992	42,372†	63.3	Scott N.P.*	Con	17,471	65.1	+0.5
			Horton R.E. Ms.	Lab	4,682	17.5	+2.0
			Broidy S.N. Ms.	LD	4,101	15.3	-2.7
			Kortvelyessy N. Ms.	Green	485	1.8*	-0.2
			Armstrong D.G.F.	AFL	88	0.3*	
					12,789	47.7	

CHELTENHAM [131]

Election	Electors	T'out	Candidate	Party	Votes	% Sh	% Ch
1983	76,068	75.9	Irving C.G.*	Con	29,187	50.6	
			Holme R.G.	Lib	23,669	41.0	
			James J.M. Ms.	Lab	4,390	7.6*	
			Swindley D.G.	Green	479	0.8*	
					5,518	9.6	
1987	79,234	78.9	Irving C.G.*	Con	31,371	50.2	-0.4
			Holme R.G.	Lib	26,475	42.3	+1.3
			Luker M.N.	Lab	4,701	7.5	-0.1
					4,896	7.8	
1992	79,806†	80.3	Jones N.D.	LD	30,351	47.3	+5.0
			Taylor J.D.B.	Con	28,683	44.7	-5.4
			Tatlow P.R. Ms.	Lab	4,077	6.4	-1.2
			Rendell M.D.	AFE	665	1.0*	+1.0
			Brighouse H.W.	NLP	169	0.3*	+0.3
			Bruce-Smith M.A.	Ind	162	0.3*	
					1,668	2.6	

CHERTSEY AND WALTON [132]

Election	Electors	T'out	Candidate	Party	Votes	% Sh	% Ch
1983	70,210	72.5	Pattie G.E.*	Con	29,679	58.3	
			De Ste. Croix R.J.	SDP	13,980	27.5	
			Greene D.M.	Lab	6,902	13.6	
			Barrett F.	Ind	318	0.6*	
					15,699	30.9	
1987	71,448	75.5	Pattie G.E.*	Con	32,119	59.5	+1.2
			Stapely S.K. Ms.	SDP	14,650	27.2	-0.3
			Trace H.G.	Lab	7,185	13.3	-0.2
					17,469	32.4	
1992	70,675	80.3	Pattie G.E.*	Con	34,164	60.2	+0.7
			Kremer A.L.	LD	11,344	20.0	-7.2
			Hamilton I. Ms.	Lab	10,793	19.0	+5.7
			Bennell S.A. Ms.	NLP	444	0.8*	+0.8
					22,820	40.2	

CHESHAM AND AMERSHAM [133]

Election	Electors	T'out	Candidate	Party	Votes	% Sh	% Ch
1983	69,980	75.9	Gilmour I.H.J.L. Sir., Bt.*	Con	32,425	61.0	
			Bradnock R.W.	Lib	16,556	31.2	
			Duncan C.P.	Lab	4,150	7.8*	
					15,869	29.9	
1987	71,751	77.3	Gilmour I.H.J.L. Sir., Bt.*	Con	34,504	62.2	+1.1
			Ketteringham A.T.	Lib	15,064	27.1	-4.0
			Goulding P.A.	Lab	5,170	9.3	+1.5
			Darnbrough A.G. Ms.	Green	760	1.4*	+1.4
					19,440	35.0	
1992	69,898†	81.9	Gillan C. Ms.	Con	36,273	63.3	+1.2
			Ketteringham A.T.	LD	14,053	24.5	-2.6
			Atherton C. Ms.	Lab	5,931	10.4	+1.0
			Strickland C. Ms.	Green	753	1.3*	-0.1
			Griffith-Jones M.	NLP	255	0.4*	+0.4
					22,220	38.8	

Election	Electors	T'out	Candidate	Party	Votes	% Sh	% Ch
1983	64,508	74.5	Morrison P.H. Hon.*	Con	22,645	47.1	
			Robertson D.E.	Lab	13,546	28.2	
			Stunell R.A.	Lib	11,874	24.7	
					9,099	18.9	
1987	65,845	79.8	Morrison P.H. Hon.*	Con	23,582	44.9	-2.3
			Robinson D.E.	Lab	18,727	35.6	+7.4
			Stunell R.A.	Lib	10,262	19.5	-5.2
					4,855	9.2	
1992	63,319	83.9	Brandreth G.D.	Con	23,411	44.1	-0.8
			Robinson D.E.	Lab	22,310	42.0	+6.4
			Smith J.G.	LD	6,867	12.9	-6.6
			Barker M.T.	Green	448	0.8*	+0.8
			Cross S.R.H.	NLP	98	0.2*	+0.2
					1,101	2.1	

CHESTERFIELD [135]

Election	Electors	T'out	Candidate	Party	Votes	% Sh	% Ch
1983	68,486	72.6	Varley E.G.*	Lab	23,881	48.0	
			Bourne N.H.	Con	16,118	32.4	
			Payne M.G.	Lib	9,705	19.5	
					7,763	15.6	

[Resignation]

Election	Electors	T'out	Candidate	Party	Votes	% Sh	% Ch
1984	68,942	76.9	Benn A.N.W.	Lab	24,633	46.5	-1.6
(1/3)			Payne M.G.	Lib	18,369	34.7	+15.2
			Bourne N. H.	Con	8.028	15.2	-17.2
			Maynard B.	Ind	1,355	2.6*	
			Sutch D.E.	MRLP	178	0.3*	
			Bentley D.E.	Ind	116	0.2*	
			Davey J.V.	Ind	83	0.2*	
			Layton T.A.	Ind	46	0.1*	
			Anscomb H. M. Ms.	Ind	34	0.1*	
			Bardwaj J.J.N.	Ind	33	0.1*	
			Butler D.	Ind	24	0.0	
			Nicholls-Jones P.	Ind	22	0.0*	
			Shaw S.D.	Ind	20	0.0*	
			Hill C.S.	Ind	17	0.0*	
			Piccaro G.R	Ind	15	0.0*	
			Cahill D.M.	Ind	12	0.0*	
			Connell J.	Ind	7	0.0*	
					6,264	11.8	

Election	Electors	T'out	Candidate	Party	Votes	% Sh	% Ch
1987	70,357	76.7	Benn A.N.W.	Lab	24,532	45.5	-2.6
			Rogers A.H.	Lib	15,955	29.6	+10.0
			Grant R.P.	Con	13,472	25.0	-7.5
					8,577	15.9	

Election	Electors	T'out	Candidate	Party	Votes	% Sh	% Ch
1992	71,685	78.1	Benn A.N.W.*	Lab	26,461	47.3	+1.8
			Rogers A.H.	LD	20,047	35.8	+6.2
			Lewis P.G.	Con	9,473	16.9	-8.0
					6,414	11.5	

CHICHESTER [136]

Election	Electors	T'out	Candidate	Party	Votes	% Sh	% Ch
1983	77,259	72.1	Nelson R.A.*	Con	35,482	63.7	
			Gibson H.	SDP	15,365	27.6	
			Rhodes R.H.	Lab	3,995	7.2*	
			Sherlock J.	Green	838	1.5*	
					20,117	36.1	
1987	81,015	74.5	Nelson R.A.*	Con	37,274	61.8	-1.9
			Weston P.F.	Lib	17,097	28.3	+0.7
			Morrison D.	Lab	4,751	7.9	+0.7
			Bagnall I.F.N.	Green	1,196	2.0*	+0.5
					20,177	33.5	
1992	82,126†	77.8	Nelson R.A.*	Con	37,906	59.3	-2.5
			Gardiner P.F.	LD	17,019	26.6	-1.7
			Andrewes D.M. Ms.	Lab	7,192	11.3	+3.4
			Paine E.	Green	876	1.4*	-0.6
			Weights J.L. Ms.	Lib	643	1.0*	+1.0
			Jackson J.L. Ms.	NLP	238	0.4*	+0.4
					20,887	32.7	

CHINGFORD [137]

Election	Electors	T'out	Candidate	Party	Votes	% Sh	% Ch
1983	56,228	72.7	Tebbit N.B.*	Con	22,541	55.1	
			Hoskins R.H.	Lib	10,127	24.8	
			Shepherd W.D.	Lab	7,239	17.7	
			Morgan J.E.	Green	479	1.2*	
			Cheetham B.A.	NF	380	0.9*	
			Neighbour J.C.	Ind	104	0.3*	
			Barklem S.J.A.	Ind	34	0.1*	
					12,414	30.3	
1987	56,797	76.7	Tebbit N.B.*	Con	27,110	62.3	+7.1
			Williams J.G.	Lib	9,155	21.0	-3.7
			Cosin M.I. Ms.	Lab	6,650	15.3	-2.4
			Newton E. Ms.	Green	634	1.5*	+0.3
					17,955	41.2	
1992	55,466	78.3	Duncan-Smith G.I.	Con	25,730	59.2	-3.0
			Dawe P.J.	Lab	10,792	24.8	+9.6
			Banks S.G.	LD	5,705	13.1	-7.9
			Green D.W.	Lib	602	1.4*	+1.4
			Baguley J.M.	Green	575	1.3*	-0.1
			Johns C.M. Ms.	Ind	41	0.1*	
					14,938	34.4	

76

CHIPPING BARNET [138]

Election	Electors	T'out	Candidate	Party	Votes	% Sh	% Ch
1983	58,423	70.7	Chapman S.B.*	Con	23,164	56.1	
			Perkin C.	Lib	10,771	26.1	
			Smith N.J.M.	Lab	6,599	16.0	
			Parry E.A.	Green	552	1.3*	
			Hopkins T.J.	Ind	195	0.5*	
					12,393	30.0	
1987	60,876	70.0	Chapman S.B.*	Con	24,686	57.9	+1.8
			Skinner J.S.	Lib	9,815	23.0	-3.1
			Perkin D.G.	Lab	8,115	19.0	+3.1
					14,871	34.9	
1992	57,150†	78.6	Chapman S.B.*	Con	25,589	57.0	-0.9
			Williams A.J.	Lab	11,638	25.9	+6.9
			Smith D.H.	LD	7,247	16.1	-6.9
			Derksen D. Ms.	NLP	222	0.5*	+0.5
			Johnson C.V.	Ind	213	0.5*	
					13,951	31.1	

CHISLEHURST [139]

Election	Electors	T'out	Candidate	Party	Votes	% Sh	% Ch
1983	54,567	72.7	Sims R.E.*	Con	22,108	55.7	
			Lingard P.	Lib	10,047	25.3	
			Macdonald A.H.	Lab	7,320	18.4	
			Waite A.	BNP	201	0.5*	
					12,061	30.4	
1987	55,535	75.5	Sims R.E.*	Con	24,165	57.6	+1.9
			Younger-Ross R.A.	Lib	9,658	23.0	-2.3
			Ward S.H.	Lab	8,115	19.3	+0.9
					14,507	34.6	
1992	53,783	78.9	Sims R.E.*	Con	24,761	58.4	+0.7
			Wingfield R.I.	Lab	9,485	22.4	+3.0
			Hawthorne T.W.	LD	6,683	15.8	-7.3
			Richmond I.	Lib	849	2.0*	+2.0
			Speed F.M. Ms.	Green	652	1.5*	+1.5
					15,276	36.0	

CHORLEY [140]

Election	Electors	T'out	Candidate	Party	Votes	% Sh	% Ch
1983	72,841	79.2	Dover D.R.*	Con	27,861	48.3	
			Taylor I.J.	Lab	17,586	30.5	
			O'Neill P.D.	SDP	11,691	20.3	
			Holgate A.S.	Green	451	0.8*	
			Rokas E. Ms.	Ind	114	0.2*	
					10,275	17.8	
1987	76,405	79.0	Dover D.R.*	Con	29,015	48.0	-0.2
			Watmough A.J.	Lab	20,958	34.7	+4.2
			Simpson I.E.	Lib	9,706	16.1	-4.2
			Holgate A.S.	Green	714	1.2*	+0.4
					8,057	13.3	
1992	78,514†	82.8	Dover D.R.*	Con	30,715	47.2	-0.8
			McManus R.C.	Lab	26,469	40.7	+6.0
			Ross-Mills J. Ms.	LD	7,452	11.5	-4.6
			Leadbetter P.D.N.	NLP	402	0.6*	+0.6
					4,246	6.5	

CHRISTCHURCH [141]

Election	Electors	T'out	Candidate	Party	Votes	% Sh	% Ch
1983	65,489	72.2	Adley R.J.*	Con	31,722	67.1	
			Alexander S.E.	SDP	11,984	25.3	
			Mitchell J.R.	Lab	3,590	7.6*	
					19,738	41.7	
1987	70,964	76.3	Adley R.J.*	Con	35,656	65.9	-1.2
			McKenzie H.J. Ms.	SDP	13,282	24.5	-0.8
			Longhurst C.E. Ms.	Lab	5,174	9.6	+2.0
					22,374	41.3	
1992	71,469	80.7	Adley R.J.*	Con	36,627	63.5	-2.4
			Bussey D.	LD	13,612	23.6	-0.9
			Lloyd A.	Lab	6,997	12.1	+2.6
			Barratt J.T.	NLP	243	0.4*	+0.4
			Wareham A.D.	Ind	175	0.3*	
					23,015	39.9	

[Death]

Election	Electors	T'out	Candidate	Party	Votes	% Sh	% Ch
1993	71,868	74.2	Maddock D.M. Ms.	LD	33,164	62.2	+38.6
(29/7)			Hayward R.A.	Con	16,737	31.4	-32.2
			Lickley N.	Lab	1,453	2.7*	-9.4
			Sked A. Dr.	AFL	878	1.6*	
			Sutch D.E.	MRLP	404	0.8*	
			Bannon A.	Ind	357	0.7*	
			Newman P.	Ind	80	0.1*	
			Jackson T. Ms.	Ind	67	0.1*	
			Hollyman P.	Ind	60	0.1*	
			Crockard J.	Ind	48	0.1*	
			Griffiths M.R.F.	NLP	45	0.1*	-0.3
			Belcher M.	Ind	23	0.0*	
			Fitzhugh K.	Ind	18	0.0*	
			Walley J.	Ind	16	0.0*	
					16,427	30.8	

79

CIRENCESTER AND TEWKESBURY [142]

Election	Electors	T'out	Candidate	Party	Votes	% Sh	% Ch
1983	80,067	74.9	Ridley N. Hon.*	Con	34,282	57.2	
			Beckerlegge P.T.	Lib	20,455	34.1	
			Penny T.J.R.	Lab	5,243	8.7*	
					13,827	23.1	
1987	84,071	77.9	Ridley N. Hon.*	Con	36,272	55.4	-1.8
			Beckerlegge P.T.	Lib	23,610	36.0	+1.9
			Naysmith J.D.	Lab	5,342	8.2	-0.6
			Curtis M.A.	Ind	283	0.4*	
					12,662	19.3	
1992	88,413	82.0	Clifton-Brown G.R.	Con	40,258	55.6	+0.2
			Weston E.J.	LD	24,200	33.4	-2.6
			Page T.A.	Lab	7,262	10.0	+1.9
			Clayton R.	NLP	449	0.6*	+0.6
			Trice-Rolph P.A.	Ind	287	0.4*	
					16,058	22.2	

CITY OF LONDON AND WESTMINSTER SOUTH [143]

Election	Electors	T'out	Candidate	Party	Votes	% Sh	% Ch
1983	67,773	51.8	Brooke P.L. Hon.*	Con	20,754	59.1	
			Walker-Smith A.A.	Lib	7,367	21.0	
			Jones S.P.	Lab	6,013	17.1	
			Shorter R.E.	Green	419	1.2*	
			Reeve A.	NF	258	0.7*	
			Spence A.W.	Comm	161	0.5*	
			Litvin V.	Ind	147	0.4*	
					13,387	38.1	
1987	57,428	58.3	Brooke P.L. Hon.*	Con	19,333	57.8	-1.3
			Smithard J.C.G. Ms.	SDP	7,299	21.8	+0.8
			Bush R.E. Ms.	Lab	6,821	20.4	+3.3
					12,034	36.0	
1992	54,830	63.3	Brooke P.L. Hon.*	Con	20,938	60.3	+2.5
			Smith C.	Lab	7,569	21.8	+1.4
			Smithard J.C.G. Ms.	LD	5,392	15.5	-6.3
			Herbert G.E.S.	Green	458	1.3*	+1.3
			Stockton P.F.	MRLP	147	0.4*	+0.4
			Farrell A.	Ind	107	0.3*	
			Johnson R.P.	NLP	101	0.3*	+0.3
					13,369	38.5	

CLACKMANNAN [144]

Election	Electors	T'out	Candidate	Party	Votes	% Sh	% Ch
1983	47,642	75.6	O'Neill M.J.*	Lab	16,478	45.8	
			Jones J.T. Ms.	SNP	6,839	19.0	
			Hendry C.	Con	6,490	18.0	
			Campbell H.C. Ms.	SDP	6,205	17.2	
					9,639	26.8	
1987	49,083	77.0	O'Neill M.J.*	Lab	20,317	53.7	+8.0
			Macartney W.J.A.	SNP	7,916	20.9	+1.9
			Parker J.	Con	5,620	14.9	-3.2
			Watters A.M. Ms.	SDP	3,961	10.5	-6.8
					12,401	32.8	
1992	48,362	79.3	O'Neill M.J.*	Lab	18,829	49.1	-4.6
			Brophy A.	SNP	10,326	26.9	+6.0
			Mackie J.A.	Con	6,638	17.3	+2.4
			Watters A.M. Ms.	LD	2,567	6.7	-3.8
					8,503	22.2	

CLWYD NORTH WEST [145]

Election	Electors	T'out	Candidate	Party	Votes	% Sh	% Ch
1983	62,503	73.1	Meyer A.J.C. Sir., Bt.*	Con	23,283	51.0	
			Lewis J.J.	Lib	13,294	29.1	
			Campbell C.I.	Lab	7,433	16.3	
			Rhys M. Ms.	PC	1,669	3.7*	
					9,989	21.9	
1987	66,118	75.2	Meyer A.J.C. Sir., Bt.*	Con	24,116	48.5	-2.4
			Thomas K.L.	Lab	12,335	24.8	+8.5
			Griffiths O.G.	Lib	11,279	22.7	-6.4
			Davies R.K.	PC	1,966	4.0*	+0.3
					11,781	23.7	
1992	67,352†	78.6	Richards R.	Con	24,488	46.2	-2.3
			Ruane C.S.	Lab	18,438	34.8	+10.0
			Ingham R.V.	LD	7,999	15.1	-7.6
			Taylor N.H.	PC	1,888	3.6*	-0.4
			Swift M.S. Ms.	NLP	158	0.3*	+0.3
					6,050	11.4	

CLWYD SOUTH WEST [146]

Election	Electors	T'out	Candidate	Party	Votes	% Sh	% Ch
1983	55,792	77.3	Harvey R.L.	Con	14,575	33.8	
			Ellis R.T.*	SDP	13,024	30.2	
			Carter D.B.	Lab	11,829	27.4	
			Schiavone A.O.G.	PC	3,684	8.5*	
					1,551	3.6	
1987	58,106	81.1	Jones M.D.	Lab	16,701	35.4	+8.0
			Harvey R.L.*	Con	15,673	33.2	-0.6
			Ellis R.T.	SDP	10,778	22.9	-7.3
			Jones E.L.	PC	3,987	8.5	-0.1
					1,028	2.2	
1992	60,607	81.5	Jones M.D.*	Lab	21,490	43.5	+8.1
			Owen G.G.V.	Con	16,549	33.5	+0.2
			Williams W.G.	LD	6,027	12.2	-10.7
			Jones E.L.	PC	4,835	9.8	+1.3
			Worth N.C.	Green	351	0.7*	+0.7
			Leadbetter J.B. Ms.	NLP	155	0.3*	+0.3
					4,941	10.0	

CLYDEBANK AND MILNGAVIE [147]

Election	Electors	T'out	Candidate	Party	Votes	% Sh	% Ch
1983	50,831	75.9	McCartney H.*	Lab	17,288	44.8	
			Gourlay J.	SDP	9,573	24.8	
			Graham R.F.	Con	7,852	20.3	
			Aitken A.C.W.	SNP	3,566	9.2*	
			Bollan J.D.	Comm	308	0.8*	
					7,715	20.0	
1987	50,152	78.9	Worthington A.	Lab	22,528	56.9	+12.1
			Hirstwood K.	Con	6,224	15.7	-4.6
			Ackland R.	SDP	5,891	14.9	-9.9
			Fisher S.F.	SNP	4,935	12.5	+3.2
					16,304	41.2	
1992	47,337	77.8	Worthington A.*	Lab	19,642	53.3	-3.6
			Hughes G.J.	SNP	7,207	19.6	+7.1
			Harvey W.A.	Con	6,650	18.1	+2.3
			Tough A.G.	LD	3,216	8.7	-6.2
			Barrie J. Ms.	NLP	112	0.3*	+0.3
					12,435	33.8	

CLYDESDALE [148]

Election	Electors	T'out	Candidate	Party	Votes	% Sh	% Ch
1983	60,240	76.5	Hart J. Dame.*	Lab	17,873	38.8	
			Bainbridge P.V.	Con	13,007	28.2	
			Craig M. Ms.	SDP	9,908	21.5	
			McAlpine T.	SNP	5,271	11.4*	
					4,866	10.6	
1987	61,620	78.2	Hood J.	Lab	21,826	45.3	+6.5
			Robertson R.S.	Con	11,324	23.5	-4.7
			Boyle J.	SDP	7,909	16.4	-5.1
			Russell M.W.	SNP	7,125	14.8	+3.3
					10,502	21.8	
1992	61,914	77.6	Hood J.*	Lab	21,418	44.6	-0.7
			Goodwin C.E. Ms.	Con	11,231	23.4	-0.1
			Gray I.	SNP	11,084	23.1	+8.3
			Buchanan E.M. Ms.	LD	3,957	8.2	-8.2
			Cartwright S.F.	BNP	342	0.7*	+0.7
					10,187	21.2	

COLCHESTER NORTH [149]

Election	Electors	T'out	Candidate	Party	Votes	% Sh	% Ch
1983	77,292	73.1	Buck P.A.F.*	Con	29,921	53.0	
			Montgomerie R.S.	Lib	14,873	26.3	
			Allen R.C.	Lab	10,397	18.4	
			Wilkinson D.	Ind Con	784	1.4*	
			Davies R.	Ind	510	0.9*	
					15,048	26.6	
1987	82,420	76.0	Buck P.A.F. Sir.*	Con	32,747	52.3	-0.7
			Hayman A.	SDP	19,124	30.5	+4.2
			Green R.A.	Lab	10,768	17.2	-1.2
					13,623	21.7	
1992	86,479†	79.1	Jenkin B.C.	Con	35,213	51.5	-0.8
			Raven J.R.	LD	18,721	27.4	-3.2
			Lee D.J.	Lab	13,870	20.3	+3.1
			Shabbeer M.T.	Green	372	0.5*	+0.5
			Mears M.L.	NLP	238	0.3*	+0.3
					16,492	24.1	

COLCHESTER SOUTH AND MALDON [150]

Election	Electors	T'out	Candidate	Party	Votes	% Sh	% Ch
1983	79,582	73.3	Wakeham J.*	Con	31,296	53.6	
			Stevens J.W.	SDP	19,131	32.8	
			Barnard H.J.	Lab	7,932	13.6	
					12,165	20.8	
1987	84,392	75.3	Wakeham J.*	Con	34,894	54.9	+1.3
			Stevens J.W.	SDP	19,411	30.6	-2.2
			Bigwood S. Ms.	Lab	9,229	14.5	+0.9
					15,483	24.4	
1992	86,406†	79.2	Whittingdale J.F.L.	Con	37,548	54.8	-0.1
			Thorn I.L.	LD	15,727	23.0	-7.6
			Pearson C.A.	Lab	14,158	20.7	+6.2
			Paterson M.B.	Green	1,028	1.5*	+1.5
					21,821	31.9	

COLNE VALLEY [151]

Election	Electors	T'out	Candidate	Party	Votes	% Sh	% Ch
1983	69,634	76.2	Wainwright R.S.*	Lib	21,139	39.8	
			Holt J.G.	Con	17,993	33.9	
			Williams A.D.	Lab	13,668	25.8	
			Keen T.L.	Ind	260	0.5*	
					3,146	5.9	
1987	70,199	80.1	Riddick G.E.G.	Con	20,457	36.4	+2.5
			Priestley N.J.	Lib	18,780	33.4	-6.4
			Harman J.A.	Lab	16,353	29.1	+3.3
			Mullany M.R.	Green	614	1.1*	+1.1
					1,677	3.0	
1992	72,029	82.0	Riddick G.E.G.*	Con	24,804	42.0	+5.6
			Harman J.A.	Lab	17,579	29.8	+0.7
			Priestley N.J.	LD	15,953	27.0	-6.4
			Stewart R.J.A.	Green	443	0.8*	-0.3
			Staniforth M.E. Ms.	MRLP	160	0.3*	+0.3
			Hosty J.G.	Ind	73	0.1*	
			Tattersall J.P.	NLP	44	0.1*	+0.1
					7,225	12.2	

Election	Electors	T'out	Candidate	Party	Votes	% Sh	% Ch
1983	63,897	76.9	Winterton J.A. Ms.	Con	23,895	48.7	
			Smedley C.V.	Lib	15,436	31.4	
			Gill E.C.	Lab	9,783	19.9	
					8,459	17.2	
1987	68,172	80.5	Winterton J.A. Ms.*	Con	26,513	48.3	-0.3
			Brodie-Browne I.M.	Lib	18,544	33.8	+2.4
			Knowles M.	Lab	9,810	17.9	-2.0
					7,969	14.5	
1992	70,475†	84.5	Winterton J.A. Ms.*	Con	29,163	49.0	+0.7
			Brodie-Browne I.M.	LD	18,043	30.3	-3.5
			Finnegan M.	Lab	11,927	20.0	+2.2
			Brown P.	NLP	399	0.7*	+0.7
					11,120	18.7	

Election	Electors	T'out	Candidate	Party	Votes	% Sh	% Ch
1983	51,567	76.4	Roberts I.W.P.*	Con	16,413	41.7	
			Roberts J.R. Rev.	Lib	12,145	30.8	
			Walters I.G.	Lab	6,731	17.1	
			Iwan D.	PC	4,105	10.4*	
					4,268	10.8	
1987	52,294	77.8	Roberts I.W.P.*	Con	15,730	38.7	-3.0
			Roberts J.R. Rev.	Lib	12,706	31.2	+0.4
			Williams B.H. Ms.	Lab	9,049	22.3	+5.2
			Davies R.V.	PC	3,177	7.8	-2.6
					3,024	7.4	
1992	53,668	78.7	Roberts I.W.P.*	Con	14,250	33.7	-5.0
			Roberts J.R. Rev.	LD	13,255	31.4	+0.1
			Williams B.H. Ms.	Lab	10,883	25.8	+3.5
			Davies R.V.	PC	3,108	7.4	-0.5
			Wainwright O.	Ind Con	637	1.5*	
			Hughes D.E.	NLP	114	0.3*	+0.3
					995	2.4	

COPELAND [154]

Election	Electors	T'out	Candidate	Party	Votes	% Sh	% Ch
1983	54,208	78.2	Cunningham J.A.*	Lab	18,756	44.2	
			Wilson V.B.C. Ms.	Con	16,919	39.9	
			Beasley J.	SDP	6,722	15.9	
					1,837	4.3	
1987	54,695	81.3	Cunningham J.A.*	Lab	20,999	47.2	+3.0
			Toft A.R.M.	Con	19,105	43.0	+3.1
			Colgan E.T.	SDP	4,052	9.1	-6.7
			Gibson R.A.	Green	319	0.7*	+0.7
					1,894	4.3	
1992	54,911†	83.5	Cunningham J.A.*	Lab	22,328	48.7	+1.5
			Davies P.G.	Con	19,889	43.4	+0.4
			Putman R.C.	LD	3,508	7.6	-1.5
			Sinton J.R.	NLP	148	0.3*	+0.3
					2,439	5.3	

CORBY [155]

Election	Electors	T'out	Candidate	Party	Votes	% Sh	% Ch
1983	63,067	77.5	Powell W.R.	Con	20,827	42.6	
			Homewood W.D.*	Lab	17,659	36.1	
			Whittington T.G.	Lib	9,905	20.3	
			Stanning R.J. Ms.	Green	505	1.0*	
					3,168	6.5	
1987	66,119	79.6	Powell W.R.*	Con	23,323	44.3	+1.7
			Feather H.A.	Lab	21,518	40.9	+4.8
			Whittington T.G.	Lib	7,805	14.8	-5.4
					1,805	3.4	
1992	68,334†	82.9	Powell W.R.*	Con	25,203	44.5	+0.2
			Feather H.A.	Lab	24,861	43.9	+3.0
			Roffe M.W.	LD	5,792	10.2	-4.6
			Wood J.I. Ms.	Lib	784	1.4*	+1.4
					342	0.6	

CORNWALL NORTH [156]

Election	Electors	T'out	Candidate	Party	Votes	% Sh	% Ch
1983	66,813	80.4	Neale G.A.*	Con	28,146	52.4	
			Chambers D.J.	Lib	23,087	43.0	
			Hayday J.C.	Lab	2,096	3.9*	
			Whetter J.C.A.	CNP	364	0.7*	
					5,059	9.4	
1987	72,375	79.8	Neale G.A.*	Con	29,862	51.7	-0.7
			Mitchell M.N.	Lib	24,180	41.9	-1.1
			Herries C.J. Ms.	Lab	3,719	6.4	+2.5
					5,682	9.8	
1992	76,333†	82.1	Tyler P.A.	LD	29,696	47.4	+5.5
			Neale G.A.*	Con	27,775	44.3	-7.4
			Jordan F.R.	Lab	4,103	6.6	+0.1
			Andrews P.J.	Lib	678	1.1*	+1.1
			Rowe G.	Ind	276	0.4*	
			Treadwell R.H. Ms.	NLP	112	0.2*	+0.2
					1,921	3.1	

CORNWALL SOUTH EAST [157]

Election	Electors	T'out	Candidate	Party	Votes	% Sh	% Ch
1983	65,166	78.6	Hicks R.A.*	Con	28,326	55.3	
			Blunt D.J.	Lib	19,972	39.0	
			Bebb A.J.	Lab	2,507	4.9*	
			Chadwick J.	Green	337	0.7*	
			Dent J.E. Ms.	Ind	94	0.2*	
					8,354	16.3	
1987	70,248	79.5	Hicks R.A.*	Con	28,818	51.6*	-3.7
			Tunbridge I.P.	Lib	22,211	39.8	+0.8
			Clark P.A.	Lab	4,847	8.7	+3.8
					6,607	11.8	
1992	73,028†	82.1	Hicks R.A.*	Con	30,565	51.0	-0.6
			Teverson R.	LD	22,861	38.1	-1.6
			Gilroy L.W. Ms.	Lab	5,536	9.2	+0.6
			Cook M.H. Ms.	Lib	644	1.1*	+1.1
			Quick A.O.H.	AFL	227	0.4*	+0.4
			Allen R. Ms.	NLP	155	0.3*	+0.3
					7,704	12.8	

COVENTRY NORTH EAST [158]

Election	Electors	T'out	Candidate	Party	Votes	% Sh	% Ch
1983	67,037	69.2	Park G.M.*	Lab	22,190	47.8	
			Weeks D.P.	Con	13,415	28.9	
			Simmons D.N.	SDP	10,251	22.1	
			Prince R.J.	WRP	342	0.7*	
			Meacham J.	Comm	193	0.4*	
					8,775	18.9	
1987	67,479	70.6	Hughes J.	Lab	25,832	54.3	+6.4
			Prior C.C.L.	Con	13,965	29.3	+0.4
			Wood S.	Lib	7,502	15.8	-6.3
			McNally M.A.	Comm	310	0.7*	+0.2
					11,867	24.9	
1992	64,788†	73.2	Ainsworth R.W.	Lab	24,896	52.5	-1.8
			Perrin K.R.	Con	13,220	27.9	-1.5
			McKee V.J.	LD	5,306	11.2	-4.6
			Hughes J.*	Ind Lab	4,008	8.5	
					11,676	24.6	

COVENTRY NORTH WEST [159]

Election	Electors	T'out	Candidate	Party	Votes	% Sh	% Ch
1983	52,072	74.7	Robinson G.*	Lab	17,239	44.3	
			Coombs A.M.V.	Con	14,201	36.5	
			Talbot W.J.	Lib	7,479	19.2	
					3,038	7.8	
1987	53,090	74.8	Robinson G.*	Lab	19,450	49.0	+4.7
			Powell J.	Con	13,787	34.7	-1.8
			Jones H.T.	SDP	6,455	16.3	-3.0
					5,663	14.3	
1992	50,671†	77.6	Robinson G.*	Lab	20,349	51.7	+2.7
			Hill A.A.B. Ms.	Con	13,917	35.4	+0.6
			Simpson E.A. Ms.	LD	5,070	12.9	-3.4
					6,432	16.4	

COVENTRY SOUTH EAST [160]

Election	Electors	T'out	Candidate	Party	Votes	% Sh	% Ch
1983	52,538	70.9	Nellist D.J.	Lab	15,307	41.1	
			Arnold J.A.	Con	12,625	33.9	
			Kilby G.E.	Lib	9,323	25.0	
					2,682	7.2	
1987	51,880	73.0	Nellist D.J.*	Lab	17,969	47.5	+6.4
			Grant A.	Con	11,316	29.9	-4.0
			Devine F.	SDP	8,095	21.4	-3.6
			Hutchinson N.	Green	479	1.3*	+1.3
					6,653	17.6	
1992	48,797†	74.9	Cunningham J.D.	Lab	11,902	32.6	-14.9
			Hyams M. Ms.	Con	10,591	29.0	-0.9
			Nellist D.J.*	Ind Lab	10,551	28.9	
			Armstrong A.	LD	3,318	9.1	-12.3
			Tomkinson N.D.W.	NF	173	0.5*	+0.5
					1,311	3.6	

COVENTRY SOUTH WEST [161]

Election	Electors	T'out	Candidate	Party	Votes	% Sh	% Ch
1983	65,077	75.9	Butcher J.P.*	Con	22,223	45.0	
			Edwards D.H.	Lab	15,776	31.9	
			Lyle H.M. Ms.	SDP	11,174	22.6	
			Williamson M. Ms.	Nat	214	0.4*	
					6,447	13.1	
1987	65,567	78.7	Butcher J.P.*	Con	22,318	43.3	-1.7
			Slater R.E.G.	Lab	19,108	37.0	+5.1
			Wheway R.	Lib	10,166	19.7	-2.9
					3,210	6.2	
1992	63,475†	80.1	Butcher J.P.*	Con	23,225	45.7	+2.4
			Slater R.E.G.	Lab	21,789	42.8	+5.8
			Sewards G.B.	LD	4,666	9.2	-10.5
			Wheway R.	Lib	989	1.9*	+1.9
			Morris D.S.	NLP	204	0.4*	+0.4
					1,436	2.8	

CRAWLEY [162]

Election	Electors	T'out	Candidate	Party	Votes	% Sh	% Ch
1983	70,713	76.4	Soames A.N.W. Hon.	Con	25,963	48.1	
			Allen L.	Lab	14,149	26.2	
			Forester T.	SDP	13,900	25.7	
					11,814	21.9	
1987	76,637	77.1	Soames A.N.W. Hon.*	Con	29,259	49.5	+1.5
			Leo P.J.	Lab	17,121	29.0	+2.8
			Simmons D.N.	SDP	12,674	21.5	-4.3
					12,138	20.6	
1992	78,268†	79.2	Soames A.N.W. Hon.*	Con	30,204	48.7	-0.8
			Moffatt L.J. Ms.	Lab	22,439	36.2	+7.2
			Seekings G.K.	LD	8,558	13.8	-7.7
			Wilson M.	Green	766	1.2*	+1.2
					7,765	12.5	

CREWE AND NANTWICH [163]

Election	Electors	T'out	Candidate	Party	Votes	% Sh	% Ch
1983	71,787	74.7	Dunwoody G.P. Ms. Hon.*	Lab	22,031	41.1	
			Rock P.R.J.	Con	21,741	40.6	
			Pollard J.S.	SDP	9,820	18.3	
					290	0.5	
1987	72,948	79.3	Dunwoody G.P. Ms. Hon.*	Lab	25,457	44.0	+2.9
			Browning A.F. Ms.	Con	24,365	42.1	+1.6
			Roberts K.N. Dr.	SDP	8,022	13.9	-4.5
					1,092	1.9	
1992	75,001	81.9	Dunwoody G.P. Ms. Hon.*	Lab	28,065	45.7	+1.7
			Silvester B.G.	Con	25,370	41.3	-0.8
			Griffiths G.	LD	7,315	11.9	-2.0
			Wilkinson N.J. Ms.	Green	651	1.1*	+1.1
					2,695	4.4	

CROSBY [164]

Election	Electors	T'out	Candidate	Party	Votes	% Sh	% Ch
1983	83,274	77.9	Thornton G.M.*	Con	30,604	47.2	
			Williams S.V.T.B. Ms.*	SDP	27,203	42.0	
			Waring R.D.	Lab	6,611	10.2*	
			Hussey P.M.	Green	415	0.6*	
					3,401	5.2	

Malcolm Thornton had been the member for Liverpool, Garston in the previous Parliament.

1987	83,914	79.6	Thornton G.M.*	Con	30,842	46.2*	-1.0
			Donovan A.F.S.	SDP	23,989	35.9	-6.1
			Cheetham C.W.	Lab	11,992	17.9	+7.7
					6,853	10.3	
1992	82,538†	82.5	Thornton G.M.*	Con	32,267	47.4	+0.2
			Eagle M. Ms.	Lab	17,461	25.7	+7.7
			Clucas H.F. Ms.	LD	16,562	24.3	-11.6
			Marks J.	Lib	1,052	1.5*	+1.5
			Brady F.P.S.	Green	559	0.8*	+0.2
			Paterson N.L.	NLP	152	0.2*	+0.2
					14,806	21.8	

CROYDON CENTRAL [165]

Election	Electors	T'out	Candidate	Party	Votes	% Sh	% Ch
1983	56,531	68.6	Moore J.E.M.*	Con	20,866	53.8	
			Mackinlay A.S.	Lab	9,045	23.3	
			Burgess T.	SDP	8,864	22.9	
					11,821	30.5	
1987	55,410	70.5	Moore J.E.M.*	Con	22,133	56.6	+2.8
			Prentice B.T. Ms.	Lab	9,516	24.3	+1.0
			Burgess T.	SDP	7,435	19.0	-3.8
					12,617	32.3	
1992	55,947	71.5	Beresford A.P.	Con	22,168	55.4	-1.2
			Davies G.R.	Lab	12,518	31.3	+6.9
			Richardson D.J. Ms.	LD	5,342	13.3	-5.7
					9,650	24.1	

CROYDON NORTH EAST [166]

Election	Electors	T'out	Candidate	Party	Votes	% Sh	% Ch
1983	62,923	67.5	Weatherill B.B.*	Con	22,292	52.5	
			Goldie J.D.	SDP	10,665	25.1	
			Riley K.A. Ms.	Lab	9,503	22.4	
					11,627	27.4	
1987	63,129	69.7	Weatherill B.B.*	Con	24,188	55.0	+2.5
			Patrick C.E. Ms.	Lab	11,669	26.5	+4.1
			Goldie J.D.	SDP	8,128	18.5	-6.6
					12,519	28.5	
1992	64,874	71.5	Congdon D.L.	Con	23,835	51.4	-3.6
			Walker M.M. Ms.	Lab	16,362	35.3	+8.7
			Fraser J.	LD	6,186	13.3	-5.1
					7,473	16.1	

CROYDON NORTH WEST [167]

Election	Electors	T'out	Candidate	Party	Votes	% Sh	% Ch
1983	58,333	67.6	Malins H.J.	Con	16,674	42.3	
			Pitt W.H.*	Lib	12,582	31.9	
			Smedley I.	Lab	9,561	24.2	
			Griffin N.J.	NF	336	0.9*	
			Rowe T.A.J.	Green	286	0.7*	
					4,092	10.4	
1987	57,369	69.2	Malins H.J.*	Con	18,665	47.0	+4.7
			Wicks M.H.	Lab	14,677	37.0	+12.7
			Rowe L.A.	Lib	6,363	16.0	-15.9
					3,988	10.0	
1992	57,821	70.1	Wicks M.H.	Lab	19,153	47.3	+10.3
			Malins H.J.*	Con	17,626	43.5	-3.5
			Hawkins L.F. Ms.	LD	3,728	9.2	-6.8
					1,527	3.8	

CROYDON SOUTH [168]

Election	Electors	T'out	Candidate	Party	Votes	% Sh	% Ch
1983	64,482	71.0	Clark W.G. Sir.*	Con	29,842	65.1	
			Forrest J.S.	Lib	12,402	27.1	
			Brooks R.C.E.	Lab	3,568	7.8*	
					17,440	38.1	
1987	65,085	73.7	Clark W.G. Sir.*	Con	30,732	64.1	-1.1
			Morrison G.I.	Lib	11,669	24.3	-2.8
			Davies G.R.	Lab	4,679	9.8	+2.0
			Baldwin P.C.	Green	900	1.9*	+1.9
					19,063	39.7	
1992	64,895	77.4	Ottaway R.G.J.	Con	31,993	63.7	-0.4
			Billenness P.H.	LD	11,568	23.0	-1.3
			Salmon H.S. Ms.	Lab	6,444	12.8	+3.1
			Samuel M.R.L.	Ind	239	0.5*	
					20,425	40.7	

CUMBERNAULD AND KILSYTH [169]

Election	Electors	T'out	Candidate	Party	Votes	% Sh	% Ch
1983	44,190	76.5	Hogg N.*	Lab	16,629	49.2	
			Herbison D.J.	SDP	6,701	19.8	
			Murray G.S.	SNP	5,875	17.4	
			Thomson A.E. Ms.	Con	4,590	13.6	
					9,928	29.4	
1987	45,427	78.5	Hogg N.*	Lab	21,385	60.0	+10.8
			Johnston T.R.	SNP	6,982	19.6	+2.2
			Deans C.S.	SDP	4,059	11.4	-8.4
			Thomson A.E. Ms.	Con	3,227	9.1	-4.5
					14,403	40.4	
1992	46,515	79.0	Hogg N.*	Lab	19,855	54.0	-6.0
			Johnston T.R.	SNP	10,640	28.9	+9.4
			Mitchell I.G.	Con	4,143	11.3	+2.2
			Haddow J.M. Ms.	LD	2,118	5.8	-5.6
					9,215	25.1	

CUNNINGHAME NORTH [170]

Election	Electors	T'out	Candidate	Party	Votes	% Sh	% Ch
1983	53,126	75.7	Corrie J.A.*	Con	15,559	38.7	
			Carson J.N.	Lab	13,920	34.6	
			Leishman R.M.	SDP	7,268	18.1	
			Cameron C.	SNP	3,460	8.6*	
					1,639	4.1	
1987	54,817	78.2	Wilson B.D.H.	Lab	19,016	44.4	+9.7
			Corrie J.A.*	Con	14,594	34.0	-4.7
			Herbison D.J.	SDP	5,185	12.1	-6.0
			Brown M.	SNP	4,076	9.5	+0.9
					4,422	10.3	
1992	54,856	78.1	Wilson B.D.H.*	Lab	17,564	41.0	-3.4
			Clarkson E.L. Ms.	Con	14,625	34.1	+0.1
			Crossan D.	SNP	7,813	18.2	+8.7
			Herbison D.J.	LD	2,864	6.7	-5.4
					2,939	6.9	

CUNNINGHAME SOUTH [171]

Election	Electors	T'out	Candidate	Party	Votes	% Sh	% Ch
1983	48,552	73.6	Lambie D.*	Lab	19,344	54.1	
			Gallie P.R.	Con	7,576	21.2	
			Boss J.A.	Lib	6,370	17.8	
			Ullrich K. Ms.	SNP	2,451	6.9*	
					11,768	32.9	
1987	49,842	75.0	Lambie D.*	Lab	22,728	60.8	+6.7
			Gibson E.R.	Con	6,095	16.3	-4.9
			Boss J.A.	Lib	4,426	11.8	-6.0
			Ullrich K. Ms.	SNP	4,115	11.0	+4.2
					16,633	44.5	
1992	49,025	75.9	Donohoe B.	Lab	19,687	52.9	-7.9
			Bell R.	SNP	9,007	24.2	+13.2
			Leslie S.A.	Con	6,070	16.3	+0.0
			Ashley B.J.	LD	2,299	6.2	-5.7
			Jackson W.T.	NLP	128	0.3*	+0.3
					10,680	28.7	

Election	Electors	T'out	Candidate	Party	Votes	% Sh	% Ch
1983	50,284	73.4	Evans I.L.*	Lab	20,668	56.0	
			Aubel F.F.E.	SDP	7,594	20.6	
			Arbuthnot J.N.	Con	5,240	14.2	
			Jarman P. Ms.	PC	3,421	9.3*	
					13,074	35.4	

[Death]

Election	Electors	T'out	Candidate	Party	Votes	% Sh	% Ch
1984	50,237	65.7	Clwyd A. Ms.	Lab	19,389	58.8	+2.8
(3/5)			Aubel F.F.E.	SDP	6,544	19.9	-0.7
			Jones C.F.	PC	3,619	11.0*	+1.8
			Arbuthnot J.N.	Con	2,441	7.4*	-6.8
			Winter M. Ms.	Comm	642	1.9*	
			Recontre N.E	Ind	215	0.6*	
			Nicholls-Jones P.	Ind	122	0.4*	
					12,835	38.9	

Election	Electors	T'out	Candidate	Party	Votes	% Sh	% Ch
1987	49,621	76.7	Clwyd A. Ms.	Lab	26,222	68.9	+12.9
			Butler K.D.	SDP	4,651	12.2	-8.3
			Bishop M.A.	Con	4,638	12.2	-2.0
			Richards D.L. Ms.	PC	2,549	6.7	-2.6
					21,571	56.7	

Election	Electors	T'out	Candidate	Party	Votes	% Sh	% Ch
1992	49,696†	76.5	Clwyd A. Ms.*	Lab	26,254	69.1	+0.2
			Smith A.M.	Con	4,890	12.9	+0.7
			Benney C.T.	PC	4,186	11.0	+4.3
			Verma M.K.	LD	2,667	7.0	-5.2
					21,364	56.2	

95

DAGENHAM [173]

Election	Electors	T'out	Candidate	Party	Votes	% Sh	% Ch
1983	62,960	63.4	Gould B.C.	Lab	15,665	39.3	
			Neill R.J.M.	Con	12,668	31.8	
			Horne J. Ms.	SDP	10,769	27.0	
			Pearce J.A.	NF	645	1.6*	
			Walshe D.R.	Comm	141	0.4*	
					2,997	7.5	
1987	61,714	67.3	Gould B.C.*	Lab	18,454	44.4	+5.2
			Neill R.J.M.	Con	15,985	38.5	+6.7
			Carter J.	SDP	7,088	17.1	-9.9
					2,469	5.9	
1992	59,656	70.7	Gould B.C.*	Lab	22,029	52.3	+7.8
			Rossiter D.P.	Con	15,295	36.3	-2.2
			Marquand C.N.H.	LD	4,824	11.4	-5.6
					6,734	16.0	

[Resignation]

Election	Electors	T'out	Candidate	Party	Votes	% Sh	% Ch
1994	58,123	37.0	Church J.A. Ms.	Lab	15,474	72.0	+19.7
(9/6)			Fairrie J.P.J.	Con	2,130	9.9	-26.4
			Dunphy P.G.	LD	1,804	8.4	-3.1
			Tyndall J.H.	BNP	1,511	7.0	
			Compobassi P.	UKI	457	2.1*	
			Leighton M.C.	NLP	116	0.5*	
					13,344	62.1	

DARLINGTON [174]

Election	Electors	T'out	Candidate	Party	Votes	% Sh	% Ch
1983	65,233	77.1	Fallon M.C.	Con	22,434	44.6	
			O'Brien O.*	Lab	18,996	37.8	
			Dutton R.	SDP	8,737	17.4	
			Clark A.H.	Ind	108	0.2*	
					3,438	6.8	
1987	65,940	80.8	Fallon M.C.*	Con	24,831	46.6	+2.0
			O'Brien O.	Lab	22,170	41.6	+3.8
			Collinge A.	Lib	6,289	11.8	-5.6
					2,661	5.0	
1992	66,094†	83.6	Milburn A.	Lab	26,556	48.1	+6.5
			Fallon M.C.*	Con	23,758	43.0	-3.6
			Bergg P.J.	LD	4,586	8.3	-3.5
			Clarke D.	BNP	355	0.6*	+0.6
					2,798	5.1	

96

DARTFORD [175]

Election	Electors	T'out	Candidate	Party	Votes	% Sh	% Ch
1983	71,622	76.4	Dunn R.J.*	Con	28,199	51.6	
			Townsend D.A.	Lab	14,630	26.8	
			Mills J.	Lib	11,204	20.5	
			Crockford A.H.	Ind	374	0.7*	
			Nye G.E.	NF	282	0.5*	
					13,569	24.8	
1987	72,632	79.0	Dunn R.J.*	Con	30,685	53.5	+1.9
			Clarke B.J.	Lab	15,756	27.5	+0.7
			Bruce M.G.	SDP	10,439	18.2	-2.3
			Davenport K.J.	Ind	491	0.9*	
					14,929	26.0	
1992	72,373	83.1	Dunn R.J.*	Con	31,194	51.9	-1.6
			Stoate H.G.A. Dr.	Lab	20,880	34.7	+7.2
			Bryden P.J.	LD	7,584	12.6	-5.6
			Munro A.	Ind	262	0.4*	
			Holland A. Ms.	NLP	241	0.4*	+0.4
					10,314	17.1	

DAVENTRY [176]

Election	Electors	T'out	Candidate	Party	Votes	% Sh	% Ch
1983	64,321	76.8	Prentice R.E.*	Con	26,357	53.3	
			Collins D.R.	SDP	13,221	26.8	
			Middleton D.	Lab	9,840	19.9	
					13,136	26.6	
1987	69,241	78.2	Boswell T.E.	Con	31,353	57.9	+4.6
			Miller I.R.	Lib	11,663	21.6	-5.2
			Koumi L.M.A.W. Ms.	Lab	11,097	20.5	+0.6
					19,690	36.4	
1992	71,830†	82.7	Boswell T.E.*	Con	34,734	58.4	+0.5
			Koumi L.M.A.W. Ms.	Lab	14,460	24.3	+3.8
			Rounthwaite A.S.	LD	9,820	16.5	-5.0
			France R.B.	NLP	422	0.7*	+0.7
					20,274	34.1	

DAVYHULME [177]

Election	Electors	T'out	Candidate	Party	Votes	% Sh	% Ch
1983	64,963	73.9	Churchill W.S.*	Con	22,055	46.0	
			Wrigley D.I.	Lib	13,041	27.2	
			Rogers S.	Lab	12,887	26.9	
					9,014	18.8	
1987	65,558	77.3	Churchill W.S.*	Con	23,633	46.6	+0.6
			Nicholson J.R.	Lab	15,434	30.4	+3.6
			Wrigley D.I.	Lib	11,637	23.0	-4.2
					8,199	16.2	
1992	62,667†	80.5	Churchill W.S.*	Con	24,216	48.0	+1.4
			Brotherton B.	Lab	19,790	39.2	+8.8
			Pearcey J. Ms.	LD	5,797	11.5	-11.5
			Brotheridge T.L.	NLP	665	1.3*	+1.3
					4,426	8.8	

DELYN [178]

Election	Electors	T'out	Candidate	Party	Votes	% Sh	% Ch
1983	62,483	77.8	Raffan K.W.T.	Con	20,242	41.6	
			Colbert J.J.	Lab	14,298	29.4	
			Hughes Parry J.D.	Lib	12,545	25.8	
			Hughes H.	PC	1,558	3.2*	
					5,944	12.2	
1987	63,915	82.1	Raffan K.W.T.*	Con	21,728	41.4*	-0.2
			Hanson D.G.	Lab	20,504	39.1	+9.7
			Evans D.J.	Lib	8,913	17.0	-8.8
			Owen D.J.	PC	1,339	2.6*	-0.7
					1,224	2.3	
1992	66,593†	83.4	Hanson D.G.	Lab	24,979	45.0	+5.9
			Whitby M.J.	Con	22,940	41.3	-0.1
			Dodd R.C.	LD	6,208	11.2	-5.8
			Drake A.J.	PC	1,414	2.5*	-0.0
					2,039	3.7	

DENTON AND REDDISH [179]

Election	Electors	T'out	Candidate	Party	Votes	% Sh	% Ch
1983	68,661	72.8	Bennett A.F.*	Lab	22,123	44.3	
			Snadden J.A.	Con	16,998	34.0	
			Begg J.L.	SDP	10,869	21.7	
					5,125	10.3	
1987	69,533	75.5	Bennett A.F.*	Lab	26,023	49.6	+5.3
			Slater P.	Con	17,773	33.9	-0.1
			Huffer T.I.	SDP	8,697	16.6	-5.2
					8,250	15.7	
1992	68,463†	76.8	Bennett A.F.*	Lab	29,021	55.2	+5.6
			Horswell J.	Con	16,937	32.2	-1.6
			Ridley H.F.	LD	4,953	9.4	-7.1
			Powell M.W.	Lib	1,296	2.5*	+2.5
			Fuller J.P.G.	NLP	354	0.7*	+0.7
					12,084	23.0	

DERBY NORTH [180]

Election	Electors	T'out	Candidate	Party	Votes	% Sh	% Ch
1983	70,374	72.5	Knight G.	Con	22,303	43.7	
			Whitehead P.*	Lab	18,797	36.8	
			Connolly S.F.	Lib	9,924	19.4	
					3,506	6.9	
1987	71,738	75.7	Knight G.*	Con	26,516	48.8	+5.1
			Whitehead P.	Lab	20,236	37.3	+0.4
			Connolly S.F.	Lib	7,268	13.4	-6.1
			Wall E.	Green	291	0.5*	+0.5
					6,280	11.6	
1992	73,177†	80.7	Knight G.*	Con	28,574	48.4	-0.4
			Laxton R.	Lab	24,121	40.9	+3.6
			Charlesworth R.A.	LD	5,638	9.6	-3.8
			Wall E.	Green	383	0.6*	+0.1
			Hart P.G.	NF	245	0.4*	+0.4
			Onley N.M.	NLP	58	0.1*	+0.1
					4,453	7.5	

DERBY SOUTH [181]

Election	Electors	T'out	Candidate	Party	Votes	% Sh	% Ch
1983	68,578	67.4	Beckett M.M. Ms.	Lab	18,169	39.3	
			Hales G.W.	Con	17,748	38.4	
			Smith I.W.	SDP	9,976	21.6	
			Wall E.	Green	297	0.6*	
					421	0.9	
1987	68,825	69.9	Beckett M.M. Ms.*	Lab	21,003	43.7	+4.3
			Leighton P.F.	Con	19,487	40.5	+2.1
			Mellor P.N. Ms.	SDP	7,608	15.8	-5.8
					1,516	3.2	
1992	66,329†	75.5	Beckett M.M. Ms.*	Lab	25,917	51.7	+8.1
			Brown N.P.	Con	18,981	37.9	-2.6
			Hartropp S.J.	LD	5,198	10.4	-5.4
					6,936	13.8	

DERBYSHIRE NORTH EAST [182]

Election	Electors	T'out	Candidate	Party	Votes	% Sh	% Ch
1983	68,273	75.7	Ellis R.J.*	Lab	21,094	40.8	
			Bridge I.G.	Con	19,088	36.9	
			Hardy S.P.	SDP	11,494	22.2	
					2,006	3.9	
1987	70,107	79.5	Barnes H.	Lab	24,747	44.4	+3.6
			Hayes J.H.	Con	21,027	37.7	+0.8
			Hardy S.P.	SDP	9,985	17.9	-4.3
					3,720	6.7	
1992	73,320	80.6	Barnes H.*	Lab	28,860	48.8	+4.4
			Hayes J.H.	Con	22,590	38.2	+0.5
			Stone D.	LD	7,675	13.0	-4.9
					6,270	10.6	

DERBYSHIRE SOUTH [183]

Election	Electors	T'out	Candidate	Party	Votes	% Sh	% Ch
1983	75,391	78.5	Currie E. Ms.	Con	25,909	43.8	
			Kent P.A.	Lab	17,296	29.2	
			MacFarquhar R.L.	SDP	15,959	27.0	
					8,613	14.6	
1987	80,044	81.3	Currie E. Ms.*	Con	31,927	49.1	+5.3
			Whitby J.D.	Lab	21,616	33.2	+4.0
			Edgar J.	SDP	11,509	17.7	-9.3
					10,311	15.9	
1992	83,104	84.7	Currie E. Ms.*	Con	34,266	48.7	-0.4
			Todd M.W.	Lab	29,608	42.1	+8.8
			Brass D.J. Ms.	LD	6,236	8.9	-8.8
			Mercer T.W.	NLP	291	0.4*	+0.4
					4,658	6.6	

DERBYSHIRE WEST [184]

Election	Electors	T'out	Candidate	Party	Votes	% Sh	% Ch
1983	68,668	77.4	Parris M.F.*	Con	29,695	55.9	
			Bingham V.N.	Lib	14,370	27.0	
			March J.S.	Lab	9,060	17.1	
					15,325	28.8	
[Resignation]							
1986	69,956	71.9	McLoughlin P.A.	Con	19,896	39.5	-16.4
(8/5)			Walmsley C.R.	Lib	19,796	39.4	+12.4
			Moore W.	Lab	9,952	19.8	+2.7
			Sidwell C.J.	Ind	348	0.7*	
			Goodall R.	Ind	289	0.6*	
					100	0.1	
1987	70,782	83.1	McLoughlin P.A.	Con	31,224	53.1	-2.8
			Walmsley C.R.	Lib	20,697	35.2	+8.2
			Moore W.	Lab	6,875	11.7	-5.4
					10,527	17.9	
1992	71,201†	85.0	McLoughlin P.A.*	Con	32,879	54.3	+1.2
			Fearn R.D.	LD	14,110	23.3	-11.9
			Clamp S.J.	Lab	13,528	22.4	+10.7
					18,769	31.0	

DEVIZES [185]

Election	Electors	T'out	Candidate	Party	Votes	% Sh	% Ch
1983	83,211	74.9	Morrison C.A. Hon.*	Con	33,644	53.9	
			Palmer F.E. Ms.	SDP	18,020	28.9	
			Hulme D.K.	Lab	10,468	16.8	
			Ewen G.M. Ms.	WR	234	0.4*	
					15,624	25.1	
1987	86,047	77.2	Morrison C.A. Hon.*	Con	36,372	54.8	+0.8
			Siegle L.E. Ms.	Lib	18,542	27.9	-1.0
			Buxton R.W.	Lab	11,487	17.3	+0.5
					17,830	26.9	
1992	89,746†	81.7	Ancram M.A.F.J.K.	Con	39,090	53.3	+0.5
			Mactaggart J.L. Ms.	LD	19,378	26.4	-1.5
			Berry R.J. Ms.	Lab	13,060	17.8	+0.5
			Coles S.C.	Lib	962	1.3*	+1.3
			Ripley J.D	Green	808	1.1*	+1.1
					19,712	26.9	

DEVON NORTH [186]

Election	Electors	T'out	Candidate	Party	Votes	% Sh	% Ch
1983	63,638	80.1	Speller A.*	Con	28,066	55.1	
			Blackmore R.B.	Lib	19,339	37.9	
			James P.E.	Lab	2,893	5.7*	
			Joanes R.N.	Green	669	1.3*	
					8,727	17.1	
1987	67,474	81.7	Speller A.*	Con	28,071	50.9	-4.2
			Pinney M.A.	Lib	23,602	42.8	+4.9
			Marjoram A.C. Ms.	Lab	3,467	6.3	+0.6
					4,469	8.1	
1992	68,991†	84.4	Harvey N.B.	LD	27,414	47.1	+4.3
			Speller A.*	Con	26,620	45.7	-5.2
			Donner P.B.	Lab	3,410	5.9	-0.4
			Simmons C.H. Ms.	Green	658	1.1*	+1.1
			Treadwell G.C.	NLP	107	0.2*	+0.2
					794	1.4	

DEVON WEST AND TORRIDGE [187]

Election	Electors	T'out	Candidate	Party	Votes	% Sh	% Ch
1983	70,648	76.0	Mills P.M. Sir.*	Con	31,156	58.0	
			Howell V.T.	Lib	18,805	35.0	
			Tupman W.A.	Lab	3,531	6.6*	
			Beale M.J.	Ind	116	0.2*	
			Rous H.E. Ms.	WR	113	0.2*	
					12,351	23.0	
1987	74,550	78.7	Nicholson E.H. Ms.	Con	29,484	50.3	-7.7
			Burnett J.P.A.	Lib	23,016	39.2	+4.2
			Brenton D.G.	Lab	4,990	8.5	+1.9
			Williamson F.	Green	1,168	2.0*	+2.0
					6,468	11.0	
1992	76,936†	81.5	Nicholson E.H. Ms.*	Con	29,627	47.3	-3.0
			McBride D.I.	LD	26,013	41.5	+2.3
			Brenton D.G.	Lab	5,997	9.6	+1.1
			Williamson F.	Green	898	1.4*	-0.6
			Collins D.H.	NLP	141	0.2*	+0.2
					3,614	5.8	

DEWSBURY [188]

Election	Electors	T'out	Candidate	Party	Votes	% Sh	% Ch
1983	69,734	74.0	Whitfield J.	Con	20,297	39.4	
			Ripley D.	Lab	18,211	35.3	
			Ginsburg D.*	SDP	13,065	25.3	
					2,086	4.0	
1987	70,836	78.8	Taylor W.A. Ms.	Lab	23,668	42.4	+7.1
			Whitfield J.*	Con	23,223	41.6	+2.3
			Mills A.	SDP	8,907	16.0	-9.4
					445	0.8	
1992	72,833	80.2	Taylor W.A. Ms.*	Lab	25,596	43.8	+1.4
			Whitfield J.	Con	24,962	42.7	+1.1
			Meadowcroft R.S.	LD	6,570	11.2	-4.7
			Birdwood J.P. Ms.	BNP	660	1.1*	+1.1
			Denby N.M.	Green	471	0.8*	+0.8
			Marsden J. Ms.	NLP	146	0.2*	+0.2
					634	1.1	

DONCASTER CENTRAL [189]

Election	Electors	T'out	Candidate	Party	Votes	% Sh	% Ch
1983	71,039	70.8	Walker H.*	Lab	21,154	42.0	
			Somers J.J.	Con	18,646	37.1	
			Stables T.L.	SDP	10,524	20.9	
					2,508	5.0	
1987	69,699	73.7	Walker H.*	Lab	26,266	51.2	+9.1
			Rawlings P.E. Ms.	Con	18,070	35.2	-1.9
			Gore-Browne J.A.	SDP	7,004	13.6	-7.3
					8,196	16.0	
1992	68,890†	74.2	Walker H.*	Lab	27,795	54.3	+3.2
			Glossop G.W.	Con	17,113	33.5	-1.7
			Hampson C.J.	LD	6,057	11.8	-1.8
			Driver M.R.	WRP	184	0.4*	
					10,682	20.9	

DONCASTER NORTH [190]

Election	Electors	T'out	Candidate	Party	Votes	% Sh	% Ch
1983	72,184	69.9	Welsh M.C.*	Lab	26,626	52.8	
			Stephen B.M.L.	Con	13,915	27.6	
			Orford D.	SDP	9,916	19.7	
					12,711	25.2	
1987	72,986	73.1	Welsh M.C.*	Lab	32,953	61.8	+9.0
			Shepherd R.J.	Con	13,015	24.4	-3.2
			Norwood P.R.	SDP	7,394	13.9	-5.8
					19,938	37.4	
1992	74,733†	73.9	Hughes K.M.	Lab	34,135	61.8	+0.0
			Light R.C.	Con	14,322	25.9	+1.5
			Whiting S.	LD	6,787	12.3	-1.6
					19,813	35.9	

DON VALLEY [191]

Election	Electors	T'out	Candidate	Party	Votes	% Sh	% Ch
1983	73,112	69.9	Redmond M.	Lab	23,036	45.1	
			Utting B. Ms.	Con	16,570	32.4	
			Lange D.L.	Lib	11,482	22.5	
					6,466	12.7	
1987	74,500	73.8	Redmond M.*	Lab	29,200	53.1	+8.0
			Gallagher C.H.	Con	17,733	32.3	-0.2
			Whitaker W.K.	Lib	8,027	14.6	-7.9
					11,467	20.9	
1992	76,328†	76.3	Redmond M.*	Lab	32,008	55.0	+1.9
			Paget-Brown N.	Con	18,474	31.7	-0.5
			Jevons M.	LD	6,920	11.9	-2.7
			Platt T.S.	Green	803	1.4*	+1.4
					13,534	23.3	

DORSET NORTH [192]

Election	Electors	T'out	Candidate	Party	Votes	% Sh	% Ch
1983	67,524	76.6	Baker N.B.*	Con	30,058	58.1	
			Tapper G.W. Dr.	Lib	18,678	36.1	
			Fox J.T.J. Ms.	Lab	2,710	5.2*	
			Fox D.C.T.	WR	294	0.6*	
					11,380	22.0	
1987	72,844	79.1	Baker N.B.*	Con	32,854	57.0	-1.1
			Tapper G.W. Dr.	Lib	20,947	36.4	+0.3
			Hanley J.	Lab	3,819	6.6	+1.4
					11,907	20.7	
1992	76,719†	81.8	Baker N.B.*	Con	34,234	54.6	+1.4
			Siegle L.E. Ms.	LD	24,154	38.5	+2.1
			Fitzmaurice J.F.	Lab	4,360	6.9	+0.3
					10,080	16.1	

DORSET SOUTH [193]

Election	Electors	T'out	Candidate	Party	Votes	% Sh	% Ch
1983	68,998	72.7	Cranborne Viscount*	Con	28,631	57.1	
			Head S.A.	SDP	13,533	27.0	
			Hewitt D.J.	Lab	7,831	15.6	
			Smith B.O. Ms.	Ind	151	0.3*	
					15,098	30.1	
1987	72,855	75.5	Bruce I.C.	Con	30,184	54.8	-2.3
			Ellis B.E.J.	Lib	15,117	27.5	+0.5
			Dench B.R.D. Ms.	Lab	9,494	17.2	+1.6
			Hayler A.E.	Ind	244	0.4*	
					15,067	27.4	
1992	75,802	76.9	Bruce I.C.*	Con	29,319	50.3	-4.5
			Ellis B.E.J.	LD	15,811	27.1	-0.3
			Chedzoy A.	Lab	12,298	21.1	+3.8
			Hagel J.W. Ms.	Ind	673	1.2*	
			Griffiths M.R.F.	NLP	191	0.3*	+0.3
					13,508	23.2	

DORSET WEST [194]

Election	Electors	T'out	Candidate	Party	Votes	% Sh	% Ch
1983	60,997	74.2	Spicer J.W.*	Con	27,030	59.7	
			Jones D.T.	Lib	13,078	28.9	
			Cash D.	Lab	5,168	11.4*	
					13,952	30.8	
1987	64,360	78.3	Spicer J.W.*	Con	28,305	56.2	-3.5
			Jones D.T.	Lib	15,941	31.6	+2.8
			Watson J.D.	Lab	6,123	12.2	+0.7
					12,364	24.5	
1992	67,260†	81.2	Spicer J.W.*	Con	27,766	50.8	-5.3
			Legg R.A.S.	LD	19,756	36.2	+4.5
			Mann J.P.B.	Lab	7,082	13.0	+0.8
					8,010	14.7	

DOVER [195]

Election	Electors	T'out	Candidate	Party	Votes	% Sh	% Ch
1983	67,922	77.6	Rees P.W.I.*	Con	25,454	48.3	
			Love S.S.E.W.	Lab	16,234	30.8	
			Nice G.	SDP	10,601	20.1	
			Potter M.J.	Green	404	0.8*	
					9,220	17.5	
1987	68,997	79.8	Shaw D.L.	Con	25,343	46.0	-2.3
			Love S.S.E.W.	Lab	18,802	34.1	+3.3
			Nice G.	SDP	10,942	19.9	-0.3
					6,541	11.9	
1992	68,954	83.5	Shaw D.L.*	Con	25,395	44.1	-1.9
			Prosser G.M.	Lab	24,562	42.6	+8.5
			Sole M.J.	LD	6,212	10.8	-9.1
			Sullivan A.C.W.	Green	637	1.1*	+0.3
			Sherred P.W.	Ind	407	0.7*	
			Philp B.J.	Ind Con	250	0.4*	
			Percy C.F.	NLP	127	0.2*	+0.2
					833	1.4	

Election	Electors	T'out	Candidate	Party	Votes	% Sh	% Ch
1983	61,519	66.3	Kilfedder J.A.*	UPUP	22,861	56.1	
			Cushnahan J.W.	APNI	9,015	22.1	
			McCartney R.L.	UU	8,261	20.3	
			O'Baoill C.	SDLP	645	1.6*	
					13,846	34.0	

[Seeks Re-election]

1986	64,276	60.5	Kilfedder J.A.*	UPUP	30,793	79.2	+23.1
(23/1)			Cushnahan J.W.	APNI	8,066	20.8	-1.3
					22,727	58.5	

1987	65,018	62.8	Kilfedder J.A.*	UPUP	18,420	45.1	-11.0
			McCartney R.L.	Ind UU	14,467	35.4	
			Cushnahan J.W.	APNI	7,932	19.4	-2.7
					3,953	9.7	

1992	68,662	65.5	Kilfedder J.A.*	UPUP	19,305	42.9	-2.2
			Kennedy L.	Con	14,371	32.0	+32.0
			Morrow A.J.	APNI	6,611	14.7	-4.7
			Vitty D.	UDUP	4,414	9.8	+9.8
			Wilmot A.	NLP	255	0.6*	+0.6
					4,934	11.0	

[Death]

1995	70,872	38.6	McCartney R.L.	UKU	10,124	37.0	
(15/6)			McFarland A.	UU	7,232	26.4	
			Napier O.J. Sir	APNI	6,970	25.4	+10.7
			Chambers A.	Ind U	2,170	7.9	
			Sexton S.E.	Con	583	2.1*	
			Brooks M.	Ind	108	0.4*	
			Carter C.	Ind	101	0.4*	
			Anderson J.	NLP	100	0.4*	-0.2
					2,892	10.6	

DOWN SOUTH [197]

Election	Electors	T'out	Candidate	Party	Votes	% Sh	% Ch
1983	66,923	76.7	Powell J.E.*	UU	20,693	40.3	
			McGrady E.K.	SDLP	20,145	39.2	
			Fitzsimmons P.D.	SF	4,074	7.9*	
			Harvey C.	UDUP	3,743	7.3*	
			Forde P.M.D.	APNI	1,823	3.6*	
			Magee M.T. Ms.	WP	851	1.7*	
					548	1.1	

(Seeks Re-election)

Election	Electors	T'out	Candidate	Party	Votes	% Sh	% Ch
1986 (23/1)	69,843	73.8	Powell J.E.*	UU	24,963	48.4	+8.1
			McGrady E.K.	SDLP	23,121	44.9	+5.7
			McDowell H.	SF	2,936	5.7	-2.2
			Magee S.D.	WP	522	1.0*	-0.7
					1,842	3.6	
1987	71,235	79.4	McGrady E.K.	SDLP	26,579	47.0	+7.8
			Powell J.E.*	UU	25,848	45.7	+5.4
			Ritchie G. Ms.	SF	2,363	4.2*	-3.8
			Laird S.E. Ms.	APNI	1,069	1.9*	-1.7
			O'Hagan D.	WP	675	1.2*	-0.5
					731	1.3	
1992	76,186	80.8	McGrady E.K.*	SDLP	31,523	51.2	+4.2
			Nelson D.	UU	25,181	40.9	-4.8
			Fitzpatrick S.	SF	1,843	3.0*	-1.2
			Healy M.G.	APNI	1,542	2.5*	+0.6
			McKenzie-Hill J.S. Ms.	Con	1,488	2.4*	+2.4
					6,342	10.3	

DUDLEY EAST [198]

Election	Electors	T'out	Candidate	Party	Votes	% Sh	% Ch
1983	74,765	71.3	Gilbert J.W.*	Lab	24,441	45.8	
			Gillies S.M. Ms.	Con	18,625	34.9	
			Simon D.C.A.	SDP	10,272	19.3	
					5,816	10.9	
1987	75,206	72.3	Gilbert J.W.*	Lab	24,942	45.9	+0.0
			Jones E.A. Ms.	Con	21,469	39.5	+4.6
			Monks K.J.	SDP	7,965	14.6	-4.6
					3,473	6.4	
1992	75,355†	75.0	Gilbert J.W.*	Lab	29,806	52.8	+6.9
			Holland C.J.	Con	20,606	36.5	-3.0
			Jenkins I.C.	LD	5,400	9.6	-5.1
			Cartwright G.E.	NF	675	1.2*	+1.2
					9,200	16.3	

DUDLEY WEST [199]

Election	Electors	T'out	Candidate	Party	Votes	% Sh	% Ch
1983	77,795	75.9	Blackburn J.G.*	Con	27,250	46.2	
			Price W.G.	Lab	18,527	31.4	
			Lewis G.P.T.	Lib	13,251	22.4	
					8,723	14.8	
1987	81,789	79.1	Blackburn J.G.*	Con	32,224	49.8	+3.6
			Titley G.	Lab	21,980	34.0	+2.6
			Lewis G.P.T.	Lib	10,477	16.2	-6.3
					11,503	17.8	
1992	86,633†	82.1	Blackburn J.G.*	Con	34,729	48.8	-1.0
			Lomax K.J.	Lab	28,940	40.7	+6.7
			Lewis G.P.T.	LD	7,446	10.5	-5.7
					5,789	8.1	
[Death]							
1994	87,972	47.0	Pearson I.P.	Lab	28,400	68.8	+28.1
(15/12)			Postles G.E.	Con	7,706	18.7	-30.2
			Hadley M.	LD	3,154	7.6	-2.8
			Floyd M.	UKI	590	1.4*	
			Carmichael A.	NF	561	1.4*	
			Hyde M.	Lib	548	1.3*	
			Nattrass M.	Ind	146	0.4*	
			Nicholson M. Ms.	Ind	77	0.2*	
			Oldbury J.D.	NLP	70	0.2*	
			Palmer C.R.	Ind	55	0.1*	
					20,694	50.1	

DULWICH [200]

Election	Electors	T'out	Candidate	Party	Votes	% Sh	% Ch
1983	56,596	67.2	Bowden G.F.	Con	15,424	40.5	
			Hoey C.L. Ms.	Lab	13,565	35.7	
			Taverne D.	SDP	8,376	22.0	
			Barker R.A.	NF	338	0.9*	
			Baker R.C.L.	Green	237	0.6*	
			Vero R.W.	MRLP	99	0.3*	
					1,859	4.9	
1987	56,355	69.3	Bowden G.F.*	Con	16,563	42.4	+1.9
			Hoey C.L. Ms.	Lab	16,383	42.0	+6.3
			Harris A.N.G. Dr.	SDP	5,664	14.5	-7.5
			Goldie A.	Green	432	1.1*	+0.5
					180	0.5	
1992	55,275	67.8	Jowell T.J.H.D. Ms.	Lab	17,714	47.3	+5.3
			Bowden G.F.*	Con	15,658	41.8	-0.6
			Goldie G.M.A.	LD	4,078	10.9	-3.6
					2,056	5.5	

DUMBARTON [201]

Election	Electors	T'out	Candidate	Party	Votes	% Sh	% Ch
1983	57,373	75.1	Campbell I.*	Lab	15,810	36.7	
			Lawson I.M.	Con	13,695	31.8	
			Sawyer R.G.	SDP	9,813	22.8	
			Bayne I.O.	SNP	3,768	8.7*	
					2,115	4.9	
1987	58,769	78.2	McFall J.	Lab	19,778	43.0	+6.3
			Graham R.F.	Con	14,556	31.7	-0.1
			Mowbray R.A.	SDP	6,060	13.2	-9.6
			Herriot J.M. Ms.	SNP	5,564	12.1	+3.4
					5,222	11.4	
1992	57,252	77.1	McFall J.*	Lab	19,255	43.6	+0.6
			Begg T.N.A.	Con	13,126	29.7	-1.9
			Mackechnie W.	SNP	8,127	18.4	+6.3
			Morrison J.	LD	3,425	7.8	-5.4
			Kras D. Ms.	NLP	192	0.4*	+0.4
					6,129	13.9	

111

DUMFRIES [202]

Election	Electors	T'out	Candidate	Party	Votes	% Sh	% Ch
1983	57,594	73.0	Monro H.S.P. Sir.*	Con	18,730	44.5	
			McCall J.R.	SDP	10,036	23.9	
			McAughtrie T.A.	Lab	8,764	20.8	
			Gibson E.D.	SNP	4,527	10.8*	
					8,694	20.7	
1987	59,347	75.6	Monro H.S.P. Sir.*	Con	18,785	41.9	-2.7
			Phillips C.W. Ms.	Lab	11,292	25.2	+4.3
			McCall J.R.	SDP	8,064	18.0	-5.9
			McAlpine T.	SNP	6,391	14.2	+3.5
			Thomas P.M.	Green	349	0.8*	+0.8
					7,493	16.7	
1992	61,189	79.9	Monro H.S.P. Sir.*	Con	21,089	43.1	+1.3
			Rennie P.R.	Lab	14,674	30.0	+4.8
			Morgan A.N.	SNP	6,971	14.3	+0.0
			Wallace N.C.	LD	5,749	11.8	-6.2
			McLeod G.W.S.	Ind Green	312	0.6*	
			Barlow T.	NLP	107	0.2*	+0.2
					6,415	13.1	

DUNDEE EAST [203]

Election	Electors	T'out	Candidate	Party	Votes	% Sh	% Ch
1983	62,752	73.7	Wilson R.G.*	SNP	20,276	43.8	
			Bowman C.	Lab	15,260	33.0	
			Vaughan B. Ms.	Con	7,172	15.5	
			Rottger S.W.	Lib	3,546	7.7*	
					5,016	10.8	
1987	60,805	75.9	McAllion J.	Lab	19,539	42.3	+9.4
			Wilson R.G.*	SNP	18,524	40.1	-3.7
			Cook P.S.	Con	5,938	12.9	-2.6
			Romberg M.K. Ms.	Lib	2,143	4.6*	-3.0
					1,015	2.2	
1992	58,959†	72.3	McAllion J.*	Lab	18,761	44.0	+1.7
			Coutts D.M.	SNP	14,197	33.3	-6.8
			Blackwood S.F.	Con	7,549	17.7	+4.9
			Yuill I.G.	LD	1,725	4.0*	-0.6
			Baird S.E. Ms.	Green	295	0.7*	+0.7
			Baxter R.	NLP	77	0.2*	+0.2
					4,564	10.7	

DUNDEE WEST [204]

Election	Electors	T'out	Candidate	Party	Votes	% Sh	% Ch
1983	62,703	74.4	Ross E.*	Lab	20,288	43.5	
			Senior D.N.	Con	10,138	21.7	
			Dick E.G. Ms.	SDP	7,976	17.1	
			Lynch J.	SNP	7,973	17.1	
			Marks P.S.H.	Green	302	0.6*	
					10,150	21.7	
1987	61,926	75.4	Ross E.*	Lab	24,916	53.4	+9.9
			Donnelly J.A.	Con	8,390	18.0	-3.8
			Morgan A.N.	SNP	7,164	15.3	-1.7
			Lonie R. Ms.	SDP	5,922	12.7	-4.4
			Mathewson S.R.	Comm	308	0.7*	+0.7
					16,526	35.4	
1992	59,953†	69.8	Ross E.*	Lab	20,498	49.0	-4.4
			Brown K.J.	SNP	9,894	23.6	+8.3
			Spearman A.M.	Con	7,746	18.5	+0.5
			Dick E.G. Ms.	LD	3,132	7.5	-5.2
			Hood E.C. Ms.	Green	432	1.0*	+0.4
			Arnold D.	NLP	159	0.4*	+0.4
					10,604	25.3	

DUNFERMLINE EAST [205]

Election	Electors	T'out	Candidate	Party	Votes	% Sh	% Ch
1983	49,881	72.0	Brown J.G.	Lab	18,515	51.5	
			Harcus D.T.	Lib	7,214	20.1	
			Shenton C.	Con	6,764	18.8	
			Hunter G.A.	SNP	2,573	7.2*	
			Maxwell A.	Comm	864	2.4*	
					11,301	31.5	
1987	51,175	76.6	Brown J.G.*	Lab	25,381	64.8	+13.2
			Shenton C.	Con	5,792	14.8	-4.0
			Harris E.B.A. Ms.	Lib	4,122	10.5	-9.6
			McGarry A. Ms.	SNP	3,901	10.0	+2.8
					19,589	50.0	
1992	50,180	75.6	Brown J.G.*	Lab	23,692	62.4	-2.3
			Tennant M.E.	Con	6,248	16.5	+1.7
			Lloyd J.V.	SNP	5,746	15.1	+5.2
			Little T.M. Ms.	LD	2,262	6.0	-4.6
					17,444	46.0	

DUNFERMLINE WEST [206]

Election	Electors	T'out	Candidate	Party	Votes	% Sh	% Ch
1983	49,075	73.5	Douglas R.G.*	Lab	12,998	36.0	
			Davison P.S.	Con	10,524	29.2	
			Moyes F.A.	SDP	9,434	26.2	
			Fairlie J.M.	SNP	2,798	7.8*	
			Dobson S.J.	Green	321	0.9*	
					2,474	6.9	
1987	51,063	77.0	Douglas R.G.*	Lab	18,493	47.0	+11.0
			Gallie P.R.	Con	9,091	23.1	-6.0
			Moyes F.A.	SDP	8,288	21.1	-5.1
			Hughes G.J.	SNP	3,435	8.7	+1.0
					9,402	23.9	
1992	50,949	76.4	Squire R.A. Ms.	Lab	16,374	42.0	-5.0
			Scott-Hayward M.D.A.	Con	8,890	22.8	-0.3
			Smith J.	SNP	7,563	19.4	+10.7
			Harris E.B.A. Ms.	LD	6,122	15.7	-5.4
					7,484	19.2	

DURHAM, CITY OF [207]

Election	Electors	T'out	Candidate	Party	Votes	% Sh	% Ch
1983	66,925	74.4	Hughes W.M.*	Lab	18,163	36.5	
			Stoker D.	SDP	16,190	32.5	
			Lavis M.E.	Con	15,438	31.0	
					1,973	4.0	
1987	66,518	78.2	Steinberg G.N.	Lab	23,382	44.9	+8.4
			Stoker D.	SDP	17,257	33.2	+0.6
			Colquhoun G.M.	Con	11,408	21.9	-9.1
					6,125	11.8	
1992	68,166†	74.6	Steinberg G.N.*	Lab	27,095	53.3	+8.3
			Woodroofe M.I	Con	12,037	23.7	+1.7
			Martin N.	LD	10,915	21.5	-11.7
			Banks S.J. Ms.	Green	812	1.6*	+1.6
					15,058	29.6	

DURHAM NORTH [208]

Election	Electors	T'out	Candidate	Party	Votes	% Sh	% Ch
1983	71,256	72.7	Radice G.H.*	Lab	26,404	51.0	
			Howarth D.	Lib	12,967	25.0	
			Popat S.	Con	12,418	24.0	
					13,437	25.9	
1987	72,115	76.0	Radice G.H.*	Lab	30,798	56.2	+5.2
			Jeary D. Dr.	SDP	12,365	22.6	-2.5
			Gibbon N.C.	Con	11,627	21.2	-2.8
					18,433	33.6	
1992	73,702†	76.1	Radice G.H.*	Lab	33,567	59.9	+3.7
			Sibley E.A. Ms.	Con	13,930	24.8	+3.6
			Appleby P.J.	LD	8,572	15.3	-7.3
					19,637	35.0	

DURHAM NORTH WEST [209]

Election	Electors	T'out	Candidate	Party	Votes	% Sh	% Ch
1983	60,747	70.7	Armstrong E.*	Lab	19,135	44.6	
			Middleton J.T.	Con	12,779	29.8	
			Foote Wood C.	Lib	11,008	25.6	
					6,356	14.8	
1987	61,302	73.5	Armstrong H.J. Ms.	Lab	22,947	50.9	+6.3
			Iceton D.	Con	12,785	28.4	-1.4
			Foote Wood C.	Lib	9,349	20.7	-4.9
					10,162	22.5	
1992	61,168	75.5	Armstrong H.J. Ms.*	Lab	26,734	57.9	+7.0
			May T.M. Ms.	Con	12,747	27.6	-0.8
			Farron T.J.	LD	6,728	14.6	-6.2
					13,987	30.3	

EALING ACTON [210]

Election	Electors	T'out	Candidate	Party	Votes	% Sh	% Ch
1983	62,078	72.2	Young G.S.K. Sir., Bt.*	Con	22,051	49.2	
			Daniel G.J.	Lab	11,959	26.7	
			Mitchell P.A.	SDP	10,593	23.6	
			Pulley S.	Comm	192	0.4*	
					10,092	22.5	
1987	67,176	71.1	Young G.S.K. Sir., Bt.*	Con	25,499	53.4	+4.2
			Portwood P.J.	Lab	13,266	27.8	+1.1
			Brooks S.R.D.	SDP	8,973	18.8	-4.9
					12,233	25.6	
1992	58,688†	76.0	Young G.S.K. Sir., Bt.*	Con	22,579	50.6	-2.8
			Johnson Y.E. Ms.	Lab	15,572	34.9	+7.1
			Rowe L.A.	LD	5,487	12.3	-6.5
			Seibe A.I. Ms.	Green	554	1.2*	+1.2
			Pitt-Aikens T.	Ind Con	432	1.0*	
					7,007	15.7	

EALING NORTH [211]

Election	Electors	T'out	Candidate	Party	Votes	% Sh	% Ch
1983	68,538	74.8	Greenway H.*	Con	23,128	45.1	
			Benn H.J.	Lab	16,837	32.8	
			Miller A.H.J.	Lib	11,021	21.5	
			Shaw J.	BNP	306	0.6*	
					6,291	12.3	
1987	71,634	75.1	Greenway H.*	Con	30,147	56.0	+10.9
			Benn H.J.	Lab	14,947	27.8	-5.1
			Miller A.H.J.	Lib	8,149	15.1	-6.3
			Fitzherbert K. Ms.	Green	577	1.1*	+1.1
					15,200	28.2	
1992	63,528†	78.8	Greenway H.*	Con	24,898	49.7	-6.3
			Stears M.J.	Lab	18,932	37.8	+10.0
			Hankinson P.C.D.	LD	5,247	10.5	-4.7
			Earl D.S	Green	554	1.1*	+0.0
			Hill C.J.G.	NF	277	0.6*	+0.6
			Davies R.A.	CDP	180	0.4*	+0.4
					5,966	11.9	

EALING SOUTHALL [212]

Election	Electors	T'out	Candidate	Party	Votes	% Sh	% Ch
1983	71,441	71.4	Bidwell S.J.*	Lab	26,664	52.3	
			Linacre N.G.T.	Con	15,548	30.5	
			Nadeem M.	Lib	8,059	15.8	
			Pendrous E.	NF	555	1.1*	
			Paul S.S.	Ind	150	0.3*	
					11,116	21.8	
1987	74,843	69.7	Bidwell S.J.*	Lab	26,480	50.7	-1.6
			Truman M.A.	Con	18,503	35.5	+5.0
			Howes M. Ms.	Lib	6,947	13.3	-2.5
			Lugg R.F.	WRP	256	0.5*	+0.5
					7,977	15.3	
1992	65,574 †	75.5	Khabra P.S.	Lab	23,476	47.4*	-3.3
			Treleaven P.C.	Con	16,610	33.6	-1.9
			Bidwell S.J.*	Ind Lab	4,665	9.4	
			Nandhra P.K. Ms.	LD	3,790	7.7	-5.7
			Goodwin N.	Green	944	1.9*	+1.9
					11,945	24.1	

EASINGTON [213]

Election	Electors	T'out	Candidate	Party	Votes	% Sh	% Ch
1983	65,732	67.5	Dormand J.D.*	Lab	25,912	58.4	
			Patterson F.E.	Lib	11,120	25.1	
			Coulson-Thomas C.J.	Con	7,342	16.5	
					14,792	33.3	
1987	64,866	73.4	Cummings J.S.	Lab	32,396	68.1	+9.7
			Perry W.J.	Con	7,757	16.3	-0.2
			Morpeth G.	Lib	7,447	15.6	-9.4
					24,639	51.8	
1992	65,062†	72.5	Cummings J.S.*	Lab	34,269	72.7	+4.6
			Perry W.J.	Con	7,879	16.7	+0.4
			Freitag P.	LD	5,001	10.6	-5.0
					26,390	56.0	

117

EASTBOURNE [214]

Election	Electors	T'out	Candidate	Party	Votes	% Sh	% Ch
1983	72,980	73.0	Gow I.R.E.*	Con	31,501	59.1	
			Driver P.G.	Lib	18,015	33.8	
			Clark C.A.	Lab	3,790	7.1*	
					13,486	25.3	
1987	74,144	75.6	Gow I.R.E.*	Con	33,587	59.9	+0.8
			Driver P.G.	Lib	16,664	29.7	-4.1
			Patel A.	Lab	4,928	8.8	+1.7
			Addison R. Ms.	Green	867	1.5*	+1.5
					16,923	30.2	

[Death]

Election	Electors	T'out	Candidate	Party	Votes	% Sh	% Ch
1990	75,904	60.7	Bellotti D.F.	LD	23,415	50.8	+21.1
(18/10)			Hickmet R.S.	Con	18,865	40.9	-19.0
			Atkins C.J.S. Ms.	Lab	2,308	5.0	-3.8
			Aherne D.	Green	553	1.2*	-0.3
			Williamson M-T. Ms.	Lib	526	1.1*	
			St. Clair L. Ms.	Ind	216	0.5*	
			McAuley J.C.	NF	154	0.3*	
			Page E.G.	Ind	35	0.1*	
					4,550	9.9	
1992	76,146	80.9	Waterson N.C.	Con	31,792	51.6	-8.3
			Bellotti D.F.	LD	26,311	42.7	+13.0
			Gibbons I.A.	Lab	2,834	4.6*	-4.2
			Aherne D.	Green	391	0.6*	-0.9
			Williamson M-T. Ms.	Lib	296	0.5*	+0.5
					5,481	8.9	

Election	Electors	T'out	Candidate	Party	Votes	% Sh	% Ch
1983	61,420	77.0	Miller M.S. Dr.*	Lab	17,545	37.1	
			Sullivan D.R.E.	SDP	13,199	27.9	
			Dalkeith R.	Con	11,483	24.3	
			Urquhart D.M.	SNP	4,795	10.1*	
			Doolan W.E.	Comm	256	0.5*	
					4,346	9.2	
1987	63,097	79.2	Ingram A.P.	Lab	24,491	49.0	+11.9
			Sullivan D.R.E.	SDP	11,867	23.7	-4.2
			Walker P.M.	Con	7,344	14.7	-9.6
			Taggart J.H.	SNP	6,275	12.6	+2.4
					12,624	25.3	
1992	64,100	80.0	Ingram A.P.*	Lab	24,055	46.9	-2.1
			McAlorum K. Ms.	SNP	12,063	23.5	+11.0
			Lind G.	Con	9,781	19.1	+4.4
			Grieve S.M. Ms.	LD	5,377	10.5	-13.3
					11,992	23.4	

EASTLEIGH [216]

Election	Electors	T'out	Candidate	Party	Votes	% Sh	% Ch
1983	82,447	77.0	Price D.E.C. Sir.*	Con	32,393	51.0	
			Kyrle M.J.	Lib	19,385	30.5	
			Hallmann P.	Lab	11,736	18.5	
					13,008	20.5	
1987	87,552	79.3	Price D.E.C. Sir.*	Con	35,584	51.3	+0.3
			Kyrle M.J.	Lib	22,229	32.0	+1.5
			Bull D.J.C.	Lab	11,599	16.7	-1.8
					13,355	19.2	
1992	91,760	82.9	Milligan S.D.W.	Con	38,998	51.3	+0.0
			Chidgey D.W.G.	LD	21,296	28.0	-4.0
			Sugrue J.E. Ms.	Lab	15,768	20.7	+4.0
					17,702	23.3	

[Death]

Election	Electors	T'out	Candidate	Party	Votes	% Sh	% Ch
1994	94,116	58.7	Chidgey D.W.G.	LD	24,473	44.3	+16.3
(9/6)			Birks M. Ms.	Lab	15,234	27.6	+6.8
			Reid S.	Con	13,675	24.7	-26.5
			Farage N.	UKI	952	1.7*	
			Sutch D.E.	MRLP	783	1.4*	
			Warburton P.N.	NLP	145	0.3*	
					9,239	16.7	

120

EAST LOTHIAN [217]

Election	Electors	T'out	Candidate	Party	Votes	% Sh	% Ch
1983	62,581	76.2	Home Robertson J.D.*	Lab	20,934	43.9	
			Fry M.R.G.	Con	14,693	30.8	
			Kibby M.R.	Lib	9,950	20.9	
			Knox R.T.	SNP	2,083	4.4*	
					6,241	13.1	
1987	65,014	78.7	Home Robertson J.D.*	Lab	24,583	48.0	+4.1
			Langdon S.M.	Con	14,478	28.3	-2.5
			Robinson A.W.	Lib	7,929	15.5	-5.4
			Burgon-Lyon A.	SNP	3,727	7.3	+2.9
			Marland A.E.	Green	451	0.9*	+0.9
					10,105	19.7	
1992	66,700†	82.4	Home Robertson J.D.*	Lab	25,537	46.5	-1.6
			Hepburne Scott J.P.	Con	15,501	28.2	-0.1
			Thomson G.	SNP	7,776	14.2	+6.9
			McKay T.	LD	6,126	11.2	-4.3
					10,036	18.3	

EASTWOOD [218]

Election	Electors	T'out	Candidate	Party	Votes	% Sh	% Ch
1983	59,378	76.2	Stewart J.A.*	Con	21,072	46.6	
			Pickett J.	SDP	12,477	27.6	
			McGuire J.	Lab	9,083	20.1	
			Herriot J.M. Ms.	SNP	2,618	5.8*	
					8,595	19.0	
1987	61,872	79.4	Stewart J.A.*	Con	19,388	39.5	-7.1
			Leishman R.M.	SDP	13,374	27.2	-0.3
			Grant-Hutchison P.A.	Lab	12,305	25.1	+5.0
			Findlay J.A.M.	SNP	4,033	8.2	+2.4
					6,014	12.2	
1992	63,658	81.0	Stewart J.A.*	Con	24,124	46.8	+7.3
			Grant-Hutchison P.A.	Lab	12,436	24.1	-0.9
			Craig M. Ms.	LD	8,493	16.5	-10.8
			Scott P.H.	SNP	6,372	12.4	+4.1
			Fergusson L.	NLP	146	0.3*	+0.3
					11,688	22.7	

ECCLES [219]

Election	Electors	T'out	Candidate	Party	Votes	% Sh	% Ch
1983	67,230	70.1	Carter-Jones L.*	Lab	21,644	45.9	
			Philp D.H.	Con	15,639	33.2	
			Hemsley K.A.	Lib	9,392	19.9	
			Cottam H.	Comm	485	1.0*	
					6,005	12.7	
1987	66,961	74.5	Lestor J. Ms.	Lab	25,346	50.8	+4.9
			Packalow M.E.J. Ms.	Con	15,647	31.3	-1.8
			Beatty P.C.W.	SDP	8,924	17.9	-2.0
					9,699	19.4	
1992	64,911†	74.1	Lestor J. Ms.*	Lab	27,357	56.9	+6.1
			Ling G.J.	Con	14,131	29.4	-2.0
			Reid G.C.	LD	5,835	12.1	-5.8
			Duriez R.C.	Green	521	1.1*	+1.1
			Garner J.A. Ms.	NLP	270	0.6*	+0.6
					13,226	27.5	

EDDISBURY [220]

Election	Electors	T'out	Candidate	Party	Votes	% Sh	% Ch
1983	71,506	74.3	Goodlad A.R.*	Con	28,407	53.5	
			Fletcher R.I.	Lib	13,561	25.5	
			Hanson D.G.	Lab	11,169	21.0	
					14,846	27.9	
1987	73,894	78.0	Goodlad A.R.*	Con	29,474	51.1	-2.3
			Fletcher R.I.	Lib	13,639	23.7	-1.9
			Grigg C. Ms.	Lab	13,574	23.5	+2.5
			Basden A.	Green	976	1.7*	+1.7
					15,835	27.5	
1992	75,081†	82.6	Goodlad A.R.*	Con	31,625	51.0	-0.1
			Edwards N.M. Ms.	Lab	18,928	30.5	+7.0
			Lyon D.W.	LD	10,543	17.0	-6.6
			Basden A.	Green	783	1.3*	-0.4
			Pollard N.P.J.	NLP	107	0.2*	+0.2
					12,697	20.5	

EDINBURGH CENTRAL [221]

Election	Electors	T'out	Candidate	Party	Votes	% Sh	% Ch
1983	57,064	64.9	Fletcher A.M.*	Con	14,095	38.0	
			Kerley R.	Lab	11,529	31.1	
			Macleod M. Ms.	SDP	9,498	25.6	
			Halliday R.N.F.	SNP	1,810	4.9*	
			Carson D.W.	Comm	119	0.3*	
					2,566	6.9	
1987	59,529	69.0	Darling A.M.	Lab	16,502	40.2	+9.1
			Fletcher A.M. Sir.*	Con	14,240	34.7	-3.4
			Myles A.B.	Lib	7,333	17.9	-7.8
			Shaw B.	SNP	2,559	6.2	+1.3
			Hendry L.M. Ms.	Green	438	1.1*	+1.1
					2,262	5.5	
1992	56,689	69.1	Darling A.M.*	Lab	15,189	38.8	-1.4
			Martin P.C.	Con	13,063	33.4	-1.3
			Devine L.J. Ms.	SNP	5,539	14.1	+7.9
			Myles A.B.	LD	4,500	11.5	-6.4
			Harper R.C.M.	Green	630	1.6*	+0.5
			Wilson D.	Lib	235	0.6*	+0.6
					2,126	5.4	

EDINBURGH EAST [222]

Election	Electors	T'out	Candidate	Party	Votes	% Sh	% Ch
1983	51,156	70.4	Strang G.S.*	Lab	16,169	44.9	
			Martin P.C.	Con	10,303	28.6	
			MacLeod R.J.	Lib	7,570	21.0	
			Scott P.H.	SNP	1,976	5.5*	
					5,866	16.3	
1987	48,895	74.1	Strang G.S.*	Lab	18,257	50.4	+5.5
			Renz J.F.	Con	8,962	24.7	-3.9
			Aitken J.C. Ms.	Lib	5,592	15.4	-5.6
			Bovey M.	SNP	3,434	9.5	+4.0
					9,295	25.6	
1992	45,785	73.7	Strang G.S.*	Lab	15,446	45.7	-4.6
			Ward K.F.	Con	8,235	24.4	-0.3
			McKinney D.	SNP	6,225	18.4	+9.0
			Scobie D.S.	LD	3,432	10.2	-5.3
			Farmer G.W.	Green	424	1.3*	+1.3
					7,211	21.4	

EDINBURGH, LEITH [223]

Election	Electors	T'out	Candidate	Party	Votes	% Sh	% Ch
1983	60,562	67.3	Brown R.D.M.*	Lab	16,177	39.7	
			Graham D.A.	SDP	11,204	27.5	
			Cooklin B.D.	Con	10,706	26.3	
			Young J.	SNP	2,646	6.5*	
					4,973	12.2	
1987	60,359	70.9	Brown R.D.M.*	Lab	21,104	49.3	+9.6
			Menzies D.A.Y.	Con	9,777	22.9	-3.4
			Wells S.R. Ms.	SDP	7,843	18.3	-9.2
			Morrison W.S.	SNP	4,045	9.5	+3.0
					11,327	26.5	
1992	56,654	71.1	Chisholm M.G.R.	Lab	13,790	34.2	-15.1
			Hyslop F.J. Ms.	SNP	8,805	21.8	+12.4
			Rizvi M.B.A	Con	8,496	21.1	-1.8
			Campbell H.C. Ms.	LD	4,975	12.3	-6.0
			Brown R.D.M.*	Ind Lab	4,142	10.3	
			Swan A.J.	NLP	96	0.2*	+0.2
					4,985	12.4	

EDINBURGH, PENTLANDS [224]

Election	Electors	T'out	Candidate	Party	Votes	% Sh	% Ch
1983	59,295	73.4	Rifkind M.L.*	Con	17,051	39.2	
			Smith K.A.	SDP	12,742	29.3	
			Milligan E.	Lab	10,390	23.9	
			McCormick D.N.	SNP	2,642	6.1*	
			Nicol Smith A.T.	Green	687	1.6*	
					4,309	9.9	
1987	58,125	77.7	Rifkind M.L.*	Con	17,278	38.3	-0.9
			Lazarowicz M.J.	Lab	13,533	30.0	+6.1
			Smith K.A.	SDP	11,072	24.5	-4.8
			MacCormick D.N.	SNP	3,264	7.2	+1.2
					3,745	8.3	
1992	55,646	80.1	Rifkind M.L.*	Con	18,128	40.7	+2.4
			Lazarowicz M.J.	Lab	13,838	31.1	+1.1
			Caskie K.M. Ms.	SNP	6,882	15.4	+8.2
			Smith K.A.	LD	5,597	12.6	-12.0
			Rae D.C.	NLP	111	0.2*	+0.2
					4,290	9.6	

EDINBURGH SOUTH [225]

Election	Electors	T'out	Candidate	Party	Votes	% Sh	% Ch
1983	62,517	71.7	Ancram M.A.F.J.K.*	Con	16,485	36.8	
			Godfrey J.	SDP	12,830	28.6	
			McCreadie R.A.	Lab	12,824	28.6	
			MacCallum N.R.	SNP	2,256	5.0*	
			Hendry L.M. Ms.	Green	450	1.0*	
					3,655	8.2	
1987	63,830	75.8	Griffiths N.	Lab	18,211	37.7	+9.1
			Ancram M.A.F.J.K.*	Con	16,352	33.8	-2.9
			Graham D.A.	SDP	10,900	22.5	-6.1
			Moore C.M. Ms.	SNP	2,455	5.1	+0.0
			Clark R.V. Ms.	Green	440	0.9*	-0.1
					1,859	3.8	
1992	61,547	72.4	Griffiths N.*	Lab	18,485	41.5	+3.8
			Stevenson S.J.S.	Con	14,309	32.1	-1.7
			McCreadie R.A.	LD	5,961	13.4	-9.2
			Knox R.T.	SNP	5,727	12.8	+7.8
			Manclark G.F.	NLP	108	0.2*	+0.2
					4,176	9.4	

EDINBURGH WEST [226]

Election	Electors	T'out	Candidate	Party	Votes	% Sh	% Ch
1983	61,050	75.7	Douglas-Hamilton J.A. Lord	Con	17,646	38.2	
			King D.G.	Lib	17,148	37.1	
			Wood A.	Lab	9,313	20.1	
			Nicol J.W.	SNP	2,126	4.6*	
					498	1.1	
1987	62,214	79.4	Douglas-Hamilton J.A. Lord*	Con	18,450	37.4	-0.8
			King D.G.	Lib	17,216	34.9	-2.2
			McGregor M.C.B.	Lab	10,957	22.2	+2.0
			Irons N.	SNP	2,774	5.6	+1.0
					1,234	2.5	
1992	59,078	82.6	Douglas-Hamilton J.A. Lord*	Con	18,071	37.0	-0.3
			Gorrie D.C.E.	LD	17,192	35.2	+0.4
			Kitson I.A. Ms.	Lab	8,759	18.0	-4.2
			Sutherland G.D.	SNP	4,117	8.4	+2.8
			Fleming A.R.	Lib	272	0.6*	+0.6
			Hendry L.M. Ms.	Green	234	0.5*	+0.5
			Bruce D.J.	BNP	133	0.3*	+0.3
					879	1.8	

EDMONTON [227]

Election	Electors	T'out	Candidate	Party	Votes	% Sh	% Ch
1983	64,809	68.9	Twinn I.D.	Con	18,968	42.5	
			Graham T.E.*	Lab	17,775	39.8	
			Brass L.S.	Lib	7,523	16.9	
			Bruce D.J.	BNP	372	0.8*	
					1,193	2.7	
1987	66,080	72.5	Twinn I.D.*	Con	24,556	51.2	+8.7
			Grayston B.G.	Lab	17,270	36.0	-3.8
			Lawson M.K.	SDP	6,115	12.8	-4.1
					7,286	15.2	
1992	63,053†	75.7	Twinn I.D.*	Con	22,076	46.3	-4.9
			Love A.M.	Lab	21,483	45.0	+9.0
			Jones E.V.	LD	3,940	8.3	-4.5
			Solly G.E. Ms.	NLP	207	0.4*	+0.4
					593	1.2	

ELLESMERE PORT AND NESTON [228]

Election	Electors	T'out	Candidate	Party	Votes	% Sh	% Ch
1983	69,992	75.8	Woodcook M.	Con	24,371	45.9	
			Davies A.D.	Lab	17,284	32.6	
			George L.J.	SDP	11,413	21.5	
					7,087	13.4	
1987	71,344	81.0	Woodcock M.*	Con	25,664	44.4	-1.5
			Jones H.M. Ms.	Lab	23,811	41.2	+8.6
			Holbrook S.A.	SDP	8,143	14.1	-7.4
			Carson D.J.E.	Ind	185	0.3*	
					1,853	3.2	
1992	71,622	84.1	Miller A.P.	Lab	27,782	46.1	+4.9
			Pearce D.A.	Con	25,793	42.8	-1.6
			Jewkes E.B. Ms.	LD	5,944	9.9	-4.2
			Money M.C.	Green	589	1.0*	+1.0
			Rae J.A.	NLP	105	0.2*	+0.2
					1,989	3.3	

ELMET [229]

Election	Electors	T'out	Candidate	Party	Votes	% Sh	% Ch
1983	67,008	75.4	Batiste S.L.	Con	23,909	47.3	
			Wilson R.	Lab	16,053	31.8	
			Paterson G.M. Ms.	SDP	10,589	20.9	
					7,856	15.5	
1987	69,024	79.3	Batiste S.L.*	Con	25,658	46.9	-0.4
			Burgon C.	Lab	20,302	37.1	+5.3
			Macarthur J.D.	SDP	8,755	16.0	-4.9
					5,356	9.8	
1992	70,711	82.4	Batiste S.L.*	Con	27,677	47.5	+0.6
			Burgon C.	Lab	24,416	41.9	+4.8
			Beck A. Ms.	LD	6,144	10.5	-5.5
					3,261	5.6	

ELTHAM [230]

Election	Electors	T'out	Candidate	Party	Votes	% Sh	% Ch
1983	55,062	74.1	Bottomley P.J.*	Con	19,530	47.9	
			Moore C.P.	Lab	11,938	29.3	
			Randall E.J.	Lib	9,030	22.1	
			Banks P.T.	BNP	276	0.7*	
					7,592	18.6	
1987	54,063	76.9	Bottomley P.J.*	Con	19,752	47.5	-0.4
			Vaughan R.D.	Lab	13,292	32.0	+2.7
			Randall E.J.	Lib	8,542	20.5	-1.6
					6,460	15.5	
1992	51,989†	78.7	Bottomley P.J.*	Con	18,813	46.0	-1.5
			Efford C.S.	Lab	17,147	41.9	+9.9
			McGinty C.P.	LD	4,804	11.7	-8.8
			Graham A.J.	Ind Con	165	0.4*	
					1,666	4.1	

Election	Electors	T'out	Candidate	Party	Votes	% Sh	% Ch
1983	67,980	72.4	Eggar T.J.C.*	Con	25,456	51.7	
			Grayston B.G.	Lab	13,740	27.9	
			Daly J.	SDP	9,452	19.2	
			Persighetti T.M. Ms.	Green	320	0.6*	
			Billingham J.	BNP	268	0.5*	
					11,716	23.8	
1987	69,488	74.5	Eggar T.J.C.*	Con	28,758	55.5	+3.8
			Upham M.	Lab	14,743	28.5	+0.6
			Leighter H.F. Ms.	SDP	7,633	14.7	-4.5
			Chantler E.M.	Green	644	1.2*	+0.6
					14,015	27.1	
1992	67,422†	77.9	Eggar T.J.C.*	Con	27,789	52.9	-2.6
			Upham M.	Lab	18,359	34.9	+6.5
			Tustin S.L. Ms.	LD	5,817	11.1	-3.7
			Markham J.P.	NLP	565	1.1*	+1.1
					9,430	18.0	

ENFIELD SOUTHGATE [232]

Election	Electors	T'out	Candidate	Party	Votes	% Sh	% Ch
1983	65,438	69.6	Berry A.G. Hon.*	Con	26,451	58.1	
			Morgan D.	Lib	10,652	23.4	
			Honeyball M.H.R. Ms.	Lab	8,132	17.9	
			Braithwaite M.F.	BNP	318	0.7*	
					15,799	34.7	

[Death]

Election	Electors	T'out	Candidate	Party	Votes	% Sh	% Ch
1984	66,473	50.6	Portillo M.D.X.	Con	16,684	49.6	-8.5
(13/12)			Slack T.W.	Lib	11,973	35.6	+12.2
			Hamid W.F.	Lab	4,000	11.9*	-5.9
			Polydorou A.	Ind	687	2.1*	
			Kershaw J.W.	Nat	80	0.2*	
			Shenton R.E.	Ind	78	0.2*	
			Burgess I.I.	Ind	50	0.2*	
			Weiss G.	Ind	48	0.1*	
			Anscomb H.M. Ms.	Ind	45	0.1*	
					4.711	14.3	

Election	Electors	T'out	Candidate	Party	Votes	% Sh	% Ch
1987	66,600	72.6	Portillo M.D.X.	Con	28,445	58.8	+0.8
			Harvey N.B.	Lib	10,100	20.9	-2.5
			Course A.W.	Lab	9,114	18.8	+1.0
			Rooney S.	Green	696	1.4*	+1.4
					18,345	37.9	

Election	Electors	T'out	Candidate	Party	Votes	% Sh	% Ch
1992	64,312†	76.3	Portillo M.D.X.*	Con	28,422	57.9	-0.9
			Livney K.R. Ms.	Lab	12,859	26.2	+7.4
			Keane K.J.M.	LD	7,080	14.4	-6.5
			Hollands M.C.P.H. Ms.	Green	696	1.4*	-0.0
					15,563	31.7	

Election	Electors	T'out	Candidate	Party	Votes	% Sh	% Ch
1983	66,355	73.0	Biggs-Davison J.A. Sir.*	Con	27,373	56.5	
			Pettman M.G.	SDP	11,995	24.8	
			Bryan H.J. Ms.	Lab	8,289	17.1	
			Boenke R.W.	Green	452	0.9*	
			Smith S.H.	BNP	330	0.7*	
					15,378	31.7	
1987	67,804	76.3	Biggs-Davison J.A. Sir.*	Con	31,536	60.9	+4.4
			Humphris A.J.	SDP	10,023	19.4	-5.4
			Murray S.W.	Lab	9,499	18.4	+1.2
			Denhard R.F.	Green	695	1.3*	+0.4
					21,513	41.6	

[Death]

Election	Electors	T'out	Candidate	Party	Votes	% Sh	% Ch
1988	67,991	49.1	Norris S.J.	Con	13,183	39.5	-21.4
(15/12)			Thompson A.J.	LD	8,679	26.0	+6.6
			Murray S.W.	Lab	6,261	18.7	+0.3
			Pettman M.G.	SDP	4,077	12.2	
			Simms A.M.	Green	672	2.0*	+0.7
			Wingfield T. Ms.	Ind NF	286	0.9*	
			Sutch D.E.	MRLP	208	0.6*	
			Moore J. Ms.	Ind	33	0.1*	
			Goodier B.G.	Ind	16	0.0*	
					4,504	13.5	
1992	67,600	80.5	Norris S.J.	Con	32,407	59.5	-1.4
			Murray S.W.	Lab	12,219	22.4	+4.1
			Austen B.H.M. Ms.	LD	9,265	17.0	-2.3
			O'Brien A.	Ind	552	1.0*	
					20,188	37.1	

EPSOM AND EWELL [234]

Election	Electors	T'out	Candidate	Party	Votes	% Sh	% Ch
1983	70,630	72.0	Hamilton A.G. Hon.*	Con	30,737	60.4	
			Anderson M.A.J.	Lib	13,542	26.6	
			Carpenter W.R.	Lab	6,587	12.9	
					17,195	33.8	
1987	70,682	75.4	Hamilton A.G. Hon.*	Con	33,145	62.2	+1.8
			Joachim M.J. Ms.	Lib	12,384	23.2	-3.4
			Follett D.B. Ms.	Lab	7,751	14.5	+1.6
					20,761	39.0	
1992	68,138†	80.1	Hamilton A.G. Hon.*	Con	32,861	60.2	-2.0
			Emerson M.P.	LD	12,840	23.5	+0.3
			Warren R.A.	Lab	8,577	15.7	+1.2
			Hatchard G.D.	NLP	334	0.6*	+0.6
					20,021	36.7	

EREWASH [235]

Election	Electors	T'out	Candidate	Party	Votes	% Sh	% Ch
1983	73,355	75.7	Rost P.L.*	Con	25,167	45.3	
			Moore W.	Lab	13,848	24.9	
			Corbett J.P.	SDP	12,331	22.2	
			Camm W.G.	Ind Lab	4,158	7.5*	
					11,319	20.4	
1987	76,536	77.4	Rost P.L.*	Con	28,775	48.6	+3.2
			Jones R.W.	Lab	19,021	32.1	+7.2
			Moss C.P. Ms.	SDP	11,442	19.3	-2.9
					9,754	16.5	
1992	75,729	83.7	Knight A.A. Ms.	Con	29,907	47.2	-1.4
			Stafford J.J.	Lab	24,204	38.2	+6.1
			Tuck P.R.	LD	8,606	13.6	-5.7
			Johnson L.A.	BNP	645	1.0*	+1.0
					5,703	9.0	

ERITH AND CRAYFORD [236]

Election	Electors	T'out	Candidate	Party	Votes	% Sh	% Ch
1983	56,066	73.5	Evennett D.A.	Con	15,289	37.1	
			Wellbeloved A.J.*	SDP	14,369	34.9	
			Smart M.G.	Lab	11,260	27.3	
			Hawke O.	BNP	272	0.7*	
					920	2.2	
1987	59,292	75.4	Evennett D.A.*	Con	20,203	45.2	+8.1
			Hargrave C.F.	Lab	13,209	29.5	+2.2
			Wellbeloved A.J.	SDP	11,300	25.3	-9.6
					6,994	15.6	
1992	59,214†	79.7	Evennett D.A.*	Con	21,926	46.5	+1.3
			Beard C.N.	Lab	19,587	41.5	+12.0
			Jamieson F.M. Ms.	LD	5,657	12.0	-13.3
					2,339	5.0	

ESHER [237]

Election	Electors	T'out	Candidate	Party	Votes	% Sh	% Ch
1983	61,745	73.1	Mather D.C.M.*	Con	28,577	63.3	
			Wheatley C.W.	Lib	12,665	28.0	
			Plaskow D.D. Ms.	Lab	3,250	7.2*	
			Wellie W.	MRLP	664	1.5*	
					15,912	35.2	
1987	62,117	76.9	Taylor I.C.	Con	31,334	65.6	+2.3
			Barnett A.J.	Lib	12,266	25.7	-2.4
			Lucas N.J.V.	Lab	4,197	8.8	+1.6
					19,068	39.9	
1992	58,862	80.8	Taylor I.C.*	Con	31,115	65.4	-0.1
			Richling J.H.	LD	10,744	22.6	-3.1
			Reay J.A. Ms.	Lab	5,685	12.0	+3.2
					20,371	42.8	

Election	Electors	T'out	Candidate	Party	Votes	% Sh	% Ch
1983	73,441	78.0	Hannam J.G.*	Con	26,660	46.5	
			Mennell S.J.	SDP	16,780	29.3	
			Evans R.J.	Lab	13,085	22.8	
			Frings P.R.	Green	779	1.4*	
					9,880	17.2	
1987	75,208	80.6	Hannam J.G.*	Con	26,922	44.4	-2.1
			Thomas M.S.	SDP	19,266	31.8	+2.5
			Vincent J.A.	Lab	13,643	22.5	-0.3
			Vail R.J.	Green	597	1.0*	-0.4
			Byles N.D.	Ind	209	0.3*	
					7,656	12.6	
1992	77,134	80.5	Hannam J.G.*	Con	25,543	41.1	-3.3
			Lloyd J.N.	Lab	22,498	36.2	+13.7
			Oakes G.J.	LD	12,059	19.4	-12.3
			Micklem A.C. Ms.	Lib	1,119	1.8*	+1.8
			Brenan T.J.R.	Green	764	1.2*	+0.2
			Turnbull M.J.	NLP	98	0.2*	+0.2
					3,045	4.9	

FALKIRK EAST [239]

Election	Electors	T'out	Candidate	Party	Votes	% Sh	% Ch
1983	52,045	72.3	Ewing H.*	Lab	17,956	47.7	
			Masterton D.D.M.	Con	7,895	21.0	
			Wedderburn A.A.I.	SDP	6,967	18.5	
			MacGregor J.	SNP	4,490	11.9*	
			McGregor F. Ms.	Comm	344	0.9*	
					10,061	26.7	
1987	52,564	75.0	Ewing H.*	Lab	21,379	54.2	+6.6
			Brookes K.H.	Con	7,356	18.7	-2.3
			Halliday R.N.F.	SNP	6,056	15.4	+3.4
			Dick E.G. Ms.	SDP	4,624	11.7	-6.8
					14,023	35.6	
1992	51,224	78.0	Connarty M.	Lab	18,423	46.1	-8.1
			Halliday R.N.F.	SNP	10,454	26.2	+10.8
			Harding K.	Con	8,279	20.7	+2.1
			Storr D.M. Ms.	LD	2,775	6.9	-4.8
					7,969	20.0	

FALKIRK WEST [240]

Election	Electors	T'out	Candidate	Party	Votes	% Sh	% Ch
1983	49,402	74.0	Canavan D.A.*	Lab	16,668	45.6	
			Mitchell I.G.	Con	7,690	21.0	
			Harris M.J.	Lib	7,477	20.4	
			Cochrane B.P.	SNP	4,739	13.0	
					8,978	24.5	
1987	50,222	76.7	Canavan D.A.*	Lab	20,256	53.2	+7.6
			Thomas D.R.B.	Con	6,704	17.6	-3.4
			Goldie I.R.	SNP	6,296	16.5	+3.6
			Harris M.J.	Lib	4,841	12.7	-7.7
					13,552	35.6	
1992	49,434	77.8	Canavan D.A.*	Lab	19,162	49.8	-3.4
			Houston W.	SNP	9,350	24.3	+7.8
			Macdonald M.	Con	7,558	19.6	+2.0
			Reilly M.J.	LD	2,414	6.3	-6.4
					9,812	25.5	

FALMOUTH AND CAMBOURNE [241]

Election	Electors	T'out	Candidate	Party	Votes	% Sh	% Ch
1983	65,624	75.0	Mudd W.D.*	Con	24,614	50.0	
			Fieldsend D.M.	SDP	13,589	27.6	
			Bunt A.J.L.	Lab	10,446	21.2	
			Jenkin R.G.	MK	582	1.2*	
					11,025	22.4	
1987	68,840	78.5	Mudd W.D.*	Con	23,725	43.9	-6.1
			Marks J.C.	SDP	18,686	34.6	+7.0
			Cosgrove J.D.	Lab	11,271	20.9	-0.4
			Stribley F.A.	MRLP	373	0.7*	+0.7
					5,039	9.3	
1992	70,712	81.1	Coe S.N.	Con	21,150	36.9	-7.0
			Jones T.L. Ms.	LD	17,883	31.2	-3.4
			Cosgrove J.D.	Lab	16,732	29.2	+8.3
			Holmes P.T.	Lib	730	1.3*	+1.3
			Saunders K.J.	Green	466	0.8*	+0.8
			Zapp F.	MRLP	327	0.6*	-0.1
			Pringle A.J.	NLP	56	0.1*	+0.1
					3,267	5.7	

FAREHAM [242]

Election	Electors	T'out	Candidate	Party	Votes	% Sh	% Ch
1983	71,901	73.7	Lloyd P.R.C.*	Con	32,762	61.8	
			Yolland S.	Lib	16,446	31.0	
			Somerville D.	Lab	3,808	7.2*	
					16,316	30.8	
1987	76,974	78.2	Lloyd P.R.C.*	Con	36,781	61.1	-0.7
			Slack T.W.	Lib	17,986	29.9	-1.2
			Merritt M.F.	Lab	5,451	9.1	+1.9
					18,795	31.2	
1992	81,125†	81.9	Lloyd P.R.C.*	Con	40,482	61.0	-0.1
			Thompson J.C.	LD	16,341	24.6	-5.3
			Weston E.M. Ms.	Lab	8,766	13.2	+4.1
			Brimecome M.J.	Green	818	1.2*	+1.2
					24,141	36.4	

FAVERSHAM [243]

Election	Electors	T'out	Candidate	Party	Votes	% Sh	% Ch
1983	76,467	73.5	Moate R.D.*	Con	29,849	53.1	
			Goyder E.M.	SDP	15,252	27.1	
			Bromley C.M.	Lab	11,130	19.8	
					14,597	26.0	
1987	79,148	76.8	Moate R.D.*	Con	31,074	51.1	-2.0
			Goyder E.M.	SDP	17,096	28.1	+1.0
			Dangerfield P.	Lab	12,616	20.8	+1.0
					13,978	23.0	
1992	82,037†	79.7	Moate R.D.*	Con	32,755	50.1	-1.0
			Brinton H.R. Ms.	Lab	16,404	25.1	+4.3
			Truelove R.	LD	15,896	24.3	-3.8
			Bradshaw R.M.	NLP	294	0.4*	+0.4
					16,351	25.0	

FELTHAM AND HESTON [244]

Election	Electors	T'out	Candidate	Party	Votes	% Sh	% Ch
1983	78,366	69.8	Ground R.P.	Con	23,724	43.4	
			Kerr R.W.*	Lab	21,576	39.4	
			Alagappa A.V.	Lib	8,706	15.9	
			Glass S.A.	NF	696	1.3*	
					2,148	3.9	
1987	81,062	73.7	Ground R.P.*	Con	27,755	46.5	+3.1
			Hinds C.W.V.	Lab	22,325	37.4	-2.0
			Daly J.	SDP	9,623	16.1	+0.2
					5,430	9.1	
1992	82,133	73.1	Keen A.	Lab	27,660	46.1	+8.7
			Ground R.P.*	Con	25,665	42.8	-3.7
			Hoban M.F.	LD	6,700	11.2	-5.0
					1,995	3.3	

FERMANAGH AND SOUTH TYRONE [245]

Election	Electors	T'out	Candidate	Party	Votes	% Sh	% Ch
1983	67,842	88.7	Maginnis K.	UU	28,630	47.6	
			Carron O.G.*	SF	20,954	34.8	
			Flanagan R. Ms.	SDLP	9,923	16.5	
			Kettyles D.A.	WP	649	1.1*	
					7,676	12.8	

[Seeks Re-election]

Election	Electors	T'out	Candidate	Party	Votes	% Sh	% Ch
1986 (23/1)	69,767	80.4	Maginnis K.*	UU	27,857	49.7	+2.1
			Carron O.G.	SF	15,278	27.2	-7.5
			Currie J.A.	SDLP	12,081	21.5	+5.0
			Kettyles D.A.	WP	864	1.5*	+0.4
					12,579	22.4	
1987	68,979	80.3	Maginnis K.*	UU	27,446	49.6	+2.0
			Corrigan P.E.	SF	14,623	26.4	-8.4
			Flanagan R. Ms.	SDLP	10,581	19.1	+2.6
			Kettyles D.A.	WP	1,784	3.2*	+2.1
			Haslett J.T.	APNI	941	1.7*	+1.7
					12,823	23.2	
1992	70,253	78.5	Maginnis K.*	UU	26,923	48.8	-0.7
			Gallagher T.	SDLP	12,810	23.2	+4.1
			Molloy F.	SF	12,604	22.9	-3.5
			Kettyles D.	PS	1,094	2.0*	+2.0
			Bullick E.A.H.	APNI	950	1.7*	+0.0
			Cullen G.	NA	747	1.4*	+1.4
					14,113	25.6	

FIFE CENTRAL [246]

Election	Electors	T'out	Candidate	Party	Votes	% Sh	% Ch
1983	54,389	72.5	Hamilton W.W.*	Lab	17,008	43.1	
			Little T.M. Ms.	Lib	9,214	23.4	
			Mason D.C.	Con	8,863	22.5	
			Taggart J.H.	SNP	4,039	10.2*	
			Allison D.A.	Green	297	0.8*	
					7,794	19.8	
1987	56,090	76.2	McLeish H.B.	Lab	22,827	53.4	+10.3
			Aird R.E.	Con	7,118	16.7	-5.8
			Little T.M. Ms.	Lib	6,487	15.2	-8.2
			Hood D.	SNP	6,296	14.7	+4.5
					15,709	36.8	
1992	56,092	74.4	McLeish H.B.*	Lab	21,036	50.4	-3.0
			Marwick T. Ms.	SNP	10,458	25.1	+10.3
			Cender C.E. Ms.	Con	7,353	17.6	+1.0
			Harrow C.T.A.	LD	2,892	6.9	-8.3
					10,578	25.3	

FIFE NORTH EAST [247]

Election	Electors	T'out	Candidate	Party	Votes	% Sh	% Ch
1983	50,476	73.7	Henderson J.S.B.*	Con	17,129	46.1	
			Campbell W.M.	Lib	14,944	40.2	
			Hulbert J.K.M. Dr.	SNP	2,442	6.6*	
			Caldwell D.C.	Lab	2,429	6.5*	
			Flinn T.G.P.	Green	242	0.7*	
					2,185	5.9	
1987	52,266	76.2	Campbell W.M.	Lib	17,868	44.8	+4.6
			Henderson J.S.B.*	Con	16,421	41.2	-4.9
			Gannon A.M.E.	Lab	2,947	7.4	+0.9
			Roche F.D.	SNP	2,616	6.6	-0.0
					1,447	3.6	
1992	53,836	77.7	Campbell W.M.*	LD	19,430	46.4	+1.6
			Scanlon M.E. Ms.	Con	16,122	38.5	-2.7
			Roche F.D.	SNP	3,589	8.6	+2.0
			Clark M.L. Ms.	Lab	2,319	5.5	-1.9
			Flinn T.G.P.	Green	294	0.7*	+0.1
			Senior D.M.	Lib	85	0.2*	+0.2
					3,308	7.9	

Election	Electors	T'out	Candidate	Party	Votes	% Sh	% Ch
1983	55,638	69.0	Thatcher M.H. Ms.*	Con	19,616	51.1	
			Spigel L.G.	Lab	10,302	26.8	
			Joachim M.J. Ms.	Lib	7,763	20.2	
			Wilkinson S.J. Ms.	Green	279	0.7*	
			Sutch D.E.	MRLP	235	0.6*	
			Noonan A.J.	Ind	75	0.2*	
			Anscomb H.M. Ms.	Ind	42	0.1*	
			Whitehead A.P.	Ind	37	0.1*	
			Webb D.A.	Ind	28	0.1*	
			Wareham B.C.	PAL	27	0.1*	
			Wedmore B.C.	Ind	13	0.0*	
					9,314	24.2	
1987	57,727	69.4	Thatcher M.H. Ms.*	Con	21,603	53.9	+2.9
			Davies J.R.M.	Lab	12,690	31.7	+4.9
			Howarth D.	Lib	5,580	13.9	-6.3
			Buckethead L.	Ind	131	0.3*	
			St. Vincent M.J. Ms.	Ind	59	0.1*	
					8,913	22.2	
1992	52,908†	77.6	Booth V.E.H.	Con	21,039	51.2	-2.7
			Marjoram A.C. Ms.	Lab	14,651	35.7	+4.0
			Leighter H.F. Ms.	LD	4,568	11.1	-2.8
			Gunstock A.	Green	564	1.4*	+1.4
			Johnson S.A. Ms.	Ind	130	0.3*	
			Macrae J.D.	NLP	129	0.3*	+0.3
					6,388	15.5	

Election	Electors	T'out	Candidate	Party	Votes	% Sh	% Ch
1983	67,802	70.6	Howard M.	Con	27,261	56.9	
			Macdonald J.R.	Lib	15,591	32.6	
			Lawrie L.G.R.	Lab	4,700	9.8*	
			Todd P.A.	Ind	318	0.7*	
					11,670	24.4	
1987	64,410	78.3	Howard M.*	Con	27,915	55.4	-1.6
			Macdonald J.R.	Lib	18,789	37.3	+4.7
			Anand V.S.	Lab	3,720	7.4	-2.4
					9,126	18.1	
1992	65,856†	79.6	Howard M.*	Con	27,437	52.3	-3.0
			Cufley L.W. Ms.	LD	18,527	35.3	-1.9
			Doherty P.	Lab	6,347	12.1	+4.7
			Hobbs A.R.	Ind	123	0.2*	
					8,910	17.0	

Election	Electors	T'out	Candidate	Party	Votes	% Sh	% Ch
1983	66,976	78.1	Hume J.	SDLP	24,071	46.0	
			Campbell G.L.	UDUP	15,923	30.5	
			McGuinness M.	SF	10,607	20.3	
			O'Grady G.	APNI	1,108	2.1*	
			Melaugh E.	WP	582	1.1*	
					8,148	15.6	
1987	70,519	69.0	Hume J.*	SDLP	23,743	48.8	+2.8
			Campbell G.L.	UDUP	13,883	28.5	-1.9
			McGuinness M.	SF	8,707	17.9	-2.4
			Zammitt E.A. Ms.	APNI	1,276	2.6*	+0.5
			Melaugh E.	WP	1,022	2.1*	+1.0
					9,860	20.3	
1992	74,673	69.5	Hume J.*	SDLP	26,710	51.5	+2.7
			Campbell G.L.	UDUP	13,705	26.4	-2.1
			McGuinness M.	SF	9,149	17.6	-0.3
			McIlroy L.A. Ms.	APNI	1,390	2.7*	+0.1
			MacKenzie G.	WP	514	1.0*	-1.1
			Burns J.J.P.	NLP	422	0.8*	+0.8
					13,005	25.1	

FULHAM [251]

Election	Electors	T'out	Candidate	Party	Votes	% Sh	% Ch
1983	51,833	76.1	Stevens M.*	Con	18,204	46.2	
			Powell A.F.W.	Lab	13,415	34.0	
			Rendel D.D.	Lib	7,194	18.2	
			Grimes J.M. Ms.	Green	277	0.7*	
			Pearse R.L.J.	NF	229	0.6*	
			Keats J.C.	Ind Lib	102	0.3*	
					4,789	12.1	

[Death]

Election	Electors	T'out	Candidate	Party	Votes	% Sh	% Ch
1986	52,380	70.8	Raynsford W.R.N.	Lab	16,451	44.4	+10.4
(10/4)			Carrington M.H.M.	Con	12,948	34.9	-11.3
			Liddle R.J.	SDP	6,953	18.7	+0.5
			Birdwood J.P. Lady	Ind	226	0.6*	
			Sutch D.E.	MRLP	134	0.4*	
			Creighton J.D.	Ind	127	0.3*	
			Black J.B.H.	Ind	98	0.3*	
			Rolph G.A.	FP	39	0.1*	
			Swinden J.S.	HP	38	0.1*	
			Duke L. Ms.	Ind	37	0.1*	
			Simmerson R.E.G.	Ind	33	0.1*	
					3,503	9.5	

Election	Electors	T'out	Candidate	Party	Votes	% Sh	% Ch
1987	54,498	77.1	Carrington M.H.M.	Con	21,752	51.8	+5.6
			Raynsford W.R.N.	Lab	15,430	36.7	+2.7
			Marshall P.R.C.	SDP	4,365	10.4	-7.9
			Grimes J.M. Ms.	Green	465	1.1*	+0.4
					6,322	15.0	

Election	Electors	T'out	Candidate	Party	Votes	% Sh	% Ch
1992	52,945	75.9	Carrington M.H.M.*	Con	21,438	53.4	+1.6
			Moore N.P.	Lab	14,859	37.0	+0.3
			Crystal P.M.	LD	3,339	8.3	-2.1
			Streeter E.G.A. Ms.	Green	443	1.1*	-0.0
			Darby J.V.	NLP	91	0.2*	+0.2
					6,579	16.4	

FYLDE [252]

Election	Electors	T'out	Candidate	Party	Votes	% Sh	% Ch
1983	62,238	71.2	Gardner E.L. Sir.*	Con	27,879	62.9	
			Smith E.A. Ms.	Lib	10,777	24.3	
			King D.J.	Lab	4,821	10.9*	
			Fowler H.	Ind	863	1.9*	
					17,102	38.6	
1987	65,108	74.8	Jack J.M.	Con	29,559	60.7	-2.2
			Smith E.A. Ms.	Lib	11,787	24.2	-0.1
			Smith G.W.T. Dr.	Lab	6,955	14.3	+3.4
			Fowler H.	Ind	405	0.8*	
					17,772	36.5	
1992	63,599	78.5	Jack J.M.*	Con	30,639	61.4	+0.7
			Cryer N.	LD	9,648	19.3	-4.9
			Hughes C. Ms.	Lab	9,382	18.8	+4.5
			Leadbetter P.D.N.	NLP	239	0.5*	+0.5
					20,991	42.1	

GAINSBOROUGH AND HORNCASTLE [253]

Election	Electors	T'out	Candidate	Party	Votes	% Sh	% Ch
1983	67,115	75.0	Leigh E.J.E.	Con	25,625	50.9	
			Phillips A.	Lib	20,558	40.8	
			James C.A.	Lab	3,886	7.7*	
			Dixon G.W.	Green	279	0.6*	
					5,067	10.1	
1987	69,760	76.9	Leigh E.J.E.*	Con	28,621	53.3	+2.4
			Grace D.A.	Lib	18,898	35.2	-5.6
			Naylor R.A.	Lab	6,156	11.5	+3.8
					9,723	18.1	
1992	72,038†	80.9	Leigh E.J.E.*	Con	31,444	54.0	+0.6
			Taylor N.	LD	15,199	26.1	-9.1
			Jones F.E.A. Ms.	Lab	11,619	19.9	+8.5
					16,245	27.9	

GALLOWAY AND UPPER NITHSDALE [254]

Election	Electors	T'out	Candidate	Party	Votes	% Sh	% Ch
1983	51,831	75.8	Lang I.B.*	Con	17,579	44.7	
			Thompson G.H.	SNP	12,118	30.8	
			Douglas G.	Lib	5,129	13.1	
			Miller M.B.	Lab	4,464	11.4*	
					5,461	13.9	
1987	53,429	76.8	Lang I.B.*	Con	16,592	40.4	-4.3
			Norris S.F.	SNP	12,919	31.5	+0.6
			McKerchar J.E.	Lib	6,001	14.6	+1.6
			Gray J.W.	Lab	5,298	12.9	+1.5
			Kenny D.	Ind	230	0.6*	
					3,673	8.9	
1992	54,500	81.6	Lang I.B.*	Con	18,681	42.0	+1.6
			Brown M.	SNP	16,213	36.4	+5.0
			Dowson J.	Lab	5,766	13.0	+0.1
			McKerchar J.E.	LD	3,826	8.6	-6.0
					2,468	5.5	

GATESHEAD EAST [255]

Election	Electors	T'out	Candidate	Party	Votes	% Sh	% Ch
1983	68,364	69.6	Conlan B.*	Lab	22,981	48.3	
			Rogers F.W.	Con	12,659	26.6	
			Nunn V.P.	SDP	11,920	25.1	
					10,322	21.7	
1987	67,953	71.8	Quin J.G. Ms.	Lab	28,895	59.2	+10.9
			Rogers F.W.	Con	11,667	23.9	-2.7
			Rippeth N.G.	SDP	8,231	16.9	-8.2
					17,228	35.3	
1992	64,355†	73.6	Quin J.G. Ms.*	Lab	30,100	63.5	+4.3
			Callanan M.J.	Con	11,570	24.4	+0.5
			Beadle R.W.A.L.	LD	5,720	12.1	-4.8
					18,530	39.1	

GEDLING [256]

Election	Electors	T'out	Candidate	Party	Votes	% Sh	% Ch
1983	66,656	75.4	Holland P.W.*	Con	27,207	54.1	
			Berkeley A.M.	SDP	12,543	25.0	
			Peck J.M.	Lab	10,330	20.6	
			Szatter J.	Ind	186	0.4*	
					14,664	29.2	
1987	68,398	79.1	Mitchell A.J.B.	Con	29,492	54.5	+0.4
			Coaker V.R.	Lab	12,953	23.9	+3.4
			Morton D.J.	SDP	11,684	21.6	-3.4
					16,539	30.6	
1992	68,954†	82.3	Mitchell A.J.B.*	Con	30,191	53.2	-1.3
			Coaker V.R.	Lab	19,554	34.4	+10.5
			George D.G.	LD	6,863	12.1	-9.5
			Miszewska A.K.L. Ms.	NLP	168	0.3*	+0.3
					10,637	18.7	

GILLINGHAM [257]

Election	Electors	T'out	Candidate	Party	Votes	% Sh	% Ch
1983	69,256	73.6	Couchman J.R.	Con	26,381	51.7	
			Lewcock C.P.	Lib	15,538	30.5	
			West A.S.	Lab	9,084	17.8	
					10,843	21.3	
1987	71,742	75.4	Couchman J.R.*	Con	28,711	53.1	+1.4
			Andrews L.R.	Lib	16,162	29.9	-0.6
			Bishop D.J.	Lab	9,230	17.1	-0.8
					12,549	23.2	
1992	71,851†	80.3	Couchman J.R.*	Con	30,201	52.3	-0.8
			Clark P.G.	Lab	13,563	23.5	+6.4
			Wallbank M.A.	LD	13,509	23.4	-6.5
			MacKinlay C.	Ind	248	0.4*	
			Jolicoeur D.	NLP	190	0.3*	+0.3
					16,638	28.8	

GLANFORD AND SCUNTHORPE [258]

Election	Electors	T'out	Candidate	Party	Votes	% Sh	% Ch
1983	71,962	73.5	Hickmet R.S.	Con	20,356	38.5	
			Ellis J.	Lab	19,719	37.3	
			Nottingham C.	SDP	12,821	24.2	
					637	1.2	
1987	72,816	78.0	Morley E.A.	Lab	24,733	43.5	+6.2
			Hickmet R.S.*	Con	24,221	42.6	+4.1
			Nottingham C.	SDP	7,762	13.7	-10.6
			Trivedi K.S.	Ind	104	0.2*	
					512	0.9	
1992	73,404	79.1	Morley E.A.*	Lab	30,637	52.8	+9.3
			Saywood A.M.	Con	22,226	38.3	-4.3
			Paxton W.	LD	4,186	7.2	-6.4
			Nottingham C.	SD	996	1.7*	+1.7
					8,411	14.5	

GLASGOW, CATHCART [259]

Election	Electors	T'out	Candidate	Party	Votes	% Sh	% Ch
1983	51,055	75.8	Maxton J.A.*	Lab	16,037	41.4	
			May D.J.	Con	11,807	30.5	
			Bloomer K.	SDP	8,710	22.5	
			Steven W.A.	SNP	2,151	5.6*	
					4,230	10.9	
1987	49,307	76.4	Maxton J.A.*	Lab	19,623	52.1	+10.7
			Harvey W.A.	Con	8,420	22.4	-8.1
			Craig M. Ms.	SDP	5,722	15.2	-7.3
			Steven W.A.	SNP	3,883	10.3	+4.8
					11,203	29.8	
1992	44,779	75.2	Maxton J.A.*	Lab	16,265	48.3	-3.8
			Young J.	Con	8,264	24.5	+2.2
			Steven W.A.	SNP	6,107	18.1	+7.8
			Dick G.C.	LD	2,614	7.8	-7.4
			Allan K.M. Ms.	Green	441	1.3*	+1.3
					8,001	23.7	

Election	Electors	T'out	Candidate	Party	Votes	% Sh	% Ch
1983	51,217	62.8	McTaggart R.*	Lab	17,066	53.0	
			Harvey W.A.	Con	6,104	19.0	
			Nelson I. Ms.	Lib	5,366	16.7	
			Mallan P.	SNP	3,300	10.3*	
			McGoldrick J.P.	Comm	347	1.1*	
					10,962	34.1	
1987	51,137	65.6	McTaggart R.*	Lab	21,619	64.5	+11.4
			Jenkin B.C.	Con	4,366	13.0	-5.9
			Bryden J.S. Dr.	Lib	3,528	10.5	-6.2
			Wilson A.B.	SNP	3,339	10.0	-0.3
			Brooks A.	Green	290	0.9*	+0.9
			McGoldrick J.P.	Comm	265	0.8*	-0.3
			Owen D.	RF	126	0.4*	
					17,253	51.5	

[Death]

Election	Electors	T'out	Candidate	Party	Votes	% Sh	% Ch
1989	50,254	52.8	Watson M.	Lab	14,480	54.6	-9.9
(15/6)			Neil A.	SNP	8,018	30.2	+20.2
			Hogarth A.	Con	2,028	7.6	-5.4
			Brandt I. Ms.	Green	1,019	3.8*	+2.9
			McCreadie R.A.	LD	411	1.5*	-9.0
			Kerr P.E.	SDP	253	1.0*	
			Murdoch L. Ms.	RCP	141	0.5*	
			Kidd B.	Scot Soc	137	0.5*	
			Lettice D.J.	WRP	48	0.2*	
					6,462	24.4	
1992	48,159	63.0	Watson M.	Lab	17,341	57.2	-7.3
			O'Hara B.	SNP	6,322	20.8	+10.9
			Stewart E.N.	Con	4,208	13.9	+0.9
			Rennie A.N. Dr.	LD	1,921	6.3	-4.2
			Brandt I. Ms.	Green	435	1.4*	+0.6
			Burn T.D.	Comm	106	0.3*	-0.5
					11,019	36.4	

Election	Electors	T'out	Candidate	Party	Votes	% Sh	% Ch
1983	50,589	69.1	Dewar D.C.*	Lab	19,635	56.2	
			Lyden W.	SDP	6,161	17.6	
			MacLeod K.N.	Con	5,368	15.4	
			MacLeod N.M.T.M.	SNP	3,566	10.2*	
			Barr S.A.	Comm	218	0.6*	
					13,474	38.6	
1987	47,958	71.4	Dewar D.C.*	Lab	23,178	67.7	+11.5
			Brophy A.	SNP	4,201	12.3	+2.1
			Begg T.N.A.	Con	3,660	10.7	-4.7
			Callison J.S.	SDP	3,211	9.4	-8.3
					18,977	55.4	
1992	41,214	71.3	Dewar D.C.*	Lab	18,920	64.4	-3.3
			Douglas R.G.*	SNP	5,580	19.0	+6.7
			Scott J.L.	Con	3,385	11.5	+0.8
			Brodie C.G.	LD	1,425	4.9*	-4.5
			Orr W.G.	NLP	61	0.2*	+0.2
					13,340	45.4	

Dick Douglas had been the Labour member for Dunfermline West in the previous Parliament.

GLASGOW, GOVAN [262]

Election	Electors	T'out	Candidate	Party	Votes	% Sh	% Ch
1983	51,754	71.6	Millan B.*	Lab	20,370	55.0	
			MacKenzie A.	Con	7,313	19.7	
			McDonald I.	SDP	7,180	19.4	
			Kindlen P.M.	SNP	2,207	6.0*	
					13,057	35.2	
1987	50,616	73.4	Millan B.*	Lab	24,071	64.8	+9.9
			Ferguson A.	SDP	4,562	12.3	-7.1
			Girsman J.R. Ms.	Con	4,411	11.9	-7.8
			McCabe F.	SNP	3,851	10.4	+4.4
			Chalmers D.	Comm	237	0.6*	+0.6
					19,509	52.5	

(Resignation)

Election	Electors	T'out	Candidate	Party	Votes	% Sh	% Ch
1988 (10/11)	49,994	60.2	Sillars J.	SNP	14,677	48.8	+38.4
			Gillespie R.P.	Lab	11,123	37.0	-27.8
			Hamilton G.M.	Con	2,207	7.3	-4.6
			Ponsonby B.	LD	1,246	4.1*	-8.2
			Campbell G.	Green	345	1.1*	
			Chalmers D.	Comm	281	0.9*	+0.3
			Sutch D.E.	MRLP	174	0.6*	
			Clark F.	Ind	51	0.2*	
					3,554	11.8	
1992	45,879	75.9	Davidson I.G.	Lab	17,051	48.9	-15.9
			Sillars J.	SNP	12,926	37.1	+26.7
			Donnelly J.A.	Con	3,458	9.9	-2.0
			Stewart R.	LD	1,227	3.5*	-8.8
			Spaven D.L.	Green	181	0.5*	+0.5
					4,125	11.8	

GLASGOW HILLHEAD [263]

Election	Electors	T'out	Candidate	Party	Votes	% Sh	% Ch
1983	57,016	72.0	Jenkins R.H.*	SDP	14,856	36.2	
			Carmichael N.G.*	Lab	13,692	33.3	
			Tosh N.M.	Con	9,678	23.6	
			Leslie G.A.	SNP	2,203	5.4*	
			Davidson J.P.	Ind Con	249	0.6*	
			Whitelaw A.	Green	239	0.6*	
			Robins J.F.	Ind	139	0.3*	
					1,164	2.8	

Neil Carmichael had been the member for Glasgow, Kelvingrove in the previous Parliament.

1987	57,836	72.4	Galloway G.	Lab	17,958	42.9	+9.5
			Jenkins R.H.*	SDP	14,707	35.1	-1.1
			Cooklin B.D.	Con	6,048	14.4	-9.1
			Kidd W.	SNP	2,713	6.5	+1.1
			Whitelaw A.	Green	443	1.1*	+0.5
					3,251	7.8	

1992	57,331	68.7	Galloway G.*	Lab	15,148	38.5	-4.4
			Mason C.M.	LD	10,322	26.2	-8.9
			Bates A.K. Ms.	Con	6,728	17.1	+2.6
			White S. Ms.	SNP	6,484	16.5	+10.0
			Collie L.R. Ms.	Green	558	1.4*	+0.4
			Gold H. Ms.	RCP	73	0.2*	+0.2
			Paterson D.J.	NLP	60	0.2*	+0.2
					4,826	12.3	

GLASGOW, MARYHILL [264]

Election	Electors	T'out	Candidate	Party	Votes	% Sh	% Ch
1983	51,847	65.5	Craigen J.M.*	Lab	18,724	55.2	
			Attwooll E.M-A. Ms.	Lib	7,521	22.2	
			Gibbs J.	Con	5,014	14.8	
			Morrison I.	SNP	2,408	7.1*	
			Smith P.B.	Comm	274	0.8*	
					11,203	33.0	

1987	52,371	67.5	Fyfe C.M. Ms.	Lab	23,482	66.4	+11.3
			Attwooll E.M-A. Ms.	Lib	4,118	11.7	-10.5
			Roberts G.	SNP	3,895	11.0	+3.9
			Kirk S.R.R.	Con	3,307	9.4	-5.4
			Spaven D.L.	Green	539	1.5*	+1.5
					19,364	54.8	

1992	48,479	65.1	Fyfe C.M. Ms.*	Lab	19,452	61.6	-4.8
			Williamson C.	SNP	6,033	19.1	+8.1
			Godfrey J.P.	Con	3,248	10.3	+0.9
			Alexander J.	LD	2,215	7.0	-4.6
			O'Brien P.J.	Green	530	1.7*	+0.2
			Henderson M.D.	NLP	78	0.2*	+0.2
					13,419	42.5	

148

GLASGOW, POLLOK [265]

Election	Electors	T'out	Candidate	Party	Votes	% Sh	% Ch
1983	53,217	68.2	White J.*	Lab	18,973	52.3	
			Carlaw D.J.	Con	7,441	20.5	
			McKell G.A.	Lib	6,308	17.4	
			Hannigan F.	SNP	3,585	9.9*	
					11,532	31.8	
1987	51,396	71.7	Dunnachie J.F.	Lab	23,239	63.1	+10.8
			French G.R. Ms.	Con	5,256	14.3	-6.2
			Shearer J.C.	Lib	4,445	12.1	-5.3
			Doig A.	SNP	3,528	9.6	-0.3
			Fogg D.	Green	362	1.0*	+1.0
					17,983	48.8	
1992	46,190	70.7	Dunnachie J.F.*	Lab	14,170	43.4	-19.7
			Sheridan T.	SML	6,287	19.3	+19.3
			Gray R.	Con	5,147	15.8	+1.5
			Leslie G.A.	SNP	5,107	15.6	+6.1
			Jago D.M.	LD	1,932	5.9	-6.2
					7,883	24.1	

GLASGOW, PROVAN [266]

Election	Electors	T'out	Candidate	Party	Votes	% Sh	% Ch
1983	47,706	65.2	Brown H.D.*	Lab	20,040	64.4	
			Heron A.D.	SDP	4,655	15.0	
			Gordon S.J. Ms.	Con	3,374	10.8*	
			Kennedy P. Ms.	SNP	2,737	8.8*	
			Jackson J.	Comm	294	0.9*	
					15,385	49.5	
1987	43,744	69.1	Wray J.	Lab	22,032	72.9	+8.5
			Ramsay W.	SNP	3,660	12.1	+3.3
			Strutt A. Ms.	Con	2,336	7.7	-3.1
			Morrison J.	SDP	2,189	7.2	-7.7
					18,372	60.8	
1992	36,579	65.3	Wray J.*	Lab	15,885	66.5	-6.4
			MacRae S. Ms.	SNP	5,182	21.7	+9.6
			Rosindell A.R.	Con	1,865	7.8	+0.1
			Bell C.E.	LD	948	4.0*	-3.3
					10,703	44.8	

GLASGOW, RUTHERGLEN [267]

Election	Electors	T'out	Candidate	Party	Votes	% Sh	% Ch
1983	59,209	75.2	MacKenzie J.G.*	Lab	21,510	48.3	
			Brown R.E.	Lib	12,384	27.8	
			Hodgins H.M. Ms.	Con	8,017	18.0	
			Fee K.	SNP	2,438	5.5*	
			Corrigan C.S.	WRP	148	0.3*	
					9,126	20.5	
1987	57,313	77.2	McAvoy T.M.	Lab	24,790	56.0	+7.7
			Brown R.E.	Lib	10,795	24.4	-3.4
			Hamilton G.M.	Con	5,088	11.5	-6.5
			Higgins J.	SNP	3,584	8.1	+2.6
					13,995	31.6	
1992	52,719	75.2	McAvoy T.M.*	Lab	21,962	55.4	-0.6
			Cooklin B.D.	Con	6,692	16.9	+5.4
			Higgins J.	SNP	6,470	16.3	+8.2
			Baillie D.S.	LD	4,470	11.3	-13.1
			Slaughter B.E. Ms.	ICP	62	0.2*	+0.2
					15,270	38.5	

GLASGOW, SHETTLESTON [268]

Election	Electors	T'out	Candidate	Party	Votes	% Sh	% Ch
1983	51,955	68.3	Marshall D.*	Lab	19,203	54.2	
			Henderson I.J.	Con	6,787	19.1	
			Strachan S.	Lib	6,568	18.5	
			Hood D.	SNP	2,801	7.9*	
			Hill K.J.	BNP	103	0.3*	
					12,416	35.0	
1987	53,604	70.4	Marshall D.*	Lab	23,991	63.6	+9.4
			Fisher J.M.S.	Con	5,010	13.3	-5.9
			MacVicar J.A.	SNP	4,807	12.7	+4.8
			Clarke P.A.M. Ms.	Lib	3,942	10.4	-8.1
					18,981	50.3	
1992	51,913	68.9	Marshall D.*	Lab	21,665	60.6	-3.0
			Sturgeon N. Ms.	SNP	6,831	19.1	+6.4
			Mortimer N.R.	Con	5,396	15.1	+1.8
			Orskov J.P. Ms.	LD	1,881	5.3	-5.2
					14,834	41.5	

150

GLASGOW, SPRINGBURN [269]

Election	Electors	T'out	Candidate	Party	Votes	% Sh	% Ch
1983	53,373	65.1	Martin M.J.*	Lab	22,481	64.7	
			Kelly J.	Lib	4,882	14.1	
			Tweedie D.	Con	4,565	13.1	
			McLaughlin J.F.	SNP	2,804	8.1*	
					17,599	50.7	
1987	51,563	67.5	Martin M.J.*	Lab	25,617	73.6	+8.9
			O'Hara B.	SNP	3,554	10.2	+2.1
			Call M.	Con	2,870	8.3	-4.9
			Rennie D.	Lib	2,746	7.9	-6.2
					22,063	63.4	
1992	45,831	65.7	Martin M.J.*	Lab	20,369	67.7	-6.0
			Miller S.	SNP	5,863	19.5	+9.3
			Barnett A.	Con	2,625	8.7	+0.5
			Ackland R.	LD	1,242	4.1*	-3.8
					14,506	48.2	

GLOUCESTER [270]

Election	Electors	T'out	Candidate	Party	Votes	% Sh	% Ch
1983	74,268	75.6	Oppenheim S. Ms.*	Con	27,235	48.5	
			Hinds C.W.V.	Lab	14,698	26.2	
			Golder M.D.	SDP	13,499	24.0	
			Waters J.H.	Green	479	0.9*	
			Rhodes R.L.	BNP	260	0.5*	
					12,537	22.3	
1987	76,910	78.1	French D.C.	Con	29,826	49.7	+1.2
			Hulme D.K.	Lab	17,791	29.6	+3.5
			Hilton J.E.	Lib	12,417	20.7	-3.3
					12,035	20.0	
1992	80,626	80.2	French D.C.*	Con	29,870	46.2	-3.5
			Stephens K.E.	Lab	23,801	36.8	+7.2
			Sewell J.M.	LD	10,978	17.0	-3.7
					6,069	9.4	

GLOUCESTERSHIRE WEST [271]

Election	Electors	T'out	Candidate	Party	Votes	% Sh	% Ch
1983	74,266	79.6	Marland P.*	Con	27,092	45.8	
			Watkinson J.T.	SDP	17,440	29.5	
			Hodkinson M.J.	Lab	14,572	24.7	
					9,652	16.3	
1987	77,994	81.1	Marland P.*	Con	29,257	46.2	+0.4
			Sandland-Nielsen P.E.	Lab	17,578	27.8	+3.1
			Watkinson J.T.	SDP	16,440	26.0	-3.5
					11,679	18.5	
1992	80,054	83.8	Marland P.*	Con	29,232	43.6	-2.7
			Organ D.M. Ms.	Lab	24,274	36.2	+8.4
			Boait J.E. Ms.	LD	13,366	19.9	-6.1
			Reeve A.	Ind	172	0.3*	
			Palmer C.R.	Ind	75	0.1*	
					4,958	7.4	

GORDON [272]

Election	Electors	T'out	Candidate	Party	Votes	% Sh	% Ch
1983	65,537	70.1	Bruce M.G.	Lib	20,134	43.8	
			Cran J.D.	Con	19,284	42.0	
			Grant G.	Lab	3,899	8.5*	
			Guild K.J.N.	SNP	2,636	5.7*	
					850	1.8	
1987	73,479	73.7	Bruce M.G.*	Lib	26,770	49.5	+5.6
			Leckie P.R.	Con	17,251	31.9	-10.1
			Morrell M.C. Ms.	Lab	6,228	11.5	+3.0
			Wright G.E.	SNP	3,876	7.2	+1.4
					9,519	17.6	
1992	79,672	74.3	Bruce M.G.*	LD	22,158	37.4	-12.0
			Porter J.A.	Con	21,884	37.0	+5.1
			Adam B.J.	SNP	8,445	14.3	+7.1
			Morrell P.M.	Lab	6,682	11.3	-0.2
					274	0.5	

GOSPORT [273]

Election	Electors	T'out	Candidate	Party	Votes	% Sh	% Ch
1983	64,877	71.6	Viggers P.J.*	Con	28,179	60.6	
			Chegwyn P.J.	Lib	13,728	29.5	
			Bond B.B.	Lab	4,319	9.3*	
			McMillan R.A.	Ind	241	0.5*	
					14,451	31.1	
1987	68,113	74.8	Viggers P.J.*	Con	29,804	58.5	-2.1
			Chegwyn P.J.	Lib	16,081	31.6	+2.0
			Lloyd A.	Lab	5,053	9.9	+0.6
					13,723	26.9	
1992	69,817	76.6	Viggers P.J.*	Con	31,094	58.1	-0.4
			Russell M.G.	LD	14,776	27.6	-3.9
			Angus M.F. Ms.	Lab	7,275	13.6	+3.7
			Ettie P.F.F.	Ind	332	0.6*	
					16,318	30.5	

GOWER [274]

Election	Electors	T'out	Candidate	Party	Votes	% Sh	% Ch
1983	56,693	78.7	Wardell G.L.*	Lab	16,972	38.1	
			Kenyon A.R.T. Dr.	Con	15,767	35.4	
			Jones G.G.	SDP	10,416	23.4	
			Williams N.	PC	1,444	3.2*	
					1,205	2.7	
1987	58,871	80.7	Wardell G.L.*	Lab	22,138	46.6	+8.6
			Price G.A.L.	Con	16,374	34.5	-0.9
			Elliott D.H.O.	SDP	7,645	16.1	-7.3
			Edwards J.G.M.	PC	1,341	2.8*	-0.4
					5,764	12.1	
1992	57,229	81.9	Wardell G.L.*	Lab	23,485	50.1	+3.5
			Donnelly A.L.	Con	16,437	35.1	+0.6
			Davies C.G.	LD	4,655	9.9	-6.2
			Price A.	PC	1,639	3.5*	+0.7
			Kingzett B.	Green	448	1.0*	+1.0
			Egan G.P.	MRLP	114	0.2*	+0.2
			Beresford M.S.	NLP	74	0.2*	+0.2
					7,048	15.0	

153

GRANTHAM [275]

Election	Electors	T'out	Candidate	Party	Votes	% Sh	% Ch
1983	75,047	73.5	Hogg D.M. Hon.*	Con	31,692	57.5	
			Titley S.P.	Lib	12,781	23.2	
			Savage T.E.	Lab	10,677	19.4	
					18,911	34.3	
1987	79,434	75.0	Hogg D.M. Hon.*	Con	33,988	57.1	-0.4
			Heppell J.P.	Lib	12,685	21.3	-1.9
			Gent M.B.	Lab	12,197	20.5	+1.1
			Hewis P.A. Ms.	Green	700	1.2*	+1.2
					21,303	35.8	
1992	83,535†	79.2	Hogg D.M. Hon.*	Con	37,194	56.2	-0.9
			Taggart S.	Lab	17,606	26.6	+6.1
			Heppell J.P.	LD	9,882	14.9	-6.4
			Hiley J.D.	Lib	1,500	2.3*	+2.3
					19,588	29.6	

GRAVESHAM [276]

Election	Electors	T'out	Candidate	Party	Votes	% Sh	% Ch
1983	71,150	77.6	Brinton T.D.*	Con	25,968	47.0	
			Ovenden J.F.	Lab	17,505	31.7	
			Horton M.C.	SDP	10,826	19.6	
			Sewell M.D.	Green	495	0.9*	
			Johnson P.	NF	420	0.8*	
					8,463	15.3	
1987	72,759	79.3	Arnold J.A.	Con	28,891	50.1	+3.0
			Coleman M.A.	Lab	20,099	34.8	+3.1
			Crawford R.I.	Lib	8,724	15.1	-4.5
					8,792	15.2	
1992	70,790	83.4	Arnold J.A.*	Con	29,322	49.7	-0.4
			Green G.A.	Lab	23,829	40.4	+5.5
			Deedman D.R.	LD	5,269	8.9	-6.2
			Bunstone A.J.	Ind	273	0.5*	
			Khilkoff-Boulding R.E.B.	Ind Con	187	0.3*	
			Buxton B.J.	Soc	174	0.3*	+0.3
					5,493	9.3	

154

GREAT GRIMSBY [277]

Election	Electors	T'out	Candidate	Party	Votes	% Sh	% Ch
1983	68,388	73.8	Mitchell A.V.*	Lab	18,330	36.3	
			Hancock C.A.	Con	17,599	34.9	
			Genney P.W.	SDP	14,552	28.8	
					731	1.4	
1987	68,501	75.3	Mitchell A.V.*	Lab	23,463	45.5	+9.2
			Robinson C.F.	Con	14,679	28.4	-6.4
			Genney P.W.	SDP	13,457	26.1	-2.7
					8,784	17.0	
1992	67,427†	75.3	Mitchell A.V.*	Lab	25,897	51.0	+5.5
			Jackson P.	Con	18,391	36.2	+7.8
			Frankish P. Ms.	LD	6,475	12.8	-13.3
					7,506	14.8	

GREAT YARMOUTH [278]

Election	Electors	T'out	Candidate	Party	Votes	% Sh	% Ch
1983	62,809	70.8	Carttiss M.R.H.	Con	22,423	50.4	
			Lloyd O.A.	Lab	11,223	25.2	
			Minett E.D.	Lib	10,803	24.3	
					11,200	25.2	
1987	65,770	74.5	Carttiss M.R.H.*	Con	25,336	51.7	+1.3
			Cannell J.	Lab	15,253	31.1	+5.9
			Maxwell S.D.	SDP	8,387	17.1	-7.2
					10,083	20.6	
1992	68,263†	77.9	Carttiss M.R.H.*	Con	25,505	47.9	-3.8
			Baughan B.J. Ms.	Lab	20,196	38.0	+6.8
			Scott M.J.	LD	7,225	13.6	-3.5
			Larkin P. Ms.	NLP	284	0.5*	+0.5
					5,309	10.0	

Election	Electors	T'out	Candidate	Party	Votes	% Sh	% Ch
1983	59,437	74.2	Godman N.A.	Lab	20,650	46.8	
			Blair A.J.	Lib	16,025	36.3	
			Crichton C.M.M.	Con	4,314	9.8*	
			Clayton A.H.	SNP	2,989	6.8*	
			McKinlay G.T.	WRP	114	0.3*	
					4,625	10.5	
1987	57,756	75.4	Godman N.A.*	Lab	27,848	63.9	+17.1
			Moody J.H.	Lib	7,793	17.9	-18.5
			Pearson T.J.D.	Con	4,199	9.6	-0.1
			Lenehan T.	SNP	3,721	8.5	+1.8
					20,055	46.0	
1992	52,062†	73.7	Godman N.A.*	Lab	22,258	58.0	-5.9
			Black I.	SNP	7,279	19.0	+10.4
			McCullough J.	Con	4,479	11.7	+2.0
			Lambert C.N.D.	LD	4,359	11.4	-6.5
					14,979	39.0	

Election	Electors	T'out	Candidate	Party	Votes	% Sh	% Ch
1983	51,586	67.7	Barnett N.G.*	Lab	13,361	38.2	
			Rolfe A.J.	Con	12,150	34.8	
			Ford T.G.	SDP	8,783	25.1	
			Dell I.B.	BNP	259	0.7*	
			Mallone R.S.	FP	242	0.7*	
			Hook F. Ms.	Comm	149	0.4*	
					1,211	3.5	

[Death]

Election	Electors	T'out	Candidate	Party	Votes	% Sh	% Ch
1987	50,637	68.2	Barnes R.S. Ms.	SDP	18,287	53.0	+27.9
(26/2)			Wood D.F.M. Ms.	Lab	11,676	33.8	-4.5
			Antcliffe J.G.C.	Con	3,852	11.2	-23.6
			Bell G.J.E.	Green	264	0.8*	
			Hardee M.G.	Ind	124	0.3*	
			Dell I.B.	BNP	116	0.3*	-0.4
			Pearce J.A.	NF	103	0.3*	
			Marshall K. Ms.	RCP	91	0.3*	
					6,611	19.2	

Election	Electors	T'out	Candidate	Party	Votes	% Sh	% Ch
1987	50,830	73.4	Barnes.R.S. Ms.	SDP	15,149	40.6	+15.5
			Wood D.F.M. Ms.	Lab	13,008	34.9	-3.4
			Antcliffe J.G.C.	Con	8,695	23.3	-11.5
			Thomas J. Ms.	Green	346	0.9*	+0.9
			Mallone R.S.	FP	59	0.2*	-0.5
			Clinton P. Ms.	Comm	58	0.2*	-0.3
					2,141	5.7	

Election	Electors	T'out	Candidate	Party	Votes	% Sh	% Ch
1992	47,790†	74.6	Raynsford W.R.N.	Lab	14,630	41.0	+6.2
			Barnes R.S. Ms.*	SD	13,273	37.2	-3.4
			McNair A. Ms.	Con	6,960	19.5	-3.8
			McCracken R.H.J.	Green	483	1.4*	+0.4
			Mallone R.S.	FP	147	0.4*	+0.2
			Hardee M.G.	Ind	103	0.3*	
			Small J.D.	NLP	70	0.2*	+0.2
					1,357	3.8	

Barnes contested the election as an Independent Social Democrat but the Liberal Democrats chose not to contest the seat.

GUILDFORD [281]

Election	Electors	T'out	Candidate	Party	Votes	% Sh	% Ch
1983	75,134	72.5	Howell D.A.R.*	Con	30,016	55.1	
			Sharp M.L. Ms.	SDP	18,192	33.4	
			Chesterton K.	Lab	5,853	10.7*	
			Farrell A.	PAL	425	0.8*	
					11,824	21.7	
1987	77,837	75.3	Howell D.A.R.*	Con	32,504	55.5	+0.4
			Sharp M.L. Ms.	SDP	19,897	33.9	+0.6
			Wolverson R.J.	Lab	6,216	10.6	-0.1
					12,607	21.5	
1992	77,265†	78.5	Howell D.A.R.*	Con	33,516	55.3	-0.2
			Sharp M.L. Ms.	LD	20,112	33.2	-0.8
			Mann H.	Lab	6,781	11.2	+0.6
			Law A.S.	NLP	234	0.4*	+0.4
					13,404	22.1	

HACKNEY NORTH AND STOKE NEWINGTON [282]

Election	Electors	T'out	Candidate	Party	Votes	% Sh	% Ch
1983	66,754	54.7	Roberts E.A.C.*	Lab	18,989	52.0	
			Booth V.E.H.	Con	10,444	28.6	
			Ash D.R.	Lib	5,746	15.7	
			Fitzpatrick D.J.	Green	492	1.3*	
			Goldman M.	Comm	426	1.2*	
			Field J.D.	NF	396	1.1*	
					8,545	23.4	
1987	66,771	58.1	Abbott D.J. Ms.	Lab	18,912	48.7	-3.3
			Letwin O.	Con	11,234	28.9	+0.3
			Taylor S.H.	SDP	7,446	19.2	+3.4
			Fitzpatrick D.J.	Green	997	2.6*	+1.2
			Anwar Y.T. Ms.	RF	228	0.6*	+0.6
					7,678	19.8	
1992	56,768	61.2	Abbott D.J. Ms.*	Lab	20,083	57.8	+9.1
			Manson C.D.	Con	9,356	26.9	-2.0
			Fitchett K.E.	LD	3,996	11.5	-7.7
			Hunt H.M. Ms.	Green	1,111	3.2*	+0.6
			Windsor J.G.	NLP	178	0.5*	+0.5
					10,727	30.9	

HACKNEY SOUTH AND SHOREDITCH [283]

Election	Electors	T'out	Candidate	Party	Votes	% Sh	% Ch
1983	71,304	53.9	Sedgemore B.C.J.	Lab	16,721	43.5	
			Croft P.J.P.	Con	8,930	23.2	
			Brown R.W.*	SDP	7,025	18.3	
			Roberts J.D.	Ind Lib	3,724	9.7*	
			Quilty S.J.	Ind Lab	704	1.8*	
			Ashton R.	NF	593	1.5*	
			Tyndall V.D. Ms.	BNP	374	1.0*	
			Green D.	Comm	246	0.6*	
			Goldstein R.D.	WRP	141	0.4*	
					7,791	20.3	
1987	70,873	55.4	Sedgemore B.C.J.*	Lab	18,799	47.8	+4.4
			Brown M.C.N.	Con	11,277	28.7	+5.5
			Roberts J.D.	Lib	8,812	22.4	+4.2
			Green D.	Comm	403	1.0*	+0.4
					7,522	19.1	
1992	60,220	61.4	Sedgemore B.C.J.*	Lab	19,730	53.4	+5.5
			Turner A.J.	Con	10,714	29.0	+0.3
			Wintle G.	LD	5,533	15.0	-7.5
			Lucas L.	Green	772	2.1*	+2.1
			Norman G.L. Ms.	NLP	226	0.6*	+0.6
					9,016	24.4	

HALESOWEN AND STOURBRIDGE [284]

Election	Electors	T'out	Candidate	Party	Votes	% Sh	% Ch
1983	76,403	76.4	Stokes J.H.R.*	Con	28,250	48.4	
			Clitheroe T.W.	SDP	14,934	25.6	
			Ellison C.	Lab	14,611	25.0	
			Rudd D.J.	Green	582	1.0*	
					13,316	22.8	
1987	78,017	79.4	Stokes J.H.R.*	Con	31,037	50.1	+1.7
			Sunter T.J.	Lab	17,229	27.8	+2.8
			Simon D.C.A.	SDP	13,658	22.1	-3.5
					13,808	22.3	
1992	77,644†	82.3	Hawksley P.W.	Con	32,312	50.6	+0.5
			Hankon A.B.	Lab	22,730	35.6	+7.8
			Sharma V.	LD	7,941	12.4	-9.6
			Weller T.	Green	908	1.4*	+1.4
					9,582	15.0	

Election	Electors	T'out	Candidate	Party	Votes	% Sh	% Ch
1983	72,747	75.1	Galley R.	Con	22,321	40.9	
			Summerskill S.C.W. Dr. Hon.‡	Lab	20,452	37.4	
			Cockcroft F.L.	SDP	11,868	21.7	
					1,869	3.4	
1987	73,392	77.7	Mahon A. Ms.	Lab	24,741	43.4	+6.0
			Galley R.*	Con	23,529	41.3	+0.4
			Cockcroft F.L.	SDP	8,758	15.4	-6.4
					1,212	2.1	
1992	73,402†	78.7	Mahon A. Ms.*	Lab	25,115	43.5	+0.1
			Martin T.R.	Con	24,637	42.7	+1.4
			Howell I.R.	LD	7,364	12.7	-2.6
			Pearson R.	Nat	649	1.1*	+1.1
					478	0.8	

HALTON [286]

Election	Electors	T'out	Candidate	Party	Votes	% Sh	% Ch
1983	72,743	73.3	Oakes G.J.*	Lab	24,752	46.4	
			Pedley P.M.	Con	17,923	33.6	
			Tilling T.R.	SDP	10,649	20.0	
					6,829	12.8	
1987	75,801	76.3	Oakes G.J.*	Lab	32,065	55.5	+9.1
			Hardman J.G.	Con	17,487	30.2	-3.4
			Clucas H.F. Ms.	SDP	8,272	14.3	-5.7
					14,578	25.3	
1992	74,909	78.3	Oakes G.J.*	Lab	35,005	59.7	+4.2
			Mercer G.L.	Con	16,821	28.7	-1.6
			Reaper D.	LD	6,104	10.4	-3.9
			Herley S.	MRLP	398	0.7*	+0.7
			Collins N.G. Ms.	NLP	338	0.6*	+0.6
					18,184	31.0	

HAMILTON [287]

Election	Electors	T'out	Candidate	Party	Votes	% Sh	% Ch
1983	61,430	75.7	Robertson G.I.M.*	Lab	24,384	52.4	
			Donaldson S.	Lib	9,365	20.1	
			Scott M. Ms.	Con	8,940	19.2	
			Whitehead M. Ms.	SNP	3,816	8.2*	
					15,019	32.3	
1987	62,205	76.9	Robertson G.I.M.*	Lab	28,563	59.7	+7.2
			Mond G.S.	Con	6,901	14.4	-4.8
			McKay T.	Lib	6,302	13.2	-7.0
			Crossley C.	SNP	6,093	12.7	+4.5
					21,662	45.3	
1992	61,572	76.1	Robertson G.I.M.*	Lab	25,849	55.2	-4.5
			Morrison W.	SNP	9,246	19.7	+7.0
			Mitchell J.M. Ms.	Con	8,250	17.6	+3.2
			Oswald J.	LD	3,515	7.5	-5.7
					16,603	35.4	

HAMMERSMITH [288]

Election	Electors	T'out	Candidate	Party	Votes	% Sh	% Ch
1983	46,178	71.3	Soley C.S.*	Lab	13,645	41.5	
			Mansfield N.E.S.	Con	11,691	35.5	
			Starks M.J.	SDP	4,925	15.0	
			Knott S.H.J.A.	Ind Lib	1,912	5.8*	
			Sutherland D.M. Ms.	Green	325	1.0*	
			Bennett L.E.T. Ms.	NF	250	0.8*	
			Dixon C.L. Ms.	WRP	81	0.2*	
			Dick P.S.	Ind	73	0.2*	
					1,954	5.9	
1987	48,285	72.7	Soley C.S.*	Lab	15,811	45.0	+3.5
			Deva N.J.A.	Con	13,396	38.1	+2.6
			Knott S.H.J.A.	Lib	5,241	14.9	-0.0
			Kirk D.P.	Green	453	1.3*	+0.3
			Fitzpatrick J.F.	RF	125	0.4*	+0.4
			Carrick M.M.A. Ms.	HP	98	0.3*	+0.3
					2,415	6.9	
1992	47,504	71.5	Soley C.S.*	Lab	17,329	51.0	+6.0
			Hennessy J.A.	Con	12,575	37.0	-1.1
			Bates J.H.	LD	3,380	10.0	-5.0
			Crosskey R.S.	Green	546	1.6*	+0.3
			Turner K.A.	NLP	89	0.3*	+0.3
			Szamuely H. Ms.	AFL	41	0.1*	+0.1
					4,754	14.0	

HAMPSHIRE EAST [289]

Election	Electors	T'out	Candidate	Party	Votes	% Sh	% Ch
1983	79,303	74.2	Mates M.J.*	Con	36,968	62.8	
			Bryan R.C. Ms.	Lib	18,641	31.7	
			Cowan S.J.	Lab	3,247	5.5*	
					18,327	31.1	
1987	86,373	77.4	Mates M.J.*	Con	43,093	64.5	+1.7
			Booker R.A.	Lib	19,307	28.9	-2.8
			Lloyd C.C.	Lab	4,443	6.6	+1.1
					23,786	35.6	
1992	93,393	79.3	Mates M.J.*	Con	47,541	64.2	-0.3
			Baring S.M Ms.	LD	18,376	24.8	-4.1
			Phillips J.A.	Lab	6,840	9.2	+2.6
			Foster I.C.	Green	1,113	1.5*	+1.5
			Hale S.L.	Ind	165	0.2*	
					29,165	39.4	

HAMPSHIRE NORTH WEST [290]

Election	Electors	T'out	Candidate	Party	Votes	% Sh	% Ch
1983	65,780	74.4	Mitchell D.B.*	Con	28,044	57.3	
			Willis I.H.	Lib	15,922	32.5	
			Davis M.J.	Lab	4,957	10.1*	
					12,122	24.8	
1987	69,965	77.9	Mitchell D.B.*	Con	31,470	57.8	+0.4
			Willis I.H.	Lib	18,033	33.1	+0.6
			Burnage A.B. Ms.	Lab	4,980	9.1	-1.0
					13,437	24.7	
1992	73,036	80.8	Mitchell D.B.*	Con	34,310	58.1	+0.4
			Simpson M.S.	LD	16,462	27.9	-5.2
			Stockwell M.A.D.	Lab	7,433	12.6	+3.5
			Ashley D.A. Ms.	Green	825	1.4*	+1.4
					17,848	30.2	

HAMPSTEAD AND HIGHGATE [291]

Election	Electors	T'out	Candidate	Party	Votes	% Sh	% Ch
1983	66,554	66.9	Finsberg G.*	Con	18,366	41.2	
			McDonnell J.M.	Lab	14,996	33.7	
			Sofer A. Ms.	SDP	11,038	24.8	
			Stevenson J.V.	Ind	156	0.4*	
					3,370	7.6	
1987	63,301	71.5	Finsberg G. Sir.*	Con	19,236	42.5	+1.3
			Turner P.J.	Lab	17,015	37.6	+3.9
			Sofer A. Ms.	SDP	8,744	19.3	-5.5
			Weiss G.	Ind	137	0.3*	
			Ellis S. Ms.	HP	134	0.3*	+0.3
					2,221	4.9	
1992	58,452	72.7	Jackson G.M. Ms.	Lab	19,193	45.1	+7.6
			Letwin O.	Con	17,753	41.8	-0.7
			Wrede C.D.H.	LD	4,765	11.2	-8.1
			Games S.N.	Green	594	1.4*	+1.4
			Prosser R.D.	NLP	86	0.2*	+0.2
			Wilson C.	Ind	44	0.1*	
			Hall A. Ms.	Ind	44	0.1*	
			Rizz C.	Ind	33	0.1*	
					1,440	3.4	

HARBOROUGH [292]

Election	Electors	T'out	Candidate	Party	Votes	% Sh	% Ch
1983	72,177	75.9	Farr J.A.*	Con	32,957	60.1	
			Swift T.J.	Lib	14,472	26.4	
			Upham M.	Lab	6,285	11.5*	
			Fewster B.	Green	802	1.5*	
			Taylor J.N.	BNP	280	0.5*	
					18,485	33.7	
1987	74,697	79.3	Farr J.A. Sir.*	Con	35,216	59.4	-0.7
			Swift T.J.	Lib	16,406	27.7	+1.3
			Harley P.	Lab	7,646	12.9	+1.4
					18,810	31.7	
1992	76,514†	82.1	Garnier E.H.	Con	34,280	54.6	-4.9
			Cox M.A.	LD	20,737	33.0	+5.3
			Mackay C. Ms.	Lab	7,483	11.9	-1.0
			Irwin A.P.	NLP	328	0.5*	+0.5
					13,543	21.6	

163

HARLOW [293]

Election	Electors	T'out	Candidate	Party	Votes	% Sh	% Ch
1983	69,715	76.5	Hayes J.J.J.	Con	21,924	41.1	
			Newens A.S.*	Lab	18,250	34.2	
			Bastick J.R.	Lib	12,891	24.2	
			Ward J.	Ind Green	266	0.5*	
					3,674	6.9	
1987	70,286	78.4	Hayes J.J.J.*	Con	26,017	47.2	+6.1
			Newens A.S.	Lab	20,140	36.6	+2.4
			Eden-Green M.C. Ms.	SDP	8,915	16.2	-8.0
					5,877	10.7	
1992	69,467	81.6	Hayes J.J.J.*	Con	26,608	47.0	-0.3
			Rammell W.E.	Lab	23,668	41.8	+5.2
			Spenceley L.H. Ms.	LD	6,375	11.3	-4.9
					2,940	5.2	

HARROGATE [294]

Election	Electors	T'out	Candidate	Party	Votes	% Sh	% Ch
1983	72,815	69.0	Banks R.G.*	Con	30,269	60.2	
			Burney J.	SDP	14,381	28.6	
			Dixon J.S.	Lab	5,128	10.2*	
			Kelly D.C.	Ind	316	0.6*	
			Vessey P.	NF	163	0.3*	
					15,888	31.6	
1987	75,761	74.1	Banks R.G.*	Con	31,167	55.6	-4.7
			Leach J.R.	SDP	19,265	34.3	+5.7
			Wright A.J.	Lab	5,671	10.1	-0.1
					11,902	21.2	
1992	76,250†	78.0	Banks R.G.*	Con	32,023	53.9	-1.7
			Hurren T.J.	LD	19,434	32.7	-1.7
			Wright A.J.	Lab	7,230	12.2	+2.0
			Warneken A.F.	Green	780	1.3*	+1.3
					12,589	21.2	

HARROW EAST [295]

Election	Electors	T'out	Candidate	Party	Votes	% Sh	% Ch
1983	79,926	72.5	Dykes H.J.M.*	Con	28,834	49.8	
			Hains D.	Lib	16,166	27.9	
			Brough D.J.	Lab	12,941	22.3	
					12,668	21.9	
1987	81,124	73.4	Dykes H.J.M.*	Con	32,302	54.2	+4.4
			Brough D.J.	Lab	14,029	23.5	+1.2
			Gifford Z. Ms.	Lib	13,251	22.2	-5.7
					18,273	30.7	
1992	74,837	77.7	Dykes H.J.M.*	Con	30,752	52.9	-1.3
			McNulty A.J.	Lab	19,654	33.8	+10.2
			Chamberlain V.M. Ms.	LD	6,360	10.9	-11.3
			Burrows P.J.	Lib	1,142	2.0*	+2.0
			Hamza S.J. Ms.	NLP	212	0.4*	+0.4
			Lester J.C.	AFL	49	0.1*	+0.1
					11,098	19.1	

HARROW WEST [296]

Election	Electors	T'out	Candidate	Party	Votes	% Sh	% Ch
1983	73,151	72.3	Page A.J.*	Con	28,056	53.0	
			Bayliss S.P.	SDP	17,035	32.2	
			Toms A.K.	Lab	7,811	14.8	
					11,021	20.8	
1987	74,041	74.5	Hughes R.G.	Con	30,456	55.2	+2.2
			Bayliss S.P.	SDP	15,012	27.2	-5.0
			Bastin C.	Lab	9,665	17.5	+2.8
					15,444	28.0	
1992	69,675	78.6	Hughes R.G.*	Con	30,240	55.2	-0.0
			Moraes C.A.	Lab	12,343	22.5	+5.0
			Noyce C.D.	LD	11,050	20.2	-7.1
			Aitman G.	Lib	845	1.5*	+1.5
			Argyle J.F.T. Ms.	NLP	306	0.6*	+0.6
					17,897	32.7	

HARTLEPOOL [297]

Election	Electors	T'out	Candidate	Party	Votes	% Sh	% Ch
1983	69,346	69.8	Leadbitter E.*	Lab	22,048	45.5	
			Rogers F.	Con	18,959	39.1	
			Bertram N.	SDP	7,422	15.3	
					3,089	6.4	
1987	68,686	73.0	Leadbitter E.*	Lab	24,296	48.5	+2.9
			Catchpole P.C.	Con	17,007	33.9	-5.2
			Preece A.	Lib	7,047	14.1	-1.3
			Cameron I.J.H.	Ind	1,786	3.6*	
					7,289	14.5	
1992	67,969†	76.1	Mandelson P.B.	Lab	26,816	51.9	+3.4
			Robb G.M.	Con	18,034	34.9	+1.0
			Cameron I.J.H.	LD	6,860	13.3	-0.8
					8,782	17.0	

HARWICH [298]

Election	Electors	T'out	Candidate	Party	Votes	% Sh	% Ch
1983	72,179	70.2	Ridsdale J.E. Sir.*	Con	27,422	54.1	
			Goodenough R.M.	Lib	14,920	29.5	
			Knight R.	Lab	8,302	16.4	
					12,502	24.7	
1987	77,149	73.5	Ridsdale J.E. Sir.*	Con	29,344	51.8	-2.4
			Lynne E. Ms.	Lib	17,262	30.5	+1.0
			Knight R.	Lab	9,920	17.5	+1.1
			Humphrey C.A.	Ind	161	0.3*	
					12,082	21.3	
1992	80,261†	77.7	Sproat I.M.	Con	32,369	51.9	+0.1
			Bevan P.A. Ms.	LD	15,210	24.4	-6.1
			Knight R.	Lab	14,511	23.3	+5.8
			McGrath E.P. Ms.	NLP	279	0.4*	+0.4
					17,159	27.5	

HASTINGS AND RYE [299]

Election	Electors	T'out	Candidate	Party	Votes	% Sh	% Ch
1983	69,747	68.9	Warren K.R.*	Con	25,626	53.3	
			Amies D.J.	Lib	14,646	30.5	
			Knowles N.	Lab	7,304	15.2	
			McNally G.L.	Ind	503	1.0*	
					10,980	22.8	
1987	72,758	71.8	Warren K.R.*	Con	26,163	50.1	-3.2
			Amies D.J.	Lib	18,816	36.0	+5.6
			Hurcombe J. Ms.	Lab	6,825	13.1	-2.1
			Tiverton D.H.	MRLP	242	0.5*	+0.5
			Davies S.P.	Ind	194	0.4*	
					7,347	14.1	
1992	71,839†	74.9	Lait J.A.H. Ms.	Con	25,573	47.6	-2.5
			Palmer M.E.	LD	18,939	35.2	-0.8
			Stevens R.D.	Lab	8,458	15.7	+2.7
			Phillips M.S. Ms.	Green	640	1.2*	+1.2
			Howell D.	MRLP	168	0.3*	-0.2
					6,634	12.3	

HAVANT [300]

Election	Electors	T'out	Candidate	Party	Votes	% Sh	% Ch
1983	73,096	72.1	Lloyd I.S.*	Con	29,148	55.3	
			Cleaver E.E. Ms.	SDP	17,192	32.6	
			Norris R.J.	Lab	6,335	12.0*	
					11,956	22.7	
1987	76,344	74.6	Lloyd I.S. Sir.*	Con	32,527	57.1	+1.8
			Cleaver E.E. Ms.	SDP	16,017	28.1	-4.5
			Phillips J.A.	Lab	8,030	14.1	+2.1
			Fuller G.W.	Ind	373	0.7*	
					16,510	29.0	
1992	74,245	79.0	Willetts D.L.	Con	32,233	55.0	-2.2
			Van Hagen S.F.	LD	14,649	25.0	-3.1
			Morris G.R.J.	Lab	10,968	18.7	+4.6
			Mitchell T.A.F.	Green	793	1.4*	+1.4
					17,584	30.0	

HAYES AND HARLINGTON [301]

Election	Electors	T'out	Candidate	Party	Votes	% Sh	% Ch
1983	57,620	70.9	Dicks T.P.	Con	16,451	40.3	
			Fagan P.F.	Lab	12,217	29.9	
			Sandelson N.D.*	SDP	11,842	29.0	
			Hill F.	Ind	324	0.8*	
					4,234	10.4	
1987	58,240	74.5	Dicks T.P.*	Con	21,355	49.2	+8.9
			Fagan P.F.	Lab	15,390	35.5	+5.6
			Slipman S. Ms.	SDP	6,641	15.3	-13.7
					5,965	13.7	
1992	55,024	78.9	Dicks T.P.*	Con	19,489	44.9	-4.3
			McDonnell J.M.	Lab	19,436	44.8	+9.3
			Little A.J.	LD	4,472	10.3	-5.0
					53	0.1	

HAZEL GROVE [302]

Election	Electors	T'out	Candidate	Party	Votes	% Sh	% Ch
1983	63,631	77.2	Arnold T.R.*	Con	22,627	46.1	
			Vos A.M.	Lib	20,605	41.9	
			Comyn-Platt J.	Lab	5,895	12.0*	
					2,022	4.1	
1987	65,717	81.6	Arnold T.R.*	Con	24,396	45.5	-0.6
			Vos A.M.	Lib	22,556	42.0	+0.1
			Ford J.G.	Lab	6,354	11.8	-0.2
			Chapman F.K. Ms.	Green	346	0.6*	+0.6
					1,840	3.4	
1992	64,300†	85.0	Arnold T.R.*	Con	24,479	44.8	-0.7
			Stunell R.A.	LD	23,550	43.1	+1.1
			MacAlister C.D.	Lab	6,390	11.7	-0.1
			Penn M.S.	NLP	204	0.4*	+0.4
					929	1.7	

HEMSWORTH [303]

Election	Electors	T'out	Candidate	Party	Votes	% Sh	% Ch
1983	54,323	68.6	Woodall A.*	Lab	22,081	59.3	
			Wooffindin J.D.	Lib	7,891	21.2	
			Williamson D.R.	Con	7,291	19.6	
					14,190	38.1	
1987	54,951	75.7	Buckley G.J.	Lab	27,859	67.0	+7.7
			Garnier E.H.	Con	7,159	17.2	-2.4
			Wooffindin J.D.	Lib	6,568	15.8	-5.4
					20,700	49.8	

[Death]

Election	Electors	T'out	Candidate	Party	Votes	% Sh	% Ch
1991 (7/11)	56,247	42.6	Enright D.A.	Lab	15,895	66.3	-0.7
			Megson V. Ms.	LD	4,808	20.1	+4.3
			Harrison G.	Con	2,512	10.5	-6.7
			Ablett P.A.	Ind Lab	648	2.7*	
			Smith T.J.	Ind	108	0.5*	
					11,087	46.2	
1992	55,696	75.9	Enright D.A.	Lab	29,942	70.8	+3.8
			Harrison G.	Con	7,867	18.6	+1.4
			Megson V. Ms.	LD	4,459	10.5	-5.2
					22,075	52.2	

[Death]

Election	Electors	T'out	Candidate	Party	Votes	% Sh	% Ch
1996 (1/2)	55,745	39.5	Trickett J.	Lab	15,817	71.9	+1.1
			Hazell N.J.	Con	1,942	8.8	-9.8
			Ridgway D.	LD	1,516	6.9	-3.7
			Nixon B. Ms.	SLP	1,193	5.4	
			Sutch D.E.	MRLP	652	3.0*	
			Davies P.	UKI	455	2.1*	
			Alexander P. Ms.	Green	157	0.7*	
			Cooper M.	ND	111	0.5*	
			Thomas M.	Ind	122	0.6*	
			Leighton D. Ms.	NLP	28	0.6*	
					13,875	63.1	

HENDON NORTH [304]

Election	Electors	T'out	Candidate	Party	Votes	% Sh	% Ch
1983	54,505	67.9	Gorst J.M.*	Con	18,449	49.8	
			Craig K.A.	SDP	9,474	25.6	
			Williams A.M.	Lab	8,786	23.7	
			Franklin B.F.	Nat	194	0.5*	
			Clayton R.C.	Ind	116	0.3*	
					8,975	24.2	
1987	55,095	65.8	Gorst J.M.*	Con	20,155	55.6	+5.8
			Manson J.R. Ms.	Lab	9,223	25.5	+1.7
			Davies E.J. Ms.	SDP	6,859	18.9	-6.7
					10,932	30.2	
1992	51,514†	75.1	Gorst J.M.*	Con	20,569	53.2	-2.4
			Hill D.J.	Lab	13,447	34.8	+9.3
			Kemp P.	LD	4,136	10.7	-8.2
			Duncan P.A. Ms.	Green	430	1.1*	+1.1
			Orr P.A. Ms.	NLP	95	0.2*	+0.2
					7,122	18.4	

HENDON SOUTH [305]

Election	Electors	T'out	Candidate	Party	Votes	% Sh	% Ch
1983	53,929	65.3	Thomas P.J.M.*	Con	17,115	48.6	
			Palmer M.E.	Lib	10,682	30.3	
			Neall D.N. Ms.	Lab	7,415	21.1	
					6,433	18.3	
1987	54,560	63.8	Marshall J.L.	Con	19,341	55.5	+6.9
			Palmer M.E.	Lib	8,217	23.6	-6.7
			Christian L.H. Ms.	Lab	7,261	20.9	-0.2
					11,124	31.9	
1992	48,401†	72.4	Marshall J.L.*	Con	20,593	58.8	+3.2
			Lloyd L. Ms.	Lab	8,546	24.4	+3.5
			Cohen J.B.	LD	5,609	16.0	-7.6
			Leslie J.	NLP	289	0.8*	+0.8
					12,047	34.4	

HENLEY [306]

Election	Electors	T'out	Candidate	Party	Votes	% Sh	% Ch
1983	62,120	72.9	Heseltine M.R.D.*	Con	27,039	59.7	
			Brook I.B.	Lib	13,258	29.3	
			Roxburgh I.E.	Lab	4,282	9.5*	
			Johnson R. Ms.	WFLOE	517	1.1*	
			Rogers T.E.	Ind Con	213	0.5*	
					13,781	30.4	
1987	65,443	74.9	Heseltine M.R.D.*	Con	29,978	61.1	+1.4
			Madeley J.	Lib	12,896	26.3	-3.0
			Barber M.B.	Lab	6,173	12.6	+3.1
					17,082	34.8	
1992	64,698†	79.8	Heseltine M.R.D.*	Con	30,835	59.7	-1.4
			Turner D.G.	LD	12,443	24.1	-2.2
			Russell-Swinnerton I.J.	Lab	7,676	14.9	+2.3
			Plane A.S.	Ind	431	0.8*	
			Banerji S.A. Ms.	NLP	274	0.5*	+0.5
					18,392	35.6	

HEREFORD [307]

Election	Electors	T'out	Candidate	Party	Votes	% Sh	% Ch
1983	64,051	75.8	Shepherd C.R.*	Con	23,334	48.1	
			Green C.F.	Lib	21,057	43.4	
			Evans J.R.P.	Lab	3,690	7.6*	
			Murray V.C. Ms.	Green	463	1.0*	
					2,277	4.7	
1987	67,075	78.0	Shepherd C.R.*	Con	24,865	47.5	-0.6
			Green C.F.	Lib	23,452	44.8	+1.4
			Woodell V.S.	Lab	4,031	7.7	+0.1
					1,413	2.7	
1992	69,686†	81.3	Shepherd C.R.*	Con	26,727	47.2	-0.3
			Jones G.G.	LD	23,314	41.2	-3.6
			Kelly J.E. Ms.	Lab	6,005	10.6	+2.9
			Mattingly C.T.	Green	596	1.1*	+1.1
					3,413	6.0	

171

HERTFORD AND STORTFORD [308]

Election	Electors	T'out	Candidate	Party	Votes	% Sh	% Ch
1983	68,615	75.6	Wells P.B.*	Con	29,039	56.0	
			Wotherspoon R.E.	SDP	16,110	31.0	
			Carr J.A.	Lab	6,203	12.0*	
			Wiles G.J.	BNP	314	0.6*	
			Cullen P.B.	Ind	221	0.4*	
					12,929	24.9	
1987	75,508	77.7	Wells P.B.*	Con	33,763	57.5	+1.6
			Wotherspoon R.E.	SDP	16,623	28.3	-2.7
			Sumner P.R.E. Ms.	Lab	7,494	12.8	+0.8
			Cole G.C.	Green	814	1.4*	+1.4
					17,140	29.2	
1992	76,655†	81.0	Wells P.B.*	Con	35,716	57.5	-0.0
			White C.J.	LD	15,506	25.0	-3.4
			Bovaird A.J.	Lab	10,125	16.3	+3.5
			Goth J.A.	Green	780	1.3*	-0.1
					20,210	32.5	

HERTFORDSHIRE NORTH [309]

Election	Electors	T'out	Candidate	Party	Votes	% Sh	% Ch
1983	75,439	79.2	Stewart B.H.I.H.*	Con	29,302	49.0	
			Binney G.W.	Lib	19,359	32.4	
			Reilly J.	Lab	11,104	18.6	
					9,943	16.6	
1987	78,694	81.1	Stewart B.H.I.H.*	Con	31,750	49.7	+0.7
			Binney G.W.	Lib	20,308	31.8	-0.6
			Gorst A.B.	Lab	11,782	18.5	-0.1
					11,442	17.9	
1992	80,086	84.4	Heald O.	Con	33,679	49.8	+0.1
			Liddle R.J.	LD	17,148	25.4	-6.4
			Bissett Johnson S.J. Ms.	Lab	16,449	24.3	+5.9
			Irving B.J.R.	NLP	339	0.5*	+0.5
					16,531	24.4	

HERTFORDSHIRE SOUTH WEST [310]

Election	Electors	T'out	Candidate	Party	Votes	% Sh	% Ch
1983	74,371	75.8	Page R.L.*	Con	30,217	53.6	
			Blair I.M.	Lib	18,023	32.0	
			Playfair E.	Lab	7,818	13.9	
			Lupton M.E.	Ind	307	0.5*	
					12,194	21.6	
1987	75,452	77.9	Page R.L.*	Con	32,791	55.8	+2.2
			Blair I.M.	Lib	17,007	28.9	-3.0
			Willmore I.	Lab	8,966	15.3	+1.4
					15,784	26.9	
1992	70,913	83.7	Page R.L.*	Con	33,825	57.0	+1.2
			Shaw A. Ms.	LD	13,718	23.1	-5.8
			Gale A.P.	Lab	11,512	19.4	+4.1
			Adamson C.J.	NLP	281	0.5*	+0.5
					20,107	33.9	

HERTFORDSHIRE WEST [311]

Election	Electors	T'out	Candidate	Party	Votes	% Sh	% Ch
1983	76,597	79.5	Jones R.B.	Con	28,436	46.7	
			Hollinghurst N.A.	SDP	18,860	31.0	
			Boateng P.Y.	Lab	13,583	22.3	
					9,576	15.7	
1987	79,159	80.7	Jones R.B.*	Con	31,760	49.7	+3.0
			Hollinghurst N.A.	SDP	16,836	26.3	-4.6
			McBrearty A.	Lab	15,317	24.0	+1.7
					14,924	23.4	
1992	78,554	82.4	Jones R.B.*	Con	33,340	51.5	+1.8
			McNally M.E. Ms.	Lab	19,400	30.0	+6.0
			Trevett M.J.	LD	10,464	16.2	-10.2
			Hannaway J.	Green	674	1.0*	+1.0
			McAuley J.C.	NF	665	1.0*	+1.0
			Harvey G.G.	NLP	175	0.3*	+0.3
					13,940	21.5	

HERTSMERE [312]

Election	Electors	T'out	Candidate	Party	Votes	% Sh	% Ch
1983	72,997	73.7	Parkinson C.E.*	Con	28,628	53.2	
			Gifford Z. Ms.	Lib	13,758	25.6	
			Reed I.D.D.	Lab	10,315	19.2	
			Parkinson R.W.	Ind Con	1,116	2.1*	
					14,870	27.6	
1987	73,367	75.4	Parkinson C.E.*	Con	31,278	56.6	+3.4
			Brass L.S.	Lib	13,172	23.8	-1.7
			Ward F.	Lab	10,835	19.6	+0.4
					18,106	32.8	
1992	69,952†	80.9	Clappison W. J.	Con	32,133	56.8	+0.2
			Souter D.N.	Lab	13,398	23.7	+4.1
			Gifford Z. Ms.	LD	10,681	18.9	-4.9
			Harding D.M. Ms.	NLP	373	0.7*	+0.7
					18,735	33.1	

HEXHAM [313]

Election	Electors	T'out	Candidate	Party	Votes	% Sh	% Ch
1983	54,341	76.4	Rippon A.G.F.*	Con	21,374	51.5	
			Robson E.M.	Lib	13,066	31.5	
			Byers S.J.	Lab	7,056	17.0	
					8,308	20.0	
1987	56,360	80.0	Amos A.T.	Con	22,370	49.6	-1.9
			Robson E.M.	Lib	14,304	31.7	+0.2
			Wood M.R.	Lab	8,103	18.0	+1.0
			Wood S.M. Ms.	Green	336	0.7*	+0.7
					8,066	17.9	
1992	57,812†	82.4	Atkinson P.L.	Con	24,967	52.4	+2.8
			Swithenbank I.C.F.	Lab	11,529	24.2	+6.2
			Wallace J.C.	LD	10,344	21.7	-10.0
			Hartshorne J.P.	Green	781	1.6*	+0.9
					13,438	28.2	

HEYWOOD AND MIDDLETON [314]

Election	Electors	T'out	Candidate	Party	Votes	% Sh	% Ch
1983	59,870	69.9	Callaghan J.*	Lab	18,111	43.3	
			Hodgson C.M. Ms.	Con	14,137	33.8	
			Rumbelow A.A.	SDP	9,262	22.1	
			Henderson K.	BNP	316	0.8*	
					3,974	9.5	
1987	59,475	73.8	Callaghan J.*	Lab	21,900	49.9	+6.6
			Walker R.E.	Con	15,052	34.3	+0.5
			Greenhalgh I.	SDP	6,953	15.8	-6.3
					6,848	15.6	
1992	57,177†	74.9	Callaghan J.*	Lab	22,380	52.3	+2.4
			Ollerenshaw E.	Con	14,306	33.4	-0.9
			Taylor M.B.	LD	5,252	12.3	-3.6
			Burke P.	Lib	757	1.8*	+1.8
			Scott A.M. Ms.	NLP	134	0.3*	+0.3
					8,074	18.9	

HIGH PEAK [315]

Election	Electors	T'out	Candidate	Party	Votes	% Sh	% Ch
1983	67,358	78.5	Hawkins C.J.	Con	24,534	46.4	
			Marquand D.I.	SDP	14,594	27.6	
			Wilcox D.J.	Lab	13,755	26.0	
					9,940	18.8	
1987	69,927	80.5	Hawkins C.J.*	Con	25,715	45.7	-0.7
			McCrindle J. Ms.	Lab	16,199	28.8	+2.8
			Oldham J. Dr.	SDP	14,389	25.6	-2.0
					9,516	16.9	
1992	70,793†	84.6	Hendry C.	Con	27,538	46.0	+0.3
			Levitt T.	Lab	22,719	37.9	+9.1
			Molloy S.P.	LD	8,861	14.8	-10.8
			Floyd R.	Green	794	1.3*	+1.3
					4,819	8.0	

HOLBORN AND ST. PANCRAS [316]

Election	Electors	T'out	Candidate	Party	Votes	% Sh	% Ch
1983	71,604	60.2	Dobson F.G.*	Lab	20,486	47.5	
			Kerpel A.R.	Con	13,227	30.7	
			Jones W.T.	Lib	9,242	21.4	
			Price R.	WRP	155	0.4*	
					7,259	16.8	
1987	70,589	64.3	Dobson F.G.*	Lab	22,966	50.6	+3.1
			Luff P.J.	Con	14,113	31.1	+0.4
			McGrath S.	Lib	7,994	17.6	-3.8
			Gavan M.J.	RF	300	0.7*	+0.7
					8,853	19.5	
1992	64,794	62.7	Dobson F.G.*	Lab	22,243	54.8	+4.1
			McHallam A.J.	Con	11,419	28.1	-3.0
			Horne-Roberts J. Ms.	LD	5,476	13.5	-4.1
			Wolf-Light P.	Green	959	2.4*	+2.4
			Hersey M.K.	NLP	212	0.5*	+0.5
			Headicar R.	Soc	175	0.4*	+0.4
			Lewis N.	Ind	133	0.3*	
					10,824	26.6	

HOLLAND WITH BOSTON [317]

Election	Electors	T'out	Candidate	Party	Votes	% Sh	% Ch
1983	63,562	71.0	Body R.B.F.S.*	Con	24,962	55.3	
			Le Brun C. Ms.	Lib	13,226	29.3	
			Moore J.F.A.	Lab	6,970	15.4	
					11,736	26.0	
1987	65,539	72.3	Body R.B.F.S. Sir.*	Con	27,412	57.9	+2.6
			Le Brun C. Ms.	Lib	9,817	20.7	-8.6
			Hough J.D.	Lab	9,734	20.5	+5.1
			James D.	Ind	405	0.9*	
					17,595	37.1	
1992	67,900	77.9	Body R.B.F.S. Sir.*	Con	29,159	55.1	-2.8
			Hough J.D.	Lab	15,328	29.0	+8.4
			Ley N.J.	LD	8,434	15.9	-4.8
					13,831	26.1	

HONITON [318]

Election	Electors	T'out	Candidate	Party	Votes	% Sh	% Ch
1983	72,237	74.5	Emery P.F.H. Sir.*	Con	32,602	60.6	
			Sampson A.H.	SDP	17,833	33.1	
			Sharpe R.A.C.	Lab	3,377	6.3*	
					14,769	27.4	
1987	77,259	76.4	Emery P.F.H. Sir.*	Con	34,931	59.2	-1.4
			Tatton-Brown G.D.	SDP	18,369	31.1	-2.0
			Pollentine S.P.	Lab	4,988	8.4	+2.2
			Hughes S.B.F.	MRLP	747	1.3*	+1.3
					16,562	28.1	
1992	79,224†	80.7	Emery P.F.H. Sir.*	Con	33,533	52.4	-6.7
			Sharratt J.M. Ms.	LD	17,022	26.6	-4.5
			Davison R.	Lab	8,142	12.7	+4.3
			Owen D.A.	Ind Con	2,175	3.4*	
			Hughes S.B.F.	RLGG	1,442	2.3*	+2.3
			Halliwell G.J.	Lib	1,005	1.6*	+1.6
			Tootill A.J.	Green	650	1.0*	+1.0
					16,511	25.8	

HORNCHURCH [319]

Election	Electors	T'out	Candidate	Party	Votes	% Sh	% Ch
1983	61,741	73.7	Squire R.C.*	Con	21,393	47.0	
			Williams A.R.	Lab	12,209	26.8	
			Martin J.	SDP	11,251	24.7	
			Joyce A.M. Ms.	NF	402	0.9*	
			Crowson K.M.	Green	219	0.5*	
					9,184	20.2	
1987	62,397	75.3	Squire R.C.*	Con	24,039	51.2	+4.1
			Williams A.R.	Lab	13,345	28.4	+1.5
			Long M.L.C.	Lib	9,609	20.4	-4.3
					10,694	22.8	
1992	60,484	79.8	Squire R.C.*	Con	25,817	53.5	+2.3
			Cooper L.A. Ms.	Lab	16,652	34.5	+6.1
			Oddy B.J.	LD	5,366	11.1	-9.3
			Matthews T.F.	SD	453	0.9*	+0.9
					9,165	19.0	

HORNSEY AND WOOD GREEN [320]

Election	Electors	T'out	Candidate	Party	Votes	% Sh	% Ch
1983	73,870	71.2	Rossi H.A.L.*	Con	22,323	42.4	
			Veness V.A. Ms.	Lab	18,424	35.0	
			Burrell M.I.	SDP	10,995	20.9	
			Lang P.S.I.	Green	854	1.6*	
					3,899	7.4	
1987	80,594	73.3	Rossi H.A.L. Sir.*	Con	25,397	43.0	+0.5
			Roche B.M. Ms.	Lab	23,618	40.0	+4.9
			Eden D.	SDP	8,928	15.1	-5.8
			Crosbie E.M. Ms.	Green	1,154	2.0*	+0.3
					1,779	3.0	
1992	73,668	75.7	Roche B.M. Ms.	Lab	27,020	48.5	+8.5
			Boff A.	Con	21,843	39.2	-3.8
			Dunphy P.G.	LD	5,547	10.0	-5.2
			Crosbie E.M. Ms.	Green	1,051	1.9*	-0.1
			Davies P.R.G.	NLP	197	0.4*	+0.4
			Massey W.	RCP	89	0.2*	+0.2
					5,177	9.3	

HORSHAM [321]

Election	Electors	T'out	Candidate	Party	Votes	% Sh	% Ch
1983	80,407	74.5	Hordern P.M.*	Con	37,897	63.2	
			Archibald G.C.	SDP	16,112	26.9	
			Ward G.R.	Lab	4,999	8.3*	
			Spurrier P.H.	Green	925	1.5*	
					21,785	36.3	
1987	81,574	76.6	Hordern P.M. Sir.*	Con	39,775	63.7	+0.4
			Pearce J. Ms.	SDP	15,868	25.4	-1.5
			Shrimpton M.	Lab	5,435	8.7	+0.4
			Metheringham T.E.	Green	1,383	2.2*	+0.7
					23,907	38.3	
1992	84,159†	81.3	Hordern P.M. Sir.*	Con	42,210	61.7	-2.0
			Stainton J.M. Ms.	LD	17,138	25.1	-0.3
			Uwins S.P.P.	Lab	6,745	9.9	+1.2
			Elliott J.A. Ms.	Lib	1,281	1.9*	+1.9
			King T.J.	Green	692	1.0*	-1.2
			Duggan J.J.	Ind	332	0.5*	
					25,072	36.7	

HOUGHTON AND WASHINGTON [322]

Election	Electors	T'out	Candidate	Party	Votes	% Sh	% Ch
1983	75,686	66.9	Boyes R.	Lab	26,168	51.7	
			Kenyon R.F.	SDP	12,347	24.4	
			Vane W.R.F. Hon.	Con	12,104	23.9	
					13,821	27.3	
1987	77,906	71.2	Boyes R.*	Lab	32,805	59.1	+7.4
			Callanan M.J.	Con	12,612	22.7	-1.2
			Kenyon R.F.	SDP	10,090	18.2	-6.2
					20,193	36.4	
1992	79,326†	70.6	Boyes R.*	Lab	34,733	62.0	+2.9
			Tyrie A.G.	Con	13,925	24.9	+2.1
			Dumpleton O.	LD	7,346	13.1	-5.1
					20,808	37.2	

HOVE [323]

Election	Electors	T'out	Candidate	Party	Votes	% Sh	% Ch
1983	71,918	65.8	Sainsbury T.A.D. Hon.*	Con	28,628	60.5	
			Beamish T.J.V. Ms.	Lib	11,409	24.1	
			Wright C.	Lab	6,550	13.8	
			Layton T.A.	Ind	524	1.1*	
			Lillie K.H.	Ind	189	0.4*	
					17,219	36.4	
1987	72,626	67.8	Sainsbury T.A.D. Hon.*	Con	28,952	58.8	-1.7
			Collins M.E. Ms.	SDP	10,734	21.8	-2.3
			Turner D.K.	Lab	9,010	18.3	+4.5
			Layton T.A.	Ind	522	1.1*	
					18,218	37.0	
1992	67,566	74.1	Sainsbury T.A.D. Hon.*	Con	24,525	49.0	-9.9
			Turner D.K.	Lab	12,257	24.5	+6.2
			Jones A.F. Ms.	LD	9,709	19.4	-2.4
			Furness J.N.P.	Ind Con	2,658	5.3	
			Sinclair G.S.	Green	814	1.6*	+1.6
			Morrilly J.H.	NLP	126	0.3*	+0.3
					12,268	24.5	

HUDDERSFIELD [324]

Election	Electors	T'out	Candidate	Party	Votes	% Sh	% Ch
1983	68,174	71.1	Sheerman B.J.*	Lab	20,051	41.4	
			Tweddle J.W.	Con	16,096	33.2	
			Hasler K.J.L. Ms.	Lib	12,027	24.8	
			Hirst H.	Ind	271	0.6*	
					3,955	8.2	
1987	66,413	75.5	Sheerman B.J.*	Lab	23,019	45.9	+4.5
			Hawkins N.J.	Con	15,741	31.4	-1.9
			Smithson J.R.	Lib	10,773	21.5	-3.4
			Harvey N.A.L.	Green	638	1.3*	+1.3
					7,278	14.5	
1992	67,574	72.4	Sheerman B.J.*	Lab	23,832	48.7	+2.9
			Kenyon J.M. Ms.	Con	16,574	33.9	+2.5
			Denham A.E. Ms.	LD	7,777	15.9	-5.6
			Harvey N.A.L.	Green	576	1.2*	-0.1
			Cran M.	NLP	135	0.3*	+0.3
					7,258	14.8	

HULL EAST [325]

Election	Electors	T'out	Candidate	Party	Votes	% Sh	% Ch
1983	70,037	67.6	Prescott J.L.*	Lab	23,615	49.9	
			Leng D.B.	Con	13,541	28.6	
			Gurevitch A.C. Ms.	Lib	10,172	21.5	
					10,074	21.3	
1987	68,657	70.6	Prescott J.L.*	Lab	27,287	56.3	+6.4
			Jackson P.	Con	12,598	26.0	-2.6
			Wright T.J.	Lib	8,572	17.7	-3.8
					14,689	30.3	
1992	69,078	69.3	Prescott J.L.*	Lab	30,096	62.9	+6.6
			Fareham J.L.	Con	11,373	23.8	-2.2
			Wastling J.H.	LD	6,050	12.6	-5.0
			Kinzell C.	NLP	323	0.7*	+0.7
					18,723	39.1	

HULL NORTH [326]

Election	Electors	T'out	Candidate	Party	Votes	% Sh	% Ch
1983	74,543	67.5	McNamara J.K.*	Lab	21,365	42.5	
			Hayward C.M.	Con	15,337	30.5	
			Smith T.A.	SDP	13,381	26.6	
			Tenney R.I.	Nat	222	0.4*	
					6,028	12.0	
1987	73,288	69.6	McNamara J.K.*	Lab	26,123	51.2	+8.7
			O'Brien A. Ms.	Con	13,954	27.3	-3.1
			Unwin S.W.	SDP	10,962	21.5	-5.1
					12,169	23.8	
1992	71,395	66.7	McNamara J.K.*	Lab	26,619	55.9	+4.7
			Coleman B.G.	Con	11,235	23.6	-3.7
			Meadowcroft A.P.	LD	9,504	20.0	-1.5
			Richardson G.P.	NLP	254	0.5*	+0.5
					15,384	32.3	

HULL WEST [327]

Election	Electors	T'out	Candidate	Party	Votes	% Sh	% Ch
1983	57,702	63.5	Randall S.J.	Lab	15,361	41.9	
			Humphrys M.R.C.	Con	11,707	31.9	
			Unwin S.W.	SDP	9,575	26.1	
					3,654	10.0	
1987	55,636	67.6	Randall S.J.*	Lab	19,527	51.9	+10.0
			Humphrys M.R.C.	Con	11,397	30.3	-1.6
			Bond M.A.	SDP	6,669	17.7	-8.4
					8,130	21.6	
1992	56,136	65.7	Randall S.J.*	Lab	21,139	57.3	+5.4
			Stewart D.M.	Con	10,554	28.6	-1.7
			Tress R.D.	LD	4,867	13.2	-4.5
			Franklin B.J.	NLP	308	0.8*	+0.8
					10,585	28.7	

HUNTINGDON [328]

Election	Electors	T'out	Candidate	Party	Votes	% Sh	% Ch
1983	76,668	71.6	Major J.R.*	Con	34,254	62.4	
			Gatiss S.J. Ms.	Lib	13,906	25.3	
			Slater M.	Lab	6,317	11.5*	
			Eiloart T.M.B.	Green	444	0.8*	
					20,348	37.0	
1987	86,186	74.0	Major J.R.*	Con	40,530	63.6	+1.2
			Nicholson A.J.	SDP	13,486	21.1	-4.2
			Brown D.M.	Lab	8,883	13.9	+2.4
			Lavin W.B.	Green	874	1.4*	+0.6
					27,044	42.4	
1992	92,914†	79.2	Major J.R.*	Con	48,662	66.2	+2.6
			Seckleman H.A	Lab	12,432	16.9	+3.0
			Duff A.N.	LD	9,386	12.8	-8.4
			Wiggin P.D.	Lib	1,045	1.4*	+1.4
			Birkhead D.M. Ms.	Green	846	1.2*	-0.2
			Sutch D.E.	MRLP	728	1.0*	+1.0
			Flanagan M.A.	Ind Con	231	0.3*	
			Buckethead L.	Ind	107	0.1*	
			Cockell C.S.	Ind	91	0.1*	
			Shepheard D.	NLP	26	0.0*	+0.0
					36,230	49.3	

HYNDBURN [329]

Election	Electors	T'out	Candidate	Party	Votes	% Sh	% Ch
1983	59,341	77.4	Hargreaves J.K.	Con	19,405	42.2	
			Davidson A.*	Lab	19,384	42.2	
			Bridgen J.	SDP	6,716	14.6	
			Smith F.	Green	266	0.6*	
			Gateson P.	Ind	169	0.4*	
					21	0.0	
1987	60,529	80.5	Hargreaves J.K.*	Con	21,606	44.4	+2.1
			Coombes K.C.	Lab	19,386	39.8	-2.4
			Strak J.	SDP	7,423	15.2	+0.6
			Smith F.	Green	297	0.6*	+0.0
					2,220	4.6	
1992	58,560	83.9	Pope G.J.	Lab	23,042	46.9	+7.1
			Hargreaves J.K.*	Con	21,082	42.9	-1.5
			Stars Y. Ms.	LD	4,886	9.9	-5.3
			Whittle S.J.	NLP	150	0.3*	+0.3
					1,960	4.0	

ILFORD NORTH [330]

Election	Electors	T'out	Candidate	Party	Votes	% Sh	% Ch
1983	60,248	71.3	Bendall V.W.H.*	Con	22,042	51.3	
			Gapes M.J.	Lab	10,841	25.2	
			Roxburgh I.W.	SDP	10,052	23.4	
					11,201	26.1	
1987	60,433	72.6	Bendall V.W.H.*	Con	24,110	54.9	+3.6
			Jeater P.F.	Lab	12,020	27.4	+2.1
			Tobbell G.	SDP	7,757	17.7	-5.7
					12,090	27.5	
1992	58,695	77.9	Bendall V.W.H.*	Con	24,678	54.0	-1.0
			Hilton L.R. Ms.	Lab	15,627	34.2	+6.8
			Scott R.J.	LD	5,430	11.9	-5.8
					9,051	19.8	

ILFORD SOUTH [331]

Election	Electors	T'out	Candidate	Party	Votes	% Sh	% Ch
1983	58,208	70.6	Thorne N.G.*	Con	18,672	45.4	
			Hogben J.H.	Lab	14,106	34.3	
			Scott R.J.	Lib	7,999	19.5	
			Martin R.A.	BNP	316	0.8*	
					4,566	11.1	
1987	58,572	71.8	Thorne N.G.*	Con	20,351	48.4	+2.9
			Jones K.H.	Lab	15,779	37.5	+3.2
			Scott R.J.	Lib	5,928	14.1	-5.4
					4,572	10.9	
1992	55,857	76.7	Gapes M.J.	Lab	19,418	45.3	+7.8
			Thorne N.G.*	Con	19,016	44.4	-4.0
			Hogarth G.G.	LD	4,126	9.6	-4.5
			Nandkishore B.	NLP	269	0.6*	+0.6
					402	0.9	

INVERNESS, NAIRN AND LOCHABER [332]

Election	Electors	T'out	Candidate	Party	Votes	% Sh	% Ch
1983	63,645	70.5	Johnston D.R.*	Lib	20,671	46.1	
			Maclean D.J.	Con	13,373	29.8	
			McMillan D.L.	Lab	6,448	14.4	
			Vernal H.W.	SNP	4,395	9.8*	
					7,298	16.3	
1987	66,743	70.9	Johnston D.R. Sir.*	Lib	17,422	36.8	-9.2
			Stewart D.J.	Lab	11,991	25.3	+11.0
			Keswick A.T. Ms.	Con	10,901	23.0	-6.8
			Johnson N.P.	SNP	7,001	14.8	+5.0
					5,431	11.5	
1992	69,151	73.6	Johnston D.R. Sir.*	LD	13,258	26.0	-10.8
			Stewart D.J.	Lab	12,800	25.1	-0.2
			Ewing F.	SNP	12,562	24.7	+9.9
			Scott J.	Con	11,517	22.6	-0.4
			Martin J.	Green	766	1.5*	+1.5
					458	0.9	

IPSWICH [333]

Election	Electors	T'out	Candidate	Party	Votes	% Sh	% Ch
1983	67,292	75.4	Weetch K.T.*	Lab	22,191	43.7	
			Cottrell D.E. Ms.	Con	21,114	41.6	
			Miernik P.C.A. Ms.	Lib	7,220	14.2	
			Pearson A.W.T.	BNP	235	0.5*	
					1,077	2.1	
1987	67,712	77.6	Irvine M.F.	Con	23,328	44.4	+2.8
			Weetch K.T.*	Lab	22,454	42.7	-1.0
			Nicholson H.P.	SDP	6,596	12.6	-1.7
			Lettice D.J.	WRP	174	0.3*	+0.3
					874	1.7	
1992	67,289	80.3	Cann J.C.	Lab	23,680	43.8	+1.1
			Irvine M.F.*	Con	23,415	43.3	-1.1
			White J.W.	LD	6,159	11.4	-1.2
			Scott J.E. Ms.	Green	591	1.1*	+1.1
			Kaplan E.S.	NLP	181	0.3*	+0.3
					265	0.5	

ISLE OF WIGHT [334]

Election	Electors	T'out	Candidate	Party	Votes	% Sh	% Ch
1983	94,226	80.0	Ross S.S.*	Lib	38,407	51.0	
			Bottomley V.H.B.M. Ms.	Con	34,904	46.3	
			Wilson C. Ms.	Lab	1,828	2.4*	
			McDermott T.B.J.	Ind	208	0.3*	
					3,503	4.6	
1987	98,662	79.6	Field B.J.A.	Con	40,175	51.2*	+0.2
			Young M.A.	Lib	33,733	43.0	-8.0
			Pearson K.	Lab	4,626	5.9	+3.5
					6,442	8.2	
1992	99,839†	79.8	Field B.J.A.*	Con	38,163	47.9	-3.3
			Brand P.	LD	36,336	45.6	+2.7
			Pearson K.	Lab	4,784	6.0	+0.1
			Daly C.A.	NLP	350	0.4*	+0.4
					1,827	2.3	

ISLINGTON NORTH [335]

Election	Electors	T'out	Candidate	Party	Votes	% Sh	% Ch
1983	59,984	61.6	Corbyn J.B.	Lab	14,951	40.4	
			Coleman D.A.	Con	9,344	25.3	
			Grant J.D.*	SDP	8,268	22.4	
			O'Halloran M.J.*	Ind Lab	4,091	11.1*	
			Bearsford-Walker L.A.D.	BNP	176	0.5*	
			Lincoln R.A.J.	Ind	134	0.4*	
					5,607	15.2	

John Grant had been the Labour member for Islington Central in the previous Parliament.
Michael O'Halloran had been the Labour member for Islington North in the previous Parliament.

Election	Electors	T'out	Candidate	Party	Votes	% Sh	% Ch
1987	58,917	66.5	Corbyn J.B.*	Lab	19,577	50.0	+9.5
			Noad E.G.	Con	9,920	25.3	+0.0
			Whelan A.	SDP	8,560	21.8	-0.5
			Ashby C.M.	Green	1,131	2.9*	+2.9
					9,657	24.6	
1992	56,814	66.6	Corbyn J.B.*	Lab	21,742	57.4	+7.5
			Champagnie M.L. Ms.	Con	8,958	23.7	-1.6
			Ludford S.A. Ms.	LD	5,732	15.1	-6.7
			Ashby C.M.	Green	1,420	3.8*	+0.9

Election	Electors	T'out	Candidate	Party	Votes	% Sh	% Ch
1983	59,795	62.0	Smith C.R.	Lab	13,460	36.3	
			Cunningham G.*	SDP	13,097	35.3	
			Johnston A.F.E.	Con	9,894	26.7	
			Donegan J.B.	NF	341	0.9*	
			Murphy J.P.	Ind	102	0.3*	
			Stentiford D.I.	BNP	94	0.3*	
			Slapper C.M.	SPGB	85	0.2*	
					363	1.0	
1987	57,910	71.2	Smith C.R.*	Lab	16,511	40.1	+3.8
			Cunningham G.	SDP	15,706	38.1	+2.8
			Mitchell A.R.	Con	8,482	20.6	-6.1
			Powell P.C.	Green	382	0.9*	+0.9
			Dowsett S.	SPGB	81	0.2*	-0.0
			Earley J.H. Ms.	HP	56	0.1*	+0.1
					805	2.0	
1992	57,060	70.6	Smith C.R.*	Lab	20,586	51.1	+11.0
			Jones M.V.	Con	9,934	24.7	+4.1
			Pryce C.J.	LD	9,387	23.3	-14.8
			Hersey R.G. Ms.	NLP	149	0.4*	+0.4
			Avino M. Ms.	MRLP	142	0.4*	+0.4
			Spinks M.J.	Ind	83	0.2*	
					10,652	26.4	

Election	Electors	T'out	Candidate	Party	Votes	% Sh	% Ch
1983	50,261	77.7	Kinnock N.G.*	Lab	23,183	59.3	
			Johnson D.S.	SDP	8,803	22.5	
			Bevan M.J.	Con	5,511	14.1	
			Richards A.	PC	1,574	4.0*	
					14,380	36.8	
1987	50,414	80.4	Kinnock N.G.*	Lab	28,901	71.3*	+12.0
			Twitchen J.K.	Con	5,954	14.7	+0.6
			Gasson J-A. Ms.	SDP	3,746	9.2	-13.3
			Richards A.	PC	1,932	4.8*	+0.7
					22,947	56.6	
1992	51,082†	81.4	Kinnock N.G.*	Lab	30,908	74.3	+3.0
			Bone P.W.	Con	6,180	14.9	+0.2
			Symonds M.A.	LD	2,352	5.7	-3.6
			Jones H.M. Ms.	PC	1,606	3.9*	-0.9
			Sutch D.E.	MRLP	547	1.3*	+1.3
					24,728	59.5	

[Resignation]

Election	Electors	T'out	Candidate	Party	Votes	% Sh	% Ch
1995	51,354	45.1	Touhig J.D.	Lab	16,030	69.2	-5.1
(16/2)			Davies J.M. Ms.	PC	2,933	12.7	+8.8
			Bushell J.	LD	2,488	10.6	+4.9
			Buckland R.	Con	913	3.9*	-10.9
			Sutch D.E.	MRLP	506	2.2*	
			Hughes H.	UKI	289	1.2*	
			Rees T.	NLP	47	0.2*	
					13,097	56.5	

JARROW [338]

Election	Electors	T'out	Candidate	Party	Votes	% Sh	% Ch
1983	63,770	71.4	Dixon D.*	Lab	25,151	55.3	
			Copland S. Ms.	Con	11,274	24.8	
			Lennox J.A.	Lib	9,094	20.0	
					13,877	30.5	
1987	62,845	74.4	Dixon D.*	Lab	29,651	63.4	+8.2
			Yeoman P.S.	Con	10,856	23.2	-1.5
			Freitag P.	Lib	6,230	13.3	-6.6
					18,795	40.2	
1992	62,612†	74.4	Dixon D.*	Lab	28,956	62.1	-1.3
			Ward T.F.	Con	11,049	23.7	+0.5
			Orrell J.K.	LD	6,608	14.2	+0.8
					17,907	38.4	

KEIGHLEY [339]

Election	Electors	T'out	Candidate	Party	Votes	% Sh	% Ch
1983	63,678	78.9	Waller G.P.A.*	Con	21,370	42.6	
			Cryer G.R.*	Lab	18,596	37.0	
			Wells J.H.	Lib	9,951	19.8	
			Penney M.J.	Green	302	0.6*	
					2,774	5.5	
1987	65,714	79.5	Waller G.P.A.*	Con	23,903	45.8	+3.2
			Rye A.	Lab	18,297	35.0	-2.0
			Wells J.H.	Lib	10,041	19.2	-0.6
					5,606	10.7	
1992	66,379	82.6	Waller G.P.A.*	Con	25,983	47.4	+1.7
			Flanagan T.B.	Lab	22,387	40.8	+5.8
			Simpson I.N.	LD	5,793	10.6	-8.7
			Crowson M.	Green	642	1.2*	+1.2
					3,596	6.6	

Election	Electors	T'out	Candidate	Party	Votes	% Sh	% Ch
1983	49,854	62.3	Rhys Williams B.M. Sir Bt.*	Con	14,274	46.0	
			Bousquet B.T.	Lab	9,173	29.5	
			Goodhart W.H.	SDP	6,873	22.1	
			Porritt J.E. Hon.	Green	649	2.1*	
			Knight T.F.	Ind	86	0.3*	
					5,101	16.4	
1987	48,212	64.7	Rhys Williams B.M. Sir. Bt.*	Con	14,818	47.5	+1.5
			Bousquet B.T.	Lab	10,371	33.2	+3.7
			Goodhart W.H.	SDP	5,379	17.2	-4.9
			Shorter R.E.	Green	528	1.7*	-0.4
			Carrick L.Q.Y. Ms.	HP	65	0.2*	+0.2
			Hughes M. Ms.	Ind	30	0.1*	
					4,447	14.3	

[Death]

Election	Electors	T'out	Candidate	Party	Votes	% Sh	% Ch
1988	45,830	51.6	Fishburn J.D.	Con	9,829	41.6	-5.9
(14/7)			Holmes P.A. Ms.	Lab	9,014	38.2	+5.0
			Goodhart W.H.	LD	2,546	10.8	-6.4
			Martin J.	SDP	1,190	5.0	
			Hobson P.A.D.	Green	572	2.4*	+0.7
			Payne C.D. Ms.	Ind	193	0.8*	
			Sutch D.E.	MRLP	61	0.3*	
			Duignan J.	Ind	60	0.3*	
			Goodier B.G.	Ind	31	0.1*	
			McDermott T.B.J.	Ind	31	0.1*	
			Edey R.	Ind	30	0.1*	
			Scola W.P.C.V.	Ind	27	0.1*	
			Crowley J.E.	Ind	24	0.1*	
			Connell J.	Ind	20	0.1*	
			Trivedi K.S. Dr.	Ind	5	0.0*	
					815	3.4	
1992	42,129†	73.3	Fishburn J.D.	Con	15,540	50.3	+2.8
			Holmes P.A. Ms.	Lab	11,992	38.8	+5.6
			Shirley C.K.	LD	2,770	9.0	-8.3
			Burlingham-Johnson A. Ms.	Green	415	1.3*	-0.3
			Hardy A.J.W.	NLP	90	0.3*	+0.3
			Bulloch A. Ms.	AFL	71	0.2*	+0.2
					3,548	11.5	

KENT MID [341]

Election	Electors	T'out	Candidate	Party	Votes	% Sh	% Ch
1983	66,510	71.4	Rowe A.J.B.	Con	25,400	53.5	
			Wainman A.J. Ms.	Lib	12,857	27.1	
			Hull V.A.	Lab	8,928	18.8	
			Delderfield D.W.	NBP	324	0.7*	
					12,543	26.4	
1987	72,456	71.9	Rowe A.J.B.*	Con	28,719	55.1	+1.7
			Colley G.D.	Lib	13,951	26.8	-0.3
			Hazelgrove J.A.	Lab	9,420	18.1	-0.7
					14,768	28.4	
1992	74,460†	79.7	Rowe A.J.B.*	Con	33,633	56.7	+1.6
			Robson T.J.	Lab	13,984	23.6	+5.5
			Colley G.D.	LD	11,476	19.3	-7.4
			Valente G.J.	NLP	224	0.4*	+0.4
					19,649	33.1	

KETTERING [342]

Election	Electors	T'out	Candidate	Party	Votes	% Sh	% Ch
1983	62,819	76.4	Freeman R.N.	Con	23,223	48.4	
			Goodhart C.M. Ms.	SDP	14,637	30.5	
			Gordon A.	Lab	10,119	21.1	
					8,586	17.9	
1987	65,965	78.8	Freeman R.N.*	Con	26,532	51.1	+2.7
			Goodhart C.M. Ms.	SDP	15,205	29.3	-1.2
			Minto A.M.	Lab	10,229	19.7	-1.4
					11,327	21.8	
1992	67,854†	82.6	Freeman R.N.*	Con	29,115	52.0	+0.9
			Hope P.I.	Lab	17,961	32.1	+12.4
			Denton-White R.D.	LD	8,962	16.0	-13.3
					11,154	19.9	

Election	Electors	T'out	Candidate	Party	Votes	% Sh	% Ch
1983	61,394	75.6	McKelvey W.*	Lab	20,250	43.6	
			Leckie P.R.	Con	11,450	24.7	
			Ross A.E.	SDP	10,545	22.7	
			Calman C.D.	SNP	4,165	9.0*	
					8,800	19.0	
1987	62,648	78.0	McKelvey W.*	Lab	23,713	48.5	+4.9
			Bates A.K. Ms.	Con	9,586	19.6	-5.1
			Leslie G.A.	SNP	8,881	18.2	+9.2
			Kerr P.E.	SDP	6,698	13.7	-9.0
					14,127	28.9	
1992	62,043	79.9	McKelvey W.*	Lab	22,210	44.8	-3.7
			Neil A.	SNP	15,231	30.7	+12.5
			Wilkinson R.M.	Con	9,438	19.0	-0.6
			Philbrick K.H.R. Ms.	LD	2,722	5.5	-8.2
					6,979	14.1	

Election	Electors	T'out	Candidate	Party	Votes	% Sh	% Ch
1983	59,552	71.5	Buchanan-Smith A.L. Hon.*	Con	20,293	47.7	
			Waugh A.S.	Lib	12,497	29.4	
			Morrell M.C. Ms.	Lab	6,472	15.2	
			Tuttle A.	SNP	3,297	7.7*	
					7,796	18.3	
1987	63,587	75.2	Buchanan-Smith A.L. Hon.*	Con	19,438	40.6	-7.0
			Stephen N.R.	Lib	17,375	36.3	+7.0
			Thomaneck J.K.A.	Lab	7,624	15.9	+0.7
			Duncan F.E. Ms.	SNP	3,082	6.4	-1.3
			Perica L.M. Ms.	Green	299	0.6*	+0.6
					2,063	4.3	

[Death]

Election	Electors	T'out	Candidate	Party	Votes	% Sh	% Ch
1991	65,667	64.6	Stephen N.R.	LD	20,779	49.0	+12.7
(7/11)			Humphrey J.M.M.	Con	12,955	30.6	-10.1
			Macartney W.J.A.	SNP	4,705	11.1	+4.6
			Savidge M.K.	Lab	3,271	7.7	-8.2
			Campbell S.J.	Green	683	1.6*	+1.0
					7,824	18.4	
1992	66,169	79.3	Kynoch G.A.B.	Con	22,924	43.7	+3.1
			Stephen N.R.	LD	18,429	35.1	-1.2
			Macartney W.J.A.	SNP	5,927	11.3	+4.9
			Savidge M.K.	Lab	4,795	9.1	-6.8
			Campbell S.J.	Green	381	0.7*	+0.1
					4,495	8.6	

KINGSTON UPON THAMES [345]

Election	Electors	T'out	Candidate	Party	Votes	% Sh	% Ch
1983	56,794	71.9	Lamont N.S.H.*	Con	22,094	54.1	
			Hayes R.M.	Lib	13,222	32.4	
			Smith P.J.	Lab	4,977	12.2*	
			Presant-Collins A. Ms.	Green	290	0.7*	
			Dodd P.	MRLP	259	0.6*	
					8,872	21.7	
1987	54,839	78.5	Lamont N.S.H.*	Con	24,198	56.2	+2.1
			Hayes R.M.	Lib	13,012	30.2	-2.2
			Markless R.H.	Lab	5,676	13.2	+1.0
			Baker J.	Ind	175	0.4*	
					11,186	26.0	
1992	51,078†	78.4	Lamont N.S.H.*	Con	20,675	51.6	-4.6
			Osbourne D.R.	LD	10,522	26.3	-3.9
			Markless R.H.	Lab	7,748	19.3	+6.2
			Amer A.C.	Lib	771	1.9*	+1.9
			Beaupre D.J.	MRLP	212	0.5*	+0.5
			Woollcombe G.D.	NLP	81	0.2*	+0.2
			Scholefield A.J.E.	AFL	42	0.1*	+0.1
					10,153	25.4	

KINGSWOOD [346]

Election	Electors	T'out	Candidate	Party	Votes	% Sh	% Ch
1983	72,159	77.5	Hayward R.A.	Con	22,573	40.4	
			Walker T.W.	Lab	20,776	37.1	
			Gilbert M.L.P.	SDP	12,591	22.5	
					1,797	3.2	
1987	73,089	80.2	Hayward R.A.*	Con	26,300	44.9	+4.5
			Berry R.L.	Lab	21,907	37.4	+0.3
			Whittle P. Ms.	SDP	10,382	17.7	-4.8
					4,393	7.5	
1992	71,740	83.8	Berry R.L.	Lab	26,774	44.5	+7.1
			Hayward R.A.*	Con	24,404	40.6	-4.3
			Pinkerton J.B. Ms.	LD	8,967	14.9	-2.8
					2,370	3.9	

KIRKCALDY [347]

Election	Electors	T'out	Candidate	Party	Votes	% Sh	% Ch
1983	53,078	71.9	Gourlay H.P.H.*	Lab	15,380	40.3	
			Walker I.B.	Con	10,049	26.3	
			Black M.	SDP	9,274	24.3	
			Wood D.D.	SNP	3,452	9.0*	
					5,331	14.0	
1987	53,439	76.5	Moonie L.G. Dr.	Lab	20,281	49.6	+9.3
			Mitchell I.G.	Con	8,711	21.3	-5.0
			Stewart D.	SDP	7,118	17.4	-6.9
			Mullin W.A.R.	SNP	4,794	11.7	+2.7
					11,570	28.3	
1992	51,955	74.8	Moonie L.G. Dr.*	Lab	17,887	46.0	-3.5
			Hosie S.	SNP	8,761	22.5	+10.8
			Wolsey S.P.	Con	8,476	21.8	+0.5
			Leslie S. Ms.	LD	3,729	9.6	-7.8
					9,126	23.5	

KNOWSLEY NORTH [348]

Election	Electors	T'out	Candidate	Party	Votes	% Sh	% Ch
1983	55,606	69.5	Kilroy-Silk R.*	Lab	24,949	64.5	
			Birch A.L.	Con	7,758	20.1	
			McColgan B.W.	SDP	5,715	14.8	
			Simons J.	WRP	246	0.6*	
					17,191	44.5	
[Resignation]							
1986	53,921	57.3	Howarth G.E.	Lab	17,403	56.3	-8.2
(13/11)			Cooper R.E. Ms.	Lib	10,679	34.6	+19.8
			Brown R.C.A.	Con	1,960	6.3	-13.8
			Hallsworth D. P.	RCP	664	2.1*	
			Weiss G.	Ind	111	0.4*	
			Cory R.	Ind	88	0.3*	
					6,724	21.7	
1987	52,959	74.2	Howarth G.E.	Lab	27,454	69.9	+5.4
			Cooper R. Ms.	Lib	6,356	16.2	+1.4
			Brown R.C.A.	Con	4,922	12.5	-7.5
			Hallsworth D.P.	RF	538	1.4*	+1.4
					21,098	53.7	
1992	48,783	72.8	Howarth G.E.*	Lab	27,517	77.5	+7.6
			Mabey S.J.	Con	5,114	14.4	+1.9
			Murray P.J.	LD	1,515	4.3*	-11.9
			Lappin K.M. Ms.	Lib	1,180	3.3*	+3.3
			Ruben V.	NLP	179	0.5*	+0.5
					22,403	63.1	

Election	Electors	T'out	Candidate	Party	Votes	% Sh	% Ch
1983	68,114	70.3	Hughes S.F.	Lab	25,727	53.8	
			Lamont E. Ms.	Con	13,958	29.2	
			Smith I.	Lib	8,173	17.1	
					11,769	24.6	
1987	65,643	74.1	Hughes S.F.*	Lab	31,378	64.5	+10.7
			Hall A.J.	Con	10,532	21.6	-7.5
			Watmough R. Ms.	SDP	6,760	13.9	-3.2
					20,846	42.8	

[Death]

Election	Electors	T'out	Candidate	Party	Votes	% Sh	% Ch
1992	63,433	33.4	O'Hara E	Lab	14,581	68.8	+4.3
(27/9)			Byrom L.T.	Con	3,214	15.2	-6.4
			Hancox C.V. Ms.	LD	1,809	8.5	-5.4
			Georgeson R.L.	Green	656	3.1*	
			Smith I.	Lib	628	3.0*	
			Sutch D.E.	MRLP	197	0.9*	
			St. Clair L. Ms.	Ind	99	0.5*	
					11,367	53.6	
1992	62,295	74.7	O'Hara E.	Lab	31,933	68.6	+4.1
			Byrom L.T.	Con	9,922	21.3	-0.3
			Smith I.	LD	4,480	9.6	-4.3
			Raiano M.	NLP	217	0.5*	+0.5
					22,011	47.3	

Election	Electors	T'out	Candidate	Party	Votes	% Sh	% Ch
1983	60,051	67.6	Molyneaux J.H.*	UU	24,017	59.2	
			Beattie W.J. Rev.	UDUP	6,801	16.8	
			Close S.A.	APNI	4,593	11.3*	
			Boomer C.J.	SDLP	2,603	6.4*	
			McAuley R.	SF	1,751	4.3*	
			Loughlin G.	WP	809	2.0*	
					17,216	42.4	

[Seeks Re-election]

Election	Electors	T'out	Candidate	Party	Votes	% Sh	% Ch
1986	63,244	56.7	Molyneaux J.H.*	UU	32,514	90.7	+31.5
(23/1)			Lowry J.T.	WP	3,328	9.3	+7.3
					29,186	81.4	

Election	Electors	T'out	Candidate	Party	Votes	% Sh	% Ch
1987	64,873	64.1	Molyneaux J.H.*	UU	29,101	70.0	+10.8
			Close S.A.	APNI	5,728	13.8	+2.5
			McDonnell B.	SDLP	2,888	6.9	+0.5
			Rice P.J.	SF	2,656	6.4	+2.1
			Lowry J.T.	WP	1,215	2.9*	+0.9
					23,373	56.2	

Election	Electors	T'out	Candidate	Party	Votes	% Sh	% Ch
1992	72,708	67.3	Molyneaux J.H.*	UU	29,772	60.8	-9.2
			Close S. A.	APNI	6,207	12.7	-1.1
			Lewsley H.	SDLP	4,626	9.4	+2.5
			Coleridge T.R.	Con	4,423	9.0	+9.0
			Rice P.J.	SF	3,346	6.8	+0.4
			Lowry A-M. Ms.	WP	582	1.2*	-1.7
					23,565	48.1	

LANCASHIRE WEST [351]

Election	Electors	T'out	Candidate	Party	Votes	% Sh	% Ch
1983	73,990	74.4	Hind K.H.	Con	25,458	46.3	
			Farrington J. Ms.	Lab	18,600	33.8	
			Sackville A.D.	SDP	10,983	20.0	
					6,858	12.5	
1987	76,094	79.7	Hind K.H.*	Con	26,500	43.7	-2.5
			Pickthall C.	Lab	25,147	41.5	+7.7
			Jermyn R.	SDP	8,972	14.8	-5.2
					1,353	2.2	
1992	77,463†	82.5	Pickthall C.	Lab	30,120	47.1	+5.6
			Hind K.H.*	Con	28,051	43.9	+0.2
			Reilly P.F.	LD	4,884	7.6	-7.2
			Pawley P.J.	Green	546	0.9*	+0.9
			Morris B.H.	NLP	336	0.5*	+0.5
					2,069	3.2	

LANCASTER [352]

Election	Electors	T'out	Candidate	Party	Votes	% Sh	% Ch
1983	56,040	74.7	Kellett-Bowman M.E. Ms.*	Con	21,050	50.3	
			Harkins J.C.	Lab	10,414	24.9	
			Booth W.J.	Lib	10,214	24.4	
			Leach S.R.	Ind	179	0.4*	
					10,636	25.4	
1987	57,229	79.2	Kellett-Bowman M.E. Ms.*	Con	21,142	46.7	-3.6
			Gallacher J.	Lab	14,689	32.4	+7.5
			Brooks K.C. Ms.	Lib	9,003	19.9	-4.5
			Jones P.F.F.	Green	473	1.0*	+1.0
					6,453	14.2	
1992	58,616	78.9	Kellett-Bowman M.E. Dame*	Con	21,084	45.6	-1.1
			Henig R.B. Ms.	Lab	18,131	39.2	+6.8
			Humberstone J.C.	LD	6,524	14.1	-5.8
			Dowding G. Ms.	Green	433	0.9*	-0.1
			Barcis R.	NLP	83	0.2*	+0.2
					2,953	6.4	

LANGBAURGH [353]

Election	Electors	T'out	Candidate	Party	Votes	% Sh	% Ch
1983	77,387	75.0	Holt J.R.	Con	24,239	41.7	
			Johnston J.G. Ms.	Lab	18,215	31.4	
			Ashby R.A.J.	Lib	15,615	26.9	
					6,024	10.4	
1987	79,193	78.8	Holt J.R.*	Con	26,047	41.7	-0.0
			Harford P.	Lab	23,959	38.4	+7.0
			Ashby R.A.J.	Lib	12,405	19.9	-7.0
					2,088	3.3	

[Death]

Election	Electors	T'out	Candidate	Party	Votes	% Sh	% Ch
1991	80,220	65.3	Kumar A.	Lab	22,442	42.9	+4.5
(7/11)			Bates M.W.	Con	20,467	39.1	-2.6
			Allen P.J.	LD	8,421	16.1	-3.8
			Parr G.F.	Green	456	0.9*	
			Holt R.C.	Ind	216	0.4*	
			St. Clair L. Ms.	Ind	198	0.4*	
			Downing N.	Ind	163	0.3*	
					1,975	3.8	
1992	79,563†	83.1	Bates M.W.	Con	30,018	45.4	+3.7
			Kumar A.	Lab	28,454	43.1	+4.7
			Allen P.J.	LD	7,615	11.5	-8.4
					1,564	2.4	

LEEDS CENTRAL [354]

Election	Electors	T'out	Candidate	Party	Votes	% Sh	% Ch
1983	63,299	61.7	Fatchett D.J.	Lab	18,706	47.9	
			Wrigley P.	Lib	10,484	26.9	
			Ashley-Brown M.A.	Con	9,192	23.6	
			Cummins G.	BNP	331	0.8*	
			Rodgers J.M.	Comm	314	0.8*	
					8,222	21.1	
1987	59,019	64.8	Fatchett D.J.*	Lab	21,270	55.6	+7.7
			Schofield D.	Con	9,765	25.5	+2.0
			Lee K.E. Ms.	SDP	6,853	17.9	-8.9
			Innes W.H.	Comm	355	0.9*	+0.1
					11,505	30.1	
1992	62,059	61.3	Fatchett D.J.*	Lab	23,673	62.2	+6.6
			Holdroyd T.C. Ms.	Con	8,653	22.7	-2.8
			Pratt D.	LD	5,713	15.0	-2.9
					15,020	39.5	

LEEDS EAST [355]

Election	Electors	T'out	Candidate	Party	Votes	% Sh	% Ch
1983	63,611	66.3	Healey D.W.*	Lab	18,450	43.8	
			Bell A.R.M.	Con	12,355	29.3	
			Clay M.G. Ms.	Lib	10,884	25.8	
			Brons A.H.W.	NF	475	1.1*	
					6,095	14.5	
1987	61,178	70.2	Healey D.W.*	Lab	20,932	48.7	+5.0
			Sheard J.S.W.	Con	11,406	26.5	-2.8
			Clay M.G. Ms.	Lib	10,630	24.7	-1.1
					9,526	22.2	
1992	61,720	70.0	Mudie G.E.	Lab	24,929	57.7	+9.0
			Carmichael W.N.	Con	12,232	28.3	+1.8
			Wrigley P.	LD	6,040	14.0	-10.8
					12,697	29.4	

LEEDS NORTH EAST [356]

Election	Electors	T'out	Candidate	Party	Votes	% Sh	% Ch
1983	65,226	70.7	Joseph K.S. Sir. Bt.*	Con	21,940	47.6	
			Crystal P.M.	SDP	12,945	28.1	
			Sedler R.H.	Lab	10,951	23.8	
			Tibbitts E.L.	Ind	128	0.3*	
			Holton P.J.	Ind	123	0.3*	
					8,995	19.5	
1987	64,631	75.3	Kirkhope T.J.R.	Con	22,196	45.6	-2.0
			Crystal P.M.	SDP	13,777	28.3	+0.2
			Glover O.B.	Lab	12,292	25.3	+1.5
			Nash C.D. Ms.	Green	416	0.9*	+0.9
					8,419	17.3	
1992	64,607	76.6	Kirkhope T.J.R.*	Con	22,462	45.4	-0.2
			Hamilton F.	Lab	18,218	36.8	+11.6
			Walmsley C.R.	LD	8,274	16.7	-11.6
			Noble J.	Green	546	1.1*	+0.2
					4,244	8.6	

LEEDS NORTH WEST [357]

Election	Electors	T'out	Candidate	Party	Votes	% Sh	% Ch
1983	68,004	71.3	Hampson K.*	Con	22,579	46.6	
			Jones N.H.	SDP	14,042	29.0	
			Battle J.D.	Lab	10,757	22.2	
			Laurence A.D.	Green	673	1.4*	
			Haygreen C.G.	Ind Con	437	0.9*	
					8,537	17.6	
1987	68,227	75.7	Hampson K.*	Con	22,480	43.5	-3.0
			Peters B.	Lib	17,279	33.5	+4.5
			Thomas J.M. Ms.	Lab	11,210	21.7	-0.5
			Stevens A.	Green	663	1.3*	-0.1
					5,201	10.1	
1992	69,733	72.5	Hampson K.*	Con	21,750	43.0*	-0.5
			Pearce B.A. Ms.	LD	14,079	27.8	-5.6
			Egan S. Ms.	Lab	13,782	27.3	+5.5
			Webb D.C.	Green	519	1.0*	-0.3
			Nowosielski N.A.B.	Lib	427	0.8*	+0.8
					7,671	15.2	

LEEDS SOUTH AND MORLEY [358]

Election	Electors	T'out	Candidate	Party	Votes	% Sh	% Ch
1983	60,864	67.9	Rees M.*	Lab	18,995	45.9	
			Hyde W.S.	Con	13,141	31.8	
			Burley P.M.	SDP	9,216	22.3	
					5,854	14.2	
1987	60,726	71.6	Rees M.*	Lab	21,551	49.6	+3.6
			Holdroyd T.C. Ms.	Con	14,840	34.1	+2.3
			Dawson E.J.V.	SDP	7,099	16.3	-6.0
					6,711	15.4	
1992	63,155	72.5	Gunnell J.	Lab	23,896	52.2	+2.6
			Booth G.R.	Con	16,524	36.1	+1.9
			Walmsley J.M. Ms.	LD	5,062	11.1	-5.3
			Thurston R.D.	NLP	327	0.7*	+0.7
					7,372	16.1	

LEEDS WEST [359]

Election	Electors	T'out	Candidate	Party	Votes	% Sh	% Ch
1983	67,538	69.0	Meadowcroft M.J.	Lib	17,908	38.4	
			Dean J.J.*	Lab	15,860	34.0	
			Keeble J.S. Ms.	Con	12,515	26.8	
			Braithwaite A.A.D.	BNP	334	0.7*	
					2,048	4.4	
1987	66,344	73.3	Battle J.D.	Lab	21,032	43.2	+9.2
			Meadowcroft M.J.*	Lib	16,340	33.6	-4.8
			Allott P.D.	Con	11,276	23.2	-3.7
					4,692	9.6	
1992	67,074	71.2	Battle J.D.*	Lab	26,310	55.1	+11.9
			Bartlett P.	Con	12,482	26.2	+3.0
			Howard G.W.B.	LD	4,252	8.9	-24.7
			Meadowcroft M.J.	Lib	3,980	8.3	+8.3
			Mander A.M. Ms.	Green	569	1.2*	+1.2
			Tenney R.I.	NF	132	0.3*	+0.3
					13,828	29.0	

LEICESTER EAST [360]

Election	Electors	T'out	Candidate	Party	Votes	% Sh	% Ch
1983	67,071	73.2	Bruinvels P.N.E.	Con	19,117	38.9	
			Hewitt P.H. Ms.	Lab	18,184	37.0	
			Bradley T.G.*	SDP	10,362	21.1	
			Ganatra R.V.	Ind	970	2.0*	
			Sutton R.L.	BNP	459	0.9*	
					933	1.9	
1987	66,372	78.6	Vaz N.K.A.S.	Lab	24,074	46.2	+9.1
			Bruinvels P.N.E.*	Con	22,150	42.5	+3.5
			Ayres A.M. Ms.	SDP	5,935	11.4	-9.7
					1,924	3.7	
1992	63,435†	78.7	Vaz N.K.A.S.*	Lab	28,123	56.3	+10.2
			Stevens J.C.	Con	16,807	33.7	-8.8
			Mitchell S.A. Ms.	LD	4,043	8.1	-3.3
			Frankland M.R.	Green	453	0.9*	+0.9
			Taylor D.J.	Ind	308	0.6*	
			Mahaldar A.S.K.	NLP	186	0.4*	+0.4
					11,316	22.7	

LEICESTER SOUTH [361]

Election	Electors	T'out	Candidate	Party	Votes	% Sh	% Ch
1983	73,573	72.3	Spencer D.H.	Con	21,424	40.3	
			Marshall J.*	Lab	21,417	40.3	
			Renold R.C.	Lib	9,410	17.7	
			Davies C.J.	Green	495	0.9*	
			Pickard C.	BNP	280	0.5*	
			Roberts D.P.	WKP	161	0.3*	
					7	0.0	
1987	73,236	77.0	Marshall J.	Lab	24,901	44.2	+3.9
			Spencer D.H.*	Con	23,024	40.8	+0.6
			Pritchard R.H.	Lib	7,773	13.8	-3.9
			Fewster B.	Green	390	0.7*	-0.2
			Mayat M.M.	Ind	192	0.3*	
			Manners R.F. Ms.	WRP	96	0.2*	+0.2
					1,877	3.3	
1992	71,120†	75.1	Marshall J.*	Lab	27,934	52.3	+8.1
			Dutt M.	Con	18,494	34.6	-6.2
			Crumbie A. Ms.	LD	6,271	11.7	-2.0
			McWhirter J.	Green	554	1.0*	+0.3
			Saunders P.A Ms.	NLP	154	0.3*	+0.3
					9,440	17.7	

LEICESTER WEST [362]

Election	Electors	T'out	Candidate	Party	Votes	% Sh	% Ch
1983	67,691	68.8	Janner G.E. Hon.*	Lab	20,837	44.8	
			Meacham R.K.	Con	19,125	41.1	
			Fernando S.C.	SDP	5,935	12.8	
			Hill R.	BNP	469	1.0*	
			Prangle B.J.	WRP	176	0.4*	
					1,712	3.7	
1987	67,829	73.4	Janner G.E. Hon.*	Lab	22,156	44.5	-0.3
			Cooper J.S.W.	Con	20,955	42.1	+1.0
			Edgar W.	SDP	6,708	13.5	+0.7
					1,201	2.4	
1992	65,511†	73.7	Janner G.E. Hon.*	Lab	22,574	46.8	+2.3
			Guthrie J.A.	Con	18,596	38.5	-3.5
			Walker G.F.	LD	6,402	13.3	-0.2
			Wintram C.D. Ms.	Green	517	1.1*	+1.1
			Rosta J.M. Ms.	NLP	171	0.4*	+0.4
					3,978	8.2	

LEICESTERSHIRE NORTH WEST [363]

Election	Electors	T'out	Candidate	Party	Votes	% Sh	% Ch
1983	68,511	81.1	Ashby D.G.	Con	24,760	44.6	
			Read I.M. Ms.	Lab	18,098	32.6	
			Cort G.R.	Lib	12,043	21.7	
			Freer D.G. Ms.	Green	637	1.1*	
					6,662	12.0	
1987	70,613	82.9	Ashby D.G.*	Con	27,872	47.6	+3.0
			Waddington S.A. Ms.	Lab	20,044	34.3	+1.7
			Emmerson D.S.	Lib	10,034	17.1	-4.5
			Michetschlager H.T. Ms.	Green	570	1.0*	-0.2
					7,828	13.4	
1992	72,419†	86.1	Ashby D.G.*	Con	28,379	45.5	-2.1
			Taylor D.L.	Lab	27,400	43.9	+9.7
			Beckett J.W.R.	LD	6,353	10.2	-7.0
			Fawcett D.J.	NLP	229	0.4*	+0.4
					979	1.6	

LEIGH [364]

Election	Electors	T'out	Candidate	Party	Votes	% Sh	% Ch
1983	68,063	72.2	Cunliffe L.F.*	Lab	25,477	51.9	
			Johnston P.J.	Con	13,163	26.8	
			Eccles D.T.	SDP	10,468	21.3	
					12,314	25.1	
1987	69,155	74.1	Cunliffe L.F.*	Lab	30,064	58.6	+6.8
			Browne L.B.A.	Con	13,458	26.3	-0.6
			Jones S.D.	SDP	7,745	15.1	-6.2
					16,606	32.4	
1992	70,065†	75.0	Cunliffe L.F.*	Lab	32,225	61.3	+2.7
			Egerton J.R.S.	Con	13,398	25.5	-0.8
			Bleakley R.M.	LD	6,621	12.6	-2.5
			Tayler A.P.	NLP	320	0.6*	+0.6
					18,827	35.8	

LEOMINSTER [365]

Election	Electors	T'out	Candidate	Party	Votes	% Sh	% Ch
1983	66,286	77.5	Temple-Morris P.*	Con	29,276	57.0	
			Pincham R.J.	Lib	19,490	37.9	
			Wilcox D.	Lab	1,932	3.8*	
			Norman F.M. Ms.	Green	668	1.3*	
					9,786	19.1	
1987	69,577	78.0	Temple-Morris P.*	Con	31,396	57.9	+0.9
			Morris S.C.	Lib	17,321	31.9	-6.0
			Chappell A.C.R.	Lab	4,444	8.2	+4.4
			Norman F.M. Ms.	Green	1,102	2.0*	+0.7
					14,075	25.9	
1992	70,874†	81.7	Temple-Morris P.*	Con	32,783	56.6	-1.2
			Short D.C.	LD	16,103	27.8	-4.1
			Chappell A.C.R.	Lab	6,874	11.9	+3.7
			Norman F.M. Ms.	Green	1,503	2.6*	+0.6
			Carlisle E.P.	AFL	640	1.1*	+1.1
					16,680	28.8	

LEWES [366]

Election	Electors	T'out	Candidate	Party	Votes	% Sh	% Ch
1983	67,366	74.3	Rathbone J.R.*	Con	29,261	58.4	
			Bellotti D.F.	Lib	15,357	30.7	
			Sander S.D. Ms.	Lab	4,244	8.5*	
			Mutter R.P.C.	Green	1,221	2.4*	
					13,904	27.8	
1987	73,181	77.0	Rathbone J.R.*	Con	32,016	56.8	-1.6
			Bellotti D.F.	Lib	18,396	32.6	+2.0
			Taylor R.P.	Lab	4,973	8.8	+0.4
			Sherwood A.G.P.	Green	970	1.7*	-0.7
					13,620	24.2	
1992	73,918†	81.8	Rathbone J.R.*	Con	33,042	54.6	-2.2
			Baker N.J.	LD	20,867	34.5	+1.9
			Chapman A.E. Ms.	Lab	5,758	9.5	+0.7
			Beaumont A.E.	Green	719	1.2*	-0.5
			Clinch N.F.	NLP	87	0.1*	+0.1
					12,175	20.1	

LEWISHAM DEPTFORD [367]

Election	Electors	T'out	Candidate	Party	Votes	% Sh	% Ch
1983	58,663	61.2	Silkin J.E. Hon.*	Lab	17,360	48.3	
			Wheatley R.J.P.	Con	11,328	31.5	
			Abbott D. Ms.	SDP	6,734	18.8	
			Wilson P.	BNP	317	0.9*	
			Housego S.B.	Ind	173	0.5*	
					6,032	16.8	
1987	58,151	64.9	Ruddock J.M. Ms.	Lab	18,724	49.6	+1.2
			Punyer M.C.	Con	11,953	31.7	+0.1
			Braun A-M.E. Ms.	SDP	6,513	17.2	-1.5
			Makepeace P.K.	Green	568	1.5*	+1.5
					6,771	17.9	
1992	57,062	65.0	Ruddock J.M. Ms.*	Lab	22,574	60.9	+11.3
			O'Neill T.A.J. Ms.	Con	10,336	27.9	-3.8
			Brightwell J.C. Ms.	LD	4,181	11.3	-6.0
					12,238	33.0	

LEWISHAM EAST [368]

Election	Electors	T'out	Candidate	Party	Votes	% Sh	% Ch
1983	61,216	69.5	Moynihan C.B.Hon.	Con	17,168	40.4	
			Moyle R.D. Hon.*	Lab	15,259	35.9	
			Toynbee P. Ms.	SDP	9,351	22.0	
			Edmonds R.C.	BNP	288	0.7*	
			Hassard A.J.	Green	270	0.6*	
			Roberts G.	Comm	135	0.3*	
			Gibson P.C.	WRP	71	0.2*	
					1,909	4.5	
1987	59,627	73.9	Moynihan C.B. Hon.*	Con	19,873	45.1	+4.8
			Profitt M.R.	Lab	15,059	34.2	-1.7
			Stone V.W. Ms.	SDP	9,118	20.7	-1.3
					4,814	10.9	
1992	57,725	74.7	Prentice B.T. Ms.	Lab	19,576	45.4	+11.2
			Moynihan C.B. Hon*	Con	18,481	42.8	-2.3
			Hawkins J.A.	LD	4,877	11.3	-9.4
			Mansour G.E. Ms.	NLP	196	0.5*	+0.5
					1,095	2.5	

205

LEWISHAM WEST [369]

Election	Electors	T'out	Candidate	Party	Votes	% Sh	% Ch
1983	63,043	70.3	Maples J.C.	Con	19,521	44.0	
			Price C.*	Lab	17,015	38.4	
			Mooney H.P.	Lib	7,470	16.8	
			Hoy R.F.G.	BNP	336	0.8*	
					2,506	5.7	
1987	62,923	72.3	Maples J.C.*	Con	20,995	46.2	+2.2
			Dowd J.P.	Lab	17,223	37.9	-0.5
			Titley S.C. Ms.	Lib	7,247	15.9	-0.9
					3,772	8.3	
1992	59,372	73.0	Dowd J.P.	Lab	20,378	47.0	+9.1
			Maples J.C.*	Con	18,569	42.8	-3.4
			Neale E. Ms.	LD	4,295	9.9	-6.0
			Coulam P.	AFL	125	0.3*	+0.3
					1,809	4.2	

LEYTON [370]

Election	Electors	T'out	Candidate	Party	Votes	% Sh	% Ch
1983	57,770	65.7	Cohen H.M.	Lab	16,504	43.5	
			Neilson-Hansen W.T.	Con	11,988	31.6	
			Magee B.E.*	SDP	9,448	24.9	
					4,516	11.9	
1987	57,662	69.6	Cohen H.M.*	Lab	16,536	41.2	-2.3
			Banks S.G.	Lib	11,895	29.6	+4.7
			Gilmartin D.N.	Con	11,692	29.1	-2.5
					4,641	11.6	
1992	57,272†	67.4	Cohen H.M.*	Lab	20,334	52.6	+11.4
			Smith C. Ms.	Con	8,882	23.0	-6.1
			Fryer J.H.	LD	8,180	21.2	-8.5
			De Pinna L.A.	Lib	561	1.5*	+1.5
			Pervez K.	Green	412	1.1*	+1.1
			Archer R.	NLP	256	0.7*	+0.7
					11,452	29.6	

LINCOLN [371]

Election	Electors	T'out	Candidate	Party	Votes	% Sh	% Ch
1983	72,887	74.6	Carlisle K.M.*	Con	25,244	46.4	
			Withers M.R.C.	Lab	14,958	27.5	
			Stockdale F.M.	SDP	13,631	25.1	
			Blades G.T.	Ind	523	1.0*	
					10,286	18.9	
1987	77,049	75.6	Carlisle K.M.*	Con	27,097	46.5	+0.1
			Butler N.J.	Lab	19,614	33.7	+6.1
			Zentner P.	SDP	11,319	19.4	-5.6
			Kyle T.B.	Ind	232	0.4*	
					7,483	12.8	
1992	78,944	79.1	Carlisle K.M.*	Con	28,792	46.1	-0.4
			Butler N.J.	Lab	26,743	42.8	+9.2
			Harding-Price D.	LD	6,316	10.1	-9.3
			Wiggin S.E. Ms.	Lib	603	1.0*	+1.0
					2,049	3.3	

LINDSEY EAST [372]

Election	Electors	T'out	Candidate	Party	Votes	% Sh	% Ch
1983	69,715	73.2	Tapsell P.H.B.*	Con	27,151	53.2	
			Sellick J.C.L.	Lib	19,634	38.5	
			Lowis G.R.	Lab	4,229	8.3*	
					7,517	14.7	
1987	74,027	75.2	Tapsell P.H.B. Sir.*	Con	29,048	52.2	-1.1
			Sellick J.C.L.	Lib	20,432	36.7	-1.8
			Stevenson K.	Lab	6,206	11.1	+2.9
					8,616	15.5	
1992	80,027†	78.1	Tapsell P.H.B. Sir.*	Con	31,916	51.1	-1.1
			Dodsworth J.L.	LD	20,070	32.1	-4.6
			Shepherd D.G.	Lab	9,477	15.2	+4.0
			Robinson R.E. Ms.	Green	1,018	1.6*	+1.6
					11,846	19.0	

207

Election	Electors	T'out	Candidate	Party	Votes	% Sh	% Ch
1983	58,111	75.2	Dalyell T.*	Lab	19,694	45.1	
			Jones C.I.	Con	8,333	19.1	
			Ramsay D.H.	SNP	8,026	18.4	
			Cockroft P.P.	SDP	7,432	17.0	
			Parnell M. Dr.‡	Comm	199	0.5*	
					11,361	26.0	
1987	59,542	77.6	Dalyell T.*	Lab	21,869	47.3	+2.3
			Sillars J.	SNP	11,496	24.9	+6.5
			Armstrong-Wilson T.C.R.	Con	6,828	14.8	-4.3
			McDade H.A. Ms.	SDP	5,840	12.6	-4.4
			Glassford J.	Comm	154	0.3*	-0.1
					10,373	22.5	
1992	61,082†	78.7	Dalyell T.*	Lab	21,603	45.0	-2.4
			MacAskill K.W.	SNP	14,577	30.3	+5.4
			Forbes E.A. Ms.	Con	8,424	17.5	+2.7
			Falchikov M.G.	LD	3,446	7.2	-5.5
					7,026	14.6	

Election	Electors	T'out	Candidate	Party	Votes	% Sh	% Ch
1983	64,018	74.8	Dickens G.K.*	Con	20,510	42.8	
			Knowles R.D.	Lib	14,860	31.0	
			Moore S.H.	Lab	12,106	25.3	
			Barry R.K.	Ind	398	0.8*	
					5,650	11.8	
1987	66,120	77.4	Dickens G.K.*	Con	22,027	43.1	+0.2
			Davies C.	Lib	15,825	30.9	-0.1
			Stonier P.	Lab	13,299	26.0	+0.7
					6,202	12.1	
1992	65,577†	81.6	Dickens G.K.*	Con	23,682	44.2	+1.2
			Davies C.	LD	19,188	35.9	+4.9
			Brett A.J.	Lab	10,649	19.9	-6.1
					4,494	8.4	

[Death]

Election	Electors	T'out	Candidate	Party	Votes	% Sh	% Ch
1995	65,445	64.4	Davies C.	LD	16,231	38.5	+2.7
(27/7)			Woolas P.	Lab	14,238	33.8	+13.9
			Hudson J.	Con	9,934	23.6	-20.7
			Sutch D.E.	MRLP	782	1.9*	
			Whittaker J.	UKI	549	1.3*	
			Douglas P.	Ind	193	0.5*	
			Blobby M.	Ind	105	0.2*	
			Pitts A.	Soc	46	0.1*	
			McLaren L.	Ind	33	0.1*	
			Palmer C.R.	Ind	25	0.1*	
					1,993	4.7	

LIVERPOOL, BROADGREEN [375]

Election	Electors	T'out	Candidate	Party	Votes	% Sh	% Ch
1983	63,826	72.1	Fields T.	Lab	18,802	40.9	
			Dougherty D.P.	Con	15,002	32.6	
			Pine R.	Ind Lib	7,021	15.3	
			Crawshaw R.*	SDP	5,169	11.2*	
					3,800	8.3	
1987	63,091	75.9	Fields T.*	Lab	23,262	48.6	+7.7
			Pine R.	Lib	17,215	35.9	+24.7
			Seddon M.R.G.	Con	7,413	15.5	-17.1
					6,047	12.6	
1992	60,080†	69.6	Kennedy J.E. Ms.	Lab	18,062	43.2	-5.4
			Cooper R.E. Ms.	LD	11,035	26.4	-9.6
			Fields T.*	Ind Lab	5,952	14.2	
			Roche H.L. Ms.	Con	5,405	12.9	-2.6
			Radford S.R.	Lib	1,211	2.9*	+2.9
			Brennan A. Ms.	NLP	149	0.4*	+0.4
					7,027	16.8	

LIVERPOOL, GARSTON [376]

Election	Electors	T'out	Candidate	Party	Votes	% Sh	% Ch
1983	64,326	71.6	Loyden E.	Lab	21,450	46.6	
			Ross J.S.	Con	17,448	37.9	
			Cooper R.E. Ms.	Lib	7,153	15.5	
					4,002	8.7	
1987	61,280	75.7	Loyden E.*	Lab	24,848	53.6	+7.0
			Feather P.B.	Con	11,071	23.9	-14.0
			Isaacson R.	SDP	10,370	22.4	+6.8
			Timlin K.	WRP	98	0.2*	+0.2
					13,777	29.7	
1992	57,539†	70.6	Loyden E.*	Lab	23,212	57.1	+3.6
			Backhouse J.E.	Con	10,933	26.9	+3.0
			Roberts C.W.	LD	5,398	13.3	-9.1
			Conrad W.G.A.	Lib	894	2.2*	+2.2
			Chandler P.J.	NLP	187	0.5*	+0.5
					12,279	30.2	

LIVERPOOL, MOSSLEY HILL [377]

Election	Electors	T'out	Candidate	Party	Votes	% Sh	% Ch
1983	62,789	73.4	Alton D.P.P.*	Lib	18,845	40.9	
			Keefe B.M.	Con	14,650	31.8	
			Snowden A.C.	Lab	12,352	26.8	
			Erickson-Rohrer M.A.	NF	212	0.5*	
					4,195	9.1	
1987	60,954	75.1	Alton D.P.P.*	Lib	20,012	43.7	+2.8
			Devaney J.A.	Lab	17,786	38.8	+12.0
			Lightfoot W.M.	Con	8,005	17.5	-14.3
					2,226	4.9	
1992	60,409†	68.5	Alton D.P.P.*	LD	19,809	47.9	+4.2
			Bann N.S.	Lab	17,203	41.6	+2.7
			Syder S.A.	Con	4,269	10.3	-7.2
			Rigby B.P.	NLP	114	0.3*	+0.3
					2,606	6.3	

LIVERPOOL, RIVERSIDE [378]

Election	Electors	T'out	Candidate	Party	Votes	% Sh	% Ch
1983	61,638	62.4	Parry R.*	Lab	24,978	65.0	
			Morrison T.	Con	7,600	19.8	
			Zentner P.	SDP	5,381	14.0	
			Blevin J.C.	Comm	261	0.7*	
			Latchford D.	WRP	234	0.6*	
					17,378	45.2	
1987	53,328	65.3	Parry R.*	Lab	25,505	73.2	+8.3
			Fitzsimmons S.	Con	4,816	13.8	-5.9
			Chahal B.S.	SDP	3,912	11.2	-2.8
			Gardner K.A. Dr.‡	Comm	601	1.7*	+1.0
					20,689	59.4	
1992	49,595†	54.6	Parry R.*	Lab	20,550	75.9	+2.7
			Zsigmond A.	Con	3,113	11.5	-2.3
			Ali M.A.	LD	2,498	9.2	-2.0
			Brown L.	Green	738	2.7*	+2.7
			Collins J.D.	NLP	169	0.6*	+0.6
					17,437	64.4	

LIVERPOOL, WALTON [379]

Election	Electors	T'out	Candidate	Party	Votes	% Sh	% Ch
1983	73,532	69.6	Heffer E.S.*	Lab	26,980	52.7	
			Maddox A.J.	Con	12,865	25.1	
			Croft D.M.B.	Lib	10,970	21.4	
			McKechnie D.J.	BNP	343	0.7*	
					14,115	27.6	
1987	73,118	73.6	Heffer E.S.*	Lab	34,661	64.4	+11.7
			Clark P.R.	Lib	11,408	21.2	-0.2
			Mays I.A.	Con	7,738	14.4	-10.8
					23,253	43.2	
[Death]							
1991	70,803	56.7	Kilfoyle P.	Lab	21,317	53.1	-11.3
(4/7)			Clark P.R.	LD	14,457	36.0	+14.8
			Mahmood L.E. Ms.	Ind	2,613	6.5	
			Greenwood B.R.J.	Con	1,155	2.9*	-11.5
			Sutch D.E.	MRLP	546	1.4*	
			Lee-Delisle E.G.	Ind	63	0.2*	
					6,860	17.1	
1992	70,118†	67.4	Kilfoyle P.	Lab	34,214	72.4	+8.0
			Greenwood B.R.J.	Con	5,915	12.5	-1.9
			Lang J.	LD	5,672	12.0	-9.2
			Newall T.S.	Lib	963	2.0*	+2.0
			Carson D.J.E.	Ind	393	0.8*	
			Raiano D.J. Ms.	NLP	98	0.2*	+0.2
					28,299	59.9	

LIVERPOOL, WEST DERBY [380]

Election	Electors	T'out	Candidate	Party	Votes	% Sh	% Ch
1983	63,088	69.5	Wareing R.N.	Lab	23,905	54.5	
			Trelawny W.M.	Con	12,062	27.5	
			Ogden E.*	SDP	7,871	18.0	
					11,843	27.0	
1987	60,522	73.4	Wareing R.N.*	Lab	29,021	65.3	+10.8
			Backhouse J.E.	Con	8,525	19.2	-8.3
			Ferguson M.	SDP	6,897	15.5	-2.4
					20,496	46.1	
1992	56,724†	69.8	Wareing R.N.*	Lab	27,014	68.2	+2.9
			Fitzsimmons S.	Con	6,589	16.6	-2.5
			Bundred G.S. Ms.	LD	4,838	12.2	-3.3
			Curtis D.	Lib	1,021	2.6*	+2.6
			Higgins C.J.	NLP	154	0.4*	+0.4
					20,425	51.6	

LIVINGSTON [381]

Election	Electors	T'out	Candidate	Party	Votes	% Sh	% Ch
1983	53,284	71.7	Cook R.F.*	Lab	14,255	37.3	
			Henderson A.M.	Lib	9,704	25.4	
			Campbell J.A.	Con	9,129	23.9	
			MacAskill K.W.	SNP	5,090	13.3	
					4,551	11.9	
1987	56,583	74.1	Cook R.F.*	Lab	19,110	45.6	+8.2
			McCreadie R.A.	Lib	8,005	19.1	-6.3
			Mayall M.N.A. Dr.	Con	7,860	18.7	-5.2
			MacAskill K.W.	SNP	6,969	16.6	+3.3
					11,105	26.5	
1992	61,093†	74.6	Cook R.F.*	Lab	20,245	44.4	-1.2
			Johnston P.J.B.	SNP	12,140	26.6	+10.0
			Gordon J.H.H.	Con	8,824	19.4	+0.6
			Mackintosh H.F.D.	LD	3,911	8.6	-10.5
			Ross-Smith A.G.	Green	469	1.0*	+1.0
					8,105	17.8	

LLANELLI [382]

Election	Electors	T'out	Candidate	Party	Votes	% Sh	% Ch
1983	63,826	75.4	Davies D.J.D.*	Lab	23,207	48.2	
			Kennedy N.T.	Con	9,601	19.9	
			Rees K.D.	Lib	9,076	18.9	
			Edwards H.T.	PC	5,880	12.2*	
			Hitchon R.E.	Comm	371	0.8*	
					13,606	28.3	
1987	63,775	78.2	Davies D.J.D.*	Lab	29,506	59.2	+10.9
			Circus P.J.	Con	8,571	17.2	-2.8
			Shrewsbury M.J.	Lib	6,714	13.5	-5.4
			Price A.	PC	5,088	10.2	-2.0
					20,935	42.0	
1992	65,057†	77.8	Davies D.J.D.*	Lab	27,802	54.9	-4.2
			Down G.L.	Con	8,532	16.9	-0.3
			Phillips D.M.	PC	7,878	15.6	+5.4
			Evans K.J.	LD	6,404	12.7	-0.8
					19,270	38.1	

213

LONDONDERRY EAST [383]

Election	Electors	T'out	Candidate	Party	Votes	% Sh	% Ch
1983	67,306	76.3	Ross W.*	UU	19,469	37.9	
			McClure J.W.	UDUP	12,207	23.8	
			Doherty A.	SDLP	9,397	18.3	
			Davey J.	SF	7,073	13.8	
			McGrath M.T. Ms.	APNI	2,401	4.7*	
			Donnelly F.	WP	819	1.6*	
					7,262	14.1	

[Seeks Re-election]

Election	Electors	T'out	Candidate	Party	Votes	% Sh	% Ch
1986	70,038	47.0	Ross W.*	UU	30,922	93.9	+56.0
(23/1)			Barry P.	FAIA	2,001	6.1	
					28,921	87.8	

Election	Electors	T'out	Candidate	Party	Votes	% Sh	% Ch
1987	71,031	68.7	Ross W.*	UU	29,532	60.5	+22.6
			Doherty A.	SDLP	9,375	19.2	+0.9
			Davey J.	SF	5,464	11.2	-2.6
			McGowan P.J.	APNI	3,237	6.6	+2.0
			Donnelly F.	WP	935	1.9*	+0.3
			Samuel M.H.	NIEP	281	0.6*	+0.6
					20,157	41.3	

Election	Electors	T'out	Candidate	Party	Votes	% Sh	% Ch
1992	75,587	69.8	Ross W.*	UU	30,370	57.6	-2.9
			Doherty A.	SDLP	11,843	22.5	+3.3
			Davey-Kennedy P. Ms.	SF	5,320	10.1	-1.1
			McGowan P.J.	APNI	3,613	6.9	+0.2
			Elder A.E.	Con	1,589	3.0*	+3.0
					18,527	35.1	

LOUGHBOROUGH [384]

Election	Electors	T'out	Candidate	Party	Votes	% Sh	% Ch
1983	70,668	77.7	Dorrell S.J.*	Con	29,056	52.9	
			Jones M.T.	Lab	12,876	23.4	
			Frears J.R.	SDP	12,189	22.2	
			Whitebread D.G.	Green	591	1.1*	
			Peacock J.A.	BNP	228	0.4*	
					16,180	29.5	
1987	73,660	79.2	Dorrell S.J.*	Con	31,931	54.7	+1.8
			Wrigley C.J.	Lab	14,283	24.5	+1.0
			Fox R.G.	SDP	11,499	19.7	-2.5
			Gupta R.	Green	656	1.1*	+0.0
					17,648	30.2	
1992	75,451†	78.5	Dorrell S.J.*	Con	30,064	50.7	-4.0
			Reed A.J.	Lab	19,181	32.4	+7.9
			Stott A.W.	LD	8,953	15.1	-4.6
			Sinclair I.	Green	817	1.4*	+0.3
			Reynolds P.	NLP	233	0.4*	+0.4
					10,883	18.4	

LUDLOW [385]

Election	Electors	T'out	Candidate	Party	Votes	% Sh	% Ch
1983	63,256	74.6	Cockeram E.P.*	Con	26,278	55.7	
			Lane D.C.W.	SDP	14,975	31.7	
			Davis P.M.	Lab	5,949	12.6	
					11,303	23.9	
1987	66,187	77.1	Gill C.J.F.	Con	27,499	53.9	-1.8
			Phillips I.D.	Lib	15,800	31.0	-0.8
			Harrison K.	Lab	7,724	15.1	+2.5
					11,699	22.9	
1992	68,937†	80.9	Gill C.J.F.*	Con	28,719	51.5	-2.4
			Phillips I.D.	LD	14,567	26.1	-4.8
			Mason B.O. Ms.	Lab	11,709	21.0	+5.9
			Appleton-Fox N.H.	Green	758	1.4*	+1.4
					14,152	25.4	

LUTON NORTH [386]

Election	Electors	T'out	Candidate	Party	Votes	% Sh	% Ch
1983	69,805	77.4	Carlisle J.R.*	Con	26,115	48.3	
			Hopkins K.P.	Lab	14,134	26.2	
			Stephen J.D.	SDP	13,769	25.5	
					11,981	22.2	
1987	74,235	77.6	Carlisle J.R.*	Con	30,997	53.8	+5.5
			Wright M.R.	Lab	15,424	26.8	+0.6
			Stephen J.D.	SDP	11,166	19.4	-6.1
					15,573	27.0	
1992	76,940†	81.8	Carlisle J.R.*	Con	33,777	53.7	-0.2
			McWalter A.	Lab	20,683	32.9	+6.1
			Jackson J.M. Ms.	LD	7,570	12.0	-7.4
			Jones R.P.	Green	633	1.0*	+1.0
			Buscombe K.M.	NLP	292	0.5*	+0.5
					13,094	20.8	

LUTON SOUTH [387]

Election	Electors	T'out	Candidate	Party	Votes	% Sh	% Ch
1983	71,015	75.8	Bright G.F.J.*	Con	22,531	41.9	
			Clemitson I.M.	Lab	17,910	33.3	
			Franks D.G.	Lib	13,395	24.9	
					4,621	8.6	
1987	70,850	75.6	Bright G.F.J.*	Con	24,762	46.2	+4.4
			McKenzie W.D.	Lab	19,647	36.7	+3.4
			Chapman P.	Lib	9,146	17.1	-7.8
					5,115	9.6	
1992	73,016†	79.1	Bright G.F.J.*	Con	25,900	44.8	-1.4
			McKenzie W.D.	Lab	25,101	43.5	+6.8
			Rogers D.	LD	6,020	10.4	-6.7
			Bliss L. Ms.	Green	550	1.0*	+1.0
			Cooke D.R.H	NLP	191	0.3*	+0.3
					799	1.3	

MACCLESFIELD [388]

Election	Electors	T'out	Candidate	Party	Votes	% Sh	% Ch
1983	73,082	75.0	Winterton N.R.*	Con	32,538	59.4	
			Coleman R. Ms.	Lib	11,859	21.6	
			Kelly P.B.	Lab	9,923	18.1	
			Reeman J.E.M.	Ind	488	0.9*	
					20,679	37.7	
1987	76,093	77.4	Winterton N.R.*	Con	33,208	56.4	-3.0
			Haldane A.B.	Lib	14,116	24.0	+2.3
			Pinder C. Ms.	Lab	11,563	19.6	+1.5
					19,092	32.4	
1992	76,549†	82.3	Winterton N.R.*	Con	36,447	57.9	+1.5
			Longworth M.C. Ms.	Lab	13,680	21.7	+2.1
			Beatty P.C.W.	LD	12,600	20.0	-4.0
			Penn C.A. Ms.	NLP	268	0.4*	+0.4
					22,767	36.1	

MAIDSTONE [389]

Election	Electors	T'out	Candidate	Party	Votes	% Sh	% Ch
1983	70,357	73.8	Wells J.J.*	Con	26,420	50.9	
			Burnett E.J.	Lib	19,194	37.0	
			Carey G.T.	Lab	6,280	12.1*	
					7,226	13.9	
1987	72,987	76.0	Widdecombe A.N. Ms.	Con	29,100	52.4	+1.5
			Sutton-Mattocks C.J.	Lib	18,736	33.8	-3.2
			Brooks K.P.	Lab	6,935	12.5	+0.4
			Kemp P.A. Ms.	Green	717	1.3*	+1.3
					10,364	18.7	
1992	72,862	80.1	Widdecombe A.N. Ms.*	Con	31,611	54.2	+1.7
			Yates P.G. Ms.	LD	15,325	26.3	-7.5
			Logan A.F.H. Ms.	Lab	10,517	18.0	+5.5
			Kemp P.A. Ms.	Green	707	1.2*	-0.1
			Ingram F.J.	NLP	172	0.3*	+0.3
					16,286	27.9	

MAKERFIELD [390]

Election	Electors	T'out	Candidate	Party	Votes	% Sh	% Ch
1983	69,176	73.7	McGuire M.T.F.*	Lab	25,114	49.3	
			Hay E.P.	Con	14,238	27.9	
			Grayson R.F.	Lib	11,633	22.8	
					10,876	21.3	
1987	70,819	75.8	McCartney I.	Lab	30,190	56.3	+7.0
			Robertson L.A.	Con	14,632	27.3	-0.7
			Hewer W.R.	Lib	8,838	16.5	-6.3
					15,558	29.0	
1992	71,426†	76.1	McCartney I.*	Lab	32,832	60.4	+4.1
			Dickson D.M. Ms.	Con	14,714	27.1	-0.2
			Jeffers S.T.	LD	5,097	9.4	-7.1
			Cairns S. Ms.	Lib	1,309	2.4*	+2.4
			Davies C.D.	NLP	397	0.7*	+0.7
					18,118	33.3	

MANCHESTER BLACKLEY [391]

Election	Electors	T'out	Candidate	Party	Votes	% Sh	% Ch
1983	60,106	69.7	Eastham K.*	Lab	20,132	48.1	
			Ridgway P.C.J.	Con	13,676	32.6	
			Cookson J.	Lib	8,081	19.3	
					6,456	15.4	
1987	58,814	72.9	Eastham K.*	Lab	22,476	52.4	+4.4
			Nath K.K.	Con	12,354	28.8	-3.8
			Showman H.L.	SDP	8,041	18.8	-0.5
					10,122	23.6	
1992	55,235†	69.3	Eastham K.*	Lab	23,031	60.2	+7.7
			Hobhouse W.S.	Con	10,642	27.8	-1.0
			Wheale S.D.	LD	4,324	11.3	-7.5
			Kennedy M.P.	NLP	288	0.8*	+0.8
					12,389	32.4	

MANCHESTER CENTRAL [392]

Election	Electors	T'out	Candidate	Party	Votes	% Sh	% Ch
1983	69,188	60.6	Litherland R.K.*	Lab	27,353	65.3	
			Eager D.	Con	8,868	21.2	
			Ahmed A.	SDP	4,956	11.8*	
			Coles A.	NF	729	1.7*	
					18,485	44.1	
1987	62,928	63.9	Litherland R.K.*	Lab	27,428	68.2	+2.9
			Banks M.R.W.	Con	7,561	18.8	-2.4
			McColgan B.W.	SDP	5,250	13.0	+1.2
					19,867	49.4	
1992	56,447†	56.9	Litherland R.K.*	Lab	23,336	72.7	+4.5
			Davies P.W.	Con	5,299	16.5	-2.3
			Clayton R.M.	LD	3,151	9.8	-3.2
			Buchanan A.N.	CL	167	0.5*	+0.5
			Mitchell V.C. Ms.	NLP	167	0.5*	+0.5
					18,037	56.2	

MANCHESTER, GORTON [393]

Election	Electors	T'out	Candidate	Party	Votes	% Sh	% Ch
1983	64,645	67.9	Kaufman G.B.*	Lab	22,460	51.2	
			Kershaw J.	Con	12,495	28.5	
			Whitmore K.A.	Lib	8,348	19.0	
			Cowle M.	Comm	333	0.8*	
			Andrews L.C.	BNP	231	0.5*	
					9,965	22.7	
1987	64,243	70.4	Kaufman G.B.*	Lab	24,615	54.4	+3.2
			Kershaw J.	Con	10,550	23.3	-5.2
			Whitmore K.A.	Lib	9,830	21.7	+2.7
			Lawrence P. Ms.	RF	253	0.6*	+0.6
					14,065	31.1	
1992	62,410†	60.8	Kaufman G.B.*	Lab	23,671	62.3	+7.9
			Bullock J.D.	Con	7,392	19.5	-3.8
			Harris C.P.	LD	5,327	14.0	-7.7
			Henderson T.	Lib	767	2.0*	+2.0
			Daw M.J.	Green	595	1.6*	+1.6
			Lawrence P. Ms.	RCP	108	0.3*	+0.3
			Mitchell P.D.	NLP	84	0.2*	+0.2
			Smith C.E. Ms.	ICP	30	0.1*	+0.1
					16,279	42.9	

219

MANCHESTER, WITHINGTON [394]

Election	Electors	T'out	Candidate	Party	Votes	% Sh	% Ch
1983	64,606	72.3	Silvester F.J.*	Con	18,329	39.2	
			Done F.W. Ms.	Lab	15,956	34.2	
			Lever B.L.	SDP	12,231	26.2	
			Gibson M.G.	Ind	184	0.4*	
					2,373	5.1	
1987	65,343	77.1	Bradley K.J.C.	Lab	21,650	42.9	+8.8
			Silvester F.J.*	Con	18,259	36.2	-3.0
			Jones A. Ms.	Lib	9,978	19.8	-6.4
			Abberton M.T.	Green	524	1.0*	+1.0
					3,391	6.7	
1992	63,838†	71.3	Bradley K.J.C.*	Lab	23,962	52.7	+9.7
			Farthing E.N.	Con	14,227	31.3	-5.0
			Hennell P.G.	LD	6,457	14.2	-5.6
			Candeland B.A.	Green	725	1.6*	+0.6
			Menhinick C.N.	NLP	128	0.3*	+0.3
					9,735	21.4	

MANCHESTER, WYTHENSHAWE [395]

Election	Electors	T'out	Candidate	Party	Votes	% Sh	% Ch
1983	60,995	69.6	Morris A.*	Lab	23,172	54.6	
			Jacobs J.M. Ms.	Con	12,488	29.4	
			Sandiford D.J.	Lib	6,766	15.9	
					10,684	25.2	
1987	58,287	72.1	Morris A.*	Lab	23,881	56.8	+2.2
			Sparrow D.G.	Con	12,026	28.6	-0.8
			Butterworth J. Ms.	SDP	5,921	14.1	-1.9
			Connelly S. Ms.	RF	216	0.5*	+0.5
					11,855	28.2	
1992	53,549†	69.7	Morris A.*	Lab	22,591	60.5	+3.7
			McKenna K.A.	Con	10,595	28.4	-0.2
			Fenn S.J.	LD	3,633	9.7	-4.3
			Otten G.N.	Green	362	1.0*	+1.0
			Martin E. Ms.	NLP	133	0.4*	+0.4
					11,996	32.1	

MANSFIELD [396]

Election	Electors	T'out	Candidate	Party	Votes	% Sh	% Ch
1983	65,277	70.7	Concannon J.D.*	Lab	18,670	40.5	
			Wrenn R.J.	Con	16,432	35.6	
			Taylor S.E.	SDP	11,036	23.9	
					2,238	4.9	
1987	66,764	78.4	Meale J.A.	Lab	19,610	37.5	-3.0
			Hendry C.	Con	19,554	37.4	+1.7
			Answer B.M.	SDP	11,604	22.2	-1.8
			Marshall B.	Ind Lab	1,580	3.0*	
					56	0.1	
1992	66,965†	82.2	Meale J.A.*	Lab	29,932	54.4	+16.9
			Mond G.S.	Con	18,208	33.1	-4.3
			Thompstone S.R.	LD	6,925	12.6	-9.6
					11,724	21.3	

MEDWAY [397]

Election	Electors	T'out	Candidate	Party	Votes	% Sh	% Ch
1983	63,387	72.6	Fenner P.E. Ms.*	Con	22,507	48.9	
			Bean R.E.	Lab	13,851	30.1	
			Winckless F.C.	SDP	9,658	21.0	
					8,656	18.8	
1987	64,103	73.0	Fenner P.E. Dame*	Con	23,889	51.0	+2.1
			Hull V.A.	Lab	13,960	29.8	-0.3
			Horne-Roberts J. Ms.	SDP	8,450	18.1	-2.9
			Rosser J.V. Ms.	Green	504	1.1*	+1.1
					9,929	21.2	
1992	61,737†	80.2	Fenner P.E. Dame*	Con	25,924	52.3	+1.3
			Marshall-Andrews R.G.	Lab	17,138	34.6	+4.8
			Trice C.L.	LD	4,751	9.6	-8.5
			Austin M.	Lib	1,480	3.0*	+3.0
			Kember P.A.	NLP	234	0.5*	+0.5
					8,786	17.7	

MEIRIONNYDD NANT CONWY [398]

Election	Electors	T'out	Candidate	Party	Votes	% Sh	% Ch
1983	30,459	81.3	Thomas D.E.*	PC	9,709	39.2	
			Lloyd D.G.	Con	7,066	28.5	
			Roberts D.L.	SDP	4,254	17.2	
			Williams G.	Lab	3,735	15.1	
					2,643	10.7	
1987	32,214	80.6	Thomas D.E.*	PC	10,392	40.0	+0.8
			Jones D.T.	Con	7,366	28.4	-0.2
			Roberts H.G.	Lab	4,397	16.9	+1.8
			Roberts D.L.	SDP	3,814	14.7	-2.5
					3,026	11.7	
1992	32,413†	81.5	Llwyd E.	PC	11,608	44.0	+3.9
			Lewis G.S.	Con	6,995	26.5	-1.9
			Williams R.	Lab	4,978	18.8	+1.9
			Parry R.E. Ms.	LD	2,358	8.9	-5.8
			Pritchard W.A.	Green	471	1.8*	+1.8
					4,613	17.5	

MERIDEN [399]

Election	Electors	T'out	Candidate	Party	Votes	% Sh	% Ch
1983	74,161	71.6	Mills I.C.*	Con	28,474	53.7	
			Sever E.J.*	Lab	13,456	25.4	
			Dunbar P.M. Ms.	SDP	10,674	20.1	
			Collins C.L.	NF	460	0.9*	
					15,018	28.3	
1987	78,444	73.9	Mills I.C.*	Con	31,935	55.1	+1.5
			Burden R.H.	Lab	15,115	26.1	+0.7
			Parkinson C.E. Ms.	SDP	10,896	18.8	-1.3
					16,820	29.0	
1992	77,009	78.8	Mills I.C.*	Con	33,462	55.1	+0.0
			Stephens N.J.	Lab	18,763	30.9	+4.8
			Morris J.A. Ms.	LD	8,489	14.0	-4.8
					14,699	24.2	

MERTHYR TYDFIL AND RHYMNEY [400]

Election	Electors	T'out	Candidate	Party	Votes	% Sh	% Ch
1983	59,486	72.5	Rowlands E.*	Lab	29,053	67.3	
			Owen P.C.	Lib	6,323	14.7	
			Blausten R.	Con	5,449	12.6	
			Howells G.	PC	2,058	4.8*	
			Gould R.T.	WRP	256	0.6*	
					22,730	52.7	
1987	58,285	76.2	Rowlands E.*	Lab	33,477	75.4	+8.0
			Walters N.M.	Con	5,270	11.9	-0.8
			Verma P.K.	Lib	3,573	8.0	-6.6
			Davies J.M. Ms.	PC	2,085	4.7*	-0.1
					28,207	63.5	
1992	58,430	75.8	Rowlands E.*	Lab	31,710	71.6	-3.8
			Rowland R.P.J.	LD	4,997	11.3	+3.2
			Hughes M.J.	Con	4,904	11.1	-0.8
			Cox A.G.	PC	2,704	6.1	+1.4
					26,713	60.3	

MIDDLESBROUGH [401]

Election	Electors	T'out	Candidate	Party	Votes	% Sh	% Ch
1983	62,950	66.5	Bell S.	Lab	21,220	50.7	
			Campey L.H. Ms.	Con	11,551	27.6	
			Sanders A.D. Rev.	Lib	8,871	21.2	
			Simpson M.A.	WRP	207	0.5*	
					9,669	23.1	
1987	60,789	71.0	Bell S.*	Lab	25,747	59.7	+9.0
			Orr-Ewing R.J.	Con	10,789	25.0	-2.6
			Hawley P.A.	Lib	6,594	15.3	-5.9
					14,958	34.7	
1992	58,852	69.8	Bell S.*	Lab	26,343	64.1	+4.4
			Rayner P.R.	Con	10,559	25.7	+0.7
			Jordan R. Ms.	LD	4,201	10.2	-5.1
					15,784	38.4	

Election	Electors	T'out	Candidate	Party	Votes	% Sh	% Ch
1983	60,496	75.0	Eadie A.*	Lab	19,401	42.7	
			Dewar A.R.	SDP	13,245	29.2	
			Menzies D.A.Y.	Con	9,922	21.9	
			Hird M.J. Ms.	SNP	2,826	6.2*	
					6,156	13.6	
1987	60,561	77.2	Eadie A.*	Lab	22,553	48.3	+5.5
			Dewar A.R.	SDP	10,300	22.0	-7.1
			Riddell F.G.	Con	8,527	18.2	-3.6
			Chisholm I.M.	SNP	4,947	10.6	+4.4
			Smith I.A.	Green	412	0.9*	+0.9
					12,253	26.2	
1992	60,311	77.8	Clarke E.L.	Lab	20,588	43.9	-4.4
			Lumsden A.	SNP	10,254	21.9	+11.3
			Stoddart W.J.	Con	9,443	20.1	+1.9
			Sewell P.L.	LD	6,164	13.1	-8.9
			Morrice I.D.	Green	476	1.0*	+0.1
					10,334	22.0	

Election	Electors	T'out	Candidate	Party	Votes	% Sh	% Ch
1983	79,229	74.0	Benyon W.R.*	Con	28,181	48.0	
			Nightingale J.M. Ms.	SDP	16,659	28.4	
			Thakoordin J.	Lab	13,045	22.2	
			Francis A.H.	Green	494	0.8*	
			Rickcord R.G.W.	BNP	290	0.5*	
					11,522	19.6	
1987	97,041	76.3	Benyon W.R.*	Con	35,396	47.8	-0.2
			Rodgers W.T.	SDP	21,695	29.3	+0.9
			Brownfield-Pope Y.V.A. Ms.	Lab	16,111	21.8	-0.5
			Francis A.H.	Green	810	1.1*	+0.3
					13,701	18.5	

During the 1987-1992 Parliament the boundaries of the two existing seats of Buckingham and Milton Keynes were re-drawn to create three new constituencies - Buckingham, Milton Keynes North East and Milton Keynes South West. The figures for change in share of the vote are based on the estimates of the likely 1987 'result' in the new seats.

MILTON KEYNES NORTH EAST

Election	Electors	T'out	Candidate	Party	Votes	% Sh	% Ch
1992	63,545	79.9	Butler P.	Con	26,212	51.6	+3.1
			Cosin M.I. Ms.	Lab	12,036	23.7	+7.8
			Gaskell P.K.	LD	11,693	23.0	-10.6
			Francis A.H.	Green	529	1.0*	-0.9
			Kavanagh-Dowsett M.T.M.P. Ms.	Ind Con	249	0.5*	
			Simson M.J.H.	NLP	79	0.2*	+0.2
					14,176	27.9	

MILTON KEYNES SOUTH WEST

Election	Electors	T'out	Candidate	Party	Votes	% Sh	% Ch
1992	67,365	75.9	Legg B.C.	Con	23,840	46.6	-1.4
			Wilson K.J.	Lab	19,153	37.4	+7.6
			Pym C.	LD	7,429	14.5	-7.6
			Field C. Ms.	Green	525	1.0*	+1.0
			Kelly H.W.	NLP	202	0.4*	+0.4
					4,687	9.2	

MITCHAM AND MORDEN [404]

Election	Electors	T'out	Candidate	Party	Votes	% Sh	% Ch
1983	63,535	73.1	Rumbold A.C.R. Ms.*	Con	19,827	42.7	
			Nicholas D.G.	Lab	13,376	28.8	
			Douglas-Mann B.L.H.	SDP	12,720	27.4	
			Perryman J.R.	NF	539	1.2*	
					6,451	13.9	
1987	63,089	75.7	Rumbold A.C.R. Ms.*	Con	23,002	48.2*	+5.5
			McDonagh S.A. Ms.	Lab	16,819	35.2	+6.4
			Douglas-Mann B.L.H.	SDP	7,930	16.6	-10.8
					6,183	13.0	
1992	63,752	80.3	Rumbold A.C.R. Ms.*	Con	23,789	46.5	-1.7
			McDonagh S.A. Ms.	Lab	22,055	43.1	+7.9
			Field J.C.	LD	4,687	9.2	-7.5
			Walsh T.J.	Green	655	1.3*	+1.3
					1,734	3.4	

MOLE VALLEY [405]

Election	Electors	T'out	Candidate	Party	Votes	% Sh	% Ch
1983	65,067	75.0	Baker K.W.*	Con	29,691	60.8	
			Thomas S.P. Ms.	Lib	14,973	30.7	
			Lines F. Ms.	Lab	4,147	8.5*	
					14,718	30.2	
1987	67,715	77.0	Baker K.W.*	Con	31,689	60.8	-0.1
			Thomas S.P. Ms.	Lib	15,613	29.9	-0.7
			King C.M.B.	Lab	4,846	9.3	+0.8
					16,076	30.8	
1992	66,963	82.0	Baker K.W.*	Con	32,549	59.3	-1.5
			Watson M.D.	LD	16,599	30.2	+0.3
			Walsh T.J.	Lab	5,291	9.6	+0.3
			Thomas J.M. Ms.	NLP	442	0.8*	+0.8
					15,950	29.1	

MONKLANDS EAST [406]

Election	Electors	T'out	Candidate	Party	Votes	% Sh	% Ch
1983	49,030	73.1	Smith J.*	Lab	18,358	51.2	
			Love J.	Con	8,559	23.9	
			Rennie A.N. Dr.	Lib	5,721	16.0	
			Johnston T.R.	SNP	3,185	8.9*	
					9,799	27.4	
1987	49,644	74.8	Smith J.*	Lab	22,649	61.0	+9.7
			Love J.	Con	6,260	16.9	-7.0
			Gibson K.J.	SNP	4,790	12.9	+4.0
			Grieve S.M. Ms.	Lib	3,442	9.3	-6.7
					16,389	44.1	
1992	48,430	75.0	Smith J.*	Lab	22,266	61.3	+0.3
			Wright J.	SNP	6,554	18.0	+5.1
			Walters S.	Con	5,830	16.0	-0.8
			Ross P.W.	LD	1,679	4.6*	-4.6
					15,712	43.2	
[Death] 1994 (30/6)	48,724	70.0	Liddell H. Ms.	Lab	16,960	49.8	-11.5
			Ullrich K. Ms.	SNP	15,320	44.9	+26.9
			Gallagher S.	LD	878	2.6*	-2.0
			Bell S. Ms.	Con	127	2.3*	-13.7
			Bremner A. Ms.	Ind	69	0.2*	
			Paterson D.J.	NLP	58	0.2*	
					1,640	4.8	

MONKLANDS WEST [407]

Election	Electors	T'out	Candidate	Party	Votes	% Sh	% Ch
1983	50,345	75.7	Clarke T.*	Lab	20,642	54.2	
			Cameron L.	Con	8,378	22.0	
			Ackland R.	SDP	6,605	17.3	
			Lyon G.A.	SNP	2,473	6.5*	
					12,264	32.2	
1987	50,874	77.3	Clarke T.*	Lab	24,499	62.3	+8.1
			Lind G.	Con	6,166	15.7	-6.3
			McQueen A. Ms.	SDP	4,408	11.2	-6.1
			Bovey K.S.	SNP	4,260	10.8	+4.3
					18,333	46.6	
1992	49,300	77.4	Clarke T.*	Lab	23,384	61.3	-1.0
			Bovey K.S.	SNP	6,319	16.6	+5.7
			Lownie A.J.H.	Con	6,074	15.9	+0.2
			Hamilton S. Ms.	LD	2,382	6.2	-5.0
					17,065	44.7	

227

MONMOUTH [408]

Election	Electors	T'out	Candidate	Party	Votes	% Sh	% Ch
1983	56,112	78.8	Stradling Thomas J.*	Con	21,746	49.2	
			Lindley C.D.	SDP	12,403	28.0	
			Short C.	Lab	9,593	21.7	
			Williams G.O.	PC	493	1.1*	
					9,343	21.1	
1987	58,292	80.8	Stradling Thomas J. Sir.*	Con	22,387	47.5	-1.6
			Gass K. Ms.	Lab	13,037	27.7	+6.0
			Lindley C.D.	SDP	11,313	24.0	-4.0
			Meredudd S.R. Ms.	PC	363	0.8*	-0.3
					9,350	19.9	

[Death]

Election	Electors	T'out	Candidate	Party	Votes	% Sh	% Ch
1991	59,460	75.8	Edwards H.W.E.	Lab	17,733	39.3	+11.6
(16/5)			Evans R.K.	Con	15,327	34.0	-13.5
			David F.A. Ms.	LD	11,164	24.8	+0.8
			Sutch D.E.	MRLP	314	0.7*	
			Witherden M.J.	GP/PC	277	0.6*	-0.2
			Carpenter P.R.	Ind	164	0.4*	
			St. Clair L. Ms.	Ind	121	0.3*	
					2,406	5.3	
1992	59,148†	86.1	Evans R.K.	Con	24,059	47.3	-0.3
			Edwards H.W.E.	Lab	20,855	41.0	+13.3
			David F.A. Ms.	LD	5,562	10.9	-13.1
			Witherden M.J.	GP/PC	431	0.8*	+0.2
					3,204	6.3	

MONTGOMERY [409]

Election	Electors	T'out	Candidate	Party	Votes	% Sh	% Ch
1983	37,474	79.2	Carlile A.C.	Lib	12,863	43.3	
			Williams D.J.D.*	Con	12,195	41.1	
			Wilson A.J.	Lab	2,550	8.6*	
			Clowes C.I. Dr.	PC	1,585	5.3*	
			Rowlands D.W.L.	Ind	487	1.6*	
					668	2.3	
1987	39,806	79.4	Carlile A.C.*	Lib	14,729	46.6	+3.2
			Evans D.M.	Con	12,171	38.5	-2.6
			Llewellyn Jones E.D.W.	Lab	3,304	10.5	+1.9
			Clowes C.I. Dr.	PC	1,412	4.5*	-0.9
					2,558	8.1	
1992	41,386†	79.9	Carlile A.C.*	LD	16,031	48.5	+1.9
			France-Hayhurst J. Ms.	Con	10,822	32.7	-5.8
			Wood S.J.	Lab	4,115	12.4	+2.0
			Parsons H.N.	PC	1,581	4.8*	+0.3
			Adams P.H.W.	Green	508	1.5*	+1.5
					5,209	15.8	

MORAY [410]

Election	Electors	T'out	Candidate	Party	Votes	% Sh	% Ch
1983	60,804	71.1	Pollock A.*	Con	16,944	39.2	
			Watt H.	SNP	15,231	35.2	
			Burnett M.R.	Lib	7,901	18.3	
			Kiddie J.	Lab	3,139	7.3*	
					1,713	4.0	
1987	62,201	72.6	Ewing M.A. Ms.	SNP	19,510	43.2	+7.9
			Pollock A.*	Con	15,825	35.0	-4.2
			Smith C.R.C.	Lab	5,118	11.3	+4.1
			Skene D.G.M.	Lib	4,724	10.5	-7.8
					3,685	8.2	
1992	62,605	73.2	Ewing M.A. Ms.*	SNP	20,299	44.3	+1.1
			Hossack R.L. Ms.	Con	17,455	38.1	+3.1
			Smith C.R.C.	Lab	5,448	11.9	+0.6
			Sheridan J.B.	LD	2,634	5.7	-4.7
					2,844	6.2	

MORECAMBE AND LUNESDALE [411]

Election	Electors	T'out	Candidate	Party	Votes	% Sh	% Ch
1983	53,238	72.9	Lennox-Boyd M.A. Hon.*	Con	21,968	56.6	
			Clare T.	SDP	9,774	25.2	
			Bryning A.C.	Lab	6,882	17.7	
			Woods I. Ms.	Ind	208	0.5*	
					12,194	31.4	
1987	55,718	76.1	Lennox-Boyd M.A. Hon.*	Con	22,327	52.7	-3.9
			Greenwell J. Ms.	SDP	10,542	24.9	-0.3
			Smith D.	Lab	9,535	22.5	+4.8
					11,785	27.8	
1992	56,432	78.3	Lennox-Boyd M.A. Hon.*	Con	22,507	50.9	-1.7
			Yates J.E. Ms.	Lab	10,998	24.9	+2.4
			Saville A.J.	LD	9,584	21.7	-3.2
			Turner M.A.	Ind	916	2.1*	
			Marriott R.M.	NLP	205	0.5*	+0.5
					11,509	26.0	

MOTHERWELL NORTH [412]

Election	Electors	T'out	Candidate	Party	Votes	% Sh	% Ch
1983	56,512	75.0	Hamilton J.*	Lab	24,483	57.8	
			Hargrave R.	Con	6,589	15.5	
			Whitelaw G.M.	Lib	5,970	14.1	
			Lyle R.	SNP	5,333	12.6	
					17,894	42.2	
1987	57,632	77.3	Reid J.	Lab	29,825	66.9	+9.2
			Currie A.	SNP	6,230	14.0	+1.4
			Hargrave R.	Con	4,939	11.1	-4.5
			Swift G.	Lib	3,558	8.0	-6.1
					23,595	53.0	
1992	57,140	76.9	Reid J.*	Lab	27,852	63.4	-3.6
			Clark D.A.	SNP	8,942	20.3	+6.4
			Hargrave R.	Con	5,011	11.4	+0.3
			Smith H.D. Ms.	LD	2,145	4.9*	-3.1
					18,910	43.0	

MOTHERWELL SOUTH [413]

Election	Electors	T'out	Candidate	Party	Votes	% Sh	% Ch
1983	52,183	72.9	Bray J.W.*	Lab	19,939	52.4	
			Walker P.M.	Con	7,590	20.0	
			Ashley B.J.	SDP	6,754	17.8	
			Wright J.	SNP	3,743	9.8*	
					12,349	32.5	
1987	52,127	75.5	Bray J.W.*	Lab	22,957	58.3	+5.9
			Wright J.	SNP	6,027	15.3	+5.5
			Bercow J.S.	Con	5,704	14.5	-5.5
			MacGregor W.R.	SDP	4,463	11.3	-6.4
			Somerville R.	Comm	223	0.6*	+0.6
					16,930	43.0	
1992	50,086	76.1	Bray J.W.*	Lab	21,771	57.1	-1.2
			Ullrich K. Ms.	SNP	7,758	20.4	+5.0
			McIntosh G.	Con	6,097	16.0	+1.5
			Mackie A.G.	LD	2,349	6.2	-5.2
			Lettice D.J.	Ind	146	0.4*	
					14,013	36.8	

Election	Electors	T'out	Candidate	Party	Votes	% Sh	% Ch
1983	55,272	76.5	Coleman D.R.*	Lab	22,670	53.6	
			Davies D.K.	SDP	9,066	21.4	
			Buckley R.W.	Con	7,350	17.4	
			Owen D.I.	PC	3,046	7.2*	
			Donovan J.	Ind	150	0.4*	
					13,604	32.2	
1987	55,261	78.8	Coleman D.R.*	Lab	27,612	63.4	+9.8
			Howe M.R.T.	Con	7,034	16.1	-1.2
			Warman J.	SDP	6,132	14.1	-7.4
			John H.	PC	2,792	6.4	-0.8
					20,578	47.2	

[Death]

Election	Electors	T'out	Candidate	Party	Votes	% Sh	% Ch
1991	54,482	63.7	Hain P.G.	Lab	17,962	51.8	-11.6
(4/4)			Evans D.R.	PC	8,132	23.4	+17.0
			Evans R.G.	Con	2,995	8.6	-7.5
			Lloyd D.G.B.	LD	2,000	5.8	-8.3
			Warman J.	SDP	1,826	5.3	
			Jeffreys R.V.W.	Ind Lab	1,253	3.6*	
			Sutch D.E.	MRLP	263	0.8*	
			Kirk B.	Ind	262	0.8*	
					9,830	28.4	
1992	56,355	80.6	Hain P.G.	Lab	30,903	68.0	+4.6
			Adams D.R.	Con	6,928	15.2	-0.9
			Evans D.R.	PC	5,145	11.3	+4.9
			Phillips M.	LD	2,467	5.4	-8.6
					23,975	52.8	

Election	Electors	T'out	Candidate	Party	Votes	% Sh	% Ch
1983	64,008	76.4	Alexander R.T.*	Con	26,334	53.8	
			McGuiggan J.	Lab	12,051	24.6	
			Thompstone S.R.	SDP	10,076	20.6	
			Hewis P.A. Ms.	Green	463	0.9*	
					14,283	29.2	
1987	67,225	78.0	Alexander R.T.*	Con	28,070	53.5	-0.3
			Barton D.H.	Lab	14,527	27.7	+3.1
			Emerson G.A.D.	SDP	9,833	18.8	-1.8
					13,543	25.8	
1992	68,802†	82.2	Alexander R.T.*	Con	28,494	50.4	-3.1
			Barton D.H.	Lab	20,265	35.8	+8.1
			Harris P.R.B.	LD	7,342	13.0	-5.8
			Wood P.A. Ms.	Green	435	0.8*	+0.8
					8,229	14.6	

Election	Electors	T'out	Candidate	Party	Votes	% Sh	% Ch
1983	71,343	75.2	McNair-Wilson R.M.C.*	Con	31,836	59.3	
			Richards A.G.	Lib	18,798	35.0	
			Knight R.C.	Lab	3,027	5.6*	
					13,038	24.3	
1987	75,187	78.0	McNair-Wilson R.M.C.*	Con	35,266	60.1	+0.8
			Rendel D.D.	Lib	18,608	31.7	-3.3
			Stapley R.C.	Lab	4,765	8.1	+2.5
					16,658	28.4	
1992	80,254†	82.8	Chaplin S.J. Ms.	Con	37,135	55.9	-4.2
			Rendel D.D.	LD	24,778	37.3	+5.6
			Hall R.J.E.	Lab	3,962	6.0	-2.2
			Wallis J.P.	Green	539	0.8*	+0.8
					12,357	18.6	

[Death]

Election	Electors	T'out	Candidate	Party	Votes	% Sh	% Ch
1993	81,081	71.3	Rendel D.D.	LD	37,590	65.1	+27.8
(6/5)			Davidson J.T.	Con	15,535	26.9	-29.0
			Billcliffe S.	Lab	1,151	2.0*	-4.0
			Sked A	AFL	601	1.0*	
			Bannon A.	Ind Con	561	1.0*	
			Martin S.	Ind	435	0.8*	
			Sutch D.E.	MRLP	432	0.7*	
			Wallis J	Green	341	0.6*	-0.2
			Marlar R.	Ref	338	0.6*	
			Browne J.E.D.D.	Ind Con	267	0.5*	
			St. Clair L. Ms.	Ind	170	0.3*	
			Board W.O.	Ind	84	0.1*	
			Grenville M.R.S.	NLP	60	0.1*	
			Day J.	Ind	49	0.1*	
			Palmer C.R.	Ind	40	0.1*	
			Grbin M.	Ind	33	0.1*	
			Page A.W.	SDP	33	0.1*	
			Murphy A.G. Ms.	CPGB	32	0.1*	
			Stone M.	Ind	21	0.0*	
					22,055	38.2	

Election	Electors	T'out	Candidate	Party	Votes	% Sh	% Ch
1983	65,400	77.3	Golding J.*	Lab	21,210	42.0	
			Lawrence L.	Con	18,406	36.4	
			Thomas A.L.	Lib	10,916	21.6	
					2,804	5.5	

[Resignation]

Election	Electors	T'out	Candidate	Party	Votes	% Sh	% Ch
1986	66,353	62.2	Golding L. Ms.	Lab	16,819	40.8	-1.2
(17/7)			Thomas A. L.	Lib	16,020	38.8	+17.2
			Nock J.C.B.	Con	7,863	19.0	-17.4
			Sutch D.E.	MRLP	277	0.7*	
			Gaskell J.A.	Ind	115	0.3*	
			Parker J.	Ind	83	0.2*	
			Brewester D. D'A.	Ind	70	0.2*	
					799	2.0	

Election	Electors	T'out	Candidate	Party	Votes	% Sh	% Ch
1987	66,053	80.8	Golding L. Ms.	Lab	21,618	40.5	-1.5
			Thomas A.L.	Lib	16,486	30.9	+9.3
			Ridgway P.C.J.	Con	14,863	27.9	-8.6
			Nicklin M.J.	Ind	397	0.7*	
					5,132	9.6	

Election	Electors	T'out	Candidate	Party	Votes	% Sh	% Ch
1992	66,595†	80.3	Golding L. Ms.*	Lab	25,652	47.9	+7.4
			Brierley A.D.	Con	15,813	29.6	+1.7
			Thomas A.L.	LD	11,727	21.9	-9.0
			Lines R.J.M.	NLP	314	0.6*	+0.6
					9,839	18.4	

NEWCASTLE UPON TYNE CENTRAL [418]

Election	Electors	T'out	Candidate	Party	Votes	% Sh	% Ch
1983	62,687	71.0	Merchant P.R.G.	Con	18,161	40.8	
			Todd N.R.	Lab	15,933	35.8	
			Horam J.R.*	SDP	9,923	22.3	
			Jacques D.N.	Green	478	1.1*	
					2,228	5.0	
1987	63,682	72.5	Cousins J.M.	Lab	20,416	44.2	+8.4
			Merchant P.R.G.*	Con	17,933	38.8	-2.0
			Martin N.	SDP	7,304	15.8	-6.5
			Bird R.J.	Green	418	0.9*	-0.2
			Williams K.	RF	111	0.2*	+0.2
					2,483	5.4	
1992	59,973†	71.3	Cousins J.M.*	Lab	21,123	49.4	+5.2
			Summersby M.A.	Con	15,835	37.0	-1.8
			Opik L.	LD	5,816	13.6	-2.2
					5,288	12.4	

NEWCASTLE UPON TYNE EAST [419]

Election	Electors	T'out	Candidate	Party	Votes	% Sh	% Ch
1983	59,587	71.0	Brown N.H.	Lab	19,247	45.5	
			Barnes A.T.	Con	11,755	27.8	
			Thomas M.S.*	SDP	11,293	26.7	
					7,492	17.7	
1987	59,369	70.6	Brown N.H.*	Lab	23,677	56.4	+10.9
			Riley J.G.A. Ms.	Con	11,177	26.6	-1.1
			Arnold P.J.	Lib	6,728	16.0	-10.7
			Keith J.	Comm	362	0.9*	+0.9
					12,500	29.8	
1992	57,165†	70.7	Brown N.H.*	Lab	24,342	60.2	+3.8
			Lucas J.R.	Con	10,465	25.9	-0.8
			Thompson J.A.	LD	4,883	12.1	-4.0
			Edwards G.L.N.	Green	744	1.8*	+1.8
					13,877	34.3	

NEWCASTLE UPON TYNE NORTH [420]

Election	Electors	T'out	Candidate	Party	Votes	% Sh	% Ch
1983	69,432	72.8	Brown R.C.*	Lab	18,985	37.6	
			Straw P.W.	Con	16,429	32.5	
			Shipley J.W.	Lib	15,136	29.9	
					2,556	5.1	
1987	69,178	75.9	Henderson D.J.	Lab	22,424	42.7	+5.1
			Shipley J.W.	Lib	17,181	32.7	+2.8
			Tweddle J.W.	Con	12,915	24.6	-7.9
					5,243	10.0	
1992	66,187†	76.8	Henderson D.J.*	Lab	25,121	49.4	+6.7
			Gordon I.	Con	16,175	31.8	+7.2
			Maughan P.J.	LD	9,542	18.8	-13.9
					8,946	17.6	

NEW FOREST [421]

Election	Electors	T'out	Candidate	Party	Votes	% Sh	% Ch
1983	70,033	73.5	McNair-Wilson P.M.E.D.*	Con	34,157	66.3	
			Harrison F.R.	Lib	13,262	25.8	
			James D.T.	Lab	4,075	7.9*	
					20,895	40.6	
1987	75,083	76.6	McNair-Wilson P.M.E.D.*	Con	37,188	64.7	-1.7
			Karn R.	Lib	15,456	26.9	+1.1
			Hampton J.I.	Lab	4,856	8.4	+0.5
					21,732	37.8	
1992	75,413†	80.8	McNair-Wilson P.M.E.D.*	Con	37,986	62.4	+0.5
			Vernon-Jackson J.K. Ms.	LD	17,581	28.9	+2.0
			Shutler M.J.	Lab	4,989	8.2	-0.3
			Carter F.A. Ms.	NLP	350	0.6*	+0.6
					20,405	33.5	

NEWHAM NORTH EAST [422]

Election	Electors	T'out	Candidate	Party	Votes	% Sh	% Ch
1983	62,463	62.1	Leighton R.*	Lab	19,286	49.7	
			Gardener H. Ms.	Con	10,773	27.8	
			Winfield A.C. Ms.	Lib	7,943	20.5	
			Adams F.R.	NF	796	2.1*	
					8,513	21.9	
1987	60,787	64.1	Leighton R.*	Lab	20,220	51.9	+2.2
			Davis P.R.C.	Con	11,984	30.7	+3.0
			Steele H. Ms.	Lib	6,772	17.4	-3.1
					8,236	21.1	
1992	59,610	60.3	Leighton R.*	Lab	20,952	58.3	+6.4
			Galbraith J.H.	Con	10,966	30.5	-0.2
			Aves J.J.	LD	4,020	11.2	-6.2
					9,986	27.8	

[Death]

Election	Electors	T'out	Candidate	Party	Votes	% Sh	% Ch
1994	56,228	34.8	Timms S.	Lab	14,668	74.9	+16.6
(9/6)			Hammond P.	Con	2,850	14.6	-16.0
			Kellaway A.J.	LD	821	4.2*	-7.0
			Scholefield A.J.E.	UKI	509	2.6*	
			Homeless J. Ms.	Ind	342	1.7*	
			Archer R.	NLP	228	1.2*	
			Garman V.	Ind	155	0.8*	
					11,818	60.4	

NEWHAM NORTH WEST [423]

Election	Electors	T'out	Candidate	Party	Votes	% Sh	% Ch
1983	49,814	56.1	Banks A.L.	Lab	13,042	46.6	
			Irons K.D.	Con	6,124	21.9	
			Kellaway A.J.	SDP	5,204	18.6	
			Lewis A.W.J.*	Ind Lab	3,074	11.0*	
			Hipperson M.B.	NF	525	1.9*	
					6,918	24.7	
1987	47,568	59.4	Banks A.L.*	Lab	15,677	55.4	+8.8
			Wylie J.C.	Con	7,181	25.4	+3.5
			Redden R.H.	SDP	4,920	17.4	-1.2
			de Grandis-Harrison V.A. Ms.	Green	497	1.8*	+1.8
					8,496	30.0	
1992	46,475	56.0	Banks A.L.*	Lab	15,911	61.1	+5.7
			Prisk M.	Con	6,740	25.9	+0.5
			Sawdon A.J.	LD	2,445	9.4	-8.0
			Sandford A.J. Ms.	Green	587	2.3*	+0.5
			Jug T.	RLGG	252	1.0*	+1.0
			O'Sullivan D.A.	ICP	100	0.4*	+0.4
					9,171	35.2	

NEWHAM SOUTH [424]

Election	Electors	T'out	Candidate	Party	Votes	% Sh	% Ch
1983	50,362	53.6	Spearing N.J.*	Lab	13,561	50.2	
			Reilly A.A.	SDP	6,250	23.1	
			Thompson N.A.M.	Con	6,212	23.0	
			Anderson I.H.M.	NF	993	3.7*	
					7,311	27.1	
1987	50,244	59.1	Spearing N.J.*	Lab	12,935	43.5	-6.7
			Fairrie J.P.J.	Con	10,169	34.2	+11.2
			Kellaway A.J.	SDP	6,607	22.2	-0.9
					2,766	9.3	
1992	51,110	60.2	Spearing N.J.*	Lab	14,358	46.6	+3.1
			Foster J. Ms.	Con	11,856	38.5	+4.3
			Kellaway A.J.	LD	4,572	14.9	-7.4
					2,502	8.1	

239

NEWPORT EAST [425]

Election	Electors	T'out	Candidate	Party	Votes	% Sh	% Ch
1983	52,503	76.6	Hughes R.J.*	Lab	15,931	39.6	
			Thomason K.R.	Con	13,301	33.1	
			David F.A. Ms.	SDP	10,293	25.6	
			Thomas D.J.	PC	697	1.7*	
					2,630	6.5	
1987	52,375	79.8	Hughes R.J.*	Lab	20,518	49.1	+9.5
			Webster-Gardiner G.R.	Con	13,454	32.2	-0.9
			David F.A. Ms.	SDP	7,383	17.7	-7.9
			Butler G.	PC	458	1.1*	-0.6
					7,064	16.9	
1992	51,602†	81.2	Hughes R.J.*	Lab	23,050	55.0	+5.9
			Emmett A.A. Ms.	Con	13,151	31.4	-0.8
			Oliver W.A.	LD	4,991	11.9	-5.7
			Ainley S.M.	GP/PC	716	1.7*	+0.6
					9,899	23.6	

NEWPORT WEST [426]

Election	Electors	T'out	Candidate	Party	Votes	% Sh	% Ch
1983	54,125	77.5	Robinson M.N.F.	Con	15,948	38.0	
			Davies B.	Lab	15,367	36.6	
			Jones W.R.D.	Lib	10,163	24.2	
			Watkins D.R.	PC	477	1.1*	
					581	1.4	
1987	55,455	81.8	Flynn P.P.	Lab	20,887	46.1	+9.4
			Robinson M.N.F.*	Con	18,179	40.1	+2.1
			Roddick G.W.	Lib	5,903	13.0	-11.2
			Bevan D.J.	PC	377	0.8*	-0.3
					2,708	6.0	
1992	54,872†	82.8	Flynn P.P.*	Lab	24,139	53.1	+7.1
			Taylor A.R.	Con	16,360	36.0	-4.1
			Toye J.W.A.	LD	4,296	9.5	-3.6
			Keelan P.J.	GP/PC	653	1.4*	+0.6
					7,779	17.1	

240

NEWRY AND ARMAGH [427]

Election	Electors	T'out	Candidate	Party	Votes	% Sh	% Ch
1983	62,298	76.1	Nicholson J.F.	UU	18,988	40.0	
			Mallon S.	SDLP	17,434	36.8	
			McAllister J.	SF	9,928	20.9	
			Moore T.O.	WP	1,070	2.3*	
					1,554	3.3	

[Seeks Re-election]

Election	Electors	T'out	Candidate	Party	Votes	% Sh	% Ch
1986	65,142	76.6	Mallon S.	SDLP	22,694	45.5	+8.7
(23/1)			Nicholson J.F.*	UU	20,111	40.3	+0.3
			McAllister J.	SF	6,609	13.2	-7.7
			McCusker P.	WP	515	1.0*	-1.3
					2,583	5.2	
1987	66,027	79.2	Mallon S.	SDLP	25,137	48.1	+11.3
			Nicholson J.F.*	UU	19,812	37.9	-2.1
			McAllister J.	SF	6,173	11.8	-9.1
			Jeffrey W.H.	APNI	664	1.3*	+1.3
			O'Hanlon G.	WP	482	0.9*	-1.3
					5,325	10.2	
1992	67,531	77.9	Mallon S.*	SDLP	26,073	49.6	+1.5
			Speers J.A.	UU	18,982	36.1	-1.8
			Curran B.P.	SF	6,547	12.5	+0.6
			Bell H.M. Ms.	APNI	972	1.8*	+0.6
					7,091	13.5	

NORFOLK MID [428]

Election	Electors	T'out	Candidate	Party	Votes	% Sh	% Ch
1983	68,953	75.3	Ryder R.A.	Con	29,032	55.9	
			Cargill D.H.	SDP	13,517	26.0	
			Potter L.J.	Lab	8,950	17.2	
			McNee M.M. Ms.	Ind	405	0.8*	
					15,515	29.9	
1987	73,893	78.2	Ryder R.A.*	Con	32,758	56.7	+0.8
			Graham G.J.E.	SDP	14,750	25.5	-0.5
			Luckey K.J.	Lab	10,272	17.8	+0.5
					18,008	31.2	
1992	80,525†	81.5	Ryder R.A.*	Con	35,620	54.3	-2.4
			Castle M.V.	Lab	16,672	25.4	+7.6
			Gleed M.J.	LD	13,072	19.9	-5.6
			Waite C.R. Ms.	NLP	226	0.3*	+0.3
					18,948	28.9	

NORFOLK NORTH [429]

Election	Electors	T'out	Candidate	Party	Votes	% Sh	% Ch
1983	65,101	74.6	Howell R.F.*	Con	26,230	54.0	
			Elworthy J.P.	SDP	13,007	26.8	
			Barber E.A.	Lab	9,317	19.2	
					13,223	27.2	
1987	69,790	77.5	Howell R.F.*	Con	28,822	53.3	-0.7
			Anthony N.R.	SDP	13,512	25.0	-1.8
			Earle A.	Lab	10,765	19.9	+0.7
			Filgate M.G.	Green	960	1.8*	+1.8
					15,310	28.3	
1992	73,780†	81.0	Howell R.F.*	Con	28,810	48.2	-5.1
			Lamb N.P.	LD	16,365	27.4	+2.4
			Cullingham M.A.	Lab	13,850	23.2	+3.3
			Zelter A.C. Ms.	Green	559	0.9*	-0.8
			Jenkinson S.M. Ms.	NLP	167	0.3*	+0.3
					12,445	20.8	

NORFOLK NORTH WEST [430]

Election	Electors	T'out	Candidate	Party	Votes	% Sh	% Ch
1983	69,181	77.6	Bellingham H.C.	Con	23,358	43.5	
			Brocklebank-Fowler C.*	SDP	20,211	37.6	
			Tilbury J.M.	Lab	10,139	18.9	
					3,147	5.9	
1987	73,739	78.9	Bellingham H.C.*	Con	29,393	50.6	+7.1
			Brocklebank-Fowler C.	SDP	18,568	31.9	-5.7
			Dignan F.P.	Lab	10,184	17.5	-1.4
					10,825	18.6	
1992	77,439†	80.7	Bellingham H.C.*	Con	32,554	52.1	+1.6
			Turner G.	Lab	20,990	33.6	+16.1
			Waterman A.M.	LD	8,599	13.8	-18.2
			Pink S.R.A.	NLP	330	0.5*	+0.5
					11,564	18.5	

NORFOLK SOUTH [431]

Election	Electors	T'out	Candidate	Party	Votes	% Sh	% Ch
1983	73,523	77.2	MacGregor J.R.R.*	Con	30,747	54.2	
			Carden R.A.P.	Lib	18,612	32.8	
			Holzer H.A.	Lab	7,408	13.0	
					12,135	21.4	
1987	78,372	81.0	MacGregor J.R.R.*	Con	33,912	53.4	-0.7
			Carden R.A.P.	Lib	21,494	33.9	+1.1
			Addison L.R.	Lab	8,047	12.7	-0.4
					12,418	19.6	
1992	81,647†	84.0	MacGregor J.R.R.*	Con	36,081	52.6	-0.9
			Brocklebank-Fowler C.	LD	18,516	27.0	-6.9
			Needle C.J.	Lab	12,422	18.1	+5.4
			Ross-Wagenknecht S. Ms.	Green	702	1.0*	+1.0
			Peacock R.W.	Ind	340	0.5*	
			Clark N.H.	NLP	320	0.5*	+0.5
			Watkins R.G.	Ind Con	232	0.3*	
					17,565	25.6	

NORFOLK SOUTH WEST [432]

Election	Electors	T'out	Candidate	Party	Votes	% Sh	% Ch
1983	70,398	73.1	Hawkins P.L. Sir.*	Con	28,632	55.7	
			Baxter E.B.S.	Lib	13,722	26.7	
			Rosenberg A.L.	Lab	9,072	17.6	
					14,910	29.0	
1987	74,240	76.0	Shephard G.P. Ms.	Con	32,519	57.6	+1.9
			Scott M.J.	Lib	12,083	21.4	-5.3
			Page M.E. Ms.	Lab	11,844	21.0	+3.3
					20,436	36.2	
1992	77,652†	79.3	Shephard G.P. Ms.*	Con	33,637	54.6	-3.0
			Page M.E. Ms.	Lab	16,706	27.1	+6.1
			Marsh J.T.	LD	11,237	18.2	-3.2
					16,931	27.5	

NORMANTON [433]

Election	Electors	T'out	Candidate	Party	Votes	% Sh	% Ch
1983	61,249	70.4	O'Brien W.	Lab	18,783	43.6	
			Paul A.	Con	14,599	33.9	
			Panteli P.	SDP	9,741	22.6	
					4,184	9.7	
1987	62,899	74.8	O'Brien W.*	Lab	23,303	49.5	+6.0
			Smith M.D.M.	Con	16,016	34.1	+0.2
			Macey R.J.	SDP	7,717	16.4	-6.2
					7,287	15.5	
1992	65,587	76.3	O'Brien W.*	Lab	25,936	51.8	+2.3
			Sturdy R.W.	Con	16,986	33.9	-0.1
			Galdas M.	LD	7,137	14.3	-2.1
					8,950	17.9	

NORTHAMPTON NORTH [434]

Election	Electors	T'out	Candidate	Party	Votes	% Sh	% Ch
1983	68,370	72.0	Marlow A.R.*	Con	23,129	47.0	
			Offenbach D.M.	Lab	13,269	27.0	
			Rounthwaite A.S.	Lib	12,829	26.1	
					9,860	20.0	
1987	69,294	74.6	Marlow A.R.*	Con	24,816	48.0	+1.0
			Granfield O.J.	Lab	15,560	30.1	+3.1
			Rounthwaite A.S.	Lib	10,690	20.7	-5.4
			Green M.J.	Green	471	0.9*	+0.9
			Colling S.F.	WRP	156	0.3*	+0.3
					9,256	17.9	
1992	69,140†	78.5	Marlow A.R.*	Con	24,865	45.8	-2.2
			Thomas J.M. Ms.	Lab	20,957	38.6	+8.5
			Church R.W.	LD	8,236	15.2	-5.5
			Spivack B.	NLP	232	0.4*	+0.4
					3,908	7.2	

NORTHAMPTON SOUTH [435]

Election	Electors	T'out	Candidate	Party	Votes	% Sh	% Ch
1983	68,910	72.6	Morris M.W.L.*	Con	26,824	53.6	
			Kyle J.K.	SDP	11,698	23.4	
			Coleman M.A.	Lab	11,533	23.0	
					15,126	30.2	
1987	76,071	75.2	Morris M.W.L.*	Con	31,864	55.7	+2.1
			Dickie J.	Lab	14,061	24.6	+1.5
			Hopkins G.H.	SDP	10,639	18.6	-4.8
			Hamilton M.E. Ms.	Green	647	1.1*	+1.1
					17,803	31.1	
1992	83,476†	79.9	Morris M.W.L.*	Con	36,882	55.3*	-0.4
			Dickie J.	Lab	19,909	29.8	+5.3
			Mabbutt G.A.G.	LD	9,912	14.9	-3.7
					16,973	25.5	

NORTHAVON [436]

Election	Electors	T'out	Candidate	Party	Votes	% Sh	% Ch
1983	73,553	78.0	Cope J.A.*	Con	30,790	53.7	
			Conrad G.M. Dr.	Lib	17,807	31.1	
			Norris N.P.J. Ms.	Lab	8,243	14.4	
			Radmall K.R.	Green	499	0.9*	
					12,983	22.6	
1987	78,487	80.2	Cope J.A.*	Con	34,224	54.4	+0.7
			Willmore C.J. Ms.	Lib	19,954	31.7	+0.6
			Norris D.	Lab	8,762	13.9	-0.5
					14,270	22.7	
1992	83,348	84.3	Cope J.A. Sir*	Con	35,338	50.3	-4.1
			Larkins H.R. Ms.	LD	23,477	33.4	+1.7
			Norris N.P.J. Ms.	Lab	10,290	14.6	+0.7
			Greene J.	Green	789	1.1*	+1.1
			Marx P.J.R.	Lib	380	0.5*	+0.5
					11,861	16.9	

NORWICH NORTH [437]

Election	Electors	T'out	Candidate	Party	Votes	% Sh	% Ch
1983	62,781	76.2	Thompson H.P.	Con	21,355	44.7	
			Ennals D.H.*	Lab	15,476	32.4	
			Jones G.R.	Lib	10,796	22.6	
			Cairns A.F. Ms.	WRP	194	0.4*	
					5,879	12.3	
1987	62,725	79.2	Thompson H.P.*	Con	22,772	45.8	+1.2
			Honeyball M.H.R. Ms.	Lab	14,996	30.2	-2.2
			Nicholls P.T.	Lib	11,922	24.0	+1.4
					7,776	15.6	
1992	63,309†	81.8	Thompson H.P.*	Con	22,419	43.3	-2.6
			Gibson I.	Lab	22,153	42.8	+12.6
			Harrison D.G.	LD	6,706	12.9	-11.0
			Betts L.	Green	433	0.8*	+0.8
			Arnold R.J.	NLP	93	0.2*	+0.2
					266	0.5	

NORWICH SOUTH [438]

Election	Electors	T'out	Candidate	Party	Votes	% Sh	% Ch
1983	64,100	76.4	Powley J.A.	Con	18,998	38.8	
			Garrett J.L.*	Lab	17,286	35.3	
			Hardie C.J.M.	SDP	11,968	24.4	
			Carter A.D.	Green	468	1.0*	
			Williams P.C.	NF	145	0.3*	
			Ward J.C.	Ind	91	0.2*	
					1,712	3.5	
1987	64,421	80.6	Garrett J.L.	Lab	19,666	37.9	+2.6
			Powley J.A.*	Con	19,330	37.3	-1.6
			Hardie C.J.M.	SDP	12,896	24.9	+0.4
					336	0.6	
1992	63,604†	80.6	Garrett J.L.*	Lab	24,965	48.7	+10.8
			Baxter D.S.	Con	18,784	36.6	-0.6
			Thomas C.	LD	6,609	12.9	-12.0
			Holmes A. St.J.	Green	803	1.6*	+1.6
			Parsons B.A.	NLP	104	0.2*	+0.2
					6,181	12.1	

Election	Electors	T'out	Candidate	Party	Votes	% Sh	% Ch
1983	55,663	65.6	Fraser J.D.*	Lab	16,280	44.6	
			Parfitt J.	Con	13,397	36.7	
			Noble M.M.	SDP	6,371	17.4	
			Williams C.M. Ms.	NF	343	0.9*	
			Sanderson J.C.	Ind	123	0.3*	
					2,883	7.9	
1987	56,602	67.0	Fraser J.D.*	Lab	18,359	48.4	+3.9
			Grieve D.C.R.	Con	13,636	36.0	-0.7
			Noble M.M.	SDP	5,579	14.7	-2.7
			Jackson F.M.	Ind	171	0.5*	
			Hammond R.J.	Ind	151	0.4*	
					4,723	12.5	
1992	52,290	66.1	Fraser J.D.*	Lab	18,391	53.2	+4.7
			Samways J.P.E.	Con	11,175	32.3	-3.7
			Lawman S.J. Ms.	LD	4,087	11.8	-2.9
			Collins W.S.B.	Green	790	2.3*	+2.3
			Leighton M.C.	NLP	138	0.4*	+0.4
					7,216	20.9	

NOTTINGHAM EAST [440]

Election	Electors	T'out	Candidate	Party	Votes	% Sh	% Ch
1983	68,638	63.6	Knowles M.	Con	17,641	40.4	
			Sloman M.G.M.	Lab	16,177	37.1	
			Bird M.J.	SDP	8,385	19.2	
			Merrick D.S.	Ind Con	1,421	3.3*	
					1,464	3.4	
1987	68,264	68.8	Knowles M.*	Con	20,162	42.9	+2.5
			Aslam M.	Lab	19,706	42.0	+4.9
			Parkhouse S.	Lib	6,883	14.7	-4.6
			Malik K.	RF	212	0.5*	+0.5
					456	1.0	
1992	67,939†	70.1	Heppell J.	Lab	25,026	52.6	+10.6
			Knowles M.*	Con	17,346	36.4	-6.5
			Ball T.S.	LD	3,695	7.8	-6.9
			Jones A.G.	Green	667	1.4*	+1.4
			Roylance C.W.	Lib	598	1.3*	+1.3
			Ashforth J.	NLP	283	0.6*	+0.6
					7,680	16.1	

NOTTINGHAM NORTH [441]

Election	Electors	T'out	Candidate	Party	Votes	% Sh	% Ch
1983	71,807	66.1	Ottaway R.G.J.	Con	18,730	39.4	
			Whitlock W.C.*	Lab	18,368	38.7	
			Williams L.V.	SDP	9,200	19.4	
			Peck J.H.	Comm	1,184	2.5*	
					362	0.8	
1987	69,620	72.6	Allen G.W.	Lab	22,713	44.9	+6.2
			Ottaway R.G.J.*	Con	21,048	41.6	+2.2
			Fernando S.C.	SDP	5,912	11.7	-7.7
			Peck J.H.	Comm	879	1.7*	-0.8
					1,665	3.3	
1992	69,495†	75.0	Allen G.W.*	Lab	29,052	55.7	+10.8
			Bridge I.G.	Con	18,309	35.1	-6.5
			Skelton A.	LD	4,477	8.6	-3.1
			Codman A.C.	NLP	274	0.5*	+0.5
					10,743	20.6	

NOTTINGHAM SOUTH [442]

Election	Electors	T'out	Candidate	Party	Votes	% Sh	% Ch
1983	69,059	70.2	Brandon-Bravo M.M.	Con	22,238	45.9	
			Coates K.	Lab	16,523	34.1	
			Poynter R.A.	Lib	9,697	20.0	
					5,715	11.8	
1987	72,807	73.5	Brandon-Bravo M.M.*	Con	23,921	44.7	-1.2
			Simpson A.	Lab	21,687	40.5	+6.4
			Williams L.V.	SDP	7,917	14.8	-5.2
					2,234	4.2	
1992	72,796†	74.2	Simpson A.	Lab	25,771	47.7	+7.2
			Brandon-Bravo M.M.*	Con	22,590	41.8	-2.9
			Long G.D.	LD	5,408	10.0	-4.8
			Christou J. Ms.	NLP	263	0.5*	+0.5
					3,181	5.9	

NUNEATON [443]

Election	Electors	T'out	Candidate	Party	Votes	% Sh	% Ch
1983	66,072	77.2	Stevens L.D.	Con	20,666	40.5	
			Haynes J.	Lab	15,605	30.6	
			Levitt R.L. Ms.	SDP	14,264	27.9	
			Davis G.E.	Ind Lab	504	1.0*	
					5,061	9.9	
1987	68,287	80.4	Stevens L.D.*	Con	24,630	44.9	+4.4
			Veness V.A. Ms.	Lab	18,975	34.6	+4.0
			Trembath A.F.	SDP	10,550	19.2	-8.7
			Morrissey J.R. Dr.	Green	719	1.3*	+1.3
					5,655	10.3	
1992	70,907†	83.7	Olner W.J.	Lab	27,157	45.8	+11.2
			Stevens L.D.*	Con	25,526	43.0	-1.9
			Merritt P.R. Ms.	LD	6,671	11.2	-8.0
					1,631	2.7	

OGMORE [444]

Election	Electors	T'out	Candidate	Party	Votes	% Sh	% Ch
1983	51,378	76.9	Powell R.*	Lab	23,390	59.2	
			Parsons J.H.	Lib	6,026	15.3	
			O'Sullivan R.M.S.	Con	5,806	14.7	
			Merriman E.J.	PC	3,124	7.9*	
			Thomas N.B. Dr.	Green	1,161	2.9*	
					17,364	44.0	
1987	51,631	79.5	Powell R.*	Lab	28,462	69.4	+10.2
			Barratt M.F.	Con	6,170	15.0	+0.3
			James M. Ms.	SDP	3,954	9.6	-5.6
			Jones J.G.	PC	1,791	4.4*	-3.5
			Heriot Spence T.	Ind Lab	652	1.6*	
					22,292	54.3	
1992	52,196†	80.6	Powell R.*	Lab	30,186	71.7	+2.4
			Edwards D.G.	Con	6,359	15.1	+0.1
			Warman J.	LD	2,868	6.8	-2.8
			McAllister L.J. Ms.	PC	2,667	6.3	+2.0
					23,827	56.6	

249

OLD BEXLEY AND SIDCUP [445]

Election	Electors	T'out	Candidate	Party	Votes	% Sh	% Ch
1983	50,255	74.1	Heath E.R.G.*	Con	22,422	60.2	
			Vickers P.	Lib	9,704	26.1	
			Kiff C.A.	Lab	5,116	13.7	
					12,718	34.1	
1987	50,831	77.1	Heath E.R.G.*	Con	24,350	62.1	+1.9
			Pearce T.H.	Lib	8,076	20.6	-5.4
			Stoate H.G.A. Dr.	Lab	6,762	17.3	+3.5
					16,274	41.5	
1992	49,449†	81.9	Heath E.R.G.*	Con	24,450	60.3	-1.8
			Brierly D. Ms.	Lab	8,751	21.6	+4.3
			Nicolle D.J.	LD	6,438	15.9	-4.7
			Rose B.	Ind Con	733	1.8*	
			Stephens R.T.	NLP	148	0.4*	+0.4
					15,699	38.7	

OLDHAM CENTRAL AND ROYTON [446]

Election	Electors	T'out	Candidate	Party	Votes	% Sh	% Ch
1983	67,177	66.9	Lamond J.A.*	Lab	18,611	41.4	
			Farquhar J.A.	Con	15,299	34.0	
			Jackson M.	SDP	11,022	24.5	
					3,312	7.4	
1987	65,277	69.2	Lamond J.A.*	Lab	21,759	48.1	+6.7
			Farquhar J.A.	Con	15,480	34.3	+0.2
			Dunn A. Ms.	SDP	7,956	17.6	-6.9
					6,279	13.9	
1992	61,360†	74.2	Davies B.	Lab	23,246	51.1	+2.9
			Morris P. Ms.	Con	14,640	32.2	-2.1
			Dunn A. Ms.	LD	7,224	15.9	-1.7
			Dalling I.D.	NLP	403	0.9*	+0.9
					8,606	18.9	

OLDHAM WEST [447]

Election	Electors	T'out	Candidate	Party	Votes	% Sh	% Ch
1983	57,445	69.8	Meacher M.H.*	Lab	17,690	44.1	
			Dickinson D.P.	Con	14,510	36.2	
			Smith R.A.M.	Lib	7,745	19.3	
			Street J.	Ind	180	0.4*	
					3,180	7.9	
1987	57,178	71.9	Meacher M.H.*	Lab	20,291	49.4	+5.3
			Jacobs J.M. Ms.	Con	14,324	34.9	-1.3
			Mason M.R. Ms.	Lib	6,478	15.8	-3.5
					5,967	14.5	
1992	54,075†	75.6	Meacher M.H.*	Lab	21,580	52.8	+3.4
			Gillen J.M.	Con	13,247	32.4	-2.5
			Smith J.D.	LD	5,525	13.5	-2.3
			Dalling S.J. Ms.	NLP	551	1.3*	+1.3
					8,333	20.4	

ORKNEY AND SHETLAND [448]

Election	Electors	T'out	Candidate	Party	Votes	% Sh	% Ch
1983	30,087	67.8	Wallace J.R.	Lib	9,374	45.9	
			Myles D.F.*	Con	5,224	25.6	
			Ewing W.M. Ms.	SNP	3,147	15.4	
			Goodlad R. Ms.	Lab	2,665	13.1	
					4,150	20.3	
1987	31,047	68.7	Wallace J.R.*	Lib	8,881	41.7	-4.3
			Jenkins R.W.A.H.	Con	4,959	23.3	-2.3
			Aberdein J.H.	Lab	3,995	18.7	+5.7
			Goodlad J.H.	OSM	3,095	14.5	+14.5
			Collister G.K.	Green	389	1.8*	+1.8
					3,922	18.4	
1992	31,472	65.5	Wallace J.R.*	LD	9,575	46.4	+4.8
			McCormick P.M.	Con	4,542	22.0	-1.2
			Aberdein J.H.	Lab	4,093	19.8	+1.1
			McKie F. Ms.	SNP	2,301	11.2	+11.2
			Wharton C.C. Ms.	NLP	115	0.6*	+0.6
					5,033	24.4	

ORPINGTON [449]

Election	Electors	T'out	Candidate	Party	Votes	% Sh	% Ch
1983	58,759	76.0	Stanbrook I.R.*	Con	25,569	57.3	
			Cook J.W.	Lib	15,418	34.5	
			Bean D.M.	Lab	3,439	7.7*	
			Taylor L.T.	BNP	215	0.5*	
					10,151	22.7	
1987	59,608	78.5	Stanbrook I.R.*	Con	27,261	58.2	+1.0
			Fryer J.H.	Lib	14,529	31.0	-3.5
			Cowan S.J.	Lab	5,020	10.7	+3.0
					12,732	27.2	
1992	57,352	83.6	Horam J.R	Con	27,421	57.2	-1.1
			Maines C.S.	LD	14,486	30.2	-0.8
			Cowan S.	Lab	5,512	11.5	+0.8
			Almond R.D.	Lib	539	1.1*	+1.1
					12,935	27.0	

OXFORD EAST [450]

Election	Electors	T'out	Candidate	Party	Votes	% Sh	% Ch
1983	63,613	73.9	Norris S.J.	Con	18,808	40.0	
			Smith A.D.	Lab	17,541	37.3	
			Godden M. Ms.	Lib	10,690	22.7	
					1,267	2.7	
1987	62,151	78.9	Smith A.D.	Lab	21,103	43.0	+5.7
			Norris S.J.*	Con	19,815	40.4	+0.4
			Godden M. Ms.	Lib	7,648	15.6	-7.1
			Dalton D.	Green	441	0.9*	+0.9
			Mylvaganam P.S.	Ind	60	0.1*	
					1,288	2.6	
1992	63,078†	74.6	Smith A.D.*	Lab	23,702	50.4	+7.4
			Mayall M.N.A. Dr.	Con	16,164	34.4	-6.0
			Horwood M.C.	LD	6,105	13.0	-2.6
			Lucas C. Ms.	Green	933	2.0*	+1.1
			Wilson A.M. Ms.	NLP	101	0.2*	+0.2
			Tompson K.	RCP	48	0.1*	+0.1
					7,538	16.0	

OXFORD WEST AND ABINGDON [451]

Election	Electors	T'out	Candidate	Party	Votes	% Sh	% Ch
1983	67,413	74.0	Patten J.H.C.*	Con	23,778	47.7	
			Luard D.E.T.	SDP	16,627	33.3	
			Jacottet J.H.	Lab	8,440	16.9	
			Starmer S.G. Ms.	Green	544	1.1*	
			Jones R.A.	MRLP	267	0.5*	
			Smith C.N.	Ind	95	0.2*	
			Doubleday P.M.	Ind	86	0.2*	
			Pinder R. Ms.	Ind	26	0.1*	
					7,151	14.3	
1987	69,193	78.4	Patten J.H.C.*	Con	25,171	46.4	-1.3
			Huhne C.M.P.	SDP	20,293	37.4	+4.0
			Power J.G.	Lab	8,108	14.9	-2.0
			Smith D.R.	Green	695	1.3*	+0.2
					4,878	9.0	
1992	72,328†	76.7	Patten J.H.C.*	Con	25,163	45.4	-1.0
			Goodhart W.H.	LD	21,624	39.0	+1.6
			Kent B.	Lab	7,652	13.8	-1.1
			Woodin M.E.	Green	660	1.2*	-0.1
			Jenking R.E.	Lib	194	0.3*	+0.3
			Nelson S.B. Ms.	AFL	98	0.2*	+0.2
			Wells G.A.	NLP	75	0.1*	+0.1
					3,539	6.4	

253

PAISLEY NORTH [452]

Election	Electors	T'out	Candidate	Party	Votes	% Sh	% Ch
1983	50,464	68.6	Adams A.S.*	Lab	15,782	45.6	
			McCartin E.P. Ms.	SDP	8,195	23.7	
			Townsend B.J.T.	Con	7,425	21.4	
			Morell H.	SNP	2,783	8.0*	
			Carlaw N.A. Dr.‡	Green	439	1.3*	
					7,587	21.9	
1987	49,487	73.5	Adams A.S.*	Lab	20,193	55.5	+9.9
			McCartin E.P. Ms.	SDP	5,751	15.8	-7.9
			Laing E.F.P. Ms.	Con	5,741	15.8	-5.7
			Taylor I.	SNP	4,696	12.9	+4.9
					14,442	39.7	

[Death]

Election	Electors	T'out	Candidate	Party	Votes	% Sh	% Ch
1990	48,063	53.7	Adams K. Ms.	Lab	11,353	44.0	-11.5
(29/11)			Mullin W.A.R.	SNP	7,583	29.4	+16.5
			Marwick E.	Con	3,835	14.8	-1.0
			Bannerman J.	LD	2,139	8.3	-7.5
			Mellor D.G.	Green	918	3.6*	
					3,770	14.6	
1992	46,424	73.4	Adams K. Ms.	Lab	17,269	50.7	-4.8
			Mullin W.A.R.	SNP	7,948	23.3	+10.4
			Sharpe D.J.	Con	5,576	16.4	+0.6
			McCartin E.P. Ms.	LD	2,779	8.2	-7.6
			Mellor D.G.	Green	412	1.2*	+1.2
			Brennan N.M.	NLP	81	0.2*	+0.2
					9,321	27.4	

Election	Electors	T'out	Candidate	Party	Votes	% Sh	% Ch
1983	52,031	72.5	Buchan N.F.*	Lab	15,633	41.4	
			Buchanan E.M. Ms.	Lib	9,104	24.1	
			Knox J.	Con	7,819	20.7	
			Mitchell J.R.	SNP	4,918	13.0	
			Mellor D.G.	Green	271	0.7*	
					6,529	17.3	
1987	51,127	75.3	Buchan N.F.*	Lab	21,611	56.2	+14.7
			Carmichael A.M.	Lib	5,826	15.1	-9.0
			Williamson D.A. Ms.	Con	5,644	14.7	-6.0
			Mitchell J.R.	SNP	5,398	14.0	+1.0
					15,785	41.0	

[Death]

Election	Electors	T'out	Candidate	Party	Votes	% Sh	% Ch
1990	49,199	55.0	McMaster G.	Lab	12,485	46.1	-10.1
(29/11)			Lawson I.	SNP	7,455	27.5	+13.5
			Workman J.C.	Con	3,627	13.4	-1.3
			Reid A.	LD	2,660	9.8	-5.3
			Collie L.R. Ms.	Green	835	3.1*	
					5,030	18.6	
1992	47,919	75.0	McMaster G.	Lab	18,202	50.7	-5.5
			Lawson I.	SNP	8,653	24.1	+10.1
			Laidlaw S.G. Ms.	Con	5,703	15.9	+1.2
			Reid A.	LD	3,271	9.1	-6.0
			Porter S.R.	NLP	93	0.3*	+0.3
					9,549	26.6	

PECKHAM [454]

Election	Electors	T'out	Candidate	Party	Votes	% Sh	% Ch
1983	59,128	54.5	Harman H.R. Ms.*	Lab	16,616	51.6	
			Eckersley T.W.H.	Con	7,792	24.2	
			Sawdon A.J.	SDP	7,006	21.7	
			Bailey M. Ms.	NF	800	2.5*	
					8,824	27.4	
1987	59,261	55.6	Harman H.R. Ms.*	Lab	17,965	54.5	+2.9
			Ingram L.K.F. Ms.	Con	8,476	25.7	+1.5
			Shearman R.H.	Lib	5,878	17.8	-3.9
			Robinson D. Ms.	Green	628	1.9*	+1.9
					9,489	28.8	
1992	58,320	53.8	Harman H.R. Ms.*	Lab	19,391	61.8	+7.2
			Frazer C.M.	Con	7,386	23.5	-2.2
			Colley R.E. Ms.	LD	4,331	13.8	-4.0
			Dacres G.C.	WRP	146	0.5*	
			Teh V.	Ind	140	0.4*	+0.5
					12,005	38.2	

PEMBROKE [455]

Election	Electors	T'out	Candidate	Party	Votes	% Sh	% Ch
1983	67,885	78.1	Edwards R.N.*	Con	24,860	46.9	
			Griffiths A.P.	Lab	15,504	29.2	
			Pullin J. Rev.	SDP	10,983	20.7	
			Osmond O.	PC	1,073	2.0*	
			Hoffman D.L.	Green	478	0.9*	
			Phillips G.S.	Ind	136	0.3*	
					9,356	17.6	
1987	70,358	80.8	Bennett N.J.	Con	23,314	41.0	-5.9
			Rayner B.J.	Lab	17,614	31.0	+1.7
			Jones P.E.C.	Lib	14,832	26.1	+5.4
			Osmond O.	PC	1,119	2.0*	-0.1
					5,700	10.0	
1992	73,187†	82.9	Ainger N.R.	Lab	26,253	43.3	+12.3
			Bennett N.J.*	Con	25,498	42.0	+1.1
			Sain ley Berry P.G.	LD	6,625	10.9	-15.2
			Bryant C.L.	PC	1,627	2.7*	+0.7
			Coghill R.W.	Green	484	0.8*	-0.1
			Stoddart R.M.	AFL	158	0.3*	+0.3
					755	1.2	

PENDLE [456]

Election	Electors	T'out	Candidate	Party	Votes	% Sh	% Ch
1983	64,483	79.7	Lee J.R.L.*	Con	22,739	44.2	
			Rodgers G.	Lab	16,604	32.3	
			Lishman A.G.	Lib	12,056	23.5	
					6,135	11.9	
1987	63,588	81.8	Lee J.R.L.*	Con	21,009	40.4	-3.9
			Renilson S.D. Ms.	Lab	18,370	35.3	+3.0
			Lishman A.G.	Lib	12,662	24.3	+0.9
					2,639	5.1	
1992	64,066	82.9	Prentice G.	Lab	23,497	44.2	+8.9
			Lee J.R.L.*	Con	21,384	40.3	-0.1
			Davies A.P.	LD	7,976	15.0	-9.3
			Thome V.M. Ms.	AFL	263	0.5*	+0.5
					2,113	4.0	

PENRITH AND THE BORDER [457]

Election	Electors	T'out	Candidate	Party	Votes	% Sh	% Ch
1983	68,164	73.1	Whitelaw W.S.I.*	Con	29,304	58.8	
			Young M.A.	Lib	13,883	27.9	
			Williams A.L.	Lab	6,612	13.3	
					15,421	31.0	

(Elevation to the Peerage)

Election	Electors	T'out	Candidate	Party	Votes	% Sh	% Ch
1983 (28/7)	68,329	55.7	MacLean D.J.	Con	17,530	46.0	-12.8
			Young M. A.	Lib	16,978	44.6	+16.7
			Williams A.L.	Lab	2,834	7.4*	-5.9
			Sutch D.E.	MRLP	412	1.1*	
			Morgan E.W.	Ind	150	0.4*	
			Anscomb H.M. Ms.	Ind	72	0.2*	
			Connell J.	Ind Soc	69	0.2*	
			Smith P.R.	Ind	35	0.1*	
					552	1.4	
1987	70,994	77.5	Maclean D.J.	Con	33,148	60.3	+1.4
			Ivison D.J.	Lib	15,782	28.7	+0.8
			Hutton J.M.P.	Lab	6,075	11.0	-2.2
					17,366	31.6	
1992	73,770†	79.7	Maclean D.J.*	Con	33,808	57.5	-2.7
			Walker K.G.	LD	15,359	26.1	-2.6
			Metcalfe J.	Lab	8,871	15.1	+4.0
			Gibson R.A.	Green	610	1.0*	+1.0
			Docker I.	NLP	129	0.2*	+0.2
					18,449	31.4	

Election	Electors	T'out	Candidate	Party	Votes	% Sh	% Ch
1983	61,478	72.3	Fairbairn N.H.*	Con	17,888	40.2	
			Crawford G.D.	SNP	11,155	25.1	
			Coutts J.B.	Lib	10,997	24.7	
			Stuart A.J.	Lab	4,414	9.9*	
					6,733	15.1	
1987	63,443	74.4	Fairbairn N.H.*	Con	18,716	39.6	-0.6
			Fairlie J.M.	SNP	13,040	27.6	+2.5
			Donaldson S.	Lib	7,969	16.9	-7.9
			McConnell J.W.	Lab	7,490	15.9	+5.9
					5,676	12.0	
1992	65,410†	76.9	Fairbairn N.H.*	Con	20,195	40.2	+0.5
			Cunningham R. Ms.	SNP	18,101	36.0	+8.4
			Rolfe M.J.	Lab	6,267	12.5	-3.4
			Black M.	LD	5,714	11.4	-5.5
					2,094	4.2	

[Death]

Election	Electors	T'out	Candidate	Party	Votes	% Sh	% Ch
1995	67,566	62.1	Cunningham R. Ms.	SNP	16,931	40.4	+4.4
(25/5)			Alexander D.	Lab	9,620	22.9	+10.5
			Godfrey J.P.	Con	8,990	21.4	-18.7
			Linklater V. Ms.	LD	4,952	11.8	+0.4
			Sutch D.E.	MRLP	586	1.4*	
			Linacre V.T. Ms.	UKI	504	1.2*	
			Harper R.C.M.	Green	223	0.5*	
			Halford M.	Ind	88	0.2*	
			Black G.	NLP	54	0.1*	
					7,311	17.4	

Election	Electors	T'out	Candidate	Party	Votes	% Sh	% Ch
1983	78,957	73.3	Mawhinney B.S.*	Con	27,270	47.1	
			Fish B.W.	Lab	16,831	29.1	
			Walston E. Lady	SDP	13,142	22.7	
			Callaghan N.A.	Green	511	0.9*	
			Hyland D.E.	WRP	155	0.3*	
					10,439	18.0	
1987	84,282	73.5	Mawhinney B.S.*	Con	30,624	49.4	+2.3
			Mackinlay A.S.	Lab	20,840	33.6	+4.6
			Green D.W.	Lib	9,984	16.1	-6.6
			Callaghan N.A.	Green	506	0.8*	-0.1
					9,784	15.8	
1992	87,639†	75.1	Mawhinney B.S.*	Con	31,827	48.3	-1.1
			Owens J. Ms.	Lab	26,451	40.2	+6.5
			Taylor A.J. Ms.	LD	5,208	7.9	-8.2
			Murat E.	Lib	1,557	2.4*	+2.4
			Heaton R.L.H.	BNP	311	0.5*	
			Beasley P.I. Ms.	Ind	271	0.4*	
			Brettell C.R.	NLP	215	0.3*	+0.3
					5,376	8.2	

Election	Electors	T'out	Candidate	Party	Votes	% Sh	% Ch
1983	61,813	76.1	Owen D.A.L. Dr.*	SDP	20,843	44.3	
			Widdecombe A.N. Ms.	Con	15,907	33.8	
			Priestley J.G.	Lab	9,845	20.9	
			Sullivan J.E.	Ind Con	292	0.6*	
			Bearsford-Walker R.E.D.	BNP	72	0.2*	
			Hill F. Ms.	Ind	51	0.1*	
					4,936	10.5	
1987	64,487	77.2	Owen D.A.L. Dr.*	SDP	21,039	42.3	-2.1
			Jones T.F.R.	Con	14,569	29.3	-4.6
			Flintoff I.	Lab	14,166	28.5	+7.5
					6,470	13.0	
1992	65,800†	77.8	Jamieson D.C.	Lab	24,953	48.7	+20.2
			Simpson K.R.	Con	17,541	34.2	+5.0
			Mactaggart M.	LD	6,315	12.3	-29.9
			Luscombe H.M.	SD	2,152	4.2*	+4.2
			Lyons F.A.	NLP	255	0.5*	+0.5
					7,412	14.5	

PLYMOUTH, DRAKE [461]

Election	Electors	T'out	Candidate	Party	Votes	% Sh	% Ch
1983	52,383	74.3	Fookes J.E. Ms.*	Con	19,718	50.6	
			Fitzgerald W.J.	SDP	11,133	28.6	
			Cresswell S.A. Ms.	Lab	7,921	20.3	
			Bradbury C.W.	BNP	163	0.4*	
					8,585	22.0	
1987	51,186	76.6	Fookes J.E. Ms.*	Con	16,195	41.3	-9.3
			Astor D.W.	SDP	13,070	33.3	+4.7
			Jamieson D.C.	Lab	9,451	24.1	+3.8
			Barber T. Ms.	Green	493	1.3*	+1.3
					3,125	8.0	
1992	51,667†	75.6	Fookes J.E. Dame*	Con	17,075	43.7	+2.4
			Telford P.	Lab	15,062	38.6	+14.5
			Cox V.A. Ms.	LD	5,893	15.1	-18.2
			Stanbury D.M.	SD	476	1.2*	+1.2
			Harrison A.E. Ms.	Green	441	1.1*	-0.1
			Pringle T.J.	NLP	95	0.2*	+0.2
					2,013	5.2	

PLYMOUTH, SUTTON [462]

Election	Electors	T'out	Candidate	Party	Votes	% Sh	% Ch
1983	59,890	76.4	Clark A.K.M. Hon.*	Con	25,203	55.1	
			Puttick A.D.	Lib	13,516	29.6	
			Holland F. Ms.	Lab	6,538	14.3	
			Shaw S.R.	Green	470	1.0*	
					11,687	25.6	
1987	64,120	79.0	Clark A.K.M. Hon.*	Con	23,187	45.8	-9.4
			Tidy B.M.	Lib	19,174	37.8	+8.3
			Maddern R.D.	Lab	8,310	16.4	+2.1
					4,013	7.9	
1992	67,430†	81.2	Streeter G.N.	Con	27,070	49.5	+3.7
			Pawley A.	Lab	15,120	27.6	+11.2
			Brett-Freeman J.P.	LD	12,291	22.5	-15.4
			Bowler J.J.	NLP	256	0.5*	+0.5
					11,950	21.8	

Election	Electors	T'out	Candidate	Party	Votes	% Sh	% Ch
1983	64,878	67.4	Lofthouse G.*	Lab	24,990	57.1	
			Howell J.B.	Con	11,299	25.8	
			Dale D.	Lib	7,452	17.0	
					13,691	31.3	
1987	64,414	73.5	Lofthouse G.*	Lab	31,656	66.9	+9.8
			Malins J.H.	Con	10,030	21.2	-4.6
			Taylor M.F.	Lib	5,334	11.3	-5.8
			Lees D.M.	RF	295	0.6*	+0.6
					21,626	45.7	
1992	64,655	74.3	Lofthouse G.*	Lab	33,546	69.9	+3.0
			Rockall A.G.M.	Con	10,051	20.9	-0.3
			Ryan D.L.	LD	4,410	9.2	-2.1
					23,495	48.9	

PONTYPRIDD [464]

Election	Electors	T'out	Candidate	Party	Votes	% Sh	% Ch
1983	60,882	72.7	John B.T.*	Lab	20,188	45.6	
			Langridge R.	SDP	11,444	25.8	
			Evans R.H.	Con	10,139	22.9	
			Davies J.M. Ms.	PC	2,065	4.7*	
			Jones A.K.	Green	449	1.0*	
					8,744	19.7	
1987	61,105	76.8	John B.T.*	Lab	26,422	56.3	+10.7
			Swayne D.A.	Con	9,135	19.5	-3.4
			Sain ley Berry P.G.	SDP	8,865	18.9	-6.9
			Bowen I.D.	PC	2,498	5.3	+0.7
					17,287	36.8	

[Death]

Election	Electors	T'out	Candidate	Party	Votes	% Sh	% Ch
1989 (23/2)	61,193	62.2	Howells K.S.	Lab	20,549	53.4	-2.9
			Morgan S.	PC	9,755	25.3	+20.0
			Evans N.M.	Con	5,212	13.5	-6.0
			Ellis T.	LD	1,500	3.9*	-15.0
			Thomas T.	SDP	1,199	3.1*	
			Richards D.	Comm	239	0.6*	
			Black D.	Ind	57	0.2*	
					10,794	28.0	
1992	61,685†	79.3	Howells K.S.	Lab	29,722	60.8	+4.5
			Donnelly P.D.	Con	9,925	20.3	+0.8
			Bowen I.D.	PC	4,448	9.1	+3.8
			Belzak S.	LD	4,180	8.5	-10.3
			Jackson E.J. Ms.	Green	615	1.3*	+1.3
					19,797	40.5	

POOLE [465]

Election	Electors	T'out	Candidate	Party	Votes	% Sh	% Ch
1983	70,731	73.6	Ward J.D.*	Con	30,358	58.3	
			Clements B.R.	Lib	15,929	30.6	
			Castle M.V.	Lab	5,595	10.7*	
			Foster A.S.	Ind	177	0.3*	
					14,429	27.7	
1987	76,673	77.5	Ward J.D.*	Con	34,159	57.5	-0.8
			Whitley R.J.	SDP	19,351	32.6	+2.0
			Shutler M.J.	Lab	5,901	9.9	-0.8
					14,808	24.9	
1992	79,223†	79.4	Ward J.D.*	Con	33,445	53.2	-4.3
			Clements B.R.	LD	20,614	32.8	+0.2
			White H.R.	Lab	6,912	11.0	+1.1
			Steen M.	Ind Con	1,620	2.6*	
			Bailey A.L.	NLP	303	0.5*	+0.5
					12,831	20.4	

PORTSMOUTH NORTH [466]

Election	Electors	T'out	Candidate	Party	Votes	% Sh	% Ch
1983	77,923	72.9	Griffiths P.H.S.*	Con	31,413	55.3	
			Luxon S.D.	SDP	13,414	23.6	
			Beard C.N.	Lab	12,013	21.1	
					17,999	31.7	
1987	80,501	74.8	Griffiths P.H.S.*	Con	33,297	55.3	+0.0
			Mitchell E.I. Ms.	SDP	14,896	24.7	+1.1
			Miles D.G.	Lab	12,016	20.0	-1.2
					18,401	30.6	
1992	79,592†	77.1	Griffiths P.H.S.*	Con	32,240	52.6	-2.7
			Burnett A.D.	Lab	18,359	29.9	+10.0
			Bentley A.M.	LD	10,101	16.5	-8.3
			Palmer H. Ms.	Green	628	1.0*	+1.0
					13,881	22.6	

263

PORTSMOUTH SOUTH [467]

Election	Electors	T'out	Candidate	Party	Votes	% Sh	% Ch
1983	74,537	67.3	Pink R.B.*	Con	25,101	50.0	
			Hancock M.T.	SDP	12,766	25.4	
			Thomas S.T. Ms.	Lab	11,324	22.6	
			Evens A.J.	Ind Lib	554	1.1*	
			Knight G.A.	NF	279	0.6*	
			Fry D.W.	Ind	172	0.3*	
					12,335	24.6	

[Death]

Election	Electors	T'out	Candidate	Party	Votes	% Sh	% Ch
1984	74,976	54.5	Hancock M.T.	SDP	15,358	37.6	+12.2
(14/6)			Rock P.R.J.	Con	14,017	34.3	-15.7
			Thomas S.T. Ms.	Lab	10,846	26.5	+3.9
			Knight G.A.	NF	226	0.5*	-0.1
			Mitchell T.A.F.	Green	190	0.5*	
			Evens A.J.	Ind Lib	113	0.3*	-0.8
			Layton T.A.	Ind	50	0.1*	
			Andrews A.N.	Ind	42	0.1*	
			Smith P.R.	Ind	41	0.1*	
					1,341	3.3	

Election	Electors	T'out	Candidate	Party	Votes	% Sh	% Ch
1987	76,292	71.3	Martin D.J.P.	Con	23,534	43.3	-6.7
			Hancock M.T.	SDP	23,329	42.9	+17.5
			Gardiner K.	Lab	7,047	13.0	-9.6
			Hughes M.R.	Ind	455	0.8*	
					205	0.4	

Election	Electors	T'out	Candidate	Party	Votes	% Sh	% Ch
1992	77,648†	69.1	Martin D.J.P.*	Con	22,798	42.5	-0.8
			Hancock M.T.	LD	22,556	42.0	-0.9
			Rapson S.N.J.	Lab	7,857	14.6	+1.7
			Zivkovic A.	Green	349	0.7*	+0.7
			Trend W.A.	NLP	91	0.2*	+0.2
					242	0.5	

Election	Electors	T'out	Candidate	Party	Votes	% Sh	% Ch
1983	64,978	71.8	Thorne S.G.*	Lab	21,810	46.7	
			Huntley T.N.	Con	14,832	31.8	
			Connolly M.J.	SDP	10,039	21.5	
					6,978	14.9	
1987	62,672	71.0	Wise A. Ms.	Lab	23,341	52.5	+5.7
			Chandran R.T. Dr.	Con	12,696	28.5	-3.2
			Wright J.P.	Lib	8,452	19.0	-2.5
					10,645	23.9	
1992	64,159†	71.7	Wise A. Ms.*	Lab	24,983	54.3	+1.8
			O'Toole S.G.	Con	12,808	27.8	-0.7
			Chadwick W.D.	LD	7,897	17.2	-1.8
			Ayliffe J. Ms.	NLP	341	0.7*	+0.7
					12,175	26.5	

Election	Electors	T'out	Candidate	Party	Votes	% Sh	% Ch
1983	70,583	75.8	Shaw J.G.D.*	Con	24,455	45.7	
			Cummins J.P.F.	Lib	19,141	35.8	
			Price S.M. Ms.	Lab	9,542	17.8	
			Smith R.	Ind	387	0.7*	
					5,314	9.9	
1987	71,681	78.0	Shaw J.G.D.*	Con	25,457	45.5	-0.2
			Cummins J.P.F.	Lib	19,021	34.0	-1.8
			Taggart N.	Lab	11,461	20.5	+2.7
					6,436	11.5	
1992	70,996	80.8	Shaw J.G.D.*	Con	25,067	43.7	-1.8
			Giles A.	Lab	16,695	29.1	+8.6
			Shutt D.T.	LD	15,153	26.4	-7.6
			Wynne J.L. Ms.	Green	466	0.8*	+0.8
					8,372	14.6	

PUTNEY [470]

Election	Electors	T'out	Candidate	Party	Votes	% Sh	% Ch
1983	63,853	73.6	Mellor D.J.*	Con	21,863	46.5	
			Hain P.G.	Lab	16,844	35.9	
			Welchman C.S.	Lib	7,668	16.3	
			Connolly M.J.	NF	290	0.6*	
			Baillie-Grohman F.R. Ms.	Green	190	0.4*	
			Chalk L.A.W.	Soc	88	0.2*	
			Williams W.T.K.P.	Ind PC	41	0.1*	
					5,019	10.7	
1987	63,108	75.9	Mellor D.J.*	Con	24,197	50.5	+4.0
			Hain P.G.	Lab	17,290	36.1	+0.2
			Harlow S.A. Ms.	Lib	5,934	12.4	-3.9
			Desorgher S.J.	Green	508	1.1*	+0.7
					6,907	14.4	
1992	61,915†	77.9	Mellor D.J.*	Con	25,188	52.2*	+1.7
			Chegwidden J.M. Ms.	Lab	17,662	36.6	+0.5
			Martyn J.D.F.	LD	4,636	9.6	-2.8
			Hagenbach K.M.	Green	618	1.3*	+0.2
			Levy P.	NLP	139	0.3*	+0.3
					7,526	15.6	

RAVENSBOURNE [471]

Election	Electors	T'out	Candidate	Party	Votes	% Sh	% Ch
1983	58,811	73.2	Hunt J.L.*	Con	27,143	63.0	
			Boston C.M. Ms.	SDP	11,631	27.0	
			Holbrook J.R.	Lab	4,037	9.4*	
			Shotton A.T.	BNP	242	0.6*	
					15,512	36.0	
1987	59,365	75.7	Hunt J.L.*	Con	28,295	63.0	-0.1
			Campbell G.W.	SDP	11,376	25.3	-1.7
			D'Arcy M.J.	Lab	5,087	11.3	+1.9
			Waite A.	BNP	184	0.4*	-0.2
					16,919	37.6	
1992	57,285	81.2	Hunt J.L.*	Con	29,506	63.4	+0.5
			Booth P.J.H.	LD	9,792	21.0	-4.3
			Dyer E.W.	Lab	6,182	13.3	+2.0
			Mouland I.J.	Green	617	1.3*	+1.3
			White P.	Lib	318	0.7*	+0.7
			Shepheard J.W.	NLP	105	0.2*	+0.2
					19,714	42.4	

266

Election	Electors	T'out	Candidate	Party	Votes	% Sh	% Ch
1983	67,511	70.4	Vaughan G.F. Dr.*	Con	24,516	51.6	
			Huhne C.M.P.	SDP	13,008	27.4	
			Boyle K.J.	Lab	9,218	19.4	
			Darnton G.	Green	519	1.1*	
			Baker P.	BNP	147	0.3*	
			Shone A.B.	Ind	113	0.2*	
					11,508	24.2	
1987	74,744	70.9	Vaughan G.F. Sir.*	Con	28,515	53.8	+2.2
			Baring S.M. Ms.	SDP	12,298	23.2	-4.2
			Salter M.J.	Lab	11,371	21.5	+2.1
			Unsworth P.J.	Green	667	1.3*	+0.2
			Shone A.B.	Ind	125	0.2*	
					16,217	30.6	
1992	72,152†	75.0	Vaughan G.F. Sir.*	Con	29,148	53.8	+0.0
			Parker G. Ms.	Lab	14,593	27.0	+5.5
			Thair D.A.	LD	9,528	17.6	-5.6
			McCubbin A.M. Ms.	Green	861	1.6*	+0.3
					14,555	26.9	

READING WEST [473]

Election	Electors	T'out	Candidate	Party	Votes	% Sh	% Ch
1983	66,080	72.5	Durant R.A.B.*	Con	24,948	52.1	
			Day R.J.	Lib	13,549	28.3	
			Evans R.	Lab	9,220	19.3	
			Lilley E.G.	Ind	161	0.3*	
					11,399	23.8	
1987	70,391	72.2	Durant R.A.B.*	Con	28,122	55.3	+3.2
			Lock K.H.	Lib	11,369	22.4	-5.9
			Orton M.E.	Lab	10,819	21.3	+2.0
			Wilson E.P.	Green	542	1.1*	+1.1
					16,753	32.9	
1992	67,938†	78.0	Durant R.A.B.*	Con	28,048	52.9	-2.4
			Ruhemann P.M.	Lab	14,750	27.8	+6.6
			Lock K.H.	LD	9,572	18.1	-4.3
			Unsworth P.J.	Green	613	1.2*	+0.1
					13,298	25.1	

REDCAR [474]

Election	Electors	T'out	Candidate	Party	Votes	% Sh	% Ch
1983	63,447	71.3	Tinn J.*	Lab	18,348	40.6	
			Bassett P.J.	Con	15,244	33.7	
			Nightingale G.	SDP	11,614	25.7	
					3,104	6.9	
1987	63,393	76.1	Mowlam M. Ms.	Lab	22,824	47.3	+6.8
			Bassett P.J.	Con	15,089	31.3	-2.4
			Nightingale G.	SDP	10,298	21.4	-4.3
					7,735	16.0	
1992	62,494†	77.7	Mowlam M. Ms.*	Lab	27,184	56.0	+8.6
			Goodwill R.	Con	15,607	32.1	+0.8
			Abbott C.M.	LD	5,789	11.9	-9.4
					11,577	23.8	

REIGATE [475]

Election	Electors	T'out	Candidate	Party	Votes	% Sh	% Ch
1983	70,320	72.1	Gardiner G.A.*	Con	29,932	59.0	
			Pamplin E.A. Ms.	SDP	13,625	26.9	
			Symons B.	Lab	6,114	12.1*	
			Newell D.R.	Green	1,029	2.0*	
					16,307	32.2	
1987	71,940	72.5	Gardiner G.A.*	Con	30,925	59.3	+0.2
			Pamplin E.A. Ms.	SDP	12,752	24.4	-2.4
			Spencer R.P.	Lab	7,460	14.3	+2.2
			Brand G.F.	Green	1,026	2.0*	-0.1
					18,173	34.8	
1992	71,876	78.5	Gardiner G.A.*	Con	32,220	57.1	-2.2
			Newsome B.	LD	14,566	25.8	+1.4
			Young H. Ms.	Lab	9,150	16.2	+1.9
			Bilcliff M.	SD	513	0.9*	+0.9
					17,654	31.3	

RENFREW WEST AND INVERCLYDE [476]

Election	Electors	T'out	Candidate	Party	Votes	% Sh	% Ch
1983	53,510	78.1	McCurley A.A. Ms.	Con	13,669	32.7	
			Mabon J.D. Dr.*	SDP	12,347	29.5	
			Doherty G.	Lab	12,139	29.0	
			Taylor W.	SNP	3,653	8.7*	
					1,322	3.2	
1987	56,189	80.5	Graham T.	Lab	17,525	38.7	+9.7
			McCurley A.A. Ms.*	Con	13,462	29.8	-2.9
			Mabon J.D. Dr.	SDP	9,669	21.4	-8.2
			Campbell C.M.	SNP	4,578	10.1	+1.4
					4,063	9.0	
1992	58,164	80.3	Graham T.*	Lab	17,085	36.6	-2.2
			Goldie A.M. Ms.	Con	15,341	32.9	+3.1
			Campbell C.	SNP	9,448	20.2	+10.1
			Nimmo A.	LD	4,668	10.0	-11.4
			Maltman D.L.	NLP	149	0.3*	+0.3
					1,744	3.7	

RHONDDA [477]

Election	Electors	T'out	Candidate	Party	Votes	% Sh	% Ch
1983	62,587	76.2	Rogers A.R.	Lab	29,448	61.7	
			Lloyd A.W.	SDP	8,078	16.9	
			Davies G.R.	PC	4,845	10.2*	
			Meyer P.J.H.	Con	3,973	8.3*	
			True A.	Comm	1,350	2.8*	
					21,370	44.8	
1987	60,931	78.0	Rogers A.R.*	Lab	34,857	73.3	+11.6
			Davies G.R.	PC	4,261	9.0	-1.2
			York-Williams J.R.	SDP	3,935	8.3	-8.7
			Reid S.H.	Con	3,612	7.6	-0.7
			True A.	Comm	869	1.8*	-1.0
					30,596	64.4	
1992	59,955†	76.6	Rogers A.R.*	Lab	34,243	74.5	+1.2
			Davies G.R.	PC	5,427	11.8	+2.9
			Richards J.W.	Con	3,588	7.8	+0.2
			Nicholls-Jones P.	LD	2,431	5.3	-3.0
			Fischer M.W.	Comm	245	0.5*	-1.3
					28,816	62.7	

Election	Electors	T'out	Candidate	Party	Votes	% Sh	% Ch
1983	59,982	76.8	Waddington D.C.*	Con	29,223	63.4	
			Carr M.	SDP	10,632	23.1	
			Saville E.A.	Lab	6,214	13.5	
					18,591	40.4	
1987	62,571	79.2	Waddington D.C.*	Con	30,136	60.9	-2.6
			Carr M.	SDP	10,608	21.4	-1.7
			Pope G.J.	Lab	8,781	17.7	+4.2
					19,528	39.4	

[Elevation to the peerage]

Election	Electors	T'out	Candidate	Party	Votes	% Sh	% Ch
1991	64,878	71.2	Carr M.	LD	22,377	48.5	+27.1
(7/3)			Evans N.M.	Con	17,776	38.5	-22.4
			Farrington J. Ms.	Lab	4,356	9.4	-8.3
			Brass D.A.	Ind Con	611	1.3*	
			Ingham H.G. Ms.	Green	466	1.0*	
			Sutch D.E.	MRLP	278	0.6*	
			Taylor S.C.	Lib	133	0.3*	
			St. Clair L. Ms.	Ind	72	0.2*	
			Hughes S.B.F.	Ind	60	0.1*	
					4,601	10.0	
1992	65,552	85.0	Evans N.M.	Con	29,178	52.4	-8.5
			Carr M.	LD	22,636	40.6	+19.2
			Pickup R.	Lab	3,649	6.5	-11.2
			Beesley D.	RLGG	152	0.3*	+0.3
			Holmes N.M. Ms.	NLP	112	0.2*	+0.2
					6,542	11.7	

RICHMOND AND BARNES [479]

Election	Electors	T'out	Candidate	Party	Votes	% Sh	% Ch
1983	55,845	79.6	Hanley J.J.	Con	20,695	46.5	
			Watson A.J.	Lib	20,621	46.4	
			Vaz N.K.A.S.	Lab	3,156	7.1*	
					74	0.2	
1987	54,700	83.2	Hanley J.J.*	Con	21,729	47.7	+1.2
			Watson A.J.	Lib	19,963	43.8	-2.5
			Gold M.D.	Lab	3,227	7.1	-0.0
			Mathews C.M. Ms.	Green	610	1.3*	+1.3
					1,766	3.9	
1992	53,138	84.9	Hanley J.J.*	Con	22,894	50.7	+3.0
			Tonge J.L. Ms.	LD	19,025	42.2	-1.7
			Touhig J.D.	Lab	2,632	5.8	-1.3
			Maciejowska J.S.M. Ms.	Green	376	0.8*	-0.5
			Cunningham C.H.	NLP	89	0.2*	+0.2
			Meacock R.	Ind	62	0.1*	
			Ellis-Jones A.K.F. Ms.	AFL	47	0.1*	+0.1
					3,869	8.6	

RICHMOND (YORKS) [480]

Election	Electors	T'out	Candidate	Party	Votes	% Sh	% Ch
1983	75,196	68.7	Brittan L.*	Con	32,373	62.6	
			Raw J.D.	Lib	14,307	27.7	
			Hawkins B.L.M. Ms.	Lab	4,997	9.7*	
					18,066	35.0	
1987	79,277	72.1	Brittan L.*	Con	34,995	61.2	-1.4
			Lloyd-Williams D.	Lib	15,419	27.0	-0.7
			Robson F.	Lab	6,737	11.8	+2.1
					19,576	34.3	

[Resignation]

Election	Electors	T'out	Candidate	Party	Votes	% Sh	% Ch
1989	81,568	64.4	Hague W.J.	Con	19,543	37.2	-24.0
(23/2)			Potter M.	SDP	16,909	32.2	
			Pearce B.A. Ms.	LD	11,589	22.1	-4.9
			Robson F.	Lab	2,591	4.9*	-6.9
			Upshall R.	Green	1,473	2.8*	
			Sutch D.E.	MRLP	167	0.3*	
			Millns A.	Ind	113	0.2*	
			St. Clair L. Ms.	Ind	106	0.2*	
			Watkins N.	Ind	70	0.1*	
					2,634	5.0	
1992	82,880†	78.4	Hague W.J.	Con	40,202	61.9	+0.6
			Irwin G.	LD	16,698	25.7	-1.3
			Cranston R.F.	Lab	7,523	11.6	-0.2
			Barr A.M.	Ind	570	0.9*	
					23,504	36.2	

ROCHDALE [481]

Election	Electors	T'out	Candidate	Party	Votes	% Sh	% Ch
1983	66,976	70.8	Smith C.*	Lib	21,858	46.1	
			Broom V.E. Ms.	Lab	14,271	30.1	
			Fearn A.d'A.	Con	10,616	22.4	
			Barker P.	NF	463	1.0*	
			Courtney P.B.	Ind	204	0.4*	
					7,587	16.0	
1987	68,693	74.6	Smith C.*	Lib	22,245	43.4	-2.7
			Williams A.D.	Lab	19,466	38.0	+7.9
			Condie C.W.	Con	9,561	18.6	-3.7
					2,779	5.4	
1992	69,522†	76.5	Lynne E. Ms.	LD	22,776	42.8	-0.6
			Williams A.D.	Lab	20,937	39.4	+1.4
			Goldie-Scot D.J.	Con	8,626	16.2	-2.4
			Henderson K.	BNP	620	1.2*	+1.2
			Lucker V.J.	NLP	211	0.4*	+0.4
					1,839	3.5	

ROCHFORD [482]

Election	Electors	T'out	Candidate	Party	Votes	% Sh	% Ch
1983	69,392	73.5	Clark M.	Con	29,495	57.8	
			Boyd R.H.	Lib	16,393	32.1	
			Witzer H.M.	Lab	5,105	10.0*	
					13,102	25.7	
1987	76,048	78.1	Clark M.*	Con	35,872	60.4	+2.6
			Young P.	Lib	16,178	27.3	-4.9
			Weir D.A.	Lab	7,308	12.3	+2.3
					19,694	33.2	
1992	76,869†	83.0	Clark M.*	Con	38,967	61.1	+0.6
			Harris N.	LD	12,931	20.3	-7.0
			Quinn D.	Lab	10,537	16.5	+4.2
			Farmer L. Ms.	Lib	1,362	2.1*	+2.1
					26,036	40.8	

ROMFORD [483]

Election	Electors	T'out	Candidate	Party	Votes	% Sh	% Ch
1983	55,758	69.8	Neubert M.J.*	Con	20,771	53.4	
			Bates J.H.	Lib	10,197	26.2	
			Hoepelman J.	Lab	7,494	19.3	
			Caine M.P. Ms.	NF	432	1.1*	
					10,574	27.2	
1987	55,668	72.9	Neubert M.J.*	Con	22,745	56.0	+2.6
			Smith N.J.M.	Lab	9,274	22.8	+3.6
			Bates J.H.	Lib	8,195	20.2	-6.0
			Gibson F.J.	Green	385	0.9*	+0.9
					13,471	33.2	
1992	53,981	78.0	Neubert M.J.*	Con	23,834	56.6	+0.6
			Gordon E. Ms.	Lab	12,414	29.5	+6.6
			Atherton P.A. Ms.	LD	5,329	12.7	-7.5
			Gibson F.J.	Green	546	1.3*	+0.3
					11,420	27.1	

ROMSEY AND WATERSIDE [484]

Election	Electors	T'out	Candidate	Party	Votes	% Sh	% Ch
1983	70,782	75.8	Colvin M.K.B.*	Con	30,361	56.6	
			Bloss A.T.	SDP	16,671	31.1	
			Knight M.W.	Lab	6,604	12.3*	
					13,690	25.5	
1987	79,136	79.0	Colvin M.K.B.*	Con	35,303	56.4	-0.2
			Bloss A.T.	SDP	20,031	32.0	+0.9
			Roberts S.J.	Lab	7,213	11.5	-0.8
					15,272	24.4	
1992	82,628†	83.2	Colvin M.K.B.*	Con	37,375	54.4	-2.0
			Dawson G.	LD	22,071	32.1	+0.1
			Mawle A. Ms.	Lab	8,688	12.6	+1.1
			Spottiswood J.C.T.	Green	577	0.8*	+0.8
					15,304	22.3	

ROSS, CROMARTY AND SKYE [485]

Election	Electors	T'out	Candidate	Party	Votes	% Sh	% Ch
1983	48,401	72.6	Kennedy C.P.	SDP	13,528	38.5	
			Gray J.H.N.*	Con	11,824	33.7	
			Elder T.M.	Lab	4,901	14.0	
			Matheson K.B. Ms.	SNP	4,863	13.8	
					1,704	4.9	
1987	52,369	72.7	Kennedy C.P.*	SDP	18,809	49.4	+10.9
			Spencer Nairn C.F.	Con	7,490	19.7	-14.0
			MacMillan M.M.	Lab	7,287	19.1	+5.2
			Gibson R.M.	SNP	4,492	11.8	-2.1
					11,319	29.7	
1992	55,771	73.6	Kennedy C.P.*	LD	17,066	41.6	-7.8
			Gray J.W.	Con	9,436	23.0	+3.3
			Gibson R.M.	SNP	7,618	18.6	+6.8
			MacDonald J.T.	Lab	6,275	15.3	-3.8
			Jardine D.M.	Green	642	1.6*	+1.6
					7,630	18.6	

ROSSENDALE AND DARWEN [486]

Election	Electors	T'out	Candidate	Party	Votes	% Sh	% Ch
1983	74,401	77.8	Trippier D.A.*	Con	27,214	47.0	
			Robinson C.B.	Lab	18,393	31.8	
			Taylor M.F.	Lib	12,246	21.2	
					8,821	15.2	
1987	75,038	80.3	Trippier D.A.*	Con	28,056	46.6	-0.5
			Anderson J. Ms.	Lab	23,074	38.3	+6.5
			Hulse P.J.	Lib	9,097	15.1	-6.1
					4,982	8.3	
1992	76,926	83.0	Anderson J. Ms.	Lab	28,028	43.9	+5.6
			Trippier D.A.*	Con	27,908	43.7	-2.9
			Connor K.	LD	7,226	11.3	-3.8
			Gaffney J.E.	Green	596	0.9*	+0.9
			Gorrod P.N.	NLP	125	0.2*	+0.2
					120	0.2	

ROTHERHAM [487]

Election	Electors	T'out	Candidate	Party	Votes	% Sh	% Ch
1983	61,165	67.0	Crowther J.S.*	Lab	22,236	54.3	
			Middleton C.N.	Con	10,523	25.7	
			Bowler P.J.	Lib	8,192	20.0	
					11,713	28.6	
1987	61,521	69.2	Crowther J.S.*	Lab	25,422	59.7	+5.4
			Stevens J.C.C.	Con	9,410	22.1	-3.6
			Bowler P.J.	Lib	7,766	18.2	-1.8
					16,012	37.6	
1992	60,937†	71.7	Boyce J.	Lab	27,933	63.9	+4.3
			Yorke S.J.D.	Con	10,372	23.7	+1.7
			Wildgoose D.B.	LD	5,375	12.3	-5.9
					17,561	40.2	

[Death]

Election	Electors	T'out	Candidate	Party	Votes	% Sh	% Ch
1994	61,327	43.7	MacShane D	Lab	14,912	55.6	-8.3
(5/5)			Wildgoose D.B.	LD	7,958	29.7	+17.4
			Gibb N.J.	Con	2.649	9.9	-13.9
			Sutch D.E.	MRLP	1,114	4.2*	
			Laycock K.	NLP	173	0.6*	
					6,954	25.9	

ROTHER VALLEY [488]

Election	Electors	T'out	Candidate	Party	Votes	% Sh	% Ch
1983	65,127	71.9	Barron K.J.	Lab	21,781	46.5	
			Derrick J.G.	Con	13,156	28.1	
			Boddy J.R.	SDP	11,903	25.4	
					8,625	18.4	
1987	66,416	75.6	Barron K.J.*	Lab	28,292	56.4	+9.9
			Rayner P.R.	Con	12,502	24.9	-3.2
			Boddy J.R.	SDP	9,240	18.4	-7.0
			Driver M.R.	WRP	145	0.3*	+0.3
					15,790	31.5	
1992	68,304†	75.0	Barron K.J.*	Lab	30,977	60.5	+4.1
			Horton G.T.A.W.	Con	13,755	26.9	+1.9
			Smith K.A.	LD	6,483	12.7	-5.8
					17,222	33.6	

276

ROXBURGH AND BERWICKSHIRE [489]

Election	Electors	T'out	Candidate	Party	Votes	% Sh	% Ch
1983	41,702	75.8	Kirkwood A.J.	Lib	15,920	50.3	
			Sproat I.M.*	Con	12,524	39.6	
			Briggs D.A.	Lab	2,326	7.4*	
			Shirley R.	SNP	852	2.7*	
					3,396	10.7	
1987	43,172	77.1	Kirkwood A.J.*	Lib	16,388	49.2	-1.1
			Fox L. Dr.	Con	12,380	37.2	-2.4
			Luckhurst T.C.H.	Lab	2,944	8.8	+1.5
			Douglas M.N.	SNP	1,586	4.8*	+2.1
					4,008	12.0	
1992	43,572†	77.6	Kirkwood A.J.*	LD	15,852	46.9	-2.3
			Finlay-Maxwell C.S. Ms.	Con	11,595	34.3	-2.9
			Douglas M.N.	SNP	3,437	10.2	+5.4
			Lambert S.	Lab	2,909	8.6	-0.2
					4,257	12.6	

RUGBY AND KENILWORTH [490]

Election	Electors	T'out	Candidate	Party	Votes	% Sh	% Ch
1983	74,501	78.1	Pawsey J.F.*	Con	29,622	50.9	
			Owen-Jones D.R.	Lib	15,381	26.4	
			Blundell P.A.	Lab	13,180	22.7	
					14,241	24.5	
1987	76,654	79.6	Pawsey J.F.*	Con	31,485	51.6	+0.7
			Airey J.	Lab	15,221	24.9	+2.3
			Owen-Jones D.R.	Lib	14,343	23.5	-2.9
					16,264	26.6	
1992	77,767†	83.7	Pawsey J.F.*	Con	34,110	52.4	+0.8
			Airey J.	Lab	20,862	32.0	+7.1
			Roodhouse J.M.	LD	9,934	15.3	-8.2
			Withers S.H.	NLP	202	0.3*	+0.3
					13,248	20.3	

RUISLIP-NORTHWOOD [491]

Election	Electors	T'out	Candidate	Party	Votes	% Sh	% Ch
1983	56,378	72.9	Wilkinson J.A.D.*	Con	24,498	59.6	
			Stephenson G.R.	Lib	11,516	28.0	
			O'Brien M.	Lab	5,105	12.4*	
					12,982	31.6	
1987	56,365	77.7	Wilkinson J.A.D.*	Con	27,418	62.6	+3.1
			Darby D. Ms.	Lib	10,447	23.9	-4.1
			Smith H.A. Ms.	Lab	5,913	13.5	+1.1
					16,971	38.8	
1992	54,033	82.1	Wilkinson J.A.D.*	Con	28,097	63.3	+0.7
			Brooks R.M. Ms.	Lab	8,306	18.7	+5.2
			Davies H.	LD	7,739	17.4	-6.4
			Sheehan M.G.	NLP	214	0.5*	+0.5
					19,791	44.6	

RUSHCLIFFE [492]

Election	Electors	T'out	Candidate	Party	Votes	% Sh	% Ch
1983	70,333	76.9	Clarke K.H.*	Con	33,253	61.5	
			Hamilton J.E.	Lib	13,033	24.1	
			Coaker V.R.	Lab	7,290	13.5	
			Pook M. Ms.	Green	518	1.0*	
					20,220	37.4	
1987	72,799	80.0	Clarke K.H.*	Con	34,214	58.8	-2.7
			George L.C.T.	SDP	13,375	23.0	-1.1
			Tipping S.P.	Lab	9,631	16.5	+3.1
			Wright H.J. Ms.	Green	991	1.7*	+0.7
					20,839	35.8	
1992	76,284	83.0	Clarke K.H.*	Con	34,448	54.4	-4.4
			Chewings A.D.	Lab	14,682	23.2	+6.6
			Wood A.M.	LD	12,660	20.0	-3.0
			Anthony S.R.	Green	775	1.2*	-0.5
			Maelor-Jones M.	Ind Con	611	1.0*	
			Richards D.	NLP	150	0.2*	+0.2
					19,766	31.2	

RUTLAND AND MELTON [493]

Election	Electors	T'out	Candidate	Party	Votes	% Sh	% Ch
1983	75,180	73.3	Latham M.A.*	Con	33,262	60.3	
			Farrer D.J.	Lib	14,909	27.0	
			Whitby J.D.	Lab	6,414	11.6*	
			Goddard H.A. Ms.	Green	532	1.0*	
					18,353	33.3	
1987	77,856	76.8	Latham M.A.*	Con	37,073	62.0	+1.6
			Renold R.C.	Lib	14,051	23.5	-3.6
			Burke L.C.	Lab	8,680	14.5	+2.9
					23,022	38.5	
1992	80,975†	80.8	Duncan A.J.C.	Con	38,603	59.0	-3.0
			Taylor J. Ms.	Lab	13,068	20.0	+5.5
			Lustig R.E.	LD	12,682	19.4	-4.1
			Berreen J.M.	Green	861	1.3*	+1.3
			Gray R.	NLP	237	0.4*	+0.4
					25,535	39.0	

RYEDALE [494]

Election	Electors	T'out	Candidate	Party	Votes	% Sh	% Ch
1983	78,388	71.8	Spence J.D.*	Con	33,312	59.2	
			Shields E.L. Ms.	Lib	17,170	30.5	
			Bloom P.R.	Lab	5,816	10.3*	
					16,142	28.7	

[Death]

1986	81,647	67.3	Shields E. L. Ms.	Lib	27,612	50.3	+19.8
(8/5)			Balfour N.R.	Con	22,672	41.3	-17.9
			Haines S. Ms.	Lab	4,633	8.4	-1.9
					4,940	9.0	
1987	83,205	79.2	Greenway J.R.	Con	35,149	53.3	-5.8
			Shields E.L. Ms.	Lib	25,409	38.6	+8.1
			Beighton J.	Lab	5,340	8.1	-2.2
					9,740	14.8	
1992	87,063	81.7	Greenway J.R.*	Con	39,888	56.1	+2.8
			Shields E.L. Ms.	LD	21,449	30.1	-8.4
			Healey J.	Lab	9,812	13.8	+5.7
					18,439	260	

SAFFRON WALDEN [495]

Election	Electors	T'out	Candidate	Party	Votes	% Sh	% Ch
1983	69,385	76.9	Haselhurst A.G.B.*	Con	30,869	57.8	
			Torode J.A.	SDP	15,620	29.3	
			Trory R.P.	Lab	6,078	11.4*	
			Smedley W.O.	FTACMP	797	1.5*	
					15,249	28.6	
1987	73,185	79.0	Haselhurst A.G.B.*	Con	33,354	57.7	-0.2
			Hayes M.P.	Lib	16,752	29.0	-0.3
			Gifford R.U.	Lab	6,674	11.5	+0.2
			Hannah G.B.	Green	816	1.4*	+1.4
			Smedley W.O.	Ind	217	0.4*	
					16,602	28.7	
1992	74,940	83.2	Haselhurst A.G.B.*	Con	35,272	56.6	-1.1
			Hayes M.P.	LD	17,848	28.6	-0.3
			Kotz J.	Lab	8,933	14.3	+2.8
			Miller M.D.	NLP	260	0.4*	+0.4
					17,424	28.0	

ST. ALBANS [496]

Election	Electors	T'out	Candidate	Party	Votes	% Sh	% Ch
1983	72,849	78.2	Lilley P.B.	Con	29,676	52.1	
			Walkington A.S.B.	Lib	21,115	37.0	
			Austin R. Ms.	Lab	6,213	10.9*	
					8,561	15.0	
1987	75,281	80.2	Lilley P.B.*	Con	31,726	52.5	+0.5
			Walkington A.S.B.	Lib	20,845	34.5	-2.5
			McWalter A.	Lab	6,922	11.5	+0.6
			Field E.V. Ms.	Green	788	1.3*	+1.3
			Pass W.H.	Ind	110	0.2*	
					10,881	18.0	
1992	74,189†	83.5	Lilley P.B.*	Con	32,709	52.8	+0.3
			Howes M. Ms.	LD	16,305	26.3	-8.2
			Pollard K.P.	Lab	12,016	19.4	+7.9
			Simmons C.	Green	734	1.2*	-0.1
			Lucas D.	NLP	161	0.3*	+0.3
					16,404	26.5	

ST. HELENS NORTH [497]

Election	Electors	T'out	Candidate	Party	Votes	% Sh	% Ch
1983	71,059	74.5	Evans J.*	Lab	25,334	47.9	
			Rhodes A.	Con	16,075	30.4	
			Derbyshire N.P.	Lib	11,525	21.8	
					9,259	17.5	
1987	70,836	76.3	Evans J.*	Lab	28,989	53.7	+5.8
			Libby M.J. Ms.	Con	14,729	27.3	-3.1
			Derbyshire N.P.	Lib	10,300	19.1	-2.7
					14,260	26.4	
1992	71,262†	77.4	Evans J.*	Lab	31,930	57.9	+4.3
			Anderson B.J.	Con	15,686	28.5	+1.2
			Beirne J.	LD	7,224	13.1	-6.0
			Lynch A.M. Ms.	NLP	287	0.5*	+0.5
					16,244	29.5	

ST. HELENS SOUTH [498]

Election	Electors	T'out	Candidate	Party	Votes	% Sh	% Ch
1983	69,172	70.6	Bermingham G.E.	Lab	22,906	46.9	
			Bull R.G.	Con	13,244	27.1	
			Briers P.J.	SDP	10,939	22.4	
			Davies M.H.	Ind Con	1,780	3.6*	
					9,662	19.8	
1987	69,449	71.3	Bermingham G.E.*	Lab	27,027	54.6	+7.7
			Brown J.A.	Con	13,226	26.7	-0.4
			Briers P.J.	SDP	9,252	18.7	-3.7
					13,801	27.9	
1992	67,521†	73.8	Bermingham G.E.*	Lab	30,391	61.0	+6.4
			Buzzard P.M. Ms.	Con	12,182	24.5	-2.3
			Spencer B.T.	LD	6,933	13.9	-4.8
			Jump H.S. Ms.	NLP	295	0.6*	+0.6
					18,209	36.6	

ST. IVES [499]

Election	Electors	T'out	Candidate	Party	Votes	% Sh	% Ch
1983	64,012	73.8	Harris D.A.	Con	24,297	51.4	
			Carter H.H.J.	SDP	16,438	34.8	
			Crowley M. Ms.	Lab	5,310	11.2*	
			Prior P.G.	MK	569	1.2*	
			Hoptrough H.S.	Green	439	0.9*	
			Horner W.A.N.	Ind	219	0.5*	
					7,859	16.6	
1987	67,207	77.5	Harris D.A.*	Con	25,174	48.3	-3.0
			Carter H.H.J.	SDP	17,619	33.8	-0.9
			Hope I.	Lab	9,275	17.8	+6.6
					7,555	14.5	
1992	71,154†	80.3	Harris D.A.*	Con	24,528	42.9	-5.4
			George A.H.	LD	22,883	40.1	+6.2
			Warran S.	Lab	9,144	16.0	-1.8
			Stephens F.G.	Lib	577	1.0*	+1.0
					1,645	2.9	

SALFORD EAST [500]

Election	Electors	T'out	Candidate	Party	Votes	% Sh	% Ch
1983	63,946	62.3	Orme S.*	Lab	21,373	53.7	
			Cole J.S.M.	Con	11,832	29.7	
			Williams A.C.	SDP	6,190	15.5	
			Carter S.M.	WRP	417	1.0*	
					9,541	24.0	
1987	58,087	66.0	Orme S.*	Lab	22,555	58.8	+5.1
			McFall C.W.H.	Con	10,499	27.4	-2.4
			Keaveney P.	SDP	5,105	13.3	-2.2
			Murray S.G.	WRP	201	0.5*	-0.5
					12,056	31.4	
1992	52,616†	64.4	Orme S.*	Lab	20,327	60.0	+1.2
			Berens D.	Con	9,092	26.8	-0.5
			Owen N.J.	LD	3,836	11.3	-2.0
			Stanley M.T.	Green	463	1.4*	+1.4
			Craig C.C.B.	NLP	150	0.4*	+0.4
					11,235	33.2	

SALISBURY [501]

Election	Electors	T'out	Candidate	Party	Votes	% Sh	% Ch
1983	74,189	72.8	Key S.R.	Con	28,876	53.5	
			Lakeman J.F.	Lib	21,702	40.2	
			Lamberth C.K. Ms.	Lab	3,139	5.8*	
			Kemp M. Ms.	WR	182	0.3*	
			Abbott T.I.	Ind	86	0.2*	
					7,174	13.3	
1987	76,221	75.6	Key S.R.*	Con	31,612	54.9*	+1.4
			Mitchell P.A.	SDP	20,169	35.0	-5.2
			Seabourne T.E. Ms.	Lab	5,455	9.5	+3.7
			Fletcher S.W.	Ind	372	0.6*	
					11,443	19.9	
1992	75,917†	79.9	Key S.R.*	Con	31,546	52.0	-2.9
			Sample P.W.L.	LD	22,573	37.2	+2.2
			Fear S.R.	Lab	5,483	9.0	-0.4
			Elcock S.M.	Green	609	1.0*	+1.0
			Fletcher S.W.	Ind	233	0.4*	
			Abbott T.I.	Ind	117	0.2*	
			Martell A. Ms.	NLP	93	0.2*	+0.2
					8,973	14.8	

SCARBOROUGH [502]

Election	Electors	T'out	Candidate	Party	Votes	% Sh	% Ch
1983	72,362	71.3	Shaw M.N. Sir.*	Con	27,977	54.3	
			Jordan R. Ms.	SDP	14,048	27.2	
			Battersby J.	Lab	9,545	18.5	
					13,929	27.0	
1987	74,612	73.2	Shaw M.N. Sir.*	Con	27,672	50.7	-3.6
			Callan H.M.W. Ms.	SDP	14,046	25.7	-1.5
			Wolstenholme M.C.	Lab	12,913	23.6	+5.1
					13,626	24.9	
1992	76,364	77.2	Sykes J.D.	Con	29,334	49.8	-0.9
			Billing D.L.	Lab	17,600	29.9	+6.2
			Davenport A.B	LD	11,133	18.9	-6.8
			Richardson R.C.	Green	876	1.5*	+1.5
					11,734	19.9	

SEDGEFIELD [503]

Election	Electors	T'out	Candidate	Party	Votes	% Sh	% Ch
1983	61,702	72.9	Blair A.C.L.	Lab	21,401	47.6	
			Horton G.T.A.W.	Con	13,120	29.2	
			Shand D.L.	SDP	10,183	22.6	
			Logan-Salton M.E.	Ind	298	0.7*	
					8,281	18.4	
1987	60,872	76.1	Blair A.C.L.*	Lab	25,965	56.0	+8.5
			Hawkins N.B.S.	Con	12,907	27.8	-1.3
			Andrew R.I.	SDP	7,477	16.1	-6.5
					13,058	28.2	
1992	61,029†	77.1	Blair A.C.L.*	Lab	28,453	60.5	+4.5
			Jopling N.M.F.	Con	13,594	28.9	+1.1
			Huntington J.G.	LD	4,982	10.6	-5.5
					14,859	31.6	

SELBY [504]

Election	Electors	T'out	Candidate	Party	Votes	% Sh	% Ch
1983	65,365	72.1	Alison M.J.H.*	Con	26,712	56.7	
			Whitaker W.K.	Lib	10,747	22.8	
			Haines S. Ms.	Lab	9,687	20.5	
					15,965	33.9	
1987	71,378	77.7	Alison M.J.H.*	Con	28,611	51.6	-5.1
			Grogan J.T.	Lab	14,832	26.7	+6.2
			Longman J.E.F.	Lib	12,010	21.7	-1.1
					13,779	24.8	
1992	77,180†	80.2	Alison M.J.H.*	Con	31,067	50.2	-1.4
			Grogan J.T.	Lab	21,559	34.8	+8.1
			Batty T.	LD	9,244	14.9	-6.7
					9,508	15.4	

SEVENOAKS [505]

Election	Electors	T'out	Candidate	Party	Votes	% Sh	% Ch
1983	71,327	73.7	Wolfson G.M.*	Con	30,722	58.4	
			Jakobi S.R.	Lib	15,016	28.6	
			Gooding R.	Lab	6,439	12.2*	
			Burnett G.L.	NF	416	0.8*	
					15,706	29.9	
1987	73,179	76.4	Wolfson G.M.*	Con	32,945	58.9	+0.5
			Jakobi S.R.	Lib	15,600	27.9	-0.7
			Green G.A.	Lab	7,379	13.2	+1.0
					17,345	31.0	
1992	71,092	81.3	Wolfson G.M.*	Con	33,245	57.5	-1.4
			Walshe R.F.C.	LD	14,091	24.4	-3.5
			Evans J.S. Ms.	Lab	9,470	16.4	+3.2
			Lawrence M.E. Ms.	Green	786	1.4*	+1.4
			Wakeling P.L.	NLP	210	0.4*	+0.4
					19,154	33.1	

SHEFFIELD, ATTERCLIFFE [506]

Election	Electors	T'out	Candidate	Party	Votes	% Sh	% Ch
1983	64,203	69.7	Duffy A.E.P.	Lab	23,067	51.5	
			Millward G.R.	Con	11,455	25.6	
			Addison I.M. Ms.	SDP	10,241	22.9	
					11,612	25.9	
1987	67,051	72.9	Duffy A.E.P.*	Lab	28,266	57.8	+6.3
			Perry G.J.	Con	11,075	22.7	-2.9
			Woolley H.E. Ms.	SDP	9,549	19.5	-3.3
					17,191	35.2	
1992	69,177†	71.8	Betts C.J.C.	Lab	28,563	57.5	-0.3
			Millward G.R.	Con	13,083	26.3	+3.7
			Woolley H.E. Ms.	LD	7,283	14.7	-4.9
			Ferguson G.D.	Green	751	1.5*	+1.5
					15,480	31.2	

SHEFFIELD, BRIGHTSIDE [507]

Election	Electors	T'out	Candidate	Party	Votes	% Sh	% Ch
1983	67,260	65.5	Maynard V.J. Ms.*	Lab	25,531	58.0	
			Butler F.R.	Lib	10,322	23.4	
			Grayson D.R.	Con	7,888	17.9	
			Spink P.A.	NF	286	0.6*	
					15,209	34.5	
1987	64,982	68.7	Blunkett D.	Lab	31,208	69.9	+11.9
			Glyn M.C. Ms.	Con	7,017	15.7	-2.2
			Leeman J.A.	Lib	6,434	14.4	-9.0
					24,191	54.2	
1992	63,810†	66.3	Blunkett D.*	Lab	29,771	70.4	+0.5
			Loughton T.P.	Con	7,090	16.8	+1.1
			Franklin R.K.	LD	5,273	12.5	-1.9
			Hyland D.E.	ICP	150	0.4*	+0.4
					22,681	53.6	

SHEFFIELD CENTRAL [508]

Election	Electors	T'out	Candidate	Party	Votes	% Sh	% Ch
1983	66,769	61.6	Caborn R.G.	Lab	24,759	60.2	
			Major P.W. Ms.	SDP	7,969	19.4	
			Rawlings P.E. Ms.	Con	7,908	19.2	
			Gill V.A. Ms.	Comm	296	0.7*	
			Barrett C. Ms.	RCP	226	0.5*	
					16,790	40.8	
1987	61,156	62.5	Caborn R.G.*	Lab	25,872	67.7	+7.6
			Oxley B.W.	Con	6,530	17.1	-2.1
			Hornby F.C. Ms.	SDP	5,314	13.9	-5.4
			Dingle C.T. Ms.	RF	278	0.7*	+0.7
			Petts K.E.	Comm	203	0.5*	-0.2
					19,342	50.6	
1992	59,060†	56.1	Caborn R.G.*	Lab	22,764	68.7	+0.9
			Davies V.J.E.	Con	5,470	16.5	-0.6
			Sangar A.P.	LD	3,856	11.6	-2.3
			Wroe G.S.	Green	750	2.3*	+2.3
			Clark M.C.	Ind	212	0.6*	
			O'Brien J. Ms.	CL	92	0.3*	+0.3
					17,294	52.2	

SHEFFIELD, HALLAM [509]

Election	Electors	T'out	Candidate	Party	Votes	% Sh	% Ch
1983	72,878	72.8	Osborn J.H.*	Con	26,851	50.6	
			Johnson M.S.	Lib	15,077	28.4	
			McCrindle J. Ms.	Lab	10,463	19.7	
			Booler P.	Ind Con	656	1.2*	
					11,774	22.2	
1987	74,158	74.7	Patnick C.I.	Con	25,649	46.3	-4.3
			Gold P.J.	Lib	18,012	32.5	+4.1
			Savani M.C.	Lab	11,290	20.4	+0.7
			Spencer L.M. Ms.	Green	459	0.8*	+0.8
					7,637	13.8	
1992	76,585†	70.8	Patnick C.I.*	Con	24,693	45.5	-0.8
			Gold P.J.	LD	17,952	33.1	+0.6
			Hardstaff V.M. Ms.	Lab	10,930	20.1	-0.2
			Baker M.A.	Green	473	0.9*	+0.0
			Hurford R.E.	NLP	101	0.2*	+0.2
			Clifford T.M. Ms.	RCP	99	0.2*	
					6,741	12.4	

SHEFFIELD, HEELEY [510]

Election	Electors	T'out	Candidate	Party	Votes	% Sh	% Ch
1983	74,659	70.5	Michie W.	Lab	24,111	45.8	
			Cordle S.C.	Con	15,743	29.9	
			Day J.M.	SDP	12,813	24.3	
					8,368	15.9	
1987	73,931	72.0	Michie W.*	Lab	28,425	53.4	+7.6
			Mearing-Smith N.P.	Con	13,985	26.3	-3.6
			Moore P.	SDP	10,811	20.3	-4.0
					14,440	27.1	
1992	70,953†	70.9	Michie W.*	Lab	28,005	55.7	+2.3
			Beck D.R.	Con	13,051	25.9	-0.3
			Moore P.	LD	9,247	18.4	-1.9
					14,954	29.7	

SHEFFIELD, HILLSBOROUGH [511]

Election	Electors	T'out	Candidate	Party	Votes	% Sh	% Ch
1983	74,422	75.4	Flannery M.H.*	Lab	20,901	37.2	
			Chadwick D.	Lib	19,355	34.5	
			Smith C.M.L. Ms.	Con	15,881	28.3	
					1,546	2.8	
1987	76,312	78.0	Flannery M.H.*	Lab	26,208	44.0	+6.8
			Chadwick D.	Lib	22,922	38.5	+4.0
			Sykes J.D.	Con	10,396	17.5	-10.8
					3,286	5.5	
1992	77,343†	77.2	Jackson H.M. Ms.	Lab	27,563	46.2	+2.1
			Chadwick D.	LD	20,500	34.3	-4.2
			Cordle S.C.	Con	11,640	19.5	+2.0
					7,063	11.8	

SHERWOOD [512]

Election	Electors	T'out	Candidate	Party	Votes	% Sh	% Ch
1983	69,091	76.3	Stewart A.S.	Con	21,595	41.0	
			Bach W.S.G.	Lab	20,937	39.7	
			Cooper M.E.B. Ms.	SDP	10,172	19.3	
					658	1.2	
1987	71,853	81.4	Stewart A.S.*	Con	26,816	45.9	+4.9
			Bach W.S.G.	Lab	22,321	38.2	-1.6
			Thompstone S.R.	SDP	9,343	16.0	-3.3
					4,495	7.7	
1992	73,355†	85.5	Tipping S.P.	Lab	29,788	47.5	+9.3
			Stewart A.S.*	Con	26,878	42.9	-3.0
			Howard J.W.	LD	6,039	9.6	-6.3
					2,910	4.6	

Election	Electors	T'out	Candidate	Party	Votes	% Sh	% Ch
1983	67,584	77.0	Fox J.M.*	Con	25,866	49.7	
			Wallace W.J.L.	Lib	14,421	27.7	
			Leathley M.	Lab	11,218	21.6	
			Shepherd S.	Green	521	1.0*	
					11,445	22.0	
1987	68,705	79.2	Fox J.M. Sir.*	Con	26,941	49.5	-0.2
			Wallace W.J.L.	Lib	14,311	26.3	-1.4
			Butler C.R.B.	Lab	12,669	23.3	+1.7
			Harris C.M. Dr.	Green	507	0.9*	-0.1
					12,630	23.2	
1992	68,827	82.1	Fox J.M. Sir.*	Con	28,463	50.4	+0.9
			Lockwood A.E. Ms.	Lab	16,081	28.5	+5.2
			Cole J.M.C.	LD	11,288	20.0	-6.3
			Harris C.M. Dr.	Green	680	1.2*	+0.3
					12,382	21.9	

SHOREHAM [514]

Election	Electors	T'out	Candidate	Party	Votes	% Sh	% Ch
1983	69,720	73.7	Luce R.N.*	Con	31,679	61.6	
			Ingram J.A.	Lib	15,913	31.0	
			Hurcombe J. Ms.	Lab	3,794	7.4*	
					15,766	30.7	
1987	72,601	76.2	Luce R.N.*	Con	33,660	60.9	-0.8
			Ingram J.A.	Lib	16,590	30.0	-1.0
			Godwin P.	Lab	5,053	9.1	+1.8
					17,070	30.9	
1992	71,252†	81.2	Stephen B.M.L.	Con	32,670	56.5	-4.4
			King M.	LD	18,384	31.8	+1.8
			Godwin P.	Lab	6,123	10.6	+1.4
			Weights B.	Lib	459	0.8*	+0.8
			Dreben J.I.	NLP	200	0.3*	+0.3
					14,286	24.7	

SHREWSBURY AND ATCHAM [515]

Election	Electors	T'out	Candidate	Party	Votes	% Sh	% Ch
1983	66,554	74.0	Conway D.L.	Con	24,397	49.5	
			Bowen A.J.	Lib	15,773	32.0	
			Mosley A.N.	Lab	9,080	18.4	
					8,624	17.5	
1987	70,689	77.0	Conway D.L.*	Con	26,027	47.8	-1.7
			Hutchinson D.R.D.	Lib	16,963	31.2	-0.9
			Owen E. Ms.	Lab	10,797	19.8	+1.4
			Hardy G.A.	Green	660	1.2*	+1.2
					9,064	16.6	
1992	70,636	82.4	Conway D.L.*	Con	26,681	45.8	-2.0
			Hemsley K.A.	LD	15,716	27.0	-4.2
			Owen E. Ms.	Lab	15,157	26.0	+6.2
			Hardy G.A.	Green	677	1.2*	-0.0
					10,965	18.8	

SHROPSHIRE NORTH [516]

Election	Electors	T'out	Candidate	Party	Votes	% Sh	% Ch
1983	73,331	72.7	Biffen W.J.*	Con	28,496	53.4	
			Evans D.J.	Lib	16,829	31.6	
			Jones H.M. Ms.	Lab	7,860	14.7	
			Phillimore J.L.	Ind	135	0.3*	
					11,667	21.9	
1987	77,122	75.5	Biffen W.J.*	Con	30,385	52.2	-1.3
			Smith J.G.	Lib	15,970	27.4	-4.1
			Hawkins R.J.	Lab	11,866	20.4	+5.6
					14,415	24.8	
1992	82,676†	77.7	Biffen W.J.*	Con	32,443	50.5	-1.7
			Stevens H.J.	LD	16,232	25.3	-2.2
			Hawkins R.J.	Lab	15,550	24.2	+3.8
					16,211	25.2	

SKIPTON AND RIPON [517]

Election	Electors	T'out	Candidate	Party	Votes	% Sh	% Ch
1983	69,421	74.9	Watson J.G.B.*	Con	31,509	60.6	
			Brooks K.C. Ms.	Lib	16,463	31.6	
			Billing M.A. Ms.	Lab	4,044	7.8*	
					15,046	28.9	
1987	72,316	77.7	Curry D.M.	Con	33,128	59.0	-1.6
			Cooksey S.J.	Lib	15,954	28.4	-3.2
			Whitfield T.L.	Lab	6,264	11.2	+3.4
			Williams L.S. Ms.	Green	825	1.5*	+1.5
					17,174	30.6	
1992	75,629†	81.3	Curry D.M.*	Con	35,937	58.4	-0.6
			Hall R.	LD	16,607	27.0	-1.4
			Allott K.R. Ms.	Lab	8,978	14.6	+3.4
					19,330	31.4	

SLOUGH [518]

Election	Electors	T'out	Candidate	Party	Votes	% Sh	% Ch
1983	71,907	71.5	Watts J.A.	Con	22,064	42.9	
			Lestor J. Ms.*	Lab	18,958	36.9	
			Bosanquet N.F.G.	SDP	9,519	18.5	
			John G.	NF	528	1.0*	
			Flindall I.E.	Green	325	0.6*	
					3,106	6.0	
1987	73,424	75.9	Watts J.A.*	Con	26,166	46.9	+4.0
			Lopez A.E.	Lab	22,076	39.6	+2.7
			Goldstone M.	SDP	7,490	13.4	-5.1
					4,090	7.3	
1992	74,103	78.0	Watts J.A.*	Con	25,793	44.6	-2.3
			Lopez A.E.	Lab	25,279	43.7	+4.1
			Mapp P.G.D.	LD	4,041	7.0	-6.4
			Clark J.S.	Lib	1,426	2.5*	+2.5
			Alford D.	Ind Lab	699	1.2*	
			Carmichael A.	NF	290	0.5*	+0.5
			Creese M.R.	NLP	153	0.3*	+0.3
			Smith E.A. Ms.	Ind	134	0.2*	
					514	0.9	

291

SOLIHULL [519]

Election	Electors	T'out	Candidate	Party	Votes	% Sh	% Ch
1983	73,677	71.4	Taylor J.M.	Con	31,947	60.8	
			Gillett I.K.	Lib	14,553	27.7	
			Jamieson I.J.	Lab	6,075	11.6*	
					17,394	33.1	
1987	78,123	75.1	Taylor J.M.*	Con	35,844	61.1	+0.3
			Gadie G.C.	Lib	14,058	24.0	-3.7
			Knowles S.E. Ms.	Lab	8,791	15.0	+3.4
					21,786	37.1	
1992	77,332	81.6	Taylor J.M.*	Con	38,385	60.8	-0.2
			Southcombe M.J.	LD	13,239	21.0	-3.0
			Kutapan N. Ms.	Lab	10,544	16.7	+1.7
			Hards C.G.	Green	925	1.5*	+1.5
					25,146	39.9	

SOMERTON AND FROME [520]

Election	Electors	T'out	Candidate	Party	Votes	% Sh	% Ch
1983	64,695	76.7	Boscawen R.T. Hon.*	Con	26,988	54.4	
			Hinton N.J.	SDP	17,761	35.8	
			Osborn J.B.	Lab	4,867	9.8*	
					9,227	18.6	
1987	68,773	79.4	Boscawen R.T. Hon.*	Con	29,351	53.7	-0.7
			Morgan R.G.	Lib	19,813	36.3	+0.5
			Kelly I.S.	Lab	5,461	10.0	+0.2
					9,538	17.5	
1992	71,358	82.7	Robinson M.N.F.	Con	28,052	47.5	-6.2
			Heath D.	LD	23,711	40.2	+3.9
			Ashford R.	Lab	6,154	10.4	+0.4
			Graham L.A. Ms.	Green	742	1.3*	+1.3
			Pollock J. Ms.	Lib	388	0.7*	+0.7
					4,341	7.4	

SOUTHAMPTON, ITCHEN [521]

Election	Electors	T'out	Candidate	Party	Votes	% Sh	% Ch
1983	72,233	73.2	Chope C.R.	Con	21,937	41.5	
			Mitchell R.C.*	SDP	16,647	31.5	
			Denham J.Y.	Lab	14,324	27.1	
					5,290	10.0	
1987	72,687	75.8	Chope C.R.*	Con	24,419	44.3	+2.8
			Denham J.Y.	Lab	17,703	32.1	+5.0
			Mitchell R.C.	SDP	13,006	23.6	-7.9
					6,716	12.2	
1992	72,105†	76.9	Denham J.Y	Lab	24,402	44.0	+11.9
			Chope C.R.*	Con	23,851	43.0	-1.3
			Hodgson J.R.T.	LD	7,221	13.0	-10.6
					551	1.0	

SOUTHAMPTON, TEST [522]

Election	Electors	T'out	Candidate	Party	Votes	% Sh	% Ch
1983	74,668	73.1	Hill S.J.A.*	Con	24,657	45.2	
			Whitehead A.P.V.	Lab	15,311	28.1	
			Vinson A.J.	SDP	14,592	26.7	
					9,346	17.1	
1987	73,918	76.4	Hill S.J.A.*	Con	25,722	45.6	+0.4
			Whitehead A.P.V.	Lab	18,768	33.3	+5.2
			Rayner V.A. Ms.	Lib	11,950	21.2	-5.6
					6,954	12.3	
1992	72,932†	77.4	Hill S.J.A.*	Con	24,504	43.4	-2.2
			Whitehead A.P.V.	Lab	23,919	42.4	+9.1
			Maddock D.M. Ms.	LD	7,391	13.1	-8.1
			Michaelis J.M.	Green	535	0.9*	+0.9
			Plummer D.	NLP	101	0.2*	+0.2
					585	1.0	

SOUTHEND EAST [523]

Election	Electors	T'out	Candidate	Party	Votes	% Sh	% Ch
1983	57,690	67.6	Taylor E.M.*	Con	21,743	55.8	
			George C.	SDP	11,052	28.4	
			O'Brien C.	Lab	6,188	15.9	
					10,691	27.4	
1987	59,073	69.3	Taylor E.M.*	Con	23,753	58.0	+2.2
			Berkeley H.J.	SDP	9,906	24.2	-4.2
			Scully D.R.	Lab	7,296	17.8	+1.9
					13,847	33.8	
1992	56,709†	73.8	Taylor Sir E.M.*	Con	24,591	58.8	+0.8
			Bramley G.	Lab	11,480	27.4	+9.6
			Horne J. Ms.	LD	5,107	12.2	-12.0
			Lynch B.T.	Lib	673	1.6*	+1.6
					13,111	31.3	

SOUTHEND WEST [524]

Election	Electors	T'out	Candidate	Party	Votes	% Sh	% Ch
1983	67,486	71.7	Channon H.P.G.*	Con	26,360	54.5	
			Grant G.	Lib	18,327	37.9	
			Nisbet J. Ms.	Lab	3,675	7.6*	
					8,033	16.6	
1987	68,415	75.3	Channon H.P.G.*	Con	28,003	54.4	-0.1
			Grant G.	Lib	19,603	38.1	+0.2
			Smith A.E. Ms.	Lab	3,899	7.6	-0.0
					8,400	16.3	
1992	64,199†	77.8	Channon H.P.G.*	Con	27,319	54.7	+0.3
			Stimson N.J. Ms.	LD	15,417	30.9	-7.2
			Viney G.P.	Lab	6,139	12.3	+4.7
			Farmer A.J.	Lib	495	1.0*	+1.0
			Keene C.R.	Green	451	0.9*	+0.9
			Warburton P.N.	NLP	127	0.3*	+0.3
					11,902	23.8	

SOUTH HAMS [525]

Election	Electors	T'out	Candidate	Party	Votes	% Sh	% Ch
1983	74,276	74.9	Steen A.D.*	Con	31,855	57.2	
			Rogers A.H.	Lib	19,454	35.0	
			Morris G.J.	Lab	3,824	6.9*	
			Morgan W.J. Ms.	Green	518	0.9*	
					12,401	22.3	
1987	78,839	78.4	Steen A.D.*	Con	34,218	55.4	-1.9
			Chave R.F.	Lib	21,072	34.1	-0.9
			Hamilton W.W.*	Lab	5,060	8.2	+1.3
			Titmuss C.G.	Green	1,178	1.9*	+1.0
			Langsford T.C.	MRLP	277	0.4*	+0.4
					13,146	21.3	

William Hamilton had been the member for Fife Central in the previous Parliament.

Election	Electors	T'out	Candidate	Party	Votes	% Sh	% Ch
1992	83,140	81.0	Steen A.D.*	Con	35,951	53.4	-2.0
			Evans R.V.	LD	22,240	33.0	-1.1
			Cohen E. Ms.	Lab	8,091	12.0	+3.8
			Titmuss C.G.	Green	846	1.3*	-0.6
			Somerville L.J. Ms.	NLP	227	0.3*	+0.3
					13,711	20.4	

SOUTHPORT [526]

Election	Electors	T'out	Candidate	Party	Votes	% Sh	% Ch
1983	70,089	72.5	Percival W.I. Sir.*	Con	25,612	50.4	
			Brodie-Browne I.M.	Lib	20,573	40.5	
			Brady F.P.	Lab	4,233	8.3*	
			Wood K.L.	Ind	374	0.7*	
					5,039	9.9	
1987	71,443	76.3	Fearn R.C.	Lib	26,110	47.9	+7.4
			Thomas N.M.	Con	24,261	44.5	-5.9
			Moore A. Ms.	Lab	3,483	6.4	-1.9
			Walker J.R.G.	Green	653	1.2*	+1.2
					1,849	3.4	
1992	71,444†	77.6	Banks M.R.W.	Con	26,081	47.0	+2.5
			Fearn R.C.*	LD	23,018	41.5	-6.4
			King J.	Lab	5,637	10.2	+3.8
			Walker J.R.G.	Green	545	1.0*	-0.2
			Clements G.	NLP	159	0.3*	+0.3
					3,063	5.5	

SOUTH RIBBLE [527]

Election	Electors	T'out	Candidate	Party	Votes	% Sh	% Ch
1983	72,401	77.7	Atkins R.J.*	Con	27,625	49.1	
			Duffy F.	Lab	14,966	26.6	
			Walker R.	Lib	13,690	24.3	
					12,659	22.5	
1987	74,643	79.8	Atkins R.J.*	Con	28,133	47.2	-1.9
			Roebuck D.F.	Lab	19,703	33.1	+6.5
			Holleran J.A.	Lib	11,746	19.7	-4.6
					8,430	14.1	
1992	78,171†	83.0	Atkins R.J.*	Con	30,828	47.5	+0.3
			Smith G.W.T.	Lab	24,855	38.3	+5.2
			Jones S.N.	LD	8,928	13.8	-6.0
			Decter R.D.	NLP	269	0.4*	+0.4
					5,973	9.2	

SOUTH SHIELDS [528]

Election	Electors	T'out	Candidate	Party	Votes	% Sh	% Ch
1983	61,924	66.2	Clark D.G.*	Lab	19,055	46.5	
			Groves P.J.	Con	12,653	30.9	
			Angus P.J.	SDP	9,288	22.7	
					6,402	15.6	
1987	60,754	70.7	Clark D.G.*	Lab	24,882	57.9	+11.4
			Fabricant M.L.D.	Con	11,031	25.7	-5.2
			Meling M.M. Ms.	SDP	6,654	15.5	-7.2
			Dunn E.G.	Ind	408	0.9*	
					13,851	32.2	
1992	59,392†	70.1	Clark D.G.*	Lab	24,876	59.8	+1.9
			Howard J.L.	Con	11,399	27.4	+1.7
			Preece A.	LD	5,344	12.8	-2.6
					13,477	32.4	

SOUTHWARK AND BERMONDSEY [529]

Election	Electors	T'out	Candidate	Party	Votes	% Sh	% Ch
1983	55,839	61.7	Hughes S.H.W.*	Lib	17,185	49.9	
			Tilley J.V.*	Lab	12,021	34.9	
			Hughes R.G.	Con	4,481	13.0	
			Sneath J.S.	NF	474	1.4*	
			Mason K.T.	NBP	154	0.4*	
			Farehk A.	RCP	54	0.2*	
			McKenzie S.C. Ms.	Nat	50	0.1*	
			Keen T.L.	Ind	50	0.1*	
					5,164	15.0	

John Tilley had been the member for Lambeth Central in the previous Parliament.

Election	Electors	T'out	Candidate	Party	Votes	% Sh	% Ch
1987	55,438	64.9	Hughes S.H.W.*	Lib	17,072	47.4	-2.4
			Bryan J.D.	Lab	14,293	39.7	+4.8
			Heald O.	Con	4,522	12.6	-0.4
			Power P.N.	Comm	108	0.3*	+0.3
					2,779	7.7	
1992	60,564	62.3	Hughes S.H.W.*	LD	21,459	56.9	+9.4
			Balfe R.A.	Lab	11,614	30.8	-8.9
			Raca A.	Con	3,794	10.1	-2.5
			Tyler S.J.	BNP	530	1.4*	+1.4
			Blackham T.S.	NF	168	0.4*	+0.4
			Barnett G.H.	NLP	113	0.3*	+0.3
			Grogan J.B.	CL	56	0.1*	+0.1
					9,845	26.1	

SPELTHORNE [530]

Election	Electors	T'out	Candidate	Party	Votes	% Sh	% Ch
1983	72,236	71.0	Atkins H.E.G.*	Con	26,863	52.4	
			Layton A.W.	SDP	13,357	26.0	
			Rowlands M.C.	Lab	7,926	15.5	
			Adams R.G.	Ind Con	2,816	5.5*	
			Butterfield E.J.	FTACMP	325	0.6*	
					13,506	26.3	
1987	72,967	74.1	Wilshire D.	Con	32,440	60.0	+7.6
			Cunningham M. Ms.	SDP	12,390	22.9	-3.1
			Welfare D.F.J.	Lab	9,227	17.1	+1.6
					20,050	37.1	
1992	69,344†	80.4	Wilshire D.*	Con	32,627	58.5	-1.5
			Leedham A.E. Ms.	Lab	12,784	22.9	+5.9
			Roberts R.D.C.	LD	9,202	16.5	-6.4
			Wassell J.D. Ms.	Green	580	1.0*	+1.0
			Rea D.J.	MRLP	338	0.6*	+0.6
			Ellis D.A.	NLP	195	0.3*	+0.3
					19,843	35.6	

Election	Electors	T'out	Candidate	Party	Votes	% Sh	% Ch
1983	70,570	76.5	Fraser H.C.P.J. Hon. Sir.*	Con	27,639	51.2	
			Dunn D.J.	SDP	13,362	24.7	
			Poulter M.J.D.	Lab	12,789	23.7	
			Caruso G.M.J.	Ind	212	0.4*	
					14,277	26.4	

[Death]

1984	70,635	65.6	Cash W.N.P.	Con	18,713	40.4	-10.8
(3/5)			Dunn D.J.	SDP	14,733	31.8	+7.1
			Poulter M.J.D.	Lab	12,677	27.4	+3.7
			Teesdale C.D.	Ind	210	0.4*	
					3,980	8.6	
1987	72,431	79.5	Cash W.N.P.	Con	29,541	51.3	+0.1
			Phipps C.B.	SDP	15,834	27.5	+2.8
			Hafeez N. Ms.	Lab	12,177	21.2	-2.5
					13,707	23.8	
1992	74,668	82.9	Cash W.N.P.*	Con	30,876	49.9	-1.5
			Kidney D.N.	Lab	19,976	32.3	+11.1
			Calder J.M.	LD	10,702	17.3	-10.2
			Peat C.A.	Ind	178	0.3*	
			Lines P.D.M.	NLP	176	0.3*	+0.3
					10,900	17.6	

Election	Electors	T'out	Candidate	Party	Votes	% Sh	% Ch
1983	67,425	77.5	Heddle B.J.*	Con	27,210	52.1	
			Jones T.A.	Lib	13,330	25.5	
			Lane P.W.	Lab	11,720	22.4	
					13,880	26.6	
1987	71,252	79.4	Heddle B.J.*	Con	28,644	50.6	-1.4
			St. Hill C.R.	Lab	13,990	24.7	+2.3
			Jones T.A.	Lib	13,114	23.2	-2.3
			Bazeley J.G.	Ind Con	836	1.5*	
					14,654	25.9	

[Death]

Election	Electors	T'out	Candidate	Party	Votes	% Sh	% Ch
1990	72,728	77.5	Heal S.L. Ms.	Lab	27,649	49.1	+24.4
(22/3)			Prior C.C.L.	Con	18,200	32.3	-18.3
			Jones T.	LD	6,315	11.2	-12.0
			Wood I.	SDP	1,422	2.5*	
			Saunders R.T.C.	Green	1,215	2.2*	
			Bazeley J.G.	Ind	547	1.0*	
			Sutch D.E.	MRLP	336	0.6*	
			Hill C.J.G.	NF	311	0.6*	
			Abell C.	Ind	102	0.2*	
			Parker-Jervis N.	Ind	71	0.1*	
			Hughes S.B.F.	Ind	59	0.1*	
			St.Clair L. Ms.	Ind	51	0.1*	
			Mildwater B.	Ind	42	0.1*	
			Black D.	Ind	39	0.1*	
					9,449	16.8	
1992	73,435	85.6	Fabricant M.L.D.	Con	31,227	49.7	-0.9
			Heal S.L. Ms.	Lab	24,991	39.8	+15.0
			Stamp B.J.	LD	6,402	10.2	-13.0
			Grice D. Ms.	NLP	239	0.4*	+0.4
					6,236	9.9	

STAFFORDSHIRE MOORLANDS [533]

Election	Electors	T'out	Candidate	Party	Votes	% Sh	% Ch
1983	72,466	77.2	Knox D.L.*	Con	30,079	53.7	
			Campbell B.	Lab	13,513	24.1	
			Gubbins P.P.	SDP	12,370	22.1	
					16,566	29.6	
1987	74,302	80.4	Knox D.L.*	Con	31,613	52.9	-0.8
			Ivers V. Ms.	Lab	17,186	28.8	+4.6
			Corbett J.P.	SDP	10,950	18.3	-3.8
					14,427	24.1	
1992	75,037†	83.7	Knox D.L.*	Con	29,240	46.6	-6.3
			Siddelley J.E.	Lab	21,830	34.8	+6.0
			Jebb C.R. Ms.	LD	9,326	14.9	-3.5
			Howson M.C.	Ind Con	2,121	3.4*	
			Davies P.	NLP	261	0.4*	+0.4
					7,410	11.8	

STAFFORDSHIRE SOUTH [534]

Election	Electors	T'out	Candidate	Party	Votes	% Sh	% Ch
1983	73,038	75.8	Cormack P.T.*	Con	32,764	59.2	
			Chambers R.J.	Lib	13,004	23.5	
			Cartwright M.J.	Lab	9,568	17.3	
					19,760	35.7	
1987	79,261	78.2	Cormack P.T.*	Con	37,708	60.9	+1.7
			Oborski F.M. Ms.	Lib	12,440	20.1	-3.4
			Bateman P.T.A.	Lab	11,805	19.1	+1.8
					25,268	40.8	
1992	82,759†	81.5	Cormack P.T.*	Con	40,266	59.7	-1.2
			Wylie B.A.	Lab	17,633	26.1	+7.1
			Sadler I.L.	LD	9,584	14.2	-5.9
					22,633	33.5	

Election	Electors	T'out	Candidate	Party	Votes	% Sh	% Ch
1983	63,324	76.5	Lightbown D.L.	Con	24,556	50.7	
			Crawley C.M. Ms.	Lab	13,658	28.2	
			Lynch M.J.	SDP	10,220	21.1	
					10,898	22.5	
1987	66,174	80.4	Lightbown D.L.*	Con	25,115	47.2	-3.5
			Gluck E.A. Ms.	SDP	14,230	26.7	+5.6
			Spilsbury D.E.	Lab	13,874	26.1	-2.1
					10,885	20.5	
1992	70,207†	82.0	Lightbown D.L.*	Con	29,180	50.7	+3.5
			Jenkins B.D.	Lab	21,988	38.2	+12.1
			Penlington G.N.	LD	5,540	9.6	-17.1
			Taylor J. Ms.	SD	895	1.6*	+1.6
					7,192	12.5	

[Death]

Election	Electors	T'out	Candidate	Party	Votes	% Sh	% Ch
1996	73,013	59.6	Jenkins B.D.	Lab	26,155	60.1	+22.0
(11/4)			James J.	Con	12,393	28.5	-22.2
			Davy J. Ms.	LD	2,042	4.7*	-4.9
			Smith A.	UKI	1,272	2.9*	
			Sutch D.E.	MRLP	506	1.2*	
			Edwards S. Ms.	ND	358	0.8*	
			Mountford S.	Lib	332	0.8*	
			Tucker L.	Ind	123	0.3*	
			Bunny N.	Ind	85	0.2*	
			Samuelson N.	Ind	80	0.2*	
			Lucas D.	NLP	53	0.1*	
			Sandy F.	Ind	53	0.1*	
			Wood A.	Ind	45	0.1*	
					13,762	31.6	

STALYBRIDGE AND HYDE [536]

Election	Electors	T'out	Candidate	Party	Votes	% Sh	% Ch
1983	67,916	70.5	Pendry T.*	Lab	21,798	45.5	
			Silvester B.G.	Con	17,436	36.4	
			Hughes J.G.	Lib	8,339	17.4	
			Nylan B.M.	NF	294	0.6*	
					4,362	9.1	
1987	67,983	74.2	Pendry T.*	Lab	24,401	48.4	+2.8
			Greenwood R.N.	Con	18,738	37.1	+0.7
			Ashenden P.J.	SDP	7,311	14.5	-2.9
					5,663	11.2	
1992	68,192†	73.5	Pendry T.*	Lab	26,207	52.3	+3.9
			Mort T.S.R.	Con	17,376	34.7	-2.5
			Kirk I.M.	LD	4,740	9.5	-5.0
			Powell R.G.J.	Lib	1,199	2.4*	+2.4
			Poyzer D.J.	MRLP	337	0.7*	+0.7
			Blomfield E.J.	NLP	238	0.5*	+0.5
					8,831	17.6	

STAMFORD AND SPALDING [537]

Election	Electors	T'out	Candidate	Party	Votes	% Sh	% Ch
1983	65,955	74.4	Lewis K. Sir.*	Con	27,728	56.5	
			Lee P.C.	SDP	15,972	32.6	
			Mullender A.E. Ms.	Lab	5,354	10.9*	
					11,756	24.0	
1987	70,560	77.8	Davies J.Q.	Con	31,016	56.5	-0.0
			Bryan R.C. Ms.	Lib	17,009	31.0	-1.6
			Lowe P.E.	Lab	6,882	12.5	+1.6
					14,007	25.5	
1992	75,154†	81.2	Davies J.Q.*	Con	35,965	59.0	+2.5
			Burke L.C.	Lab	13,096	21.5	+8.9
			Lee B.	LD	11,939	19.6	-11.4
					22,869	37.5	

STEVENAGE [538]

Election	Electors	T'out	Candidate	Party	Votes	% Sh	% Ch
1983	67,706	77.9	Wood T.J.R.	Con	20,787	39.4	
			Stoneham B.R.M.	SDP	19,032	36.1	
			Reeves S.A. Ms.	Lab	12,673	24.0	
			Bowmaker D.R.	BNP	236	0.4*	
					1,755	3.3	
1987	69,525	80.5	Wood T.J.R.*	Con	23,541	42.1	+2.6
			Stoneham B.R.M.	SDP	18,201	32.5	-3.6
			Withers M.R.C.	Lab	14,229	25.4	+1.4
					5,340	9.5	
1992	70,229	83.0	Wood T.J.R.*	Con	26,652	45.7	+3.6
			Church J.A. Ms.	Lab	21,764	37.3	+11.9
			Reilly A.A.	LD	9,668	16.6	-15.9
			Calcraft A.	NLP	233	0.4*	+0.4
					4,888	8.4	

STIRLING [539]

Election	Electors	T'out	Candidate	Party	Votes	% Sh	% Ch
1983	56,302	75.7	Forsyth M.B.	Con	17,039	40.0	
			Connarty M.	Lab	11,906	27.9	
			Finnie J.R.	Lib	10,174	23.9	
			Houston W.	SNP	3,488	8.2*	
					5,133	12.0	
1987	58,035	78.5	Forsyth M.B.*	Con	17,191	37.8	-2.2
			Connarty M.	Lab	16,643	36.5	+8.6
			Macfarlane I.B.	Lib	6,804	14.9	-8.9
			Lawson I.M.	SNP	4,897	10.8	+2.6
					548	1.2	
1992	58,267†	82.3	Forsyth M.B.*	Con	19,174	40.0	+2.2
			Phillips K. Ms.	Lab	18,471	38.5	+2.0
			Fisher G.A.	SNP	6,558	13.7	+2.9
			Robertson W.B.	LD	3,337	7.0	-8.0
			Thomson W.R.	Green	342	0.7*	+0.7
			Sharp R.	MRLP	68	0.1*	+0.1
					703	1.5	

STOCKPORT [540]

Election	Electors	T'out	Candidate	Party	Votes	% Sh	% Ch
1983	58,909	74.6	Favell A.R.	Con	18,517	42.1	
			Ward P.R.	Lab	12,731	29.0	
			McNally T.*	SDP	12,129	27.6	
			Shipley M.J.	Green	369	0.8*	
			Walker K.S.	Nat	194	0.4*	
					5,786	13.2	
1987	60,059	78.1	Favell A.R.*	Con	19,410	41.4	-0.8
			Haines S. Ms.	Lab	16,557	35.3	+6.3
			Begg J.L.	SDP	10,365	22.1	-5.5
			Shipley M.J.	Green	573	1.2*	+0.4
					2,853	6.1	
1992	58,096†	82.3	Coffey A. Ms.	Lab	21,096	44.1	+8.8
			Favell A.R.*	Con	19,674	41.2	-0.2
			Corris A.C. Ms.	LD	6,539	13.7	-8.4
			Filmore J.A. Ms.	Green	436	0.9*	-0.3
			Saunders D.N.	NLP	50	0.1*	+0.1
					1,422	3.0	

STOCKTON NORTH [541]

Election	Electors	T'out	Candidate	Party	Votes	% Sh	% Ch
1983	70,277	70.3	Cook F.	Lab	18,339	37.1	
			Davies H.L.	Con	16,469	33.3	
			Rodgers W.T.*	SDP	14,630	29.6	
					1,870	3.8	
1987	70,410	75.3	Cook F.*	Lab	26,043	49.1	+12.0
			Faber D.J.C.	Con	17,242	32.5	-0.8
			Bosanquet N.F.G.	SDP	9,712	18.3	-11.3
					8,801	16.6	
1992	69,458†	76.8	Cook F.*	Lab	27,918	52.3	+3.2
			Brocklebank-Fowler S.E.	Con	17,444	32.7	+0.2
			Fletcher S. Ms.	LD	7,454	14.0	-4.4
			McGarvey K.	Ind Lab	550	1.0*	
					10,474	19.6	

STOCKTON SOUTH [542]

Election	Electors	T'out	Candidate	Party	Votes	% Sh	% Ch
1983	73,790	72.1	Wrigglesworth I.W.*	SDP	19,551	36.7	
			Finnegan T.M.	Con	19,448	36.6	
			Griffiths F.J.	Lab	13,998	26.3	
			Fern D.N.	Ind	205	0.4*	
					103	0.2	
1987	75,279	79.0	Devlin T.R.	Con	20,833	35.0	-1.5
			Wrigglesworth I.W.*	SDP	20,059	33.7	-3.0
			Scott J.M.	Lab	18,600	31.3	+5.0
					774	1.3	
1992	75,959†	82.8	Devlin T.R.*	Con	28,418	45.2	+10.2
			Scott J.M.	Lab	25,049	39.8	+8.6
			Kirkham K. Ms.	LD	9,410	15.0	-18.8
					3,369	5.4	

STOKE-ON-TRENT CENTRAL [543]

Election	Electors	T'out	Candidate	Party	Votes	% Sh	% Ch
1983	66,934	65.9	Fisher M.	Lab	21,194	48.1	
			Mans K.D.R.	Con	12,944	29.4	
			Freeman V.L. Ms.	SDP	9,458	21.4	
			Cook C.S.	MRLP	504	1.1*	
					8,250	18.7	
1987	65,987	68.8	Fisher M.*	Lab	23,842	52.5	+4.5
			Stone D.	Con	14,072	31.0	+1.7
			Cundy I.	SDP	7,462	16.4	-5.0
					9,770	21.5	
1992	65,528†	68.1	Fisher M.*	Lab	25,897	58.0	+5.5
			Gibb N.J.	Con	12,477	27.9	-3.1
			Dent M.J.	LD	6,073	13.6	-2.8
			Pullen N.A.	NLP	196	0.4*	+0.4
					13,420	30.1	

305

STOKE-ON-TRENT NORTH [544]

Election	Electors	T'out	Candidate	Party	Votes	% Sh	% Ch
1983	75,251	71.0	Forrester J.S.*	Lab	24,721	46.3	
			Ibbs R.M.	Con	16,518	30.9	
			Beswick T.R.	SDP	12,186	22.8	
					8,203	15.4	
1987	74,184	72.9	Walley J.L. Ms.	Lab	25,459	47.1	+0.8
			Davies R.	Con	16,946	31.3	+0.4
			Simmonds S.J.	SDP	11,665	21.6	-1.2
					8,513	15.7	
1992	73,141†	73.4	Walley J.L. Ms.*	Lab	30,464	56.7	+9.6
			Harris L.M.	Con	15,687	29.2	-2.1
			Redfern J.P.	LD	7,167	13.3	-8.2
			Morrison A.H.	NLP	387	0.7*	+0.7
					14,777	27.5	

STOKE-ON-TRENT SOUTH [545]

Election	Electors	T'out	Candidate	Party	Votes	% Sh	% Ch
1983	70,600	69.6	Ashley J.*	Lab	23,611	48.0	
			Maxwell P.G.C.	Con	16,506	33.6	
			Walley W.J.	Lib	9,050	18.4	
					7,105	14.5	
1987	70,806	73.7	Ashley J.*	Lab	24,794	47.5	-0.5
			Hartshorne D.	Con	19,741	37.8	+4.2
			Wild P.	Lib	7,669	14.7	-3.7
					5,053	9.7	
1992	71,317†	74.3	Stevenson G.W.	Lab	26,380	49.8	+2.3
			Ibbs R.M.	Con	19,471	36.7	-1.1
			Jones F.A.	LD	6,870	13.0	-1.7
			Lines E.A. Ms.	NLP	291	0.5*	+0.5
					6,909	13.0	

STRANGFORD [546]

Election	Electors	T'out	Candidate	Party	Votes	% Sh	% Ch
1983	60,179	65.0	Taylor J.D.	UU	19,086	48.8	
			Gibson H.J.S.	UDUP	11,716	30.0	
			Morrow A.J.	APNI	6,171	15.8	
			Curry J.	SDLP	1,713	4.4*	
			Heath S.R.	Ind Lab	430	1.1*	
					7,370	18.8	

[Seeks Re-election]

1986	62,854	55.1	Taylor J.D.*	UU	32,627	94.2	+45.4
(23/1)			Barry P.	FAIA	1,993	5.8	
					30,634	88.5	
1987	64,429	57.6	Taylor J.D.*	UU	28,199	75.9	+27.1
			Morrow A.J.	APNI	7,553	20.3	+4.6
			Hynds I.E. Ms.	WP	1,385	3.7*	+3.7
					20,646	55.6	
1992	68,901	65.0	Taylor J.D.*	UU	19,517	43.6	-32.4
			Wilson S.	UDUP	10,606	23.7	+23.7
			McCarthy K.	APNI	7,585	16.9	-3.4
			Eyre S.J.A.	Con	6,782	15.1	+15.1
			Shaw D.	NLP	295	0.7*	+0.7
					8,911	19.9	

STRATFORD-ON-AVON [547]

Election	Electors	T'out	Candidate	Party	Votes	% Sh	% Ch
1983	76,649	72.9	Howarth A.T.	Con	34,041	60.9	
			Taylor W.J.B.	Lib	16,124	28.8	
			Hooley F.O.*	Lab	5,731	10.3*	
					17,917	32.1	
1987	81,263	76.5	Howarth A.T.*	Con	38,483	61.9	+1.0
			Cowcher D.G.	Lib	17,318	27.9	-1.0
			Rhodes R.H.	Lab	6,335	10.2	-0.1
					21,165	34.1	
1992	82,818†	82.1	Howarth A.T.*	Con	40,251	59.2	-2.7
			Fogg J.N.	LD	17,359	25.5	-2.3
			Brookes S.M. Ms.	Lab	8,932	13.1	+2.9
			Roughan R.G.	Green	729	1.1*	+1.1
			Saunders A.J.	Ind Con	573	0.8*	
			Twite M.R.	NLP	130	0.2*	+0.2
					22,892	33.7	

STRATHKELVIN AND BEARSDEN [548]

Election	Electors	T'out	Candidate	Party	Votes	% Sh	% Ch
1983	60,500	79.4	Hirst M.W.	Con	17,501	36.4	
			Waddell R.M.	Lib	13,801	28.7	
			Ingram A.P.	Lab	12,308	25.6	
			Bain M.A. Ms.	SNP	4,408	9.2*	
					3,700	7.7	
1987	62,676	82.2	Galbraith S.L. Dr.	Lab	19,639	38.1	+12.5
			Hirst M.W.*	Con	17,187	33.4	-3.1
			Bannerman J.	Lib	11,034	21.4	-7.3
			Paterson G.	SNP	3,654	7.1	-2.1
					2,452	4.8	
1992	61,210	82.2	Galbraith S.L. Dr.*	Lab	21,267	42.3	+4.1
			Hirst M.W.	Con	18,105	36.0	+2.6
			Chalmers T.	SNP	6,275	12.5	+5.4
			Waterfield B Ms.	LD	4,585	9.1	-12.3
			Whitley D.F.	NLP	90	0.2*	+0.2
					3,162	6.3	

STREATHAM [549]

Election	Electors	T'out	Candidate	Party	Votes	% Sh	% Ch
1983	60,032	65.4	Shelton W.J.M.*	Con	18,264	46.5	
			Long M.M. Ms.	Lab	12,362	31.5	
			Billenness P.H.	Lib	8,321	21.2	
			Handy K.D.	NF	321	0.8*	
					5,902	15.0	
1987	60,519	69.5	Shelton W.J.M.*	Con	18,916	44.9	-1.6
			Tapsell E.A. Ms.	Lab	16,509	39.2	+7.7
			Tuffrey M.W.	Lib	6,663	15.8	-5.4
					2,407	5.7	
1992	57,212	70.3	Hill T.K.	Lab	18,925	47.0	+7.8
			Shelton W.J.M. Sir*	Con	16,608	41.3	-3.7
			Pindar M.J.	LD	3,858	9.6	-6.2
			Baker R.C.L.	Green	443	1.1*	+1.1
			Hankin A.	Islam	154	0.4*	+0.4
			Payne C.D. Ms.	Ind	145	0.4*	
			Parsons J.V.	NLP	97	0.2*	+0.2
					2,317	5.8	

STRETFORD [550]

Election	Electors	T'out	Candidate	Party	Votes	% Sh	% Ch
1983	57,448	70.0	Lloyd A.J.	Lab	18,028	44.9	
			Sweeney W.E.	Con	13,686	34.1	
			Wilks D.R.	SDP	8,141	20.3	
			Ala-ud-Din S.	Ind Lab	336	0.8*	
					4,342	10.8	
1987	57,568	71.9	Lloyd A.J.*	Lab	22,831	55.2	+10.3
			Dougherty D.P.	Con	13,429	32.4	-1.6
			Lee D.S.	SDP	5,125	12.4	-7.9
					9,402	22.7	
1992	54,468†	68.8	Lloyd A.J.*	Lab	22,300	59.5	+4.4
			Rae J.C.B.	Con	11,163	29.8	-2.6
			Beswick F.C.	LD	3,722	9.9	-2.4
			Boyton L.A.	NLP	268	0.7*	+0.7
					11,137	29.7	

STROUD [551]

Election	Electors	T'out	Candidate	Party	Votes	% Sh	% Ch
1983	77,528	77.7	Kershaw J.A. Sir.*	Con	30,896	51.3	
			Fallon G.T.	Lib	19,182	31.9	
			Parsons D.	Lab	10,141	16.8	
					11,714	19.5	
1987	81,275	80.6	Knapman R.M.	Con	32,883	50.2	-1.1
			Walker-Smith A.A.	Lib	20,508	31.3	-0.6
			Levitt T.	Lab	12,145	18.5	+1.7
					12,375	18.9	
1992	82,553†	84.5	Knapman R.M.*	Con	32,201	46.2	-4.0
			Drew D.E.	Lab	18,796	26.9	+8.4
			Robinson M.P.	LD	16,751	24.0	-7.3
			Atkinson S.M. Ms.	Green	2,005	2.9*	+2.9
					13,405	19.2	

SUFFOLK CENTRAL [552]

Election	Electors	T'out	Candidate	Party	Votes	% Sh	% Ch
1983	75,641	74.4	Lord M.N.	Con	30,096	53.5	
			Baldwin N.D.J.	Lib	15,365	27.3	
			Sierakowski D.M. Ms.	Lab	10,828	19.2	
					14,731	26.2	
1987	79,199	76.2	Lord M.N.*	Con	32,422	53.7	+0.2
			Dale T.E.	Lib	16,132	26.7	-0.6
			Walker M.S.	Lab	11,817	19.6	+0.3
					16,290	27.0	
1992	82,735	80.3	Lord M.N.*	Con	32,917	49.6	-4.1
			Henniker-Major L.A. Ms.	LD	16,886	25.4	-1.3
			Harris J.W.	Lab	15,615	23.5	+3.9
			Matthissen J.E.	Green	800	1.2*	+1.2
			Wilmot J.C. Ms.	NLP	190	0.3*	+0.3
					16,031	24.1	

SUFFOLK COASTAL [553]

Election	Electors	T'out	Candidate	Party	Votes	% Sh	% Ch
1983	71,521	75.0	Gummer J.S.*	Con	31,240	58.2	
			Houseley D.	SDP	15,618	29.1	
			Ballentyne D.W.G.	Lab	6,780	12.6	
					15,622	29.1	
1987	75,684	77.9	Gummer J.S.*	Con	32,834	55.7	-2.6
			Miller J.M. Ms.	SDP	17,554	29.8	+0.6
			Reeves S.A. Ms.	Lab	7,534	12.8	+0.1
			Holloway J.W.	Green	1,049	1.8*	+1.8
					15,280	25.9	
1992	79,334†	81.6	Gummer J.S.*	Con	34,680	53.6	-2.1
			Monk P.D.	LD	15,395	23.8	-6.0
			Hodgson T.E.	Lab	13,508	20.9	+8.1
			Slade A.C.	Green	943	1.5*	-0.3
			Kaplan F.B. Ms.	NLP	232	0.4*	+0.4
					19,285	29.8	

SUFFOLK SOUTH [554]

Election	Electors	T'out	Candidate	Party	Votes	% Sh	% Ch
1983	76,209	76.3	Yeo T.S.K.	Con	29,469	50.6	
			Kemp R.E.	Lib	18,200	31.3	
			Billcliffe S.	Lab	10,516	18.1	
					11,269	19.4	
1987	81,954	77.6	Yeo T.S.K.*	Con	33,972	53.4	+2.8
			Bradford C.M.N.	Lib	17,729	27.9	-3.4
			Bavington A.C.	Lab	11,876	18.7	+0.6
					16,243	25.5	
1992	84,835†	81.7	Yeo T.S.K.*	Con	34,773	50.2	-3.2
			Pollard A.K. Ms.	LD	17,504	25.3	-2.6
			Hesford S.	Lab	16,623	24.0	+5.3
			Aisbitt T.	NLP	420	0.6*	+0.6
					17,269	24.9	

SUNDERLAND NORTH [555]

Election	Electors	T'out	Candidate	Party	Votes	% Sh	% Ch
1983	78,520	66.5	Clay R.A.	Lab	24,179	46.3	
			Lewis C.N.P.	Con	16,983	32.5	
			McCourt D.	Lib	11,090	21.2	
					7,196	13.8	
1987	75,674	70.5	Clay R.A.*	Lab	29,767	55.8	+9.5
			Picton I.S.	Con	15,095	28.3	-4.2
			Jenkinson T.	Lib	8,518	16.0	-5.3
					14,672	27.5	
1992	72,874†	68.9	Etherington W.	Lab	30,481	60.7	+5.0
			Barnes J.V. Ms.	Con	13,477	26.9	-1.4
			Halom V.L.	LD	5,389	10.7	-5.2
			Lundgren W.E. Ms.	Lib	841	1.7*	+1.7
					17,004	33.9	

SUNDERLAND SOUTH [556]

Election	Electors	T'out	Candidate	Party	Votes	% Sh	% Ch
1983	75,124	66.6	Bagier G.A.T.*	Lab	22,869	45.7	
			Mitchell A.J.B.	Con	17,321	34.6	
			Anderson J.R.	SDP	9,865	19.7	
					5,548	11.1	
1987	74,947	71.1	Mullin C.J.	Lab	28,823	54.1	+8.4
			Howe G.E.	Con	16,210	30.4	-4.2
			Hudson K.H.	SDP	7,768	14.6	-5.1
			Jacques D.N.	Green	516	1.0*	+1.0
					12,613	23.7	
1992	72,608†	69.9	Mullin C.J.*	Lab	29,399	57.9	+3.9
			Howe G.E.	Con	14,898	29.4	-1.0
			Lennox J.A.	LD	5,844	11.5	-3.1
			Scouler T.	Green	596	1.2*	+0.2
					14,501	28.6	

SURBITON [557]

Election	Electors	T'out	Candidate	Party	Votes	% Sh	% Ch
1983	46,949	71.3	Tracey R.P.	Con	18,245	54.5	
			Nowakowski C.	SDP	9,496	28.4	
			Waskett N.D.	Lab	5,173	15.5	
			Maclellan J.	Green	551	1.6*	
					8,749	26.1	
1987	45,428	78.3	Tracey R.P.*	Con	19,861	55.9	+1.3
			Burke D.T.	SDP	10,120	28.5	+0.1
			McGowan A.H.	Lab	5,111	14.4	-1.1
			Vidler J. Ms.	Green	465	1.3*	-0.3
					9,741	27.4	
1992	42,422†	82.4	Tracey R.P.*	Con	19,033	54.4	-1.4
			Janke B. Ms.	LD	9,394	26.9	-1.6
			Hutchinson R.T.	Lab	6,384	18.3	+3.9
			Parker W.	NLP	161	0.5*	+0.5
					9,639	27.6	

SURREY EAST [558]

Election	Electors	T'out	Candidate	Party	Votes	% Sh	% Ch
1983	58,485	74.1	Howe R.E.G. Sir.*	Con	27,272	62.9	
			Liddell S.M. Ms.	Lib	11,836	27.3	
			Pincott H.	Lab	4,249	9.8*	
					15,436	35.6	
1987	59,528	77.2	Howe R.E.G. Sir.*	Con	29,126	63.4	+0.5
			Anderson M.A.J.	Lib	11,000	23.9	-3.4
			Davis M.J.	Lab	4,779	10.4	+0.6
			Newell D.R.	Green	1,044	2.3*	+2.3
					18,126	39.4	
1992	58,014	82.3	Ainsworth P.M.	Con	29,767	62.3	-1.1
			Tomlin R.L.	LD	12,111	25.4	+1.4
			Roles G.M. Ms.	Lab	5,075	10.6	+0.2
			Kilpatrick I.T.	Green	819	1.7*	-0.6
					17,656	37.0	

SURREY NORTH WEST [559]

Election	Electors	T'out	Candidate	Party	Votes	% Sh	% Ch
1983	78,377	70.2	Grylls W.M.J.*	Con	35,297	64.1	
			Weedon J.P.	Lib	14,279	25.9	
			Burrow J.R.	Lab	5,452	9.9*	
					21,018	38.2	
1987	83,083	72.5	Grylls W.M.J.*	Con	38,535	64.0	-0.2
			Brodie C.G.	Lib	14,960	24.8	-1.1
			Cooper J.G.	Lab	6,751	11.2	+1.3
					23,575	39.1	
1992	83,577	78.3	Grylls W.M.J.*	Con	41,772	63.8	-0.2
			Clark C.M. Ms.	LD	13,378	20.4	-4.4
			Hayhurst R.M.	Lab	8,886	13.6	+2.4
			Hockey Y. Ms.	Green	1,441	2.2*	+2.2
					28,394	43.4	

SURREY SOUTH WEST [560]

Election	Electors	T'out	Candidate	Party	Votes	% Sh	% Ch
1983	69,875	74.5	Macmillan M.V.	Con	31,067	59.7	
			Scott G.D.	Lib	16,716	32.1	
			Williams S.E.D.	Lab	4,239	8.1*	
					14,351	27.6	

[Death]

1984	70,797	61.7	Bottomley V.H.B.M. Ms.	Con	21,545	49.3	-10.4
(3/5)			Scott G.D.	Lib	18,946	43.4	+11.3
			Roche B.M. Ms.	Lab	2,949	6.7*	-1.5
			Litvin V.	Ind	117	0.3*	
			Anscomb H.M. Ms.	Ind	82	0.2*	
			Smith P.R.	Ind	29	0.1*	
					2,599	5.9	

1987	73,018	78.4	Bottomley V.H.B.M. Ms.	Con	34,024	59.5	-0.3
			Scott G.D.	Lib	19,681	34.4	+2.3
			Evers J.K.P.	Lab	3,224	5.6	-2.5
			Green M.J.	Ind Con	299	0.5*	
					14,343	25.1	

1992	72,312	82.7	Bottomley V.H.B.M. Ms.*	Con	35,008	58.5	-0.9
			Sherlock N.R.	LD	20,033	33.5	-0.9
			Kelly P.J.	Lab	3,840	6.4	+0.8
			Bedrock N.	Green	710	1.2*	+1.2
			Campbell K.S.	NLP	147	0.2*	+0.2
			Newman D.	Ind	98	0.2*	
					14,975	25.0	

SUSSEX MID [561]

Election	Electors	T'out	Candidate	Party	Votes	% Sh	% Ch
1983	77,005	74.7	Renton R.T.*	Con	35,310	61.4	
			Campbell J.M.	Lib	18,566	32.3	
			Hawkes P.A. Ms.	Lab	3,470	6.0*	
			Bray J.	Ind	196	0.3*	
					16,744	29.1	
1987	80,143	77.2	Renton R.T.*	Con	37,781	61.1	-0.3
			Westbrook N.S.E.	Lib	19,489	31.5	-0.8
			Hughes R.S.E.	Lab	4,573	7.4	+1.4
					18,292	29.6	
1992	80,828†	82.9	Renton R.T.*	Con	39,524	59.0	-2.1
			Collins M.E. Ms.	LD	18,996	28.4	-3.1
			Gregory L.C. Ms.	Lab	6,951	10.4	+3.0
			Stevens H.G.	Green	772	1.2*	+1.2
			Berry P.B	MRLP	392	0.6*	+0.6
			Hodkin P.D	Ind	246	0.4*	
			Hankey A.M.A.	NLP	89	0.1*	+0.1
					20,528	30.6	

SUTTON AND CHEAM [562]

Election	Electors	T'out	Candidate	Party	Votes	% Sh	% Ch
1983	63,099	74.3	Macfarlane D.N.*	Con	26,782	57.1	
			Caswill C.J.	Lib	16,518	35.2	
			Dixon G.S.	Lab	3,568	7.6*	
					10,264	21.9	
1987	63,850	76.6	Macfarlane D.N.*	Con	29,710	60.8	+3.6
			Greig R.D.	Lib	13,992	28.6	-6.6
			Monk L. Ms.	Lab	5,202	10.6	+3.0
					15,718	32.1	
1992	60,995	82.3	Maitland O.H. Lady	Con	27,710	55.2	-5.6
			Burstow P.K.	LD	16,954	33.8	+5.1
			Martin G.C.	Lab	4,980	9.9	-0.7
			Duffy J.	Green	444	0.9*	+0.9
			Hatchard A.R. Ms.	NLP	133	0.3*	+0.3
					10,756	21.4	

SUTTON COLDFIELD [563]

Election	Electors	T'out	Candidate	Party	Votes	% Sh	% Ch
1983	67,695	71.8	Fowler P.N.*	Con	31,753	65.4	
			Jones A.	Lib	12,769	26.3	
			Gibbons C.C.	Lab	4,066	8.4*	
					18,984	39.1	
1987	72,329	74.5	Fowler P.N.*	Con	34,475	64.0	-1.4
			Bick T.J.	Lib	13,292	24.7	-1.6
			McLoughlin P.	Lab	6,104	11.3	+3.0
					21,183	39.3	
1992	71,444	79.5	Fowler P.N. Sir*	Con	37,001	65.2	+1.2
			Whorwood J.E.	LD	10,965	19.3	-5.4
			Bott-Obi J.M. Ms.	Lab	8,490	15.0	+3.6
			Meads H.S.	NLP	324	0.6*	+0.6
					26,036	45.9	

SWANSEA EAST [564]

Election	Electors	T'out	Candidate	Party	Votes	% Sh	% Ch
1983	57,285	71.5	Anderson D.*	Lab	22,297	54.4	
			Shrewsbury M.J.	Lib	8,762	21.4	
			O'Shaughnessy N.J.	Con	8,080	19.7	
			Reid C.B.	PC	1,531	3.7*	
			Jones W.R.	Comm	294	0.7*	
					13,535	33.0	
1987	57,200	75.4	Anderson D.*	Lab	27,478	63.7	+9.3
			Lewis R.D.	Con	8,140	18.9	-0.9
			Wynford Thomas D. Rev.	Lib	6,380	14.8	-6.6
			Reid C.B.	PC	1,145	2.7*	-1.1
					19,338	44.8	
1992	59,187	75.6	Anderson D.*	Lab	31,179	69.7	+6.0
			Davies H.L.	Con	7,697	17.2	-1.7
			Barton R.E.	LD	4,248	9.5	-5.3
			Bonner-Evans E.E. Ms.	PC	1,607	3.6*	+0.9
					23,482	52.5	

SWANSEA WEST [565]

Election	Electors	T'out	Candidate	Party	Votes	% Sh	% Ch
1983	58,237	73.5	Williams A.J.*	Lab	18,042	42.1	
			Lewis J.M.	Con	15,692	36.6	
			Sain ley Berry P.G.	SDP	8,036	18.8	
			Pennar A.M.	PC	795	1.9*	
			Oubridge G.E.	Green	265	0.6*	
					2,350	5.5	
1987	59,836	76.1	Williams A.J.*	Lab	22,089	48.5	+6.4
			Evans N.M.	Con	15,027	33.0	-3.6
			Ford M.A.	Lib	7,019	15.4	-3.3
			Williams N.	PC	902	2.0*	+0.1
			Harmon J.V. Ms.	Green	469	1.0*	+0.4
					7,062	15.5	
1992	59,791	73.3	Williams A.J.*	Lab	23,238	53.0	+4.5
			Perry R.J.	Con	13,760	31.4	-1.6
			Shrewsbury M.J.	LD	4,620	10.5	-4.9
			Lloyd D.R.	PC	1,668	3.8*	+1.8
			Oubridge G.E.	Green	564	1.3*	+0.3
					9,478	21.6	

SWINDON [566]

Election	Electors	T'out	Candidate	Party	Votes	% Sh	% Ch
1983	76,833	74.1	Coombs S.C.	Con	22,310	39.2	
			Stoddart D.L.*	Lab	20,915	36.7	
			Scott D.J.	SDP	13,743	24.1	
					1,395	2.4	
1987	86,150	77.8	Coombs S.C.*	Con	29,385	43.8	+4.7
			Johnston J.G. Ms.	Lab	24,528	36.6	-0.1
			Scott D.J.	SDP	13,114	19.6	-4.6
					4,857	7.2	
1992	90,068†	81.5	Coombs S.C.*	Con	31,749	43.3	-0.6
			D'Avila J.P.	Lab	28,923	39.4	+2.8
			Cordon S.R.	LD	11,737	16.0	-3.6
			Hughes J.V.	Green	647	0.9*	+0.9
			Gillard C.R.	MRLP	236	0.3*	+0.3
			Farrar V.F.	Ind	78	0.1*	
					2,826	3.9	

317

TATTON [567]

Election	Electors	T'out	Candidate	Party	Votes	% Sh	% Ch
1983	68,747	74.3	Hamilton M.N.	Con	27,877	54.6	
			Levy D.	SDP	13,917	27.2	
			Davies D.W.	Lab	9,295	18.2	
					13,960	27.3	
1987	71,904	76.7	Hamilton M.N.*	Con	30,128	54.6	+0.0
			Gaskin B. Ms.	SDP	13,034	23.6	-3.6
			Blears H-A. Ms.	Lab	11,760	21.3	+3.1
			Gibson M.G.	Ind	263	0.5*	
					17,094	31.0	
1992	71,085†	80.8	Hamilton M.N.*	Con	31,658	55.1	+0.5
			Kelly J.M.	Lab	15,798	27.5	+6.2
			Hancox C.V. Ms.	LD	9,597	16.7	-6.9
			Gibson M.G.	Ind	410	0.7*	
					15,860	27.6	

TAUNTON [568]

Election	Electors	T'out	Candidate	Party	Votes	% Sh	% Ch
1983	70,359	75.5	du Cann E.D.L.*	Con	28,112	52.9	
			Cocks M.A.K.	SDP	15,545	29.2	
			Gray J.F.	Lab	9,498	17.9	
					12,567	23.6	
1987	74,225	79.3	Nicholson D.J.	Con	30,248	51.4	-1.5
			Cocks M.A.K.	SDP	19,868	33.7	+4.5
			Reynolds G. Dr.	Lab	8,754	14.9	-3.0
					10,380	17.7	
1992	78,037†	82.3	Nicholson D.J.*	Con	29,576	46.0	-6.9
			Ballard J.M. Ms.	LD	26,240	40.8	+7.1
			Hole L.J. Ms.	Lab	8,151	12.7	-2.2
			Leavey P.A.	NLP	279	0.4*	+0.4
					3,336	5.2	

TAYSIDE NORTH [569]

Election	Electors	T'out	Candidate	Party	Votes	% Sh	% Ch
1983	51,972	72.6	Walker W.C.*	Con	19,269	51.0	
			Morgan A.N.	SNP	9,170	24.3	
			Skene D.G.M.	Lib	7,255	19.2	
			Wylie N.M.O.	Lab	2,057	5.4*	
					10,099	26.8	
1987	53,985	74.7	Walker W.C.*	Con	18,307	45.4	-5.7
			Guild K.J.N.	SNP	13,291	32.9	+8.6
			Regent P.F.	Lib	5,201	12.9	-6.3
			Whytock J.	Lab	3,550	8.8	+3.3
					5,016	12.4	
1992	55,970†	77.6	Walker W.C.*	Con	20,283	46.7	+1.3
			Swinney J.R.	SNP	16,288	37.5	+4.5
			Horner S.A.	LD	3,791	8.7	-4.2
			Maclennan T.A.S.	Lab	3,094	7.1	-1.7
					3,995	9.2	

TEIGNBRIDGE [570]

Election	Electors	T'out	Candidate	Party	Votes	% Sh	% Ch
1983	67,515	77.5	Nicholls P.C.M.	Con	28,265	54.0	
			Alderson J.C.	Lib	20,047	38.3	
			Loughlin M.P.	Lab	3,749	7.2*	
			Hope A.	MRLP	241	0.5*	
					8,218	15.7	
1987	71,870	80.3	Nicholls P.C.M.*	Con	30,693	53.2	-0.8
			Ryder R.H.J.D.	Lib	20,268	35.1	-3.2
			Greenwood J.R.	Lab	6,413	11.1	+3.9
			Hope A.	MRLP	312	0.5*	+0.0
					10,425	18.1	
1992	75,798†	82.4	Nicholls P.C.M.*	Con	31,274	50.0	-3.2
			Younger-Ross R.A.	LD	22,416	35.9	+0.7
			Kennedy R.A.	Lab	8,128	13.0	+1.9
			Hope A.	MRLP	437	0.7*	+0.2
			Hayes N.J.	NLP	234	0.4*	+0.4
					8,858	14.2	

319

THANET NORTH [571]

Election	Electors	T'out	Candidate	Party	Votes	% Sh	% Ch
1983	66,678	68.8	Gale R.J.	Con	26,801	58.4	
			Macmillan W.D.	SDP	12,256	26.7	
			Booth C. Ms.	Lab	6,482	14.1	
			Dobing B.	BNP	324	0.7*	
					14,545	31.7	
1987	69,811	72.1	Gale R.J.*	Con	29,225	58.0	-0.4
			Cranston N.R.M.	SDP	11,745	23.3	-3.4
			Bretman A.M.	Lab	8,395	16.7	+2.5
			Conder D.R.	Green	996	2.0*	+2.0
					17,480	34.7	
1992	70,977†	76.0	Gale R.J.*	Con	30,867	57.2	-0.8
			Bretman A.M.	Lab	12,657	23.5	+6.8
			Phillips J.L. Ms.	LD	9,563	17.7	-5.6
			Dawe H.F. Ms.	Green	873	1.6*	-0.4
					18,210	33.7	

THANET SOUTH [572]

Election	Electors	T'out	Candidate	Party	Votes	% Sh	% Ch
1983	61,989	70.0	Aitken J.W.P.*	Con	24,512	56.5	
			Josephs I.R.P.	Lib	10,461	24.1	
			Clarke M.A.	Lab	8,429	19.4	
					14,051	32.4	
1987	62,761	73.7	Aitken J.W.P.*	Con	25,135	54.3	-2.1
			Pitt W.H.	Lib	11,452	24.8	+0.7
			Wright C.	Lab	9,673	20.9	+1.5
					13,683	29.6	
1992	62,440†	78.2	Aitken J.W.P.*	Con	25,253	51.7	-2.6
			James M.S.	Lab	13,740	28.1	+7.2
			Pitt W.H.	LD	8,948	18.3	-6.4
			Peckham S. Ms.	Green	871	1.8*	+1.8
					11,513	23.6	

THURROCK [573]

Election	Electors	T'out	Candidate	Party	Votes	% Sh	% Ch
1983	66,300	67.7	McDonald O.A. Ms.*	Lab	17,600	39.2	
			Tallon J.G. Ms.	Con	15,878	35.4	
			Benson D.S.	SDP	9,761	21.7	
			Bibby M.J.	Ind	1,220	2.7*	
			Sinclair R.W.	BNP	252	0.6*	
			Paul J.R.	Comm	199	0.4*	
					1,722	3.8	
1987	67,594	71.5	Janman T.S.	Con	20,527	42.5	+7.1
			McDonald O.A. Ms.*	Lab	19,837	41.0	+1.9
			Benson D.S.	SDP	7,970	16.5	-5.2
					690	1.4	
1992	69,211	78.1	MacKinlay A.S.	Lab	24,791	45.9	+4.8
			Janman T.S.*	Con	23,619	43.7	+1.2
			Banton A.J.	LD	5,145	9.5	-7.0
			Rogers C.W.	Ind	391	0.7*	
			Compobassi P.	AFL	117	0.2*	+0.2
					1,172	2.2	

TIVERTON [574]

Election	Electors	T'out	Candidate	Party	Votes	% Sh	% Ch
1983	63,828	77.5	Maxwell-Hyslop R.J.*	Con	27,101	54.8	
			Morrish D.J.	Lib	19,215	38.8	
			Gorbutt D.A.	Lab	3,154	6.4*	
					7,886	15.9	
1987	68,218	79.7	Maxwell-Hyslop R.J.*	Con	29,875	54.9	+0.2
			Morrish D.J.	Lib	20,663	38.0	-0.8
			Northam J.A. Ms.	Lab	3,400	6.3	-0.1
			Jones W.J.	Ind	434	0.8*	
					9,212	16.9	
1992	70,742	83.3	Browning A.F. Ms.	Con	30,376	51.5	-3.4
			Cox D.N.	LD	19,287	32.7	-5.3
			Gibb S.C. Ms.	Lab	5,950	10.1	+3.8
			Morrish D.J.	Lib	2,225	3.8*	+3.8
			Foggitt P.J.	Green	1,007	1.7*	+1.7
			Rhodes B.C.	NLP	96	0.2*	+0.2
					11,089	18.8	

TONBRIDGE AND MALLING [575]

Election	Electors	T'out	Candidate	Party	Votes	% Sh	% Ch
1983	72,549	74.7	Stanley J.P.*	Con	30,417	56.1	
			Freeman R.	SDP	16,897	31.2	
			Bishop D.J.	Lab	6,896	12.7	
					13,520	24.9	
1987	76,797	77.8	Stanley J.P.*	Con	33,990	56.9	+0.8
			Ward M.J.	SDP	17,561	29.4	-1.8
			Still D.G.	Lab	7,803	13.1	+0.3
			Easter M.D.S.	BNP	369	0.6*	+0.6
					16,429	27.5	
1992	77,257	82.7	Stanley J.P.*	Con	36,542	57.2	+0.3
			Roberts P.D.	LD	14,984	23.5	-6.0
			O'Neill M.A. Ms.	Lab	11,533	18.1	+5.0
			Tidy J.	Green	612	1.0*	+1.0
			Horvath J.I.R. Ms.	NLP	221	0.3*	+0.3
					21,558	33.7	

TOOTING [576]

Election	Electors	T'out	Candidate	Party	Votes	% Sh	% Ch
1983	68,083	67.5	Cox T.M.*	Lab	19,640	42.7	
			Harris R.D.R.	Con	16,981	37.0	
			Neuberger J.B.S. Ms.	SDP	8,317	18.1	
			Berbridge P.	NF	355	0.8*	
			Shaw E.M. Ms.	Green	255	0.6*	
			Lewis R.E.	Comm	181	0.4*	
			Patel H.	Ind	146	0.3*	
			Redgrave C.W.	WRP	72	0.2*	
					2,659	5.8	
1987	68,116	71.2	Cox T.M.*	Lab	21,457	44.2	+1.5
			Winter M.A.S.	Con	20,016	41.3	+4.3
			Ambache J.N.	SDP	6,423	13.2	-4.9
			Vickery M.E. Ms.	Green	621	1.3*	+0.7
					1,441	3.0	
1992	68,307†	74.8	Cox T.M.*	Lab	24,601	48.2	+3.9
			Winter M.A.S.	Con	20,494	40.1	-1.1
			Bunce R.J.	LD	3,776	7.4	-5.8
			Martin C. Ms.	Lib	1,340	2.6*	+2.6
			Owens P.J.	Green	694	1.4*	+0.1
			Anklesaria F.	NLP	119	0.2*	+0.2
			Whitelaw M.N.	Ind	64	0.1*	
					4,107	8.0	

TORBAY [577]

Election	Electors	T'out	Candidate	Party	Votes	% Sh	% Ch
1983	67,337	72.6	Bennett F.M. Sir.*	Con	25,721	52.6	
			Mitchell M.N.	Lib	19,166	39.2	
			Rackley P.W.	Lab	3,521	7.2*	
			Murray A.M.L. Ms.	Ind	500	1.0*	
					6,555	13.4	
1987	70,435	76.3	Allason R.W.S.	Con	29,029	54.0	+1.4
			Bye N.D.	Lib	20,209	37.6	-1.6
			Taylor G.R.	Lab	4,538	8.4	+1.2
					8,820	16.4	
1992	71,184	80.6	Allason R.W.S.*	Con	28,624	49.9	-4.1
			Sanders A.M.	LD	22,837	39.8	+2.2
			Truscott P. Dr.	Lab	5,503	9.6	+1.2
			Jones R.P.	NF	268	0.5*	+0.5
			Thomas A.H. Ms.	NLP	157	0.3*	+0.3
					5,787	10.1	

TORFAEN [578]

Election	Electors	T'out	Candidate	Party	Votes	% Sh	% Ch
1983	58,739	74.4	Abse L.*	Lab	20,678	47.3	
			Blackburn G.R.	Lib	12,393	28.3	
			Martin P.J.	Con	9,751	22.3	
			Cox P.M.R. Ms.	PC	896	2.0*	
					8,285	19.0	
1987	59,896	75.6	Murphy P.P.	Lab	26,577	58.7	+11.4
			Blackburn G.R.	Lib	9,027	19.9	-8.4
			Gordon R.I.N.	Con	8,632	19.1	-3.2
			Evans J. Ms.	PC	577	1.3*	-0.8
			Witherden M.J.	Green	450	1.0*	+1.0
					17,550	38.8	
1992	61,103†	77.5	Murphy P.P.*	Lab	30,352	64.1	+5.4
			Watkins M.C.	Con	9,598	20.3	+1.2
			Hewson M.G.	LD	6,178	13.1	-6.9
			Cox J.I.	PC/GP	1,210	2.6*	+1.3
					20,754	43.8	

TOTTENHAM [579]

Election	Electors	T'out	Candidate	Party	Votes	% Sh	% Ch
1983	67,944	63.4	Atkinson N.*	Lab	22,423	52.0	
			Murphy P.L.	Con	13,027	30.2	
			L'Estrange A.S.G.	Lib	6,990	16.2	
			Hurry W.G.	Ind Con	652	1.5*	
					9,396	21.8	
1987	76,092	66.1	Grant B.A.M.	Lab	21,921	43.6	-8.4
			Murphy P.L.	Con	17,780	35.4	+5.1
			Etherington S.J.	Lib	8,983	17.9	+1.6
			Nicholls D.J.	Green	744	1.5*	+1.5
			Nealon P.J.	Ind	638	1.3*	
			Dixon C.L. Ms.	WRP	205	0.4*	+0.4
					4,141	8.2	
1992	68,404	65.5	Grant B.A.M.*	Lab	25,309	56.5	+12.9
			Charalambous A.L.	Con	13,341	29.8	-5.6
			L'Estrange A.S.G.	LD	5,120	11.4	-6.4
			Budge P.	Green	903	2.0*	+0.5
			Obomanu M. Ms.	NLP	150	0.3*	+0.3
					11,968	26.7	

TRURO [580]

Election	Electors	T'out	Candidate	Party	Votes	% Sh	% Ch
1983	68,514	79.6	Penhaligon D.C.*	Lib	31,279	57.3	
			Buddell P.D.	Con	20,799	38.1	
			Beecroft J.M. Ms.	Lab	2,479	4.5*	
					10,480	19.2	
[Death] 1987 (12/3)	72,105	70.3	Taylor M.O.J.	Lib	30,599	60.4	+3.1
			St. Aubyn N.F.	Con	15,982	31.6	-6.5
			King J.R.	Lab	3,603	7.1	+2.6
			Hoptrough H.S.	Green	403	0.8*	
			Anscomb H.M. Ms.	Ind	75	0.1*	
					14,617	28.8	
1987	72,445	79.9	Taylor M.O.J.	Lib	28,368	49.0	-8.3
			St. Aubyn N.F.	Con	23,615	40.8	+2.7
			King J.R.	Lab	5,882	10.2	+5.6
					4,753	8.2	
1992	75,119	82.3	Taylor M.O.J.*	LD	31,230	50.5	+1.5
			St. Aubyn N.F.	Con	23,660	38.3	-2.6
			Geach J.H.	Lab	6,078	9.8	-0.3
			Keating L.M.	Green	569	0.9*	+0.9
			Tankard C.M.	Lib	208	0.3*	+0.3
			Hartley M.K.F. Ms.	NLP	108	0.2*	+0.2
					7,570	12.2	

TUNBRIDGE WELLS [581]

Election	Electors	T'out	Candidate	Party	Votes	% Sh	% Ch
1983	73,709	72.7	Mayhew P.B.B.*	Con	31,199	58.3	
			Blaine P.A.	Lib	16,073	30.0	
			Casely S.J.	Lab	6,042	11.3*	
			Smith D.	NF	236	0.4*	
					15,126	28.2	
1987	76,291	74.3	Mayhew P.B.B. Sir.*	Con	33,111	58.4	+0.2
			Buckrell D.A. Ms.	Lib	16,989	30.0	-0.0
			Sloman P.L.	Lab	6,555	11.6	+0.3
					16,122	28.5	
1992	76,807†	78.1	Mayhew P.B.B. Sir*	Con	34,162	56.9	-1.5
			Clayton A.S.	LD	17,030	28.4	-1.6
			Goodman E.A.C.	Lab	8,300	13.8	+2.3
			Fenna E.W.	NLP	267	0.4*	+0.4
			Edey R.	Ind	236	0.4*	
					17,132	28.6	

TWEEDDALE, ETTRICK AND LAUDERDALE [582]

Election	Electors	T'out	Candidate	Party	Votes	% Sh	% Ch
1983	37,075	77.8	Steel D.M.S.*	Lib	16,868	58.5	
			Ballantyne A.D.	Con	8,329	28.9	
			Saren M.A.J.	Lab	2,200	7.6*	
			Macartney W.J.A.	SNP	1,455	5.0*	
					8,539	29.6	
1987	37,875	77.2	Steel D.M.S.*	Lib	14,599	49.9	-8.5
			Finlay-Maxwell C.S. Ms.	Con	8,657	29.6	+0.7
			Glen N.	Lab	3,320	11.4	+3.7
			Lumsden A.	SNP	2,660	9.1	+4.1
					5,942	20.3	
1992	39,478†	78.1	Steel Sir D.M.S.*	LD	12,296	39.9	-10.0
			Beat L.A.	Con	9,776	31.7	+2.1
			Creech C. Ms.	SNP	5,244	17.0	+7.9
			Dunton A.	Lab	3,328	10.8	-0.6
			Hein J.	Lib	177	0.6*	+0.6
					2,520	8.2	

TWICKENHAM [583]

Election	Electors	T'out	Candidate	Party	Votes	% Sh	% Ch
1983	64,116	77.8	Jessel T.F.H.*	Con	25,110	50.4	
			Waller J.	Lib	20,318	40.8	
			Nicholas P.A. Ms.	Lab	3,732	7.5*	
			Clarke J.J.	Green	424	0.9*	
			Denville-Faulkner T.J.	NF	234	0.5*	
			Kenyon R.W.	Ind	40	0.1*	
					4,792	9.6	
1987	64,661	81.5	Jessel T.F.H.*	Con	27,331	51.9	+1.5
			Waller J.	Lib	20,204	38.3	-2.4
			Vaz V.C.M. Ms.	Lab	4,415	8.4	+0.9
			Batchelor D.S.	Green	746	1.4*	+0.6
					7,127	13.5	
1992	63,152	84.2	Jessel T.F.H.*	Con	26,804	50.4	-1.4
			Cable J.V.	LD	21,093	39.7	+1.3
			Gold M.D.	Lab	4,919	9.3	+0.9
			Gill G.P.	NLP	152	0.3*	+0.3
			Griffiths D.W.	Ind Con	103	0.2*	
			Miners A.J.	Lib	85	0.2*	+0.2
					5,711	10.7	

TYNE BRIDGE [584]

Election	Electors	T'out	Candidate	Party	Votes	% Sh	% Ch
1983	60,808	61.5	Cowans H.L.*	Lab	21,127	56.5	
			Crawley R.S.	Con	9,434	25.2	
			Dawson D.A.	Lib	6,852	18.3	
					11,693	31.3	

[Death]

Election	Electors	T'out	Candidate	Party	Votes	% Sh	% Ch
1985 (5/12)	61,400	38.1	Clelland D.G.	Lab	13,517	57.8	+1.3
			Kenyon R.F.	SDP	6,942	29.7	+11.4
			Lait J.A.H. Ms.	Con	2,588	11.1	-14.1
			Connell J.	Ind	250	1.1*	
			Weiss G.	Ind	38	0.2*	
			Smith P.R.	Ind	32	0.1*	
					6,575	28.1	
1987	58,152	63.1	Clelland D.G.	Lab	23,131	63.0	+6.6
			Bates M.W.	Con	7,558	20.6	-4.6
			Mansfield J.C. Dr.	SDP	6,005	16.4	-1.9
					15,573	42.4	
1992	53,080†	62.6	Clelland D.G.*	Lab	22,328	67.2	+4.1
			Liddell-Grainger C.M.	Con	7,118	21.4	+0.8
			Burt J.S.	LD	3,804	11.4	-4.9
					15,210	45.7	

Election	Electors	T'out	Candidate	Party	Votes	% Sh	% Ch
1983	74,549	74.6	Trotter N.G.*	Con	27,029	48.6	
			Cosgrove P.J.	Lab	17,420	31.3	
			Mayhew D.F.	Lib	11,153	20.1	
					9,609	17.3	
1987	74,407	78.1	Trotter N.G.*	Con	25,113	43.2	-5.4
			Cosgrove P.J.	Lab	22,530	38.8	+7.5
			Mayhew D.F.	Lib	10,446	18.0	-2.1
					2,583	4.4	
1992	74,956†	80.4	Trotter N.G.*	Con	27,731	46.0	+2.8
			Cosgrove P.J.	Lab	27,134	45.0	+6.2
			Selby P.J.S.	LD	4,855	8.1	-9.9
			Buchanan-Smith A.	Green	543	0.9*	+0.9
					597	1.0	

327

Election	Electors	T'out	Candidate	Party	Votes	% Sh	% Ch
1983	63,831	84.4	McCrea R.T.W. Rev.	UDUP	16,174	30.0	
			Morrison D.G.	SF	16,096	29.9	
			Haughey P.D.	SDLP	12,044	22.4	
			Thompson W.J.	UU	7,066	13.1	
			Lagan J.A. Dr.	APNI	1,735	3.2*	
			Owens T.A.	WP	766	1.4*	
					78	0.1	

[Seeks Re-election]

Election	Electors	T'out	Candidate	Party	Votes	% Sh	% Ch
1986	66,757	77.0	McCrea R.T.W. Rev.*	UDUP	23,695	46.1	+16.1
(23/1)			Morrison D.G.	SF	13,998	27.2	-2.7
			Colton A.	SDLP	13,021	25.3	+2.9
			Owens T.A.	WP	691	1.3*	+0.0
					9,697	18.9	
1987	67,256	77.4	McCrea R.T.W. Rev.*	UDUP	23,004	44.2	+14.2
			Haughey P.D.	SDLP	13,644	26.2	+3.8
			Begley S.	SF	12,449	23.9	-6.0
			Bogan P.J.	APNI	1,846	3.5*	+0.3
			McClean P.J.	WP	1,133	2.2*	+0.8
					9,360	18.0	
1992	69,138	79.2	McCrea R.T.W. Rev.*	UDUP	23,181	42.3	-1.8
			Haughey P.D.	SDLP	16,994	31.0	+4.8
			McElduff B.	SF	10,248	18.7	-5.2
			McLaughlin J.	Ind	1,996	3.6*	
			Gormley A. Ms.	APNI	1,506	2.8*	-0.8
			Hutchinson H.	LTU	389	0.7*	+0.7
			Owens T.A.	WP	285	0.5*	-1.7
			Anderson J.M.	NLP	164	0.3*	+0.3
					6,187	11.3	

Election	Electors	T'out	Candidate	Party	Votes	% Sh	% Ch
1983	66,445	72.1	Bonsor N.C. Sir. Bt.*	Con	25,153	52.5	
			Osman D.A.	SDP	12,339	25.8	
			Hughes A.T.	Lab	9,829	20.5	
			Nobes-Pride G.H.	NF	566	1.2*	
					12,814	26.8	
1987	66,613	75.2	Bonsor N.C. Sir. Bt.*	Con	27,946	55.8	+3.3
			Martin J.	SDP	11,089	22.1	-3.6
			O'Flynn D.R.	Lab	11,069	22.1	+1.6
					16,857	33.6	
1992	64,125	80.5	Bonsor N.C. Sir. Bt.*	Con	28,791	55.8	+0.0
			Ward T.	Lab	14,970	29.0	+6.9
			Hurlstone T.E.	LD	7,848	15.2	-6.9
					13,821	26.8	

UPPER BANN [588]

Election	Electors	T'out	Candidate	Party	Votes	% Sh	% Ch
1983	60,734	72.0	McCusker J.H.*	UU	24,888	56.9	
			McDonald J.	SDLP	7,807	17.8	
			Wells J.H.	UDUP	4,547	10.4*	
			Curran B.P.	SF	4,110	9.4*	
			French T.	WP	2,392	5.5*	
					17,081	39.0	

[Seeks Re-election]

1986	63,484	57.2	McCusker J.H.	UU	29,311	80.8	+23.9
(23/1)			French T.	WP	6,978	19.2	+13.7
					22,333	61.5	

1987	64,540	65.6	McCusker J.H.*	UU	26,037	61.5	+4.6
			Rodgers B. Ms.	SDLP	8,676	20.5	+2.6
			Curran B.P.	SF	3,126	7.4	-2.0
			Cook M.F.A. Ms.	APNI	2,487	5.9	+5.9
			French T.	WP	2,004	4.7*	-0.7
					17,361	41.0	

[Death]

1990	66,377	53.4	Trimble W.D.	UU	20,547	58.0	-3.5
(17/5)			Rodgers B. Ms.	SDLP	6,698	18.9	-1.6
			Campbell S.T. Ms.	SF	2,033	5.7	-1.7
			Ross H.	Ind	1,534	4.3*	
			French T.	WP	1,083	3.1*	-1.6
			Jones C. Ms.	Con	1,038	3.0*	
			Ramsay W.W.	APNI	948	2.7*	-3.2
			McMichael G.J.	UDP	600	1.7*	
			Doran P.F.	Green	576	1.6*	
			Holmes J.E.	Ind	235	0.6*	
			Dunn A.	SDP	154	0.4*	
					13,849	39.1	
1992	67,460	67.4	Trimble W.D.	UU	26,824	59.0	-2.5
			Rodgers B. Ms.	SDLP	10,661	23.4	+2.9
			Curran B.P.	SF	2,777	6.1	-1.3
			Ramsay W.W.	APNI	2,541	5.6	-0.3
			Jones C. Ms.	Con	1,556	3.4*	+3.4
			French T.	WP	1,120	2.5*	-2.2
					16,163	35.5	

Election	Electors	T'out	Candidate	Party	Votes	% Sh	% Ch
1983	61,615	72.3	Shersby J.M.*	Con	23,876	53.6	
			Russell P.F.N.	SDP	11,038	24.8	
			Magee P.J.	Lab	9,611	21.6	
					12,838	28.8	
1987	63,157	76.5	Shersby J.M.*	Con	27,292	56.5	+2.8
			Keys D.M.E.	Lab	11,323	23.4	+1.8
			Goodman A.P.	SDP	9,164	19.0	-5.8
			Flindall I.E.	Green	549	1.1*	+1.1
					15,969	33.0	
1992	61,604	79.1	Shersby J.M.*	Con	27,487	56.4	-0.0
			Evans R.J.E.	Lab	14,308	29.4	+5.9
			Carey S.J.	LD	5,900	12.1	-6.8
			Flindall I.E.	Green	538	1.1*	-0.0
			O'Rourke M.R.	BNP	350	0.7*	+0.7
			Deans A.J.	NLP	120	0.2*	+0.2
					13,179	27.1	

Election	Electors	T'out	Candidate	Party	Votes	% Sh	% Ch
1983	62,885	74.2	Gower H.R. Sir.*	Con	22,421	48.0	
			Sharp M.E.	Lab	12,028	25.8	
			Evans W.A.	SDP	11,154	23.9	
			Dixon A.J.	PC	1,068	2.3*	
					10,393	22.3	
1987	65,310	79.3	Gower H.R. Sir.*	Con	24,229	46.8	-1.3
			Smith J.W.P.	Lab	17,978	34.7	+8.9
			Davies D.K.	SDP	8,633	16.7	-7.2
			Williams P.G.	PC	946	1.8*	-0.5
					6,251	12.1	

[Death]

Election	Electors	T'out	Candidate	Party	Votes	% Sh	% Ch
1989	67,549	70.7	Smith J.W.P.	Lab	23,342	48.9	+14.2
(4/5)			Richards R.	Con	17,314	36.3	-10.5
			Leavers F.	LD	2,017	4.2*	-12.5
			Dixon A.J.	PC	1,672	3.5*	+1.7
			Davies K.	SDP	1,098	2.3*	
			Wakefield M.A. Ms.	Green	971	2.0*	
			Tiarks C.	Ind	847	1.8*	
			Sutch D.E.	MRLP	266	0.6*	
			Roberts E.	Ind	148	0.3*	
			St. Clair L. Ms.	Ind	39	0.1*	
			Black D.	Ind	32	0.1*	
					6,028	12.6	
1992	66,673†	80.2	Sweeney W.E.	Con	24,220	44.3	-2.4
			Smith J.W.P.	Lab	24,201	44.3	+9.6
			Davies D.K.	LD	5,045	9.2	-7.4
			Haswell D.B.L.	PC	1,160	2.1*	+0.3
					19	0.0	

VAUXHALL [591]

Election	Electors	T'out	Candidate	Party	Votes	% Sh	% Ch
1983	64,867	60.5	Holland S.K.*	Lab	18,234	46.5	
			Manning K.G.	Con	10,454	26.7	
			Liddle R.J.	SDP	9,515	24.3	
			Wright J.G.	NF	508	1.3*	
			Lingard P.J.	MRLP	266	0.7*	
			Cook D.J.S.	Comm	199	0.5*	
			Shorter G.B.	WKP	38	0.1*	
					7,780	19.8	
1987	66,538	64.0	Holland S.K.*	Lab	21,364	50.2	+3.7
			Lidington D.R.	Con	12,345	29.0	+2.3
			Acland S.H.V.	SDP	7,764	18.2	-6.0
			Owens J. Ms.	Green	770	1.8*	+1.8
			Cook D.J.S.	Comm	223	0.5*	+0.0
			Oluremi K.	RF	117	0.3*	+0.3
					9,019	21.2	

[Resignation]

Election	Electors	T'out	Candidate	Party	Votes	% Sh	% Ch
1989	64,905	44.4	Hoey C.L. Ms.	Lab	15,191	52.8	+2.6
(15/6)			Keegan M.	Con	5,425	18.8	-10.2
			Tuffrey M.W.	LD	5,043	17.5	-0.7
			Bewley H.	Green	1,767	6.1	+4.3
			Andrew H.	Ind	302	1.0*	
			Allen D.	Ind	264	0.9*	
			Narayan R.	Ind	179	0.6*	
			Milligan D.	RCP	177	0.6*	
			Harrington P.	NF	127	0.4*	
			Sutch D.E.	MRLP	106	0.4*	
			Black D.	Ind	86	0.3*	
			Budden E.	Ind NF	83	0.3*	
			Rolph G.A.	FP	24	0.1*	
			Scola W.P.C.V.	Ind	21	0.1*	
					9,766	34.0	
1992	62,595	62.2	Hoey C.L. Ms.	Lab	21,328	54.7	+4.6
			Gentry B.A.R.	Con	10,840	27.8	-1.2
			Tuffrey M.W.	LD	5,678	14.6	-3.7
			Shepherd P.A. Ms.	Green	803	2.1*	+0.3
			Khan A.G.	Ind	156	0.4*	
			Hill S. Ms.	RCP	152	0.4*	+0.4
					10,488	26.9	

333

WAKEFIELD [592]

Election	Electors	T'out	Candidate	Party	Votes	% Sh	% Ch
1983	68,416	69.3	Harrison W.*	Lab	19,166	40.4	
			Hazell N.J.	Con	18,806	39.6	
			Carlton D.	SDP	9,166	19.3	
			Parker V. Ms.	BNP	295	0.6*	
					360	0.8	
1987	69,580	75.6	Hinchliffe D.M.	Lab	24,509	46.6	+6.2
			Hazell N.J.	Con	21,720	41.3	+1.7
			Kamal L.R.M. Dr.	SDP	6,350	12.1	-7.2
					2,789	5.3	
1992	69,825	76.2	Hinchliffe D.M.*	Lab	26,964	50.6	+4.0
			Fanthorpe D.P.	Con	20,374	38.3	-3.0
			Wright T.J.	LD	5,900	11.1	-1.0
					6,590	12.4	

WALLASEY [593]

Election	Electors	T'out	Candidate	Party	Votes	% Sh	% Ch
1983	68,462	72.6	Chalker L. Ms.*	Con	22,854	46.0	
			Robertson J.A.	Lab	16,146	32.5	
			Richardson J.K.	SDP	10,717	21.6	
					6,708	13.5	
1987	67,216	79.8	Chalker L. Ms.*	Con	22,791	42.5	-3.5
			Duffy L.	Lab	22,512	41.9	+9.5
			Richardson J.K.	SDP	8,363	15.6	-6.0
					279	0.5	
1992	65,670	82.6	Eagle A. Ms.	Lab	26,531	48.9	+7.0
			Chalker L. Ms.*	Con	22,722	41.9	-0.6
			Thomas N.R.L.	LD	4,177	7.7	-7.9
			Davis S.V. Ms.	Green	680	1.3*	+1.3
			Gay G.N.W.	NLP	105	0.2*	+0.2
					3,809	7.0	

334

WALLSEND [594]

Election	Electors	T'out	Candidate	Party	Votes	% Sh	% Ch
1983	76,268	71.1	Garrett W.E.*	Lab	26,615	49.1	
			Leigh M.D. Ms.	Con	14,101	26.0	
			Phylactou J. Ms.	SDP	13,522	24.9	
					12,514	23.1	
1987	76,688	75.0	Garrett W.E.*	Lab	32,709	56.8	+7.8
			Milburn D.	Con	13,325	23.2	-2.8
			Phylactou J. Ms.	SDP	11,508	20.0	-4.9
					19,384	33.7	
1992	77,941†	74.1	Byers S.J.	Lab	33,439	57.9	+1.0
			Gibbon M. Ms.	Con	13,969	24.2	+1.0
			Huscroft M.J.	LD	10,369	17.9	-2.1
					19,470	33.7	

WALSALL NORTH [595]

Election	Electors	T'out	Candidate	Party	Votes	% Sh	% Ch
1983	68,868	71.0	Winnick D.J.*	Lab	20,782	42.5	
			Stephens N.E.E.	Con	17,958	36.7	
			Bentley A.G.	Lib	10,141	20.7	
					2,824	5.8	
1987	68,331	73.8	Winnick D.J.*	Lab	21,458	42.6	+0.1
			Hertz L. Ms.	Con	19,668	39.0	+2.3
			Shires I.	Lib	9,285	18.4	-2.3
					1,790	3.6	
1992	69,605†	75.0	Winnick D.J.*	Lab	24,387	46.7	+4.2
			Syms R.A.R.	Con	20,563	39.4	+0.4
			Powis A.R.	LD	6,629	12.7	-5.7
			Reynolds K.A.	NF	614	1.2*	+1.2
					3,824	7.3	

335

WALSALL SOUTH [596]

Election	Electors	T'out	Candidate	Party	Votes	% Sh	% Ch
1983	67,257	74.3	George B.T.*	Lab	21,735	43.5	
			Nicholson D.J.	Con	21,033	42.1	
			Silver B.	Lib	6,586	13.2	
			Parker J.C.	BNP	632	1.3*	
					702	1.4	
1987	66,746	75.5	George B.T.*	Lab	22,629	44.9	+1.4
			Postles G.E.	Con	21,513	42.7	+0.6
			King L.A.	Lib	6,241	12.4	-0.8
					1,116	2.2	
1992	65,643†	76.3	George B.T.*	Lab	24,133	48.2	+3.3
			Jones L.C.	Con	20,955	41.9	-0.8
			Williams G.E.	LD	4,132	8.3	-4.1
			Clarke R.J.	Green	673	1.3*	+1.3
			Oldbury J.D.	NLP	167	0.3*	+0.3
					3,178	6.3	

WALTHAMSTOW [597]

Election	Electors	T'out	Candidate	Party	Votes	% Sh	% Ch
1983	48,324	68.8	Deakins E.P.*	Lab	13,241	39.8	
			Amos A.T.	Con	11,936	35.9	
			Leighton P.L.	SDP	7,192	21.6	
			Mitchell P.	NF	444	1.3*	
			Lambert S.W.	Green	424	1.3*	
					1,305	3.9	
1987	48,691	72.4	Summerson H.H.F.	Con	13,748	39.0	+3.1
			Deakins E.P.*	Lab	12,236	34.7	-5.1
			Leighton P.L.	SDP	8,852	25.1	+3.5
			Malik Z.I. Dr.	Ind	396	1.1*	
					1,512	4.3	
1992	49,347	72.0	Gerrard N.F.	Lab	16,251	45.7	+11.0
			Summerson H.H.F.*	Con	13,229	37.2	-1.8
			Leighton P.L.	LD	5,142	14.5	-10.7
			Lambert J.D. Ms.	Green	594	1.7*	+1.7
			Wilkinson V.R.	Lib	241	0.7*	+0.7
			Planton A.W.	NLP	94	0.3*	+0.3
					3,022	8.5	

WANSBECK [598]

Election	Electors	T'out	Candidate	Party	Votes	% Sh	% Ch
1983	63,398	72.9	Thompson J.	Lab	21,732	47.0	
			Thompson J.A.	Lib	13,901	30.1	
			Michell C.H.W.	Con	10,563	22.9	
					7,831	17.0	
1987	62,640	78.0	Thompson J.*	Lab	28,080	57.5	+10.4
			Mitchell S.A.G. Ms.	Lib	11,291	23.1	-7.0
			Walton D.M.	Con	9,490	19.4	-3.4
					16,789	34.4	
1992	63,502	79.2	Thompson J.*	Lab	30,046	59.7	+2.2
			Sanderson H.G.H.	Con	11,872	23.6	+4.2
			Priestley B.C.	LD	7,691	15.3	-7.8
			Best N.F.	Green	710	1.4*	+1.4
					18,174	36.1	

WANSDYKE [599]

Election	Electors	T'out	Candidate	Party	Votes	% Sh	% Ch
1983	71,094	79.0	Aspinwall J.H.*	Con	28,434	50.6	
			Denton-White R.D.	Lib	15,368	27.4	
			Williams L.	Lab	12,168	21.7	
			Stout A.	WR	213	0.4*	
					13,066	23.3	
1987	75,239	81.3	Aspinwall J.H.*	Con	31,537	51.6	+1.0
			Blackmore R.B.	Lib	15,393	25.2	-2.2
			White I.J.	Lab	14,231	23.3	+1.6
					16,144	26.4	
1992	77,245	84.2	Aspinwall J.H.*	Con	31,389	48.2	-3.3
			Norris D.	Lab	18,048	27.7	+4.5
			Darby D. Ms.	LD	14,834	22.8	-2.4
			Hayden F.E.	Green	800	1.2*	+1.2
					13,341	20.5	

337

WANSTEAD AND WOODFORD [600]

Election	Electors	T'out	Candidate	Party	Votes	% Sh	% Ch
1983	57,705	68.4	Jenkin C.P.F.*	Con	23,765	60.3	
			Crawford K.	Lib	9,411	23.9	
			Hilton L.R. Ms.	Lab	5,334	13.5	
			Warth C. Ms.	Green	476	1.2*	
			Marshall H.	NF	456	1.2*	
					14,354	36.4	
1987	57,921	72.4	Arbuthnot J.N.	Con	25,701	61.3	+1.0
			Bastick J.R.	Lib	9,289	22.1	-1.7
			Hilton L.R. Ms.	Lab	6,958	16.6	+3.1
					16,412	39.1	
1992	55,867	78.2	Arbuthnot J.N.*	Con	26,204	60.0	-1.3
			Brown L.C. Ms.	Lab	9,319	21.3	+4.7
			Staight G.P.	LD	7,362	16.8	-5.3
			Roads F.M.	Green	637	1.5*	+1.5
			Brickell A.J.	NLP	178	0.4*	+0.4
					16,885	38.6	

WANTAGE [601]

Election	Electors	T'out	Candidate	Party	Votes	% Sh	% Ch
1983	63,950	76.9	Jackson R.V.	Con	25,992	52.9	
			Tumin W.L. Ms.	SDP	15,867	32.3	
			Popper A.J.D.	Lab	7,115	14.5	
			Barrett Mockler A.P.	WR	183	0.4*	
					10,125	20.6	
1987	66,499	77.9	Jackson R.V.*	Con	27,951	54.0*	+1.1
			Tumin W.L. Ms.	SDP	15,795	30.5	-1.8
			Ladyman S.J.	Lab	8,055	15.5	+1.1
					12,156	23.5	
1992	68,329†	82.7	Jackson R.V.*	Con	30,575	54.1	+1.2
			Morgan R.M.C.	LD	14,102	25.0	-5.5
			Woodell V.S.	Lab	10,955	19.4	+3.8
			Ely R.J.	Green	867	1.5*	+1.5
					16,473	29.2	

338

WARLEY EAST [602]

Election	Electors	T'out	Candidate	Party	Votes	% Sh	% Ch
1983	57,439	68.9	Faulds A.M.W.*	Lab	18,036	45.6	
			Whitby M.J.	Con	14,645	37.0	
			Hamer J.E.B.	SDP	6,697	16.9	
			Randhawa H.S.	Comm	217	0.5*	
					3,391	8.6	
1987	55,706	69.4	Faulds A.M.W.*	Lab	19,428	50.2	+4.7
			Antoniou A.J.	Con	13,843	35.8	-1.2
			Jordan J.	SDP	5,396	14.0	-3.0
					5,585	14.4	
1992	51,725	71.7	Faulds A.M.W.*	Lab	19,891	53.6	+3.4
			Marshall G.P.B.	Con	12,097	32.6	-3.2
			Harrod A.R.A.	LD	4,547	12.3	-1.7
			Groucott A.T.	NLP	561	1.5*	+1.5
					7,794	21.0	

WARLEY WEST [603]

Election	Electors	T'out	Candidate	Party	Votes	% Sh	% Ch
1983	57,165	67.8	Archer P.K.*	Lab	18,272	47.1	
			McIntyre A.E.J. Ms.	Con	13,004	33.5	
			Baines A.G.	Lib	7,485	19.3	
					5,268 .	13.6	
1987	57,526	70.0	Archer P.K.*	Lab	19,825	49.2	+2.1
			Williams W.	Con	14,432	35.8	+2.3
			Todd E. Ms.	Lib	6,027	15.0	-4.3
					5,393	13.4	
1992	57,158	73.9	Spellar J.F.	Lab	21,386	50.6	+1.4
			Whitehouse S. Ms.	Con	15,914	37.7	+1.8
			Todd E. Ms.	LD	4,945	11.7	-3.3
					5,472	13.0	

WARRINGTON NORTH [604]

Election	Electors	T'out	Candidate	Party	Votes	% Sh	% Ch
1983	69,850	72.6	Hoyle E.D.H.*	Lab	20,873	41.2	
			Sexton S.E.	Con	15,596	30.8	
			Harrison D.S.	SDP	13,951	27.5	
			Sloan I.	BNP	267	0.5*	
					5,277	10.4	
1987	75,627	75.2	Hoyle E.D.H.*	Lab	27,422	48.2	+7.0
			Jones L.C.	Con	19,409	34.1	+3.4
			Bithel C.	SDP	10,046	17.7	-9.9
					8,013	14.1	
1992	78,654	77.3	Hoyle E.D.H.*	Lab	33,019	54.3	+6.1
			Daniels C.	Con	20,397	33.6	-0.6
			Greenhalgh I.	LD	6,965	11.5	-6.2
			Davis B.R.	NLP	400	0.7*	+0.7
					12,622	20.8	

WARRINGTON SOUTH [605]

Election	Electors	T'out	Candidate	Party	Votes	% Sh	% Ch
1983	72,803	74.5	Carlisle M.*	Con	22,740	41.9	
			Colin-Thomé D.G. Dr.	Lab	16,275	30.0	
			Marks I.G.	Lib	14,827	27.3	
			Chantrell N.S.	Green	403	0.7*	
					6,465	11.9	
1987	74,267	79.6	Butler C.J.	Con	24,809	42.0	+0.0
			Booth A.E.	Lab	21,200	35.9	+5.9
			Marks I.G.	Lib	13,112	22.2	-5.2
					3,609	6.1	
1992	77,693	82.0	Hall M.T.	Lab	27,819	43.6	+7.8
			Butler C.J.*	Con	27,628	43.3	+1.4
			Walker P.J.	LD	7,978	12.5	-9.7
			Benson S.D	NLP	321	0.5*	+0.5
					191	0.3	

WARWICK AND LEAMINGTON [606]

Election	Electors	T'out	Candidate	Party	Votes	% Sh	% Ch
1983	70,858	73.6	Smith D.G. Sir.*	Con	26,512	50.8	
			Behrens R.F.	SDP	13,480	25.9	
			Chessum R.T.	Lab	11,463	22.0	
			Charlton N.J.	Green	685	1.3*	
					13,032	25.0	
1987	72,763	76.0	Smith D.G. Sir.*	Con	27,530	49.8	-1.1
			O'Sullivan K.P.	SDP	13,548	24.5	-1.4
			Christina A. Ms.	Lab	13,019	23.5	+1.6
			Alty J.A. Ms.	Green	1,214	2.2*	+0.9
					13,982	25.3	
1992	71,260†	81.5	Smith D.G. Sir.*	Con	28,093	48.3	-1.4
			Taylor M.	Lab	19,158	33.0	+9.4
			Boad S.E. Ms.	LD	9,645	16.6	-7.9
			Alty J.A. Ms.	Green	803	1.4*	-0.8
			Newby R.	Ind	251	0.4*	
			Brewster J.L.	NLP	156	0.3*	+0.3
					8,935	15.4	

WARWICKSHIRE NORTH [607]

Election	Electors	T'out	Candidate	Party	Votes	% Sh	% Ch
1983	68,625	78.0	Maude F.A.A.	Con	22,452	41.9	
			Tomlinson J.E.	Lab	19,867	37.1	
			Kerry H.M.	SDP	11,207	20.9	
					2,585	4.8	
1987	70,687	79.9	Maude F.A.A. Hon.*	Con	25,453	45.1	+3.1
			O'Brien M.	Lab	22,624	40.1	+3.0
			Neale S.J. Ms.	SDP	8,382	14.8	-6.1
					2,829	5.0	
1992	71,473†	83.8	O'Brien M.	Lab	27,599	46.1	+6.0
			Maude F.A.A. Hon.*	Con	26,145	43.6	-1.4
			Mitchell N.R.	LD	6,167	10.3	-4.6
					1,454	2.4	

WATFORD [608]

Election	Electors	T'out	Candidate	Party	Votes	% Sh	% Ch
1983	71,992	76.1	Garel-Jones W.A.T.T.*	Con	26,273	48.0	
			Burton P.L.	SDP	14,267	26.0	
			Wilson I.S.	Lab	14,247	26.0	
					12,006	21.9	
1987	73,540	77.9	Garel-Jones W.A.T.T.*	Con	27,912	48.7	+0.8
			Jackson M.J.	Lab	16,176	28.2	+2.2
			Beckett F.M. Ms.	SDP	13,202	23.0	-3.0
					11,736	20.5	
1992	72,291†	82.3	Garel-Jones W.A.T.T.*	Con	29,072	48.8	+0.1
			Jackson M.J.	Lab	19,482	32.7	+4.5
			Oaten M.	LD	10,231	17.2	-5.9
			Hywel-Davies J.	Green	566	1.0*	+1.0
			Davis L.J.K.	NLP	176	0.3*	+0.3
					9,590	16.1	

WAVENEY [609]

Election	Electors	T'out	Candidate	Party	Votes	% Sh	% Ch
1983	77,960	75.3	Prior J.M.L.*	Con	30,371	51.8	
			Lark J.A.	Lab	16,073	27.4	
			Artis G.M. Ms.	SDP	12,234	20.8	
					14,298	24.4	
1987	81,892	78.4	Porter D.J.	Con	31,067	48.4	-3.4
			Lark J.A.	Lab	19,284	30.0	+2.6
			Beavan D.S.	SDP	13,845	21.6	+0.7
					11,783	18.4	
1992	84,181†	81.8	Porter D.J.*	Con	33,174	48.2	-0.2
			Leverett E.C.	Lab	26,472	38.4	+8.4
			Rogers A.C.	LD	8,925	13.0	-8.6
			Hook D.	NLP	302	0.4*	+0.4
					6,702	9.7	

WEALDEN [610]

Election	Electors	T'out	Candidate	Party	Votes	% Sh	% Ch
1983	69,244	71.8	Johnson Smith G. Sir.*	Con	31,926	64.2	
			Pace D.E.	SDP	14,741	29.6	
			Knight P.F.L. Ms.	Lab	3,060	6.2*	
					17,185	34.6	
1987	73,057	75.0	Johnson Smith G. Sir.*	Con	35,154	64.2	-0.0
			Sinclair D.A.	SDP	15,044	27.5	-2.2
			Ward C.E.	Lab	4,563	8.3	+2.2
					20,110	36.7	
1992	74,558	81.0	Johnson Smith G. Sir.*	Con	37,263	61.7	-2.5
			Skinner M.D.	LD	16,332	27.1	-0.4
			Billcliffe S.	Lab	5,579	9.2	+0.9
			Guy-Moore I.	Green	1,002	1.7*	+1.7
			Graham R.F.	NLP	182	0.3*	+0.3
					20,931	34.7	

WELLINGBOROUGH [611]

Election	Electors	T'out	Candidate	Party	Votes	% Sh	% Ch
1983	67,598	77.8	Fry P.D.*	Con	25,715	48.9	
			Mann J.H.	Lab	13,659	26.0	
			Stringer L.E.	Lib	12,994	24.7	
			Garnett D.M.P. Ms.	Ind	228	0.4*	
					12,056	22.9	
1987	70,450	78.1	Fry P.D.*	Con	29,038	52.7	+3.9
			Currie J.	Lab	14,968	27.2	+1.2
			Stringer L.E.	Lib	11,047	20.1	-4.6
					14,070	25.6	
1992	73,876†	81.9	Fry P.D.*	Con	32,302	53.4	+0.6
			Sawford P.A.	Lab	20,486	33.9	+6.7
			Trevor J.E. Ms.	LD	7,714	12.7	-7.3
					11,816	19.5	

343

WELLS [612]

Election	Electors	T'out	Candidate	Party	Votes	% Sh	% Ch
1983	62,161	77.6	Heathcoat-Amory D.P.	Con	25,385	52.6	
			Butt Philip A.A.S.	Lib	18,810	39.0	
			Leigh A.M.	Lab	3,747	7.8*	
			Livings G.E.	Ind	273	0.6*	
					6,575	13.6	
1987	67,229	79.5	Heathcoat-Amory D.P.*	Con	28,624	53.5	+0.9
			Butt Philip A.A.S.	Lib	20,083	37.6	-1.5
			James P.E.	Lab	4,637	8.7	+0.9
			Fish J.S.	Ind	134	0.3*	
					8,541	16.0	
1992	69,833	82.7	Heathcoat-Amory D.P.*	Con	28,620	49.6	-4.0
			Temperley H.P.N.	LD	21,971	38.0	+0.5
			Pilgrim J.W.	Lab	6,126	10.6	+1.9
			Fenner M.D.	Green	1,042	1.8*	+1.8
					6,649	11.5	

WELWYN HATFIELD [613]

Election	Electors	T'out	Candidate	Party	Votes	% Sh	% Ch
1983	72,644	79.4	Murphy C.P.Y.*	Con	27,498	47.7	
			Granshaw L.P. Ms.	SDP	15,252	26.5	
			France J.	Lab	14,898	25.8	
					12,246	21.2	
1987	73,607	80.9	Evans D.J.	Con	27,164	45.6	-2.1
			Granshaw L.P. Ms.	SDP	16,261	27.3	+0.9
			Pond C.R.	Lab	15,699	26.4	+0.5
			Dyson B.I.	Ind Con	401	0.7*	
					10,903	18.3	
1992	72,236†	84.3	Evans D.J.*	Con	29,447	48.4	+2.7
			Little R.A.	Lab	20,982	34.5	+8.1
			Parker R.G.	LD	10,196	16.7	-10.6
			Lucas E.T. Ms.	NLP	264	0.4*	+0.4
					8,465	13.9	

WENTWORTH [614]

Election	Electors	T'out	Candidate	Party	Votes	% Sh	% Ch
1983	62,057	69.7	Hardy P.*	Lab	25,538	59.1	
			Norton R.W.B.	Con	9,603	22.2	
			Tildsley D.M.	SDP	8,082	18.7	
					15,935	36.9	
1987	63,886	72.5	Hardy P.*	Lab	30,205	65.2	+6.1
			Hague W.J.	Con	10,113	21.8	-0.4
			Eglin D.M.	SDP	6,031	13.0	-5.7
					20,092	43.3	
1992	64,915†	74.0	Hardy P.*	Lab	32,939	68.5	+3.4
			Brennan M.J.	Con	10,490	21.8	+0.0
			Roderick C. Ms.	LD	4,629	9.6	-3.4
					22,449	46.7	

WEST BROMWICH EAST [615]

Election	Electors	T'out	Candidate	Party	Votes	% Sh	% Ch
1983	59,391	70.2	Snape P.C.*	Lab	15,892	38.1	
			Cole C.W.	Con	15,596	37.4	
			Smith M.G.	Lib	10,200	24.5	
					296	0.7	
1987	58,239	73.2	Snape P.C.*	Lab	18,162	42.6	+4.5
			Woodhouse R.F.	Con	17,179	40.3	+2.9
			Smith M.G.	Lib	7,268	17.1	-7.4
					983	2.3	
1992	56,945	75.7	Snape P.C.*	Lab	19,913	46.2	+3.6
			Blunt C.J.R.	Con	17,100	39.7	-0.7
			Smith M.G.	LD	5,630	13.1	-4.0
			Lord J.B.R.	NF	477	1.1*	+1.1
					2,813	6.5	

WEST BROMWICH WEST [616]

Election	Electors	T'out	Candidate	Party	Votes	% Sh	% Ch
1983	58,341	63.8	Boothroyd B. Ms.*	Lab	18,896	50.7	
			Harman D.M.	Con	12,257	32.9	
			Collingbourne A.	SDP	6,094	16.4	
					6,639	17.8	
1987	58,944	67.0	Boothroyd B. Ms.*	Lab	19,925	50.5	-0.3
			Betteridge F.A.	Con	14,672	37.2	+4.3
			Collingbourne A.	SDP	4,877	12.4	-4.0
					5,253	13.3	
1992	57,666	70.4	Boothroyd B. Ms.*	Lab	22,251	54.8	+4.3
			Swayne D.A.	Con	14,421	35.5	-1.6
			Broadbent S.E.H. Ms.	LD	3,925	9.7	-2.7
					7,830	19.3	

WESTBURY [617]

Election	Electors	T'out	Candidate	Party	Votes	% Sh	% Ch
1983	80,244	75.5	Walters D.M.*	Con	31,133	51.4	
			Hughes D.J.	Lib	22,627	37.4	
			Thomas H.W.	Lab	6,058	10.0*	
			Ekins P.W.	Green	609	1.0*	
			Banks J.C.	WR	131	0.2*	
					8,506	14.0	
1987	84,618	78.5	Walters D.M.*	Con	34,256	51.6	+0.2
			Hughes D.J.	Lib	24,159	36.4	-1.0
			Thomas H.W.	Lab	7,982	12.0	+2.0
					10,097	15.2	
1992	87,537†	82.8	Faber D.J.C.	Con	36,568	50.4	-1.1
			Rayner V.A. Ms.	LD	23,950	33.0	-3.3
			Stallard W.	Lab	9,642	13.3	+1.3
			Macdonald P.I.	Lib	1,440	2.0*	+2.0
			French P.R.	Green	888	1.2*	+1.2
					12,618	17.4	

WESTERN ISLES [618]

Election	Electors	T'out	Candidate	Party	Votes	% Sh	% Ch
1983	22,822	66.5	Stewart D.J.*	SNP	8,272	54.5	
			Wilson B.D.H.	Lab	4,560	30.1	
			Morrison M.	Con	1,460	9.6*	
			Macleod N.M.	Lib	876	5.8*	
					3,712	24.5	
1987	23,507	70.2	MacDonald C.A.	Lab	7,041	42.7	+12.6
			Smith I.	SNP	4,701	28.5	-26.0
			MacIver K.A.	SDP	3,419	20.7	+14.9
			Morrison M.	Con	1,336	8.1	-1.5
					2,340	14.2	
1992	22,785†	70.4	MacDonald C.A.*	Lab	7,664	47.8	+5.1
			MacFarlane F.M. Ms.	SNP	5,961	37.2	+8.7
			Heaney R.J.	Con	1,362	8.5	+0.4
			Mitchison N.	LD	552	3.4*	-17.3
			Price A.R.	Ind	491	3.1*	
					1,703	10.6	

WESTMINSTER NORTH [619]

Election	Electors	T'out	Candidate	Party	Votes	% Sh	% Ch
1983	68,988	64.2	Wheeler J.D.*	Con	19,134	43.2	
			Latham A.C.	Lab	17,424	39.4	
			Halliwell T.G.C.	SDP	6,956	15.7	
			Cooper T.H.	Green	527	1.2*	
			Keen T.L.	Ind	148	0.3*	
			Fisher B.	Ind	73	0.2*	
					1,710	3.9	
1987	59,263	71.1	Wheeler J.D.*	Con	19,941	47.3	+4.1
			Edwards J.F. Ms.	Lab	16,631	39.5	+0.1
			De Ste. Croix R.J.	SDP	5,116	12.1	-3.6
			Stutchfield D.	Green	450	1.1*	-0.1
					3,310	7.9	
1992	59,405	75.1	Wheeler J.D. Sir*	Con	21,828	49.0	+1.6
			Edwards J.F. Ms.	Lab	18,095	40.6	+1.1
			Wigoder L.J.	LD	3,349	7.5	-4.6
			Burke A.N. Ms.	Green	1,017	2.3*	+1.2
			Hinde J.R.	NLP	159	0.4*	+0.4
			Kelly M.F.D.	AFL	137	0.3*	+0.3
					3,733	8.4	

WESTMORLAND AND LONSDALE [620]

Election	Electors	T'out	Candidate	Party	Votes	% Sh	% Ch
1983	67,161	72.3	Jopling T.M.*	Con	29,775	61.3	
			Hulls K.	Lib	13,188	27.2	
			Stott C.C.	Lab	4,798	9.9*	
			Gibson R.A.	Green	805	1.7*	
					16,587	34.2	
1987	70,237	74.8	Jopling T.M.*	Con	30,259	57.6	-3.7
			Collins S.B.	Lib	15,339	29.2	+2.0
			Halfpenny S.P.	Lab	6,968	13.3	+3.4
					14,920	28.4	
1992	71,864†	77.8	Jopling T.M.*	Con	31,798	56.9	-0.7
			Collins S.B.	LD	15,362	27.5	-1.7
			Abbott D.J.	Lab	8,436	15.1	+1.8
			Johnstone R.A.	NLP	287	0.5*	+0.5
					16,436	29.4	

WESTON-SUPER-MARE [621]

Election	Electors	T'out	Candidate	Party	Votes	% Sh	% Ch
1983	71,439	73.0	Wiggin A.W.*	Con	27,948	53.6	
			Marks J.C.	SDP	18,457	35.4	
			Berry R.L.	Lab	5,781	11.1*	
					9,491	18.2	
1987	76,307	75.7	Wiggin A.W.*	Con	28,547	49.4	-4.1
			Crockford-Hawley J.R.	SDP	20,549	35.6	+0.2
			Loach P.J.	Lab	6,584	11.4	+0.3
			Lawson R.H. Dr.	Green	2,067	3.6*	+3.6
					7,998	13.9	
1992	78,843†	79.7	Wiggin A.W.*	Con	30,022	47.7	-1.7
			Cotter B.J.	LD	24,680	39.3	+3.7
			Murray D.E.	Lab	6,913	11.0	-0.4
			Lawson R.H. Dr.	Green	1,262	2.0*	-1.6
					5,342	8.5	

WIGAN [622]

Election	Electors	T'out	Candidate	Party	Votes	% Sh	% Ch
1983	72,390	75.6	Stott R.*	Lab	29,851	54.5	
			Pigott J.	Lib	12,554	22.9	
			Cadman H.L.	Con	12,320	22.5	
					17,297	31.6	
1987	72,064	76.6	Stott R.*	Lab	33,955	61.5	+7.0
			Wade K.R.	Con	13,493	24.5	+1.9
			White K.J.	Lib	7,732	14.0	-8.9
					20,462	37.1	
1992	72,741†	76.2	Stott R.*	Lab	34,910	63.0	+1.5
			Hess E.J.W.	Con	13,068	23.6	-0.9
			Davies G.	LD	6,111	11.0	-3.0
			White K.J.	Lib	1,116	2.0*	+2.0
			Tayler A.B. Ms.	NLP	197	0.4*	+0.4
					21,842	39.4	

WILTSHIRE NORTH [623]

Election	Electors	T'out	Candidate	Party	Votes	% Sh	% Ch
1983	76,150	76.6	Needham R.F.*	Con	30,924	53.0	
			Graham C.S.M.	Lib	23,692	40.6	
			Allsopp S.R.	Lab	2,888	5.0*	
			Barham E.	Green	678	1.2*	
			Baile de Laperriere H.C.	Ind	113	0.2*	
					7,232	12.4	
1987	80,712	79.3	Needham R.F.*	Con	35,309	55.2	+2.1
			Graham C.S.M.	Lib	24,370	38.1	-2.6
			Reid C. Ms.	Lab	4,343	6.8	+1.8
					10,939	17.1	
1992	85,852†	81.7	Needham R.F.*	Con	39,028	55.6	+0.5
			Napier C.R. Ms.	LD	22,640	32.3	-5.8
			Reid C. Ms.	Lab	6,945	9.9	+3.1
			Howitt L.H. Ms.	Green	850	1.2*	+1.2
			Hawkins G.F.J.	Lib	622	0.9*	+0.9
			Martienssen D.S.	Ind	66	0.1*	
					16,388	23.4	

WIMBLEDON [624]

Election	Electors	T'out	Candidate	Party	Votes	% Sh	% Ch
1983	64,132	72.4	Havers R.M.O. Sir.*	Con	24,169	52.1	
			Twigg D.J.	Lib	12,623	27.2	
			Tansey R.B.	Lab	8,806	19.0	
			Jones A.	Green	717	1.5*	
			Weakner E.J.	PAL	114	0.2*	
					11,546	24.9	
1987	63,353	76.1	Goodson-Wickes C. Dr.	Con	24,538	50.9	-1.2
			Slade A.C.	Lib	13,237	27.5	+0.3
			Bickerstaff C.M. Ms.	Lab	10,428	21.6	+2.7
					11,301	23.4	
1992	61,966	80.2	Goodson-Wickes C. Dr.*	Con	26,331	53.0	+2.1
			Abrams K.J.	Lab	11,570	23.3	+1.7
			Willott A.L. Ms.	LD	10,569	21.3	-6.2
			Flood V.H.	Green	860	1.7*	+1.7
			Godfrey H.R.A.	NLP	181	0.4*	+0.4
			Hadley G.W.	Ind	170	0.3*	
					14,761	29.7	

WINCHESTER [625]

Election	Electors	T'out	Candidate	Party	Votes	% Sh	% Ch
1983	72,792	76.2	Browne J.E.D.D.*	Con	31,908	57.6	
			MacDonald J.L.	SDP	18,861	34.0	
			Allchin W.H. Dr.	Lab	4,512	8.1*	
			Winkworth S.	WR	155	0.3*	
					13,047	23.5	
1987	76,507	80.4	Browne J.E.D.D.*	Con	32,195	52.3	-5.2
			MacDonald J.L.	SDP	24,716	40.2	+6.2
			Inglis F.C.	Lab	4,028	6.5	-1.6
			Walker J.P. Ms.	Green	565	0.9*	+0.9
					7,479	12.2	
1992	79,432	83.2	Malone P.G.	Con	33,113	50.1	-2.3
			Barron A.D	LD	24,992	37.8	-2.4
			Jenks P.J.	Lab	4,917	7.4	+0.9
			Browne J.E.D.D.*	Ind Con	3,095	4.7*	
					8,121	12.3	

Election	Electors	T'out	Candidate	Party	Votes	% Sh	% Ch
1983	78,619	70.3	Glyn A. Dr.	Con	32,191	58.2	
			Winner P.E.	Lib	13,988	25.3	
			Price V.I. Ms.	Lab	6,383	11.5*	
			Board W.O.	Ind Con	1,842	3.3*	
			Gillmore G.F.C.	NF	511	0.9*	
			Illesley P.B.	Ind	300	0.5*	
			Bex C.R.	WR	68	0.1*	
					18,203	32.9	
1987	79,319	75.4	Glyn A. Dr.*	Con	33,980	56.8	-1.4
			Jackson S.J.	Lib	16,144	27.0	+1.7
			De Lyon H.B. Ms.	Lab	6,678	11.2	-0.4
			Board W.O.	Ind Con	1,938	3.2*	
			Gordon P.	Green	711	1.2*	+1.2
			Stephenson P.H. Ms.	Ind	328	0.5*	
					17,836	29.8	
1992	77,427	81.6	Trend M. St.J.	Con	35,075	55.5	-1.3
			Hyde J.R.G.	LD	22,147	35.1	+8.1
			Attlee C.M.S. Ms.	Lab	4,975	7.9	-3.3
			Williams R.N.	Green	510	0.8*	-0.4
			Askwith D.N.	MRLP	236	0.4*	+0.4
			Bigg E. Ms.	Ind	110	0.2*	
			Grenville M.R.S.	NLP	108	0.2*	+0.2
					12,928	20.5	

Election	Electors	T'out	Candidate	Party	Votes	% Sh	% Ch
1983	60,864	75.8	Porter G.B.*	Con	24,766	53.7	
			Hollingworth P.J.M.	SDP	10,928	23.7	
			Rimmer K.S.J.	Lab	10,411	22.6	
					13,838	30.0	
1987	62,251	79.4	Porter G.B.*	Con	24,821	50.2	-3.5
			Swarbrooke J.S.	Lab	13,858	28.0	+5.4
			Gilchrist P.N.	Lib	10,779	21.8	-1.9
					10,963	22.2	
1992	61,135	82.3	Porter G.B.*	Con	25,590	50.8	+0.6
			Southworth H.M. Ms.	Lab	17,407	34.6	+6.6
			Cunniffe E.T.	LD	6,581	13.1	-8.7
			Birchenough N.	Green	584	1.2*	+1.2
			Griffiths G.	NLP	182	0.4*	+0.4
					8,183	16.3	

[Death]

Election	Electors	T'out	Candidate	Party	Votes	% Sh	% Ch
1997	59,288	73.0	Chapman B.	Lab	22,767	52.6	+18.0
(27/2)			Byrom L.T.	Con	14,879	34.4	-16.5
			Clucas H.F. Ms.	LD	4,347	10.1	-3.0
			North R.	UKI	410	0.9*	
			Bence, H.	Ind	184	0.4*	
			Cullen M.	SLP	156	0.4*	
			Gott P.	Ind	148	0.3*	
			Taylor R.	Ind	132	0.3*	
			Samuelson T.	Ind	124	0.3*	
			Mead G.	NLP	52	0.1*	-0.3
			Palmer C.R.	Ind	44	0.1*	
			Astbury F.	Ind	40	0.1*	
					7,888	18.2	

WIRRAL WEST [628]

Election	Electors	T'out	Candidate	Party	Votes	% Sh	% Ch
1983	61,646	73.4	Hunt D.J.F.*	Con	25,276	55.9	
			Mulholland S.J.	Lib	10,125	22.4	
			McCabe J.F.	Lab	9,855	21.8	
					15,151	33.5	
1987	63,597	77.9	Hunt D.J.F.*	Con	25,736	51.9	-3.9
			Dunn A.H.	Lab	13,013	26.3	+4.5
			Brame A.J.	Lib	10,015	20.2	-2.2
			Burton D.	Green	806	1.6*	+1.6
					12,723	25.7	
1992	62,471	81.6	Hunt D.J.F.*	Con	26,852	52.7	+0.8
			Stephenson K. Ms.	Lab	15,788	31.0	+4.7
			Thornton J.L.	LD	7,420	14.6	-5.6
			Bowler G.M. Ms.	Green	700	1.4*	-0.3
			Broome N.J.	NLP	188	0.4*	+0.4
					11,064	21.7	

WITNEY [629]

Election	Electors	T'out	Candidate	Party	Votes	% Sh	% Ch
1983	69,362	74.7	Hurd D.R. Hon.*	Con	28,695	55.4	
			Baston P.J.	Lib	15,983	30.8	
			Douse C.B. Ms.	Lab	7,145	13.8	
					12,712	24.5	
1987	75,358	77.2	Hurd D.R. Hon.*	Con	33,458	57.5	+2.1
			Burton M.E. Ms.	Lib	14,994	25.8	-5.1
			Collette C.F. Ms.	Lab	9,733	16.7	+2.9
					18,464	31.7	
1992	78,541	81.9	Hurd D.R. Hon*	Con	36,256	56.4	-1.1
			Plaskitt J.	Lab	13,688	21.3	+4.6
			Blair I.M.	LD	13,393	20.8	-4.9
			Beckford C. Ms.	Green	716	1.1*	+1.1
			Catling S.B. Ms.	NLP	134	0.2*	+0.2
			Brown M.C.C. Ms.	Ind	119	0.2*	
					22,568	35.1	

Election	Electors	T'out	Candidate	Party	Votes	% Sh	% Ch
1983	78,327	71.7	Onslow C.G.D.*	Con	32,748	58.3	
			Goldenberg P.	Lib	16,511	29.4	
			Broer D.B. Ms.	Lab	6,566	11.7*	
			Comens D.M.	PAL	368	0.7*	
					16,237	28.9	
1987	82,471	75.1	Onslow C.G.D.*	Con	35,990	58.1	-0.2
			Goldenberg P.	Lib	19,446	31.4	+2.0
			Pollack A.J. Ms.	Lab	6,537	10.5	-1.1
					16,544	26.7	
1992	80,814†	79.2	Onslow C.G.D.*	Con	37,744	58.9	+0.9
			Buckrell D.A. Ms.	LD	17,902	28.0	-3.4
			Dalgleish J.M.	Lab	8,080	12.6	+2.1
			MacIntyre T.A. Ms.	NLP	302	0.5*	+0.5
					19,842	31.0	

WOKINGHAM [631]

Election	Electors	T'out	Candidate	Party	Votes	% Sh	% Ch
1983	71,725	76.0	van Straubenzee W.R. Sir	Con	32,925	60.4	
			Leston J.C.	Lib	17,227	31.6	
			Orton M.E.	Lab	4,362	8.0*	
					15,698	28.8	
1987	83,062	78.1	Redwood J.A.	Con	39,808	61.4	+1.0
			Leston J.C.	Lib	19,421	29.9	-1.7
			Morgan P.J.	Lab	5,622	8.7	+0.7
					20,387	31.4	
1992	86,545†	81.8	Redwood J.A.*	Con	43,497	61.4	+0.0
			Simon P.G.	LD	17,788	25.1	-4.8
			Bland N.T.G.	Lab	8,846	12.5	+3.8
			Owen P.	MRLP	531	0.7*	+0.7
			Harriss P.E.	Ind	148	0.2*	
					25,709	36.3	

WOLVERHAMPTON NORTH EAST [632]

Election	Electors	T'out	Candidate	Party	Votes	% Sh	% Ch
1983	63,716	70.3	Short R. Ms.*	Lab	17,941	40.1	
			Burnside A.T.	Con	17,727	39.6	
			Yarnell R.C.	Lib	8,524	19.0	
			Baugh C.	NF	585	1.3*	
					214	0.5	
1987	63,464	74.3	Hicks M.P. Ms.	Con	19,857	42.1	+2.5
			Purchase K.	Lab	19,653	41.7	+1.6
			Pearson M.A.	Lib	7,623	16.2	-2.9
					204	0.4	
1992	62,701	78.0	Purchase K.	Lab	24,106	49.3	+7.6
			Hicks M.P. Ms.*	Con	20,167	41.2	-0.9
			Gwinnett M.	LD	3,546	7.3	-8.9
			Bullman K.E.J.	Lib	1,087	2.2*	+2.2
					3,939	8.1	

WOLVERHAMPTON SOUTH EAST [633]

Election	Electors	T'out	Candidate	Party	Votes	% Sh	% Ch
1983	56,428	69.1	Edwards R.*	Lab	17,440	44.7	
			McLoughlin P.A.	Con	12,428	31.9	
			Wernick J.A.	Lib	9,112	23.4	
					5,012	12.9	
1987	55,710	72.5	Turner D.	Lab	19,760	48.9	+4.2
			Mellor J.P.	Con	13,362	33.1	+1.2
			Whitehouse R.F.	Lib	7,258	18.0	-5.4
					6,398	15.8	
1992	56,170	72.9	Turner D.*	Lab	23,215	56.7	+7.8
			Bradbourn P.C.	Con	12,975	31.7	-1.4
			Whitehouse R.F.	LD	3,881	9.5	-8.5
			Twelvetrees C. Ms.	Lib	850	2.1*	+2.1
					10,240	25.0	

WOLVERHAMPTON SOUTH WEST [634]

Election	Electors	T'out	Candidate	Party	Votes	% Sh	% Ch
1983	68,847	72.4	Budgen N.W.*	Con	25,214	50.6	
			Jones R.M.	Lab	13,694	27.5	
			Harwood E.	SDP	10,724	21.5	
			Deary J.	Ind	201	0.4*	
					11,520	23.1	
1987	68,586	75.5	Budgen N.W.*	Con	26,235	50.7	+0.1
			Lawrence R.C.	Lab	15,917	30.7	+3.3
			Lamb B.J.	SDP	9,616	18.6	-2.9
					10,318	19.9	
1992	67,368	78.2	Budgen N.W.*	Con	25,969	49.3	-1.4
			Murphy S.F.	Lab	21,003	39.9	+9.1
			Wiggin M.	LD	4,470	8.5	-10.1
			Hallmark C.G.	Lib	1,237	2.3*	+2.3
					4,966	9.4	

WOODSPRING [635]

Election	Electors	T'out	Candidate	Party	Votes	% Sh	% Ch
1983	71,282	77.8	Dean A.P.*	Con	31,932	57.6	
			Morgan R.G.	Lib	16,800	30.3	
			White D.H.	Lab	6,536	11.8*	
			Robyns D.M.	WR	177	0.3*	
					15,132	27.3	
1987	76,289	79.1	Dean A.P. Sir.*	Con	34,134	56.6	-1.0
			Coleman C.R. Ms.	Lib	16,282	27.0	-3.3
			Chapple D.L.T.	Lab	8,717	14.4	+2.7
			Keeble B.R.	Green	1,208	2.0*	+2.0
					17,852	29.6	
1992	77,532†	83.2	Fox L.	Con	35,175	54.5	-2.1
			Kirsen N.E. Ms.	LD	17,666	27.4	+0.4
			Stone R.E.	Lab	9,942	15.4	+1.0
			Brown N.E.	Lib	836	1.3*	+1.3
			Knifton R.J. Ms.	Green	801	1.2*	-0.8
			Lee B.D.	NLP	100	0.2*	+0.2
					17,509	27.1	

Election	Electors	T'out	Candidate	Party	Votes	% Sh	% Ch
1983	56,297	68.0	Cartwright J.C.*	SDP	15,492	40.5	
			Wise A. Ms.	Lab	12,767	33.4	
			Drummond-Brown P.M. Ms.	Con	9,616	25.1	
			Fitz-Gerald T.C.	BNP	384	1.0*	
					2,725	7.1	
1987	58,071	70.7	Cartwright J.C.*	SDP	17,137	41.7	+1.2
			Austin-Walker J.E.	Lab	15,200	37.0	+3.6
			Salter A.R.	Con	8,723	21.2	-3.9
					1,937	4.7	
1992	55,977†	70.9	Austin-Walker J.E.	Lab	17,551	44.2	+7.2
			Cartwright J.C.*	SD	15,326	38.6	-3.1
			Walmsley K.J.T.	Con	6,598	16.6	-4.6
			Hayward S.J.E. Ms.	NLP	220	0.6*	+0.6
					2,225	5.6	

Cartwright contested the election as an Independent Social Democrat but the Liberal Democrats chose not to contest the seat.

Election	Electors	T'out	Candidate	Party	Votes	% Sh	% Ch
1983	66,531	74.1	Walker P.E.*	Con	24,381	49.4	
			Phipps C.B.	SDP	13,510	27.4	
			Rudd J.C.	Lab	11,208	22.7	
			Axon K.A.	BNP	208	0.4*	
					10,871	22.0	
1987	68,980	76.7	Walker P.E.*	Con	25,504	48.2	-1.3
			Webb M.J.	Lab	15,051	28.4	+5.7
			Caiger J.J.	SDP	12,386	23.4	-4.0
					10,453	19.7	
1992	74,201†	81.0	Luff P.J.	Con	27,883	46.4	-1.8
			Berry R.E.	Lab	21,731	36.2	+7.7
			Caiger J.J.	LD	9,561	15.9	-7.5
			Foster M.J.	Green	592	1.0*	+1.0
			Soden M.C.	Ind	343	0.6*	
					6,152	10.2	

WORCESTERSHIRE MID [638]

Election	Electors	T'out	Candidate	Party	Votes	% Sh	% Ch
1983	74,254	74.6	Forth E.	Con	28,159	50.9	
			Maher R.E.	Lab	13,954	25.2	
			Fairhead M.E. Ms.	SDP	12,866	23.2	
			Fletcher D.W.	Ind	386	0.7*	
					14,205	25.7	
1987	80,591	76.6	Forth E.*	Con	31,854	51.6	+0.7
			Pinfield P.J.	Lab	16,943	27.4	+2.2
			Harwood E.	SDP	12,954	21.0	-2.3
					14,911	24.1	
1992	84,290	81.1	Forth E.*	Con	33,964	49.7	-1.9
			Smith J.J. Ms.	Lab	24,094	35.3	+7.8
			Barwick D.J.	LD	9,745	14.3	-6.7
			Davis P.	NLP	520	0.8*	+0.8
					9,870	14.4	

WORCESTERSHIRE SOUTH [639]

Election	Electors	T'out	Candidate	Party	Votes	% Sh	% Ch
1983	73,278	73.6	Spicer W.M.H.*	Con	30,095	55.8	
			Phillips I.D.	Lib	18,706	34.7	
			Sandland-Nielsen P.E.	Lab	4,183	7.8*	
			Woodford G.H.M.	Green	866	1.6*	
			Pass G.R.G.	Ind	113	0.2*	
					11,389	21.1	
1987	77,237	75.6	Spicer W.M.H.*	Con	32,277	55.3	-0.5
			Chandler P.J.	Lib	18,632	31.9	-2.7
			Garnett R.J.	Lab	6,374	10.9	+3.2
			Woodford G.H.M.	Green	1,089	1.9*	+0.3
					13,645	23.4	
1992	80,157	80.3	Spicer W.M.H.*	Con	34,792	54.1	-1.2
			Chandler P.J.	LD	18,641	29.0	-2.9
			Knowles N.	Lab	9,727	15.1	+4.2
			Woodford G.H.M.	Green	1,178	1.8*	-0.0
					16,151	25.1	

WORKINGTON [640]

Election	Electors	T'out	Candidate	Party	Votes	% Sh	% Ch
1983	56,119	79.6	Campbell-Savours D.N.*	Lab	23,239	52.0	
			Smith M.D.M.	Con	16,111	36.1	
			Blackshaw N.L.	Lib	5,311	11.9*	
					7,128	16.0	
1987	56,911	80.6	Campbell-Savours D.N.*	Lab	24,019	52.4	+0.3
			McIntosh A.C.B. Ms.	Con	17,000	37.1	+1.0
			Badger G.W.	Lib	4,853	10.6	-1.3
					7,019	15.3	
1992	57,608	81.5	Campbell-Savours D.N.*	Lab	26,719	56.9	+4.5
			Sexton S.E.	Con	16,270	34.7	-2.4
			Neale C.A. Ms.	LD	3,028	6.4	-4.1
			Langstaff D.	MRLP	755	1.6*	+1.6
			Escott N.M. Ms.	NLP	183	0.4*	+0.4
					10,449	22.3	

WORSLEY [641]

Election	Electors	T'out	Candidate	Party	Votes	% Sh	% Ch
1983	71,987	74.7	Lewis T.	Lab	21,675	40.3	
			Windle S.	Con	17,536	32.6	
			Roper J.F.H.*	SDP	14,545	27.1	
					4,139	7.7	
1987	73,231	77.1	Lewis T.*	Lab	27,157	48.1	+7.8
			Horman V. Ms.	Con	19,820	35.1	+2.5
			Cowpe D.A.	Lib	9,507	16.8	-10.2
					7,337	13.0	
1992	72,244†	77.7	Lewis T.*	Lab	29,418	52.4	+4.3
			Cameron N. St.C.	Con	19,406	34.6	-0.5
			Boyd R.D.	LD	6,490	11.6	-5.3
			Connolly P.J.	Green	677	1.2*	+1.2
			Phillips G.D.	NLP	176	0.3*	+0.3
					10,012	17.8	

WORTHING [642]

Election	Electors	T'out	Candidate	Party	Votes	% Sh	% Ch
1983	75,772	71.2	Higgins T.L.*	Con	32,807	60.9	
			Clare A.R.	Lib	17,554	32.6	
			Minto A.M.	Lab	3,158	5.9*	
			Wingfield M.	NF	292	0.5*	
			Monks D.M.	BNP	103	0.2*	
					15,253	28.3	
1987	76,998	72.8	Higgins T.L.*	Con	34,573	61.7	+0.9
			Clare A.R.	Lib	16,072	28.7	-3.9
			Deen J.L.W.	Lab	5,387	9.6	+3.8
					18,501	33.0	
1992	77,550	77.4	Higgins T.L.*	Con	34,198	57.0	-4.7
			Bucknall S. Ms.	LD	17,665	29.4	+0.7
			Deen J.L.W.	Lab	6,679	11.1	+1.5
			Beever P.J. Ms.	Green	806	1.3*	+1.3
			Goble N.J.	Lib	679	1.1*	+1.1
					16,533	27.5	

WREKIN, THE [643]

Election	Electors	T'out	Candidate	Party	Votes	% Sh	% Ch
1983	77,226	75.5	Hawksley P.W.*	Con	22,710	39.0	
			Grocott B.J.	Lab	21,379	36.7	
			Biltcliffe M.	SDP	14,208	24.4	
					1,331	2.3	
1987	82,520	78.3	Grocott B.J.	Lab	27,681	42.8	+6.1
			Hawksley P.W.*	Con	26,225	40.6	+1.6
			Cook G.	SDP	10,737	16.6	-7.8
					1,456	2.3	
1992	90,893†	77.1	Grocott B.J.*	Lab	33,865	48.3	+5.5
			Holt E.J. Ms.	Con	27,217	38.8	-1.8
			West A.C.	LD	8,032	11.5	-5.2
			Saunders R.T.C.	Green	1,008	1.4*	+1.4
					6,648	9.5	

WREXHAM [644]

Election	Electors	T'out	Candidate	Party	Votes	% Sh	% Ch
1983	60,707	77.5	Marek J.	Lab	16,120	34.3	
			Wood C.K. Ms.	Con	15,696	33.4	
			Thomas A.M.	Lib	13,974	29.7	
			Thomas J.R.	PC	1,239	2.6*	
					424	0.9	
1987	62,381	80.9	Marek J.*	Lab	22,144	43.9	+9.6
			Graham-Palmer R.H.W.	Con	17,992	35.6	+2.3
			Thomas A.M.	Lib	9,808	19.4	-10.3
			Watkins D.R.	PC	539	1.1*	-1.6
					4,152	8.2	
1992	63,729	80.7	Marek J.*	Lab	24,830	48.3	+4.4
			Paterson O.W.	Con	18,114	35.2	-0.4
			Thomas A.M.	LD	7,074	13.8	-5.7
			Wheatley W.G.	PC	1,415	2.8*	+1.7
					6,716	13.1	

WYCOMBE [645]

Election	Electors	T'out	Candidate	Party	Votes	% Sh	% Ch
1983	70,065	71.7	Whitney R.W.*	Con	27,221	54.2	
			Page A.W.	SDP	14,024	27.9	
			Bastin C.	Lab	8,636	17.2	
			Amin M.	Ind	327	0.7*	
					13,197	26.3	
1987	71,918	72.8	Whitney R.W.*	Con	28,209	53.9	-0.4
			Hayhoe T.E.G.	SDP	14,390	27.5	-0.5
			Huddart J.R.W.	Lab	9,773	18.7	+1.5
					13,819	26.4	
1992	72,565†	78.0	Whitney R.W.*	Con	30,081	53.1	-0.7
			Andrews T.W.	LD	13,005	23.0	-4.5
			Huddart J.R.W.	Lab	12,222	21.6	+2.9
			Laker J.	Green	686	1.2*	+1.2
			Page A.W.	SD	449	0.8*	+0.8
			Anton T.P.	NLP	168	0.3*	+0.3
					17,076	30.2	

WYRE [646]

Election	Electors	T'out	Candidate	Party	Votes	% Sh	% Ch
1983	65,934	71.4	Clegg W. Sir.*	Con	26,559	56.4	
			Murdoch I.C.	SDP	11,748	25.0	
			Goldsmith W.	Lab	8,743	18.6	
					14,811	31.5	
1987	67,066	75.4	Mans K.D.R.	Con	26,800	53.0	-3.4
			Murdoch I.C.	SDP	12,139	24.0	-0.9
			Ainscough P.W.E.	Lab	10,725	21.2	+2.6
			Brown A.R.C.	Green	874	1.7*	+1.7
					14,661	29.0	
1992	67,778†	79.5	Mans K.D.R.*	Con	29,449	54.6	+1.6
			Borrow D.S.	Lab	17,785	33.0	+11.8
			Ault J.A.	LD	6,420	11.9	-12.1
			Perry R.V.	NLP	260	0.5*	+0.5
					11,664	21.6	

WYRE FOREST [647]

Election	Electors	T'out	Candidate	Party	Votes	% Sh	% Ch
1983	68,298	75.1	Bulmer J.E.*	Con	24,809	48.4	
			Batchelor A.J.	Lib	16,632	32.4	
			Williams R.D.	Lab	9,850	19.2	
					8,177	15.9	
1987	70,784	77.6	Coombs A.M.V.	Con	25,877	47.1	-1.2
			Batchelor A.J.	Lib	18,653	34.0	+1.6
			Knowles N.	Lab	10,365	18.9	-0.3
					7,224	13.2	
1992	73,602	82.3	Coombs A.M.V.*	Con	28,983	47.8	+0.7
			Maden R.	Lab	18,642	30.8	+11.9
			Jones M.D.	LD	12,958	21.4	-12.6
					10,341	17.1	

YEOVIL [648]

Election	Electors	T'out	Candidate	Party	Votes	% Sh	% Ch
1983	66,102	79.8	Ashdown J.J.D.	Lib	26,608	50.5	
			Martin D.J.P.	Con	23,202	44.0	
			Brushett P.J.	Lab	2,928	5.6*	
					3,406	6.5	
1987	70,390	79.7	Ashdown J.J.D.*	Lib	28,841	51.4	+1.0
			Sandeman G.D.S.	Con	23,141	41.3	-2.7
			Fitzmaurice J.F.	Lab	4,099	7.3	+1.8
					5,700	10.2	
1992	73,060	82.0	Ashdown J.J.D.*	LD	30,958	51.7	+0.3
			Davidson J.T.	Con	22,125	36.9	-4.3
			Nelson V. Ms.	Lab	5,765	9.6	+2.3
			Risbridger J.O.	Green	639	1.1*	+1.1
			Sutch D.E.	MRLP	338	0.6*	+0.6
			Simmerson R.E.G.	Ind	70	0.1*	
					8,833	14.7	

YNYS MON [649]

Election	Electors	T'out	Candidate	Party	Votes	% Sh	% Ch
1983	50,359	79.6	Best K.L.*	Con	15,017	37.5	
			Jones I.W.	PC	13,333	33.3	
			Williams T.	Lab	6,791	16.9	
			Thomas D.E.	SDP	4,947	12.3*	
					1,684	4.2	
1987	52,633	81.7	Jones I.W.	PC	18,580	43.2	+10.0
			Evans R.K.	Con	14,282	33.2	-4.2
			Parry C.	Lab	7,255	16.9	-0.1
			Evans I.W.	SDP	2,863	6.7	-5.7
					4,298	10.0	
1992	53,412†	80.6	Jones I.W.*	PC	15,984	37.1	-6.1
			Rowlands G.P.	Con	14,878	34.6	+1.3
			Jones R.O.	Lab	10,126	23.5	+6.6
			Badger P.E. Ms.	LD	1,891	4.4*	-2.3
			Parry S.M. Ms.	NLP	182	0.4*	+0.4
					1,106	2.6	

Election	Electors	T'out	Candidate	Party	Votes	% Sh	% Ch
1983	78,311	75.1	Gregory C.R.	Con	24,309	41.3	
			Lyon A.W.*	Lab	20,662	35.1	
			Cable J.V.	SDP	13,523	23.0	
			Lister A.J.	Ind	204	0.3*	
			Brattan T.G.	BNP	148	0.3*	
					3,647	6.2	
1987	79,297	78.4	Gregory C.R.*	Con	25,880	41.6	+0.3
			Bayley H.	Lab	25,733	41.4	+6.3
			Cable J.V.	SDP	9,898	15.9	-7.1
			Dunnett A.D.	Green	637	1.0*	+1.0
					147	0.2	
1992	79,242†	81.0	Bayley H.	Lab	31,525	49.1	+7.7
			Gregory C.R.*	Con	25,183	39.2	-2.4
			Anderson K.J. Ms.	LD	6,811	10.6	-5.3
			Kenwright S.N.	Green	594	0.9*	-0.1
			Orr P.S. Ms.	NLP	54	0.1*	+0.1
					6,342	9.9	

GENERAL ELECTION STATISTICS

GENERAL ELECTION 1983

	Total Votes	%	Cands	Elected
England				
C	11,711,519	46.0	523	362
L	3,658,903	14.4	267	10
SDP	3,056,054	12.0	256	3
(Total L/SDP)	6,714,957	26.4	523	13
Lab	6,862,422	26.9	523	148
BNP	14,364	0.1	52	0
Comm	6,368	0.0	22	0
Green	46,484	0.2	90	0
NF	27,065	0.1	60	0
WRP	3,280	0.0	18	0
Others	86,187	0.3	189	0
Total	25,472,646		2,000	523
Electorate	35,143,479	72.5% turnout		
Wales				
C	499,310	31.0	38	14
L	194,988	12.1	19	2
SDP	178,370	11.1	19	0
(Total L/SDP)	373,358	23.2	38	2
Lab	603,858	37.5	38	20
BNP	154	0.0	1	0
Comm	2,015	0.1	3	0
Green	3,510	0.2	7	0
PC	125,309	7.8	38	2
WRP	256	0.0	1	0
Others	1,216	0.1	5	0
Total	1,608,986		169	38
Electorate	2,113,855	76.1% turnout		
Scotland				
C	801,487	28.4	72	21
L	356,224	12.6	36	5
SDP	336,410	11.9	36	3
(Total L/SDP)	692,634	24.5	72	8
Lab	990,654	35.1	72	41
BNP	103	0.0	1	0
Comm	3,223	0.1	10	0
Green	3,854	0.1	11	0
SNP	331,975	11.8	72	2
WRP	262	0.0	2	0
Others	388	0.0	2	0
Total	2,824,580		314	72
Electorate	3,886,899	72.7% turnout		

	Total Votes	%	Cands	Elected
N. Ireland				
UDUP	152,749	20.0	14	3
UPUP	22,861	3.0	1	1
UU	259,952	34.0	16	11
Others	1,134	0.1	1	0
(Total 'Loyalist')	436,696	57.1	32	15
APNI	61,275	8.0	12	0
Green	451	0.1	1	0
SDLP	137,012	17.9	17	1
SF	102,701	13.4	14	1
WP	14,650	1.9	14	0
Others	12,140	1.6	5	0
Total	764,925	100.0	95	17
Electorate	1,048,766	72.9% turnout		
Great Britain				
C	13,012,316	43.5	633	397
L	4,210,115	14.1	322	17
SDP	3,570,834	11.9	311	6
(Total L/SDP)	7,780,949	26.0	633	23
Lab	8,456,934	28.3	633	209
BNP	14,621	0.0	54	0
Comm	11,606	0.0	35	0
Green	53,848	0.2	108	0
NF	27,065	0.1	60	0
PC	125,309	0.4	38	2
SNP	331,975	1.1	72	2
WRP	3,798	0.0	21	0
Others	87,791	0.3	196	0
Total	29,906,212		2,483	633
Electorate	41,144,233	72.7% turnout		
United Kingdom				
C	13,012,316	42.4	633	397
L	4,210,115	13.7	322	17
SDP	3,570,834	11.6	311	6
(Total L/SDP)	7,780,949	25.4	633	23
Lab	8,456,934	27.6	633	209
BNP	14,621	0.0	54	0
Comm	11,606	0.0	35	0
Green	53,848	0.2	108[1]	0
NF	27,065	0.1	60	0
PC	125,309	0.4	38	2
SNP	331,975	1.1	72	2
WRP	3,798	0.0	21	0
Others	852,716	2.8	291[2]	17[3]
Total	30,671,137		2,578[4]	650
Electorate	42,192,999	72.7% turnout		

1. Including three joint Green/WFLOE candidates who polled 1,341 votes, but excluding one candidate in Northern Ireland who polled 451 votes.
2. Including all candidates in Northern Ireland and 11 MRLP, 10 WR, 5 Nat Pty, 4 PAL, 4 Rev CP, 2 FTACMP, 2 MK, 2 NBP, 2 Wk P, 1 CNP, 1 FP, 1 N Lab P, 1 SPGB, 1 WFLOE.
3. The seventeen members for Northern Ireland constituencies (11 UU, 3 UDUP, 1 SDLP, 1 SF, 1 UPUP).
4. The number of persons seeking election was 2,574 as one candidate contested five constituencies.

GENERAL ELECTION 1987

	Total Votes	%	Cands	Elected
England				
C	12,546,186	46.2	523	358
L	3,684,813	13.6	271	7
SDP	2,782,537	10.3	252	3
(Total L/SDP)	6,467,350	23.8	523	10
Lab	8,006,466	29.5	523	155
Comm	4,022	0.0	13	0
Green	82,787	0.3	117	0
Others	26,711	0.1	83	0
Total	27,133,522		1,782	523
Electorate	35,987,776	75.4% turnout		
Wales				
C	501,316	29.5	38	8
L	181,427	10.7	20	3
SDP	122,803	7.2	18	0
(Total L/SDP)	304,230	17.9	38	3
Lab	765,209	45.1	38	24
Comm	869	0.1	1	0
Green	2,221	0.1	4	0
PC	123,599	7.3	38	3
Others	652	0.0	1	0
Total	1,698,096		158	38
Electorate	2,151,352	78.9% turnout		
Scotland				
C	713,081	24.0	72	10
L	307,210	10.4	36	7
SDP	262,843	8.9	36	2
(Total L/SDP)	570,053	19.2	72	9
Lab	1,258,132	42.4	72	50
Comm	1,187	0.0	5	0
Green	4,745	0.2	12	0
SNP	416,473	14.0	71	3
Others	4,137	0.1	4	0
Total	2,967,808		308	72
Electorate	3,952,465	75.1% turnout		

	Total Votes	%	Cands	Elected
N. Ireland				
UDUP	85,642	11.7	4	3
UPUP	18,420	2.5	1	1
UU	276,230	37.8	12	9
Others	20,138	2.8	2	0
(Total 'Loyalist')	400,430	54.8	19	13
APNI	72,671	10.0	16	0
NIEP	281	0.0	1	0
SDLP	154,087	21.1	13	3
SF	83,389	11.4	14	1
WP	19,294	2.6	14	0
Total	730,152		77	17
Electorate	1,089,160	67.0% turnout		
Great Britain				
C	13,760,583	43.3	633	376
L	4,173,450	13.1	327	17
SDP	3,168,183	10.0	306	5
(Total L/SDP)	7,341,633	23.1	633	22
Lab	10,029,807	31.5	633	229
Comm	6,078	0.0	19	0
Green	89,753	0.3	133	0
PC	123,599	0.4	38	3
SNP	416,473	1.3	71	3
Others	31,500	0.1	88	0
Total	31,799,426		2,248	633
Electorate	42,091,593	75.5% turnout		
United Kingdom				
C	13,760,583	42.3	633	376
L	4,173,450	12.8	327	17
SDP	3,168,183	9.7	306	5
(Total L/SDP)	7,341,633	22.6	633	22
Lab	10,029,807	30.8	633	229
Comm	6,078	0.0	19	0
Green	89,753	0.3	133	0
PC	123,599	0.4	38	3
SNP	416,473	1.3	71	3
Others	761,652	2.3	165[1]	17[2]
Total	32,529,578		2,325	650
Electorate	43,180,753	75.3% turnout		

1. Including all candidates in Northern Ireland and 14 RF, 10 WRP, 5 MRLP, 4 HP, 2 BNP, 1 FP, 1 OSM, 1 SPGB.
2. The seventeen members for Northern Ireland constituencies (9 UU, 3 UDUP, 1UPUP, 3 SDLP, 1 SF).

GENERAL ELECTION 1992

	Total Votes	%	Cands	Elected
England				
C	12,796,772	45.5	524	319
Lab	9,551,910	33.9	524	195
LD	5,398,293	19.2	522	10
Green	156,463	0.6	223	0
NLP	57,415	0.2	272	0
Others	187,653	0.7	263	0
Total	28,148,506		2328	524
Electorate	36,071,067	78.0% turnout		
Wales				
C	499,677	28.6	38	6
Lab	865,663	49.5	38	27
LD	217,457	12.4	38	1
PC	154,947	8.9	35	4
Green	7,073	0.4	14	0
NLP	1,231	0.1	9	0
Others	2,729	0.2	8	0
Total	1,748,777		180	38
Electorate	2,194,218	79.7% turnout		
Scotland				
C	751,950	25.6	72	11
Lab	1,142,911	39.0	72	49
LD	383,856	13.1	72	9
SNP	629,564	21.5	72	3
Green	8,391	0.3	19	0
NLP	2,095	0.1	19	0
Others	12,931	0.4	15	0
Total	2,931,698		341	72
Electorate	3,885,131	75.5% turnout		

	Total Votes	%	Cands	Elected
N. Ireland				
C	44,608	5.7	11	0
UU	271,049	34.5	13	9
DUP	103,039	13.1	7	3
UPUP	19,305	2.5	1	1
SDLP	184,445	23.5	13	4
AP	68,665	8.7	16	0
SF	78,291	10.0	14	0
NLP	2,147	0.3	9	0
Others	13,544	1.7	16	0
Total	785,093		100	17
Electorate	1,124,900	69.8% turnout		
Great Britain				
C	14,048,399	42.8	634	336
Lab	11,560,484	35.2	634	271
LD	5,999,606	18.3	632	20
PC	154,947	0.5	35	4
SNP	629,564	1.9	72	3
Green	171,927	0.5	256	0
NLP	60,741	0.2	300	0
Others	203,313	0.6	286	0
Total	32,828,981		2849	634
Electorate	42,150,416	77.9% turnout		
United Kingdom				
C	14,093,007	41.9	645	336
Lab	11,560,484	34.4	634	271
LD	5,999,606	17.8	632	20
PC	154,947	0.5	35	4
SNP	629,564	1.9	72	3
Green	171,927	0.5	256	0
NLP	62,888	0.2	309	0
Others	941,651	2.8	366[1]	17[2]
Total	33,614,074		2949	651
Electorate	43,275,316	77.7% turnout		

1. Including all candidates in Northern Ireland except the 11 Conservative and 9 NLP candidates.
2. The seventeen members for Northern Ireland constituencies (9 UU, 3 DUP, 1UPUP, 4 SDLP).

APPENDICES

Appendix 1

Craig's listing of Parliamentary Constituencies and Constituency Number

Greater London

Barking (22), Battersea (32), Beckenham (34), Bethnal Green & Stepney (44), Bexleyheath (47), Bow & Poplar (78), Brent East (84), Brent North (85), Brent South (86), Brentford & Isleworth (87), Carshalton & Wallington (125), Chelsea (130), Chingford (137), Chipping Barnet (138), Chislehurst (139), City Of London & Westminster South (143), Croydon Central (165), Croydon North East (166), Croydon North West (167), Croydon South (168), Dagenham (173), Dulwich (200), Ealing Acton (210), Ealing North (211), Ealing Southall (212), Edmonton (227), Eltham (230), Enfield North (231), Enfield Southgate (232), Erith & Crayford (236), Feltham & Heston (244), Finchley (248), Fulham (251), Greenwich (280), Hackney North & Stoke Newington (282), Hackney South & Shoreditch (283), Hammersmith (288), Hampstead & Highgate (291), Harrow East (295), Harrow West (296), Hayes & Harlington (301), Hendon North (304), Hendon South (305), Holborn & St. Pancras (316), Hornchurch (319), Hornsey & Wood Green (320), Ilford North (330), Ilford South (331), Islington North (335), Islington South & Finsbury (336), Kensington (340), Kingston-Upon-Thames (345), Lewisham Deptford (367), Lewisham East (368), Lewisham West (369), Leyton (370), Mitcham & Morden (404), Newham North East (422), Newham North West (423), Newham South (424), Norwood (439), Old Bexley & Sidcup (445), Orpington (449), Peckham (454), Putney (470), Ravensbourne (471), Richmond & Barnes (479), Romford (483), Ruislip-Northwood (491), Southwark & Bermondsey (529), Streatham (549), Surbiton (557), Sutton & Cheam (562), Tooting (576), Tottenham (579), Twickenham (583), Upminster (587), Uxbridge (589), Vauxhall (591), Walthamstow (597), Wanstead & Woodford (600), Westminster North (619), Wimbledon (624), Woolwich (636)

England (excluding Greater London)

Aldershot (4), Aldridge-Brownhills (5), Altrincham & Sale (6), Amber Valley (8), Arundel (14), Ashfield (15), Ashford (16), Ashton-Under-Lyne (17), Aylesbury (18), Banbury (20), Barnsley Central (23), Barnsley East (24), Barnsley West & Pensistone (25), Barrow & Furness (26), Basildon (27), Basingstoke (28), Bassetlaw (29), Bath (30), Batley & Spen (31), Beaconsfield (33), Bedfordshire Mid (35), Bedford-shire North (36), Bedfordshire South West (37), Berkshire East (42), Berwick-Upon-Tweed (43), Beverley (45), Bexhill & Battle (46), Billericay (48), Birkenhead (49), Birmingham Edgbaston (50), Birmingham Erdington (51), Birmingham Hall Green (52), Birmingham Hodge Hill (53), Birmingham Ladywood (54), Birmingham Northfield (55), Birmingham Perry Barr (56), Birmingham Selly Oak (57), Birmingham Small Heath (58), Birmingham Sparkbrook (59), Birmingham Yardley (60), Bishop Auckland (61), Blaby (62), Blackburn (63), Blackpool North (64), Blackpool South (65), Blaydon (67), Blyth Valley (68), Bolsover (69), Bolton North East (70), Bolton South East (71), Bolton West (72), Boothferry (73), Bootle (74), Bosworth (75), Bournemouth East (76), Bournemouth West (77), Bradford North (79), Bradford South (80), Bradford West (81), Braintree (82), Brentwood & Ongar (88), Bridgwater (90), Bridlington (91), Brigg & Cleethorpes (92), Brighton Kemptown (93), Brighton Pavilion (94), Bristol East (95), Bristol North West (96), Bristol South (97), Bristol West (98), Bromsgrove (99), Broxbourne (100), Broxtowe (101), Buckingham (102), Burnley (103), Burton (104), Bury North (105), Bury South (106), Bury St Edmunds (107), Calder Valley (111), Cambridge (112), Cambridgeshire North East (113), Cambridgeshire South East (114), Cambridgeshire South West (115), Cannock & Burntwood (116), Canterbury (117), Carlisle (122), Castle Point (126), Cheadle (128), Chelmsford (129), Cheltenham (131), Chertsey & Walton (132), Chesham & Amersham (133), Chester (134), Chesterfield (135), Chichester (136), Chorley (140), Christchurch (141), Cirencester & Tewkesbury (142), Colchester North (149), Colchester South & Maldon (150), Colne Valley (151), Congleton (152), Copeland (154), Corby (155), Cornwall North (156), Cornwall South East (157), Coventry North East (158), Coventry North West (159), Coventry South East (160), Coventry South West (161), Crawley (162), Crewe & Nantwich (163), Crosby (164), Darlington (174), Dartford (175), Daventry (176), Davyhulme (177), Denton & Reddish (179), Derby North (180), Derby South (181), Derbyshire North East (182), Derbyshire South

(183), Derbyshire West (184), Devizes (185), Devon North (186), Devon West & Torridge (187), Dewsbury (188), Don Valley (191), Doncaster Central (189), Doncaster North (190), Dorset North (192), Dorset South (193), Dorset West (194), Dover (195), Dudley East (198), Dudley West (199), Durham North (208), Durham North West (209), Durham, City Of (207), Easington (213), Eastbourne (214), Eastleigh (216), Eccles (219), Eddisbury (220), Ellesmere Port & Neston (228), Elmet (229), Epping Forest (233), Epsom & Ewell (234), Erewash (235), Esher (237), Exeter (238), Falmouth & Cambourne (241), Fareham (242), Faversham (243), Folkestone & Hythe (249), Fylde (252), Gainsborough & Horncastle (253), Gateshead East (255), Gedling (256), Gillingham (257), Glanford & Scunthorpe (258), Gloucester (270), Gloucester West (271), Gosport (273), Grantham (275), Gravesham (276), Great Grimsby (277), Great Yarmouth (278), Guildford (281), Halesowen & Stourbridge (284), Halifax (285), Halton (286), Hampshire East (289), Hampshire North West (290), Harborough (292), Harlow (293), Harrogate (294), Hartlepool (297), Harwich (298), Hastings & Rye (299), Havant (300), Hazel Grove (302), Hemsworth (303), Henley (306), Hereford (307), Hertford & Stortford (308), Hertfordshire North (309), Hertfordshire South West (310), Hertfordshire West (311), Hertsmere (312), Hexham (313), Heywood & Middleton (314), High Peak (315), Holland With Boston (317), Honiton (318), Horsham (321), Houghton & Washington (322), Hove (323), Huddersfield (324), Hull East (325), Hull North (326), Hull West (327), Huntingdon (328), Hyndburn (329), Ipswich (333), Isle Of Wight (334), Jarrow (338), Keighley (339), Kent Mid (341), Kettering (342), Kingswood (346), Knowsley North (348), Knowsley South (349), Lanbaurgh (353), Lancashire West (351), Lancaster (352), Leeds Central (354), Leeds East (355), Leeds North East (356), Leeds North West (357), Leeds South & Morley (358), Leeds West (359), Leicester East (360), Leicester North West (363), Leicester South (361), Leicester West (362), Leigh (364), Leominster (365), Lewes (366), Lincoln (371), Lindsey East (372), Littleborough & Saddleworth (374), Liverpool Broadgreen (375), Liverpool Garston (376), Liverpool Mossley Hill (377), Liverpool Riverside (378), Liverpool Walton (379), Liverpool West Derby (380), Loughborough (384), Ludlow (385), Luton North (386), Luton South (387), Macclesfield (388), Maidstone (389), Makerfield (390), Manchester Blackley (391), Manchester Central (392), Manchester Gorton (393), Manchester Withington (394), Manchester Wythenshawe (395), Mansfield (396), Medway (397), Meriden (399), Middlesbrough (401), Milton Keynes (403), Mole Valley (405), Morecombe & Lunesdale (411), New Forest (421), Newark (415), Newbury (416), Newcastle-Under-Lyme (417), Newcastle-Upon-Tyne Central (418), Newcastle-Upon-Tyne East (419), Newcastle-Upon-Tyne North (420), Norfolk Mid (428), Norfolk North (429), Norfolk North West (430), Norfolk South (431), Norfolk South West (432), Normanton (433), Northampton North (434), Northampton South (435), Northavon (436), Norwich North (437), Norwich South (438), Nottingham East (440), Nottingham North (441), Nottingham South (442), Nuneaton (443), Oldham Central & Royton (446), Oldham West (447), Oxford East (450), Oxford West & Abingdon (451), Pendle (456), Penrith & The Border (457), Peterborough (459), Plymouth Devonport (460), Plymouth Drake (461), Plymouth Sutton (462), Pontefract & Castleford (463), Poole (465), Portsmouth North (466), Portsmouth South (467), Preston (468), Pudsey (469), Reading East (472), Reading West (473), Redcar (474), Reigate (475), Ribble Valley (478), Richmond (Yorks) (480), Rochdale (481), Rochford (482), Romsey & Waterside (484), Rossendale & Darwen (486), Rother Valley (488), Rotherham (487), Rugby & Kenilworth (490), Rushcliffe (492), Rutland & Melton (493), Ryedale (494), Saffron Walden (495), Salford East (500), Salisbury (501), Scarborough (502), Sedgefield (503), Selby (504), Sevenoaks (505), Sheffield Attercliffe (506), Sheffield Brightside (507), Sheffield Central (508), Sheffield Hallam (509), Sheffield Heeley (510), Sheffield Hillsborough (511), Sherwood (512), Shipley (513), Shoreham (514), Shrewsbury & Atcham (515), Shropshire North (516), Skipton & Ripon (517), Slough (518), Solihull (519), Somerton & Frome (520), South Hams (525), South Ribble (527), South Shields (528), Southampton Itchen (521), Southampton Test (522), Southend East (523), Southend West (524), Southport (526), Spelthorne (530), St Albans (496), St Helens North (497), St Helens South (498), St Ives (499), Stafford (531), Staffordshire Mid (532), Staffordshire Moorlands (533), Staffordshire South (534), Staffordshire South East (535), Stalybridge & Hyde (536), Stamford & Spalding (537), Stevenage (538), Stockport (540), Stockton North (541), Stockton South (542), Stoke-On-Trent Central (543), Stoke-On-Trent North (544), Stoke-On-Trent South (545), Stratford-On-Avon (547), Stretford (550), Stroud (551), Suffolk Central (552), Suffolk Coastal (553), Suffolk South (554), Sunderland North (555), Sunderland South (556), Surrey East (558), Surrey North West (559), Surrey South West (560), Sussex Mid (561), Sutton Coldfield (563), Swindon (566), Tatton (567), Taunton (568), Teignbridge (570),

Thanet North (571), Thanet South (572), Thurrock (573), Tiverton (574), Tonbridge & Malling (575), Torbay (577), Truro (580), Tunbridge Wells (581), Tyne Bridge (584), Tynemouth (585), Wakefield (592), Wallasey (593), Wallsend (594), Walsall North (595), Walsall South (596), Wansbeck (598), Wansdyke (599), Wantage (601), Warley East (602), Warley West (603), Warrington North (604), Warrington South (605), Warwick & Leamington (606), Warwickshire North (607), Watford (608), Waveney (609), Wealden (610), Wellingborough (611), Wells (612), Welwyn Hatfield (613), Wentworth (614), West Bromwich East (615), West Bromwich West (616), Westbury (617), Westmorland & Lonsdale (620), Weston-Super-Mare (621), Wigan (622), Wiltshire North (623), Winchester (625), Windsor & Maidenhead (626), Wirral South (627), Wirral West (628), Witney (629), Woking (630), Wokingham (631), Wolverhampton North East (632), Wolverhampton South East (633), Wolverhampton South West (634), Woodspring (635), Worcester (637), Worcestershire Mid (638), Worcestershire South (639), Workington (640), Worsley (641), Worthing (642), Wrekin, The (643), Wycombe (645), Wyre (646), Wyre Forest (647), Yeovil (648), York (650)

Wales

Aberavon (1), Alyn & Deeside (7), Blaenau Gwent (66), Brecon & Radnor (83), Bridgend (89), Caernarfon (108), Caerphilly (109), Cardiff Central (118), Cardiff North (119), Cardiff South & Penarth (120), Cardiff West (121), Carmarthen (123), Ceredigion & Pembroke North (127), Clwyd North West (145), Clwyd South West (146), Conwy (153), Cynon Valley (172), Delyn (178), Gower (274), Islwyn (337), Llanelli (382), Meirionnydd Nant Conwy (398), Merthyr Tydfil & Rhymney (400), Monmouth (408), Montgomery (409), Neath (414), Newport East (425), Newport West (426), Ogmore (444), Pembroke (455), Pontypridd (464), Rhondda (477), Swansea East (564), Swansea West (565), Torfaen (578), Vale Of Glamorgan (590), Wrexham (644), Ynys Mon (649)

Scotland

Aberdeen North (2), Aberdeen South (3), Angus East (9), Argyll & Bute (13), Ayr (19), Banff & Buchan (21), Caithness & Sutherland (110), Carrick, Cumnock & Doon Valley (124), Clackmannan (144), Clydebank & Milngavie (147), Clydesdale (148), Cumbernauld & Kilsyth (169), Cunninghame North (170), Cunninghame South (171), Dumbarton (201), Dumfries (202), Dundee East (203), Dundee West (204), Dunfermline East (205), Dunfermline West (206), East Kilbride (215), East Lothian (217), Eastwood (218), Edinburgh Central (221), Edinburgh East (222), Edinburgh Leith (223), Edinburgh Pentlands (224), Edinburgh South (225), Edinburgh West (226), Falkirk East (239), Falkirk West (240), Fife Central (246), Fife North East (247), Galloway & Upper Nithsdale (254), Glasgow Cathcart (259), Glasgow Central (260), Glasgow Garscadden (261), Glasgow Govan (262), Glasgow Hillhead (263), Glasgow Maryhill (264), Glasgow Pollok (265), Glasgow Provan (266), Glasgow Rutherglen (267), Glasgow Shettleston (268), Glasgow Springburn (269), Gordon (272), Greenock & Port Glasgow (279), Hamilton (287), Inverness, Nairn & Lochaber (332), Kilmarnock & Loudoun (343), Kincardine & Deeside (344), Kirkcaldy (347), Linlithgow (373), Livingston (381), Midlothian (402), Monklands East (406), Monklands West (407), Moray (410), Motherwell North (412), Motherwell South (413), Orkney & Shetland (448), Paisley North (452), Paisley South (453), Perth & Kinross (458), Renfrew West & Inverclyde (476), Ross, Cromarty & Skye (485), Roxburgh & Berwickshire (489), Stirling (539), Strathkelvin & Bearsden (548), Tayside North (569), Tweedale, Ettrick & Lauderdale (582), Western Isles (618)

Northern Ireland

Antrim East (10), Antrim North (11), Antrim South (12), Belfast East (38), Belfast North (39), Belfast South (40), Belfast West (41), Down North (196), Down South (197), Fermanagh & South Tyrone (245), Foyle (250), Lagan Valley (350), Londonderry East (383), Newry & Armagh (427), Strangford (546), Ulster Mid (586), Upper Bann (588)

Appendix 2

List of candidates who fought as Labour/Co-operative Party

* indicates candidate was elected

1983

Craigen J.M.*, Glasgow, Maryhill
Douglas R.G.*, Dunfermline West
Edwards R.*, Wolverhampton S.E.
Evans I.L.*, Cynon Valley
Foulkes G.*, Carrick, Cumnock & Doon Valley
Graham T.E., Edmonton
Hawkins B.L.M. Ms., Richmond (Yorks)
Jones M.T., Loughborough
Morris A.*, Manchester Wythenshawe
Newens A.S., Harlow
O'Brien O., Darlington
Palmer S.R. Ms., Bristol N.W.
Pavitt L.A.*, Brent South
Robertson J.A., Wallasey
Sheerman B.J.*, Huddersfield
Sloman M.G.M., Nottingham East
Tomlinson J.E., Warwickshire N.

1987

Douglas R.G.*, Dunfermline West
Foulkes G.*, Carrick, Cumnock & Doon Valley
Harkin G.J., Bolton West
Jones H.M. Ms., Ellesmere Port & Neston
Loach P.J., Weston-super-Mare
McAvoy T.M.*, Glasgow, Rutherglen
McFall J.*, Dumbarton
McWalter A., St. Albans
Michael A.E.*, Cardiff South & Penarth
Miles D.G., Portsmouth North
Moonie L.G.*, Kirkcaldy
Morris A.*, Manchester Wythenshawe
Newens A.S., Harlow
O'Brien O., Darlington
Sheerman B.J.*, Huddersfield
Smith A.E. Ms., Southend West
Sumner P.R.E. Ms., Hertford & Stortford
Turner D.*, Wolverhampton S.E.
Wrigley C.J., Loughborough

1992

Balfe R.A., Southwark & Bermondsey
Davidson I.G.*, Glasgow Govan
Foulkes G.*, Carrick, Cumnock & Doon Valley
Gapes M.J.*, Ilford South
Gilroy L.W. Ms., Cornwall South East
Hope P.I., Kettering
Jones J.O.*, Cardiff Central
Keen A.*, Feltham & Heston
Lazarowicz M.J., Edinburgh Pentlands
Love A.M., Edmonton
McAvoy T.M.*, Glasgow, Rutherglen
McFall J.*, Dumbarton
McMaster G.*, Paisley South
Michael A.E.*, Cardiff South & Penarth
Moonie L.G.*, Kirkcaldy
Morris A.*, Manchester Wythenshawe
Naysmith J.D., Bristol N.W.
Purchase K.*, Wolverhampton N.E.
Sheerman B.J.*, Huddersfield
Shutler M.J., New Forest
Stears M.J., Ealing North
Stephens N.J., Meriden
Taggart S., Grantham
Telford P., Plymouth Drake
Turner D.*, Wolverhampton S.E.
Whitemore M.F., Canterbury
Woodell V.S., Wantage

INDEX TO CANDIDATES

This index lists the names of all the candidates at General Elections from 1983 to 1992 and at intervening by-elections up to end April 1997. The number or numbers following the name of each candidate indicates the constituency reference number which is given following the name of each constituency.

385

Crowley J.E. 340
Crowley M. Ms. 499
Crowson K.M. 319, 339
Crowther J.S. 487
Cruden A.H. 106
Crumbie A. Ms. 361
Cryer G.R. 80, 339
Cryer N. 252
Crystal P.M. 251, 356
Cufley L.W. Ms. 249
Cullen M. 627
Cullen F.J. 38
Cullen G. 245
Cullen P.B. 308
Cullingham M.A. 429
Cummings J.S. 213
Cummins G. 354
Cummins J.P.F. 469
Cummins M. 84
Cundy I. 543
Cundy R.W.C. 47
Cunliffe L.F. 364
Cunniffe E.T. 627
Cunning W.A. 10
Cunningham C.H. 479
Cunningham G. 336
Cunningham J.A. 154
Cunningham J.D. 160
Cunningham J.J. 74
Cunningham L. Ms. 126
Cunningham M. Ms. 530
Cunningham R. Ms. 458
Curphey S.E. Ms. 117
Curran B.P. 427, 588
Currie A. 412
Currie E. Ms. 183
Currie J. 611
Currie J.A. 245
Curry D.M. 517
Curry J. 546
Curtis C.I. 28
Curtis D. 380
Curtis M.A. 142
Cushinan H.J. 12
Cushnahan J.W. 196
Cutcher P.S. 97
Cutts S.M. Ms. 1

D

D'Arcy B.H.M. 18
D'Arcy M.J. 471
D'Avila J.P. 566
Dacres G.C. 454

Daden P.F. 28
Dafis C.G. (Davies) 127
Dale D. 463
Dale T.E. 552
Dalgleish J.M. 630
Dalkeith R. 215
Dalling I.D. 446
Dalling S.J. Ms. 447
Dalton D. 450
Daly C.A. 334
Daly J. 231, 244
Dalyell T. 373
Dangerfield P. 243
Daniel G.J. 210
Daniels C. 604
Darby D. Ms. 491, 599
Darby J.V. 251
Darling A.M. 221
Darnbrough A.G. Ms. 133
Darnton G. 472
Darracott C.G. 34
Davenport A.B 502
Davenport K.J. 175
Davey J. 383
Davey J.V. 135
Davey L. 120
Davey-Kennedy P. Ms. 383
David F.A. Ms. 408, 425
Davids T.F. 85
Davidson A. 329
Davidson I.G. 262
Davidson J.C. 3
Davidson J.P. 263
Davidson J.T. 648
Davies A.D. 228
Davies A.P. 456
Davies B. 426, 446
Davies C. 374
Davies C.D. 390
Davies C.G. 274
Davies C.J. 361
Davies D.J.D. 382
Davies D.K. 414, 590
Davies D.W. 567
Davies E.J. Ms. 304
Davies G. 622
Davies G.R. (Lab) 165, 168
Davies G.R. (PC) 477
Davies H. 491
Davies H.L. 541, 564
Davies J.D. Ms. 73
Davies J.H. 83
Davies J.M. Ms. (PC) 83,
.... 337, 400, 464

Davies J.M. Ms. (LD) 100
Davies J.Q. 537
Davies J.R. 127
Davies J.R.M. 248
Davies K. 590
Davies M.H. 498
Davies P 303
Davies P. 533
Davies P.G. 154
Davies P.R.G. 320
Davies P.W. 392
Davies R. (Lab) 109
Davies R. (Ind) 149
Davies R. (Con) 544
Davies R.A. 211
Davies R.K. 145
Davies R.T. 118
Davies R.V. 153
Davies S.P. 299
Davies T.A.R. 66
Davies V.J.E. 508
Davis B.R. 604
Davis D.M. 73
Davis G.E. 443
Davis L.J.K. 608
Davis M.J. 290, 558
Davis P. 638
Davis P.A. Ms. 50
Davis P.M. 385
Davis P.R.C. 422
Davis S.V. Ms. 593
Davis T.A.G. 53
Davison P.S. 206
Davison R. 318
Davy J. Ms. .̇..................... 535
Daw M.J. 393
Dawe H.F. Ms. 571
Dawe P.J. 137
Dawe S.M. 117
Dawson D.A. 584
Dawson E.J.V. 358
Dawson G. 484
Day J. 416
Day J.M. 510
Day R.J. 473
Day S.R. 81, 128
De Grandis-Harrison V.A. Ms. .. 423
De Lyon H.B. Ms. 626
De Pinna L.A. 370
De Ste. Croix R.J. 132, 619
Deakins E.P. 597
Deal W.A. 126
Dean A.P. 635
Dean J.J. 359

387

E

F

H

393

398

400

N

407

408

410

411

414

415